# Lecture Notes in Computer Science 14384

The series Lecture Notes in Computer Science (LNCS), including its subseries Lecture Notes in Artificial Intelligence (LNAI) and Lecture Notes in Bioinformatics (LNBI), has established itself as a medium for the publication of new developments in computer science and information technology research, teaching, and education.

LNCS enjoys close cooperation with the computer science R & D community, the series counts many renowned academics among its volume editors and paper authors, and collaborates with prestigious societies. Its mission is to serve this international community by providing an invaluable service, mainly focused on the publication of conference and workshop proceedings and postproceedings. LNCS commenced publication in 1973.

Lissa Holloway-Attaway · John T. Murray
Editors

# Interactive Storytelling

## 16th International Conference on Interactive Digital Storytelling, ICIDS 2023
## Kobe, Japan, November 11–15, 2023
## Proceedings, Part II

Springer

*Editors*
Lissa Holloway-Attaway
University of Skövde
Skövde, Sweden

John T. Murray
University of Central Florida
Orlando, FL, USA

ISSN 0302-9743 ISSN 1611-3349 (electronic)
Lecture Notes in Computer Science
ISBN 978-3-031-47657-0 ISBN 978-3-031-47658-7 (eBook)
https://doi.org/10.1007/978-3-031-47658-7



This Springer imprint is published by the registered company Springer Nature Switzerland AG
The registered company address is: Gewerbestrasse 11, 6330 Cham, Switzerland

Paper in this product is recyclable.

# Preface

This volume constitutes the proceedings of the 16th International Conference on Interactive Digital Storytelling (ICIDS 2023). ICIDS is the premier conference for researchers and practitioners concerned with studying digital interactive narrative forms from various perspectives, including theoretical, technological, and applied design lenses. The annual conference is an interdisciplinary gathering that combines technology-focused approaches with humanities-inspired theoretical inquiry, empirical research, and artistic expression.

The theme for the conference this year was "Traversing Boundaries, Barriers and Borders." We were motivated to consider the varied border and boundary crossings enabled by the current state of Interactive Digital Storytelling. At a time when our fields for reflection and making have matured and deepened, particularly in the complex intra-disciplinary modes of creative/critical design and research within our ICIDS communities, we asked authors to reflect on their own situated-ness, displacements, and modes and means of travel. We asked in particular for them to reflect on key questions: "Where are you located in relation to interactive digital story-making and reflection, and how does that enable or hinder your perspectives? In what ways, and how, do you navigate around and through disciplinary fields, making-practices, users, nations, cultures, and other environments for engagement? Who is included and excluded from these bounded territories, freshly mapped worlds, and/or open sites for play and interaction?" We suggested they might consider maps and mapping as a strategic entry point to the topic. Maps can describe a variety of features from different perspectives of physical, social, and economic significance. We envision the act of traversing as both wayfinding and trailblazing and cartography of a burgeoning field that requires multiple, intersectional perspectives, and we invited authors also to consider how they might act as cartographers of the disciplines from which they come. We asked them, "What are your cartographic tools and how do they allow you to map-make to find new routes and passages that are open for all?" We encouraged contributions from diverse perspectives, including but not limited to: decolonial thinking, cross-disciplinary collaboration or resistance, multinational design as well as development critique and practice, and/or around issues of diversity and inclusion across communities and tools.

These proceedings represent the latest work from a wide range of researchers, with representation from around the world. The program was divided into six main areas based on the tracks to which authors submitted their research: Applications and Case Studies; Interactive Narrative Design; Social and Cultural Contexts; Theory, History and Foundations; Tools and Systems; and Virtual Worlds, Performance, Games and Play. Each subject area represents an important domain for exploring the theories, contexts, histories, practices, and designs for interactive digital storytelling. Collectively the papers in this volume present a range of intriguing and thoughtful reflections on how these unique digital narrative forms may be critiqued, developed, and designed.

ICIDS 2023 was hosted in Kobe, Japan, and sponsored by Kansai University and Ritsumeikan University, but it was also organized as a hybrid event, with participants either attending on-site, or joining the conference remotely. Care was taken to ensure that all aspects of the program were equally accessible to those who were attending physically and virtually.

This year, we received 101 submissions (45 full papers, 22 short papers and 34 Late Breaking Works papers). Following the review process, the Program Committee accepted 30 full papers, 9 short papers, and 22 Late Breaking Works (61 total). The total acceptance rate was 0.61. We also accepted 15 submissions to the Doctoral Consortium.

As in the past, the review process for Papers and Late Breaking Works was strictly double-blind and used a structured and detailed review form. A minimum of three reviews per paper were requested before the decision, with additional reviews solicited on the recommendations of reviewers. In addition, we included a rebuttal phase for long and short papers, and final decisions were made at virtual program chairs' meetings, which included the area chairs. However, we still welcome feedback from both authors and reviewers to help us continue to refine and strengthen the way that we run the conference. We want to thank our area chairs for their hard work and participation in the meta-review process: Mattia Bellini, Colette Daiute, Joshua Fisher, Emily Johnson, Hartmut Koenitz, Vincenzo Lombardo, Sandy Louchart, Mark Marino, Frank Nack, Christian Roth, Rebecca Rouse, and Anastasia Salter.

Finally, we want to thank the members of the ICIDS community who served as reviewers this year. The commitment of our reviewers to provide high-quality reviews and constructive and insightful discussions is a credit to our community, and helps to maintain the rigor and integrity of the ongoing development of this exciting and growing field.

November 2023

Lissa Holloway-Attaway
John T. Murray

# ARDIN, The Association for Research in Interactive Digital Narratives

ARDIN's purpose is to support research in Interactive Digital Narratives (IDN), in a wide range of forms, be that video and computer games, interactive documentaries and fiction, journalistic interactives, art projects, educational titles, transmedia, virtual reality and augmented reality titles, or any emerging novel forms of IDN.

ARDIN provides a home for an interdisciplinary community and for various activities that connect, support, grow, and validate said community. The long- term vision for the suite of activities hosted by ARDIN includes membership services, such as a community platform, job postings, and support for local gatherings, but also conferences, publication opportunities, research fellowships, and academic/professional awards. ARDIN publishes a monthly newsletter and holds a monthly online social, where both established researchers and graduate students share their ongoing work in an informal setting. A new journal (Journal for Interactive Narrative Research), published in collaboration with ETC press, is currently being prepared, with a first issue planned to be available soon. There are also several committees and task forces, listed below.

ICIDS is the main academic conference of ARDIN. Additional international and local conferences are welcome to join the organization. The Zip-Scene conference, focused on eastern Europe, is the first associated conference.

Diversity is important to ARDIN. The organization will strive towards gender balance and the representation of different people from different origins. Diversity also means to represent scholars at different levels of their careers.

No ARDIN member shall discriminate against any other ARDIN member or others outside of the organization in any way, including but not limited to gender, nationality, race, religion, sexuality, or ability. Discrimination against these principles will not be tolerated and membership in ARDIN can be withdrawn based on evidence of such behavior.

The association is incorporated as a legal entity in Amsterdam, the Netherlands. First proposed during the ICIDS 2017 conference in Madeira, Portugal, the association was officially announced at ICIDS 2018 in Dublin, Ireland. During its foundational year, members of the former ICIDS Steering Committee continued to serve as the ARDIN board as approved by the first general assembly at ICIDS 2018. The current board structure and membership were approved at the second general assembly at ICIDS 2019 in Utah, and, as of October 2023, ARDIN has more than 160 members.

More information about ARDIN can be found at https://ardin.online/. ARDIN is also on Facebook (https://www.facebook.com/ARDINassociation), X (@ARDIN_online), and Discord (https://discord.gg/jNg5b5dWP4).

## Committees

The Promotion and Advancement committee is led by Hartmut Koenitz and Josh Fisher with the help of Luis Bruni and Colette Daiute. The aim of this committee is to create a tenure equivalency document and recruit a team of expert reviewers for tenure and examination. Those interested should reach out to Hartmut Koenitz (hkoenitz at gmail.com). The IDN in Education committee is led by Jonathon Barbara. This committee will be looking into how IDN can become a part of school (K-12) curricula and will be producing a white paper with recommendations. Students are also welcome to join as task force members! Those interested should reach out to Jonathon Barbara (barbaraj at tcd.ie).

## Task Forces

The Task Force on Inclusive Pricing Structure is led by Agnes Bakk. This task force will be looking into how to adjust registration for membership and conference registration according to GDP. Those interested should reach out to Agnes Bakk (bakk at mome.hu). The Task Force on ARDIN Outreach is led by Maria Cecilia Reyes. Aims of this task force are to create awareness about IDN and around ARDIN, and to build partnerships with industry, art, and education institutions, among others key stakeholders. Contact Maria Cecilia Reyes (mariaceciliareyesr at gmail.com) for more information or to get involved.

# Organization

## Organization Committee

### General Chairs

| | |
|---|---|
| Ryosuke Yamanishi | Kansai University, Japan |
| Ruck Thawonmas | Ritsumeikan University, Japan |

### Program Committee Chairs

| | |
|---|---|
| Lissa Holloway-Attaway | University of Skövde, Sweden |
| John T. Murray | University of Central Florida, USA |

### Financial Management Chairs

| | |
|---|---|
| Akiko Yamanobe | May Project, Japan |
| Frank Nack | University of Amsterdam, The Netherlands |

### Art Exhibition Chairs

| | |
|---|---|
| Iva Georgieva | Bulgarian Academy of Sciences, Bulgaria |
| Mondheera Pituxcoosuvarn | Ritsumeikan University, Japan |

### Workshop Chair

| | |
|---|---|
| Frederic Seraphine | University of Tokyo, Japan |

### Doctoral Consortium Chairs

| | |
|---|---|
| Hartmut Koenitz | Södertörn University, Sweden |
| Ágnes Bakk Moholy-Nagy | University of Art and Design, Hungary |

### Online Chair

| | |
|---|---|
| Liang Li | Ritsumeikan University, Japan |

## ARDIN Officers and Board

### Executive Board

| | |
|---|---|
| Hartmut Koenitz (President) | Södertörn University, Sweden |
| Frank Nack | University of Amsterdam, The Netherlands |
| Lissa Holloway-Attaway | University of Skövde, Sweden |
| Alex Mitchell | National University of Singapore, Singapore |
| Ágnes Bakk Moholy-Nagy | University of Art and Design, Hungary |

### General Board

| | |
|---|---|
| Luis Bruni | Aalborg University, Denmark |
| Clara Fernandez-Vara | NYU, USA |
| Josh Fisher | Columbia College Chicago, USA |
| Andrew Gordon | University of Southern California, USA |
| Mads Haahr | Trinity College Dublin, Ireland |
| Michael Mateas | UC Santa Cruz, USA |
| Valentina Nisi | University of Madeira, Portugal, and Carnegie Mellon University, USA |
| Mirjam Palosaari Eladhari | Södertörn University, Sweden |
| Tess Tanenbaum | UC Irvine, USA |
| David Thue | Carleton University, Canada, and Reykjavik University, Iceland |

## ICIDS Program Committee Area Chairs

### Theory, History, and Foundations

| | |
|---|---|
| Hartmut Koenitz | Södertörn University, Sweden |
| Mattia Bellini | University of Tartu, Latvia |

### Social and Cultural Contexts

| | |
|---|---|
| Anastasia Salter | University of Central Florida, USA |
| Rebecca Rouse | University of Skövde, Sweden |

**Tools and Systems**

| | |
|---|---|
| Frank Nack | University of Amsterdam, The Netherlands |
| Vincenzo Lombardo | University of Torino, Italy |

**Interactive Narrative Design**

| | |
|---|---|
| Mark Marino | University of Southern California, USA |
| Christian Roth | HKU University of the Arts, The Netherlands |

**Virtual Worlds, Performance, Games and Play**

| | |
|---|---|
| Sandy Louchart | Glasgow School of Art, UK |
| Emily Johnson | University of Central Florida, USA |

**Applications and Case Studies**

| | |
|---|---|
| Colette Daiute | City University of New York, USA |
| Joshua Fisher | Ball State University, USA |

**Late Breaking Works**

| | |
|---|---|
| Hartmut Koenitz | Södertörn University, Sweden |
| Joshua Fisher | Ball State University, USA |

## Program Committee

| | |
|---|---|
| Febri Abdullah | Ritsumeikan University, Japan |
| Alberto Alvarez | Malmö University, Sweden |
| Gabriele Aroni | Manchester Metropolitan University, UK |
| Pratama Atmaja | University of Pembangunan Nasional "Veteran" Jawa Timur, Indonesia |
| Byung-Chull Bae | Hongik University, South Korea |
| Sojung Bahng | Queen's University, Canada |
| Agnes Bakk | Moholy-Nagy University of Art and Design, Hungary |
| Jonathan Barbara | Saint Martin's Institute of Higher Education, Malta |
| Mattia Bellini | University of Tartu, Estonia |
| Jessica L. Bitter | Hochschule RheinMain, Germany |
| Alex Calderwood | Montana State University, USA |

| | |
|---|---|
| Elin Carstensdottir | University of California Santa Cruz, USA |
| Sherol Chen | Passion Talks, USA |
| Laureline Chiapello | NAD UQAC Université du Québec à Chicoutimi, Canada |
| Dan Cox | University of Central Florida, USA |
| Danilo Croce | Univ. of Roma Tor Vergata, Italy |
| Colette Daiute | City University of New York, USA |
| Rossana Damiano | Università di Torino, Italy |
| Steven Dashiell | American University, USA |
| Sam Davern | Trinity College Dublin, Ireland |
| Carl Erez | University of California, Santa Cruz, USA |
| Mury Fajar Dewantoro | Ritsumeikan University, Japan |
| Jamie Fawcus | Skövde University, Sweden |
| Joshua Fisher | Ball State University, USA |
| Terra-Mae Gasque | Georgia Institute of Technology, USA |
| Georgi V. Georgiev | University of Oulu, Finland |
| Iva Georgieva | Bulgarian Academy of Sciences, Bulgaria |
| Zhengya Gong | University of Oulu, Finland |
| Kyle Gonzalez | University of California, Santa Cruz, USA |
| Andrew Gordon | University of Southern California, USA |
| Srushti Goud | University of Torino, Italy |
| Lindsay Grace | University of Miami, USA |
| Mads Haahr | Trinity College Dublin, Ireland |
| Wolfgang Heiden | Bonn-Rhein-Sieg University of Applied Sciences, Germany |
| Kenton Howard | University of Central Florida, USA |
| Ido Aharon Iurgel | Hochschule Rhein-Waal, Germany |
| Emily Johnson | University of Central Florida, USA |
| Shi Johnson-Bey | University of California Santa Cruz, USA |
| Akrivi Katifori | University of Athens, Greece |
| Jonas Knochelmann | University of Utah, USA |
| Hartmut Koenitz | Södertörn University, Sweden |
| David Lamas | Tallinn University, Estonia |
| Bjarke Alexander Larsen | UC Santa Cruz, USA |
| Vittorio Lauro | Università di Torino, Italy |
| Vincenzo Lombardo | Università di Torino, Italy |
| Sandy Louchart | Glasgow School of Art, UK |
| Péter Kristóf Makai | Kazimierz Wielki University, Poland |
| Mark Marino | University of Southern California, USA |
| James Minogue | North Carolina State University, USA |
| Alex Mitchell | National University of Singapore, Singapore |
| Kevin Moloney | Ball State University, USA |

# Contents – Part II

# Contents – Part I

**Tools and Systems**



**Interactive Narrative Design**

# Applications and Case Studies

# *Bury Me, My Love*: The Boundary Between Reality and Fiction in IDNs for Smartphone

Serge Bouchardon(✉)

Université de Technologie de Compiègne, Compiègne, France
serge.bouchardon@utc.fr

**Abstract.** Interactive digital narratives for telephones, described as *smartfictions*, are based on our ordinary practices with a smartphone, in particular instant messaging and notifications. Using the example of *Bury me, my Love,* the paper analyses the play on the boundary between reality and fiction, but also what these narratives reveal about our own use of the smartphone and the ethical issues they raise.

**Keywords:** Interactive narrative · smartfiction · smartphone · notification · fiction · reality

## 1 Introduction

If we think of all the digital works that are inserted into the social media, whether it be twitterature or novels on Instagram, to mention only these examples[1], it is the frontier between reality and fiction that is constantly being re-interrogated. These narratives provoke an intrusion of fiction into spaces that are not originally intended for it. To what extent does the digital reconfigure the boundary between reality and fiction, and to what extent are interactive digital narratives a good indicator of this?

On smartphone application platforms (Google Play and App Store), there are more and more interactive narratives for smartphones, "smartfictions" [1]. These fictions are based on ordinary, everyday practices with a smartphone, such as instant chat, but also notifications (such as *Lifeline* or *Somewhere*). These fictions introduce the reader's *real time* into the fictional setting. The time of the smartphone and the time that passes are data that are fictionalised.

Based on a close reading of *Bury me, my Love*[2], the aim of this paper is to understand what is at stake in this blurring of the boundary between reality and fiction, but also what these stories tell us about our own use of the smartphone and the ethical issues they raise.

[1] One might also think of the whole online tradition of ARGs, *Alternate Reality Games*, or the "fictional profiles" on which Alexandra Saemmer and Bertrand Gervais are working (author's note). Actually, pretending veracity goes back a long time and has been used in regular fiction for centuries, e.g., in Gothic stories.

[2] http://enterremoimonamour.arte.tv/. In Arabic, "Bury me, my Love" means "take care of yourself", "don't you dare die before me".


L. Holloway-Attaway and J. T. Murray (Eds.): ICIDS 2023, LNCS 14384, pp. 3–13, 2023.
https://doi.org/10.1007/978-3-031-47658-7_1

## 2 *Bury Me, My Love*: Crossing Borders

The "narrative game"[3] *Bury me, my Love* (*Enterre-moi, mon amour* for the original French version), published in 2017, is the result of a collaboration between the studio *The Pixel Hunt* and the television channel *Arte France*. The starting point for this creation was a testimonial story published by the newspaper *Le Monde* in 2016 and entitled "Le Journal d'une migrante"[4]. This diary consists of the Whatsapp feed of a young Syrian woman migrating to Germany. This testimonial story was later transformed into an fictional story, *Bury me, my Love*[5] (see Fig. 1).

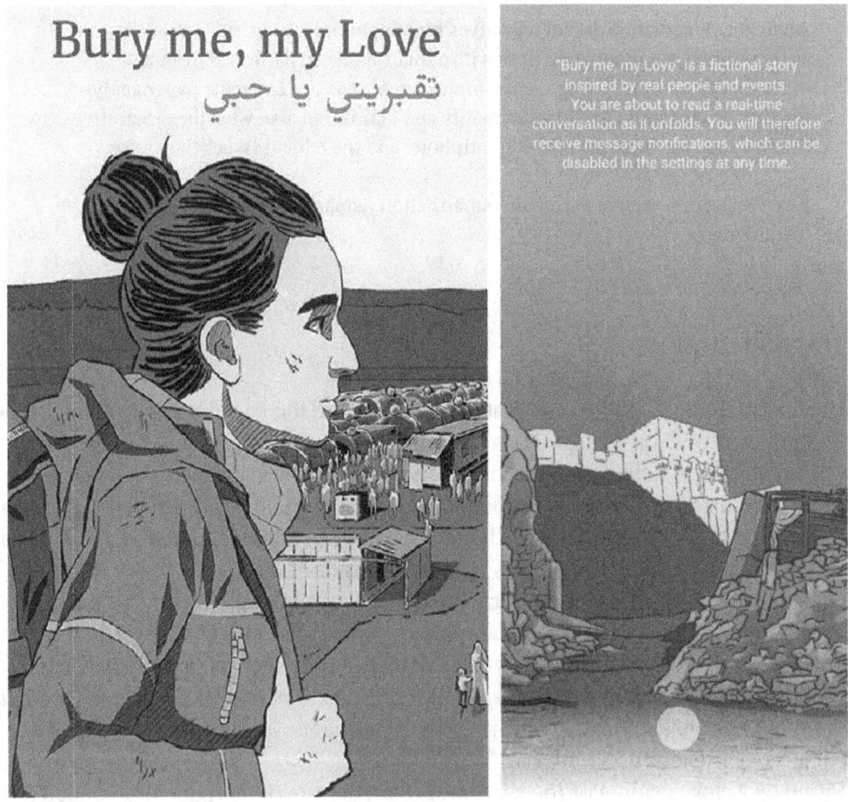


**Fig. 1.** Intro screens of "Bury me, my Love".

[3] It is under this category that this creation is marketed.

[4] https://www.lemonde.fr/international/visuel/2015/12/18/dans-le-telephone-D-une-migrante-syrienne_4834834_3210.html.

[5] The interactive prologue is playable here: http://enterremoimonamour.arte.tv/prologue.

In this interactive digital narrative, we play the character of Majd, the husband of Nour, a young Syrian woman trying to reach Europe. We exchange with Nour via instant messaging. We try to advise her and to support her morally (see Fig. 2). The journey between Syria and Europe has no set duration. The journey can last several days.

The play on chronology and temporality is combined with a play on cartography and spatiality. The reader can access the progress of Nour's journey via a geolocation tag, located at the top right of the instant discussion space (see Fig. 2). The reader can thus visualise the character's progress in real time on a map. This temporality is also an indication of the reader's progress in the story. The closer Nour gets to one of the European countries, the closer the reader gets to the end of the reading experience. It is therefore both a spatial and temporal marker of the character's progress as well as that of the reader in his/her reading journey.

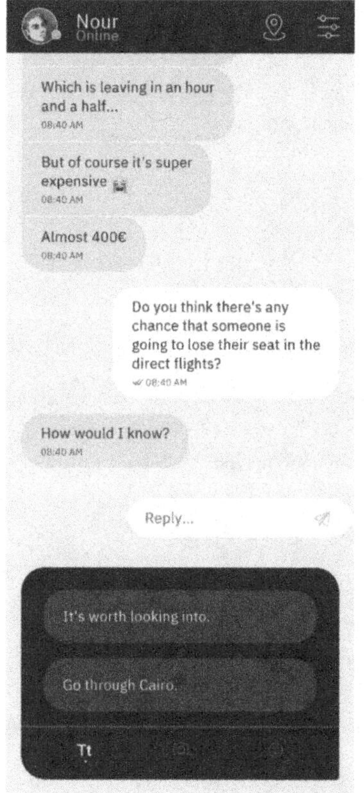


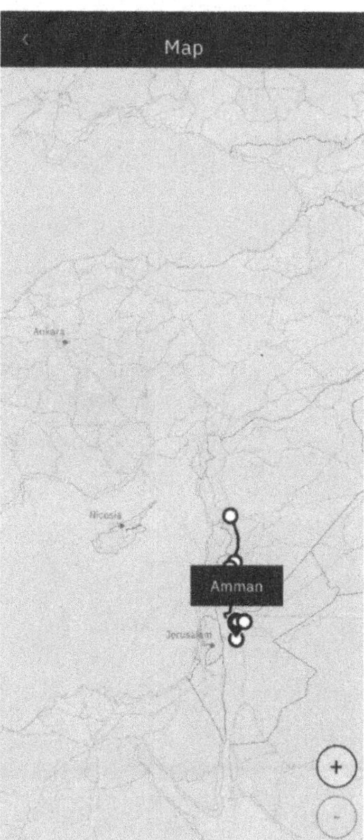


**Fig. 2.** Map (right) showing the character's route.

Along each route (there are 19 different endings in this IDN), a counter indicates the days that pass. The border may be temporarily closed, Nour may have an appointment with an acquaintance who does not arrive… In this case, should we wait or reconsider our plans? "Your communications will be in pseudo-real time: if Nour has to do something that is supposed to take her a few hours, you will not be able to reach her during that time. When she returns, you will be notified that she is available again - and that she may need you"[6] (Fig. 3).

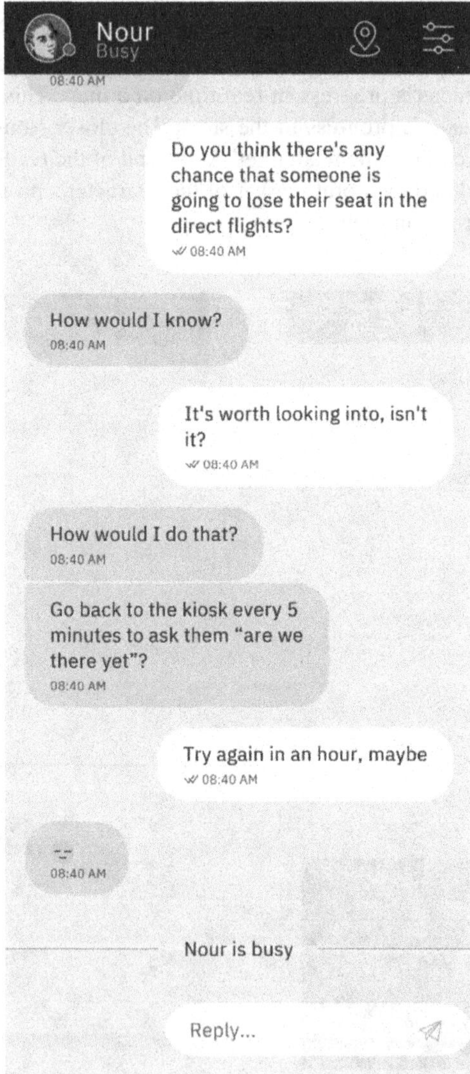


**Fig. 3.** The character Nour is no longer available. The reader must wait for a notification from her.

[6] http://enterremoimonamour.arte.tv/.

## 3 The Reader's *Real Time*

It is this "real time" mode that interests us here (see Fig. 4). It should be noted that the reader can deactivate the "real time" notifications if he or she wishes, as this mode is activated by default.

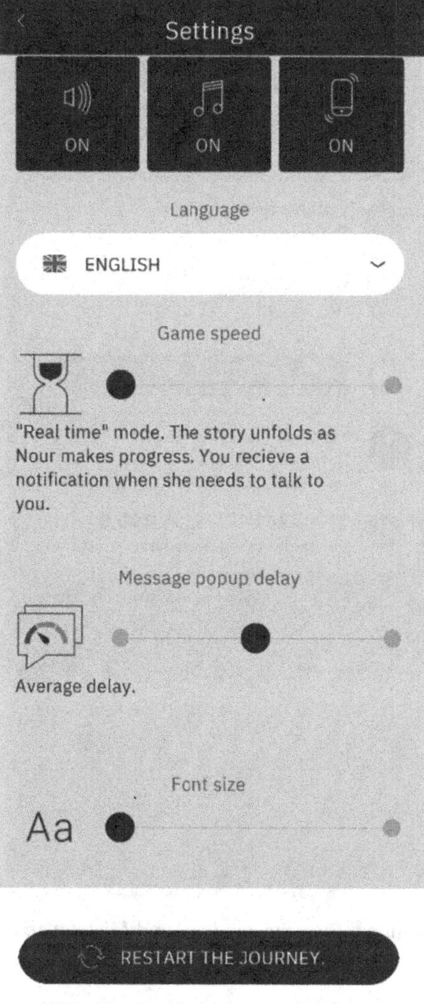


**Fig. 4.** *Real-time* mode settings.

There is a play on temporality with the intrusion of the reader's (and the fictional character's) "real time". The relationship to reading time is thus different with the intrusion of notifications: when he or she receives a notification from Nour, among other notifications (see Fig. 5), the user is encouraged to dive back into the fiction to dialogue with the character. From a phenomenological point of view, there is an interruption with the injunction of the notification. Notification-based fictions[7] thus go quite far in disrupting the user's time, but at the same time reintroduce the user's "real time" into the fictional setting. Manon Picard has referred to these fictional notifications as "notifictions" [1].

**Fig. 5.** Fictional notifications (*Bury me, my Love* and *Lifeline*) among other notifications.

Just as *locative narratives*[8] play on the boundary between fictional space and the reader's real space, encouraging the reader to physically move to a given place to advance the narrative, notification-based narratives play on the boundary between fictional time and the reader's real time.

[7] These include *Lifeline* (2015) and *Somewhere* (2017).

[8] For example *The Cartographer's Confession* (2017), by James Attlee, set in London.

What do these smartfictions that involve notifications bring? They give us the impression of co-presence. As readers/actors of smartfiction, when we make a choice, we somehow make the fictional character present through our actions. But this notion of presence is further reinforced when we respond to the character's call via a notification. We make the time of the other (as well as that of the fiction) happen. The temporality of the character (and of the events) coincides, via the notifications, with the temporality of the reader, who then fully appropriates the duration of the story. Note that for some readers, having to leave the story to wait for a notification can be a disengagement factor from the story (in this case, it is always possible to deactivate the notifications).

For Paul Ricoeur, "time becomes human time insofar as it is articulated in a narrative manner; in turn, narrative is significant insofar as it draws the features of temporal experience" [2]. Narrative is, according to this perspective, our main tool for situating ourselves in time - and for situating time in us. Furthermore, the digital can be characterised as a "tool for the phenomenal deconstruction of temporality" [3]. Indeed, it translates into two trends: real-time calculation, giving the impression of immediacy; universality of access[9], giving the impression of availability. The digital, in its availability and immediacy, would thus lead to a permanent present, without any temporal flow [3].

The smartfictions that play with notifications could allow a retemporalisation of human time de-temporised by computation.

## 4 An Indicator of Smartphone Use

The play on notifications is based in particular on the fact that the smartphone device is our device for everyday communication and writing practices. The blurring between reality and fiction is all the more effective because it is the same device that we use to communicate in everyday life and to read/act in fiction. This blurring can be found in all the *Lost Phone* type smartfictions (*A Normal Lost Phone*, *Another Lost Phone*, *Ana the Game*...): the user is supposed to have found a phone in which he or she can rummage (email, photos, diary...) to understand the character's story.

If this gives the fiction an effect of reality, we also perceive, through the fictional notifications that blur the real, that the smartphone is in a way itself a medium of derealisation: it builds a layer of fiction outside the real world. Thanks to these fictions, we thus understand that the smartphone device is already a medium of fiction (and narration) introducing a new relationship to temporality (and probably also reminding us that the fiction/reality distinction must be overcome in this case).

Smartfiction thus has a reflexive dimension. It invites us to reflect on the daily use of the medium and device that is the smartphone. There are few devices that are used daily and that serve as narrative devices. The aesthetic diversion, which is carried out in an artistic gesture, shifts the focus and thus reveals the relationship that we have with the smartphone on a daily basis. Our everyday uses are always filled with fiction and narrative. Smartfiction, which exploits the possibilities of the device, thus reveals a power at work in all the uses of the smartphone: isn't any use of the smartphone in

[9] While it can indeed be said that the smartphone has reached near global ubiquity, it is not universal nor are smartfictions universally accessible.

some way a smartfiction, thus tainted by absence and fiction? It is our own relationship to the blurring of the boundary between fiction and reality that interactive smartphone narratives bring to the fore, and about which they encourage us to question ourselves.

## 5 Fictions and Ethical Issues

Many smartfictions emphasise the fact that they are based on real data (for example, the *Whatsapp* feed of the Syrian migrant, Dana, published by the *Le Monde* website, and the real testimonies of migrants that fed into *Bury me, my Love*). Florent Maurin, co-writer and game designer of *Bury me, my Love*, also speaks of a "game of reality". In his speeches and interviews, he addresses the question of reality/fiction, insisting on the fact that *Bury me, my Love* is a fiction and that this creation must be taken as such… But at the same time he insists on the fact that "everything we tell is based on reality, on concrete testimonies, and first and foremost Dana's. We didn't want to tell something that couldn't have happened"[10]. In *Bury me, my Love*, we thus have a hybrid between fact and fiction. Françoise Lavocat has argued that "what is factual is referential, and what is fictional is not" [4]. This is undoubtedly reductive, as fiction seems most of the time - if not always - to have a referential value (political, social, historical…), even though Thomas Pavel [5] underlines that what matters about fiction is its relation to the human capacity of invention and the complex requirements of imagination.

In *Fait et fiction. Pour une frontière* [4], Françoise Lavocat sets out to deconstruct the blurring of the boundaries between reality and fiction, seeking to "show the existence and the cognitive, conceptual and political necessity of the boundaries of fiction" in all the arts of fiction. There is thus a tension between the need to establish the boundaries between reality and fiction[11] and the perpetual blurring practiced by the creators of digital fictions, in particular smartphone IDNs such as *Bury me, my Love*. This blurring of the boundaries between reality and fiction is often a commercial argument: "The application chooses one alternative over another depending on your location, the time of day and even the weather around you. The story should thus come as close as possible to your context to enhance immersion."[12]

The *ultra-personalisation* of certain digital fictions for smartphones (for example, if it is raining when I am reading the story, it is raining in the story I am reading…) has a consequence: the reader is not invited to de-centre himself or herself in order to immerse him or herself in an imaginary experience; on the contrary, it is the story that is moulded into the sphere of his or her identity.

More broadly, there is a current trend in storytelling, embodied in particular by the fashion for autofiction. The narrative is not seen as an opening to the other, but as an extension of oneself, for the author as well as for the reader. Often, one no longer tells a story, that is, what happened to others than me, or to me as another, but extends one's present identity into fiction. In a way, in many contemporary fictions, the other is now

[10] *Bury me, my Love*: a split/screen documentary: https://youtu.be/JGF1z8sSv9s.

[11] One can think of the proliferation of *fake news* on the internet as part of a form of grand conspiracy narrative.

[12] "*Chronique(s) d'Abîme*, a novel that adapts to your context": https://www.igen.fr/app-store/2016/06/chroniques-dabime-un-roman-qui-sadapte-votre-contexte-96253 (2016).

only approached as a mirror of the self. Digital technology is part of this trend, but not the source of it. Digital technology introduces a presentism (content is consulted as if it were simultaneous with my consultation, there is no longer any marker of past time), and proposes a role as actor/player and not only as reader. In addition to presentism and interactivity, another feature of the digital world accentuates this trend, namely the blurring of the boundaries between reality and fiction, particularly in smartfictions that use the smartphone as a medium for fictionalisation.

If, in *Bury me, my Love*, Nour's story is an extension of myself, what allows me to pretend to live what she lives? One can understand the ethical resistance of some readers. The question of ethical issues arises when the role of a migrant (or the role of a parent of a migrant) is played by a reader comfortably seated in front of his or her computer or smartphone, especially when the experience is presented as a "narrative game". It is thus conceivable that some users may be reluctant to "fictionalise" [6] such a story.

However, in *Bury me, my Love*, the feeling of helplessness experienced by the readers/players when they have only one possible answer, or when they have two and none of them suit them, reminds them that it is not their stories, but that of Majd (who is jealous, somewhat racist towards Iraqis in particular…). Majd's character is strongly characterised, in a somewhat counter-intuitive way compared to many video games in which the character we play is intentionally neutral, without any marked personality, so that the player can more easily embody him or her (think for example of the character of Gordon Freeman in *Half-Life*). The aesthetics of *Bury me, my Love*, in stylized drawing, also introduces distance and goes against the idea of a "game of reality". There is therefore a whole play on distance, in relation to the character and in relation to the story.

Hartmut Koenitz [6] mentions that "the study by Scott Parrot et al. [7] provides evidence for the positive effects of an IDN to combat prejudices against migrants", even though "empathy is a problematic category when it comes to intended prosocial effects, as for example Rebecca Rouse has pointed out" [8]. The "impeded desire to help the character", which according to Françoise Lavocat [4] characterises empathy in fiction, works well in *Bury me, my Love*, all the more so because the main character (Nour) is not the one we embody. Moreover, the fact that the fate of the character ends up partly eluding the reader, despite the promises of the interactive device, can also be seen as a way of re-establishing a certain otherness of the not-me. In smartfiction, there is a sense that the interactive device can increase the possibility of empathy tenfold.

Jean-Marie Schaeffer [9] tells us that "fictional universes, far from being illusory appearances or deceptive constructions, are one of the major aspects of our relationship with reality". And no doubt the digital – and IDNs in particular - opens up possibilities in this play on the boundary between reality and fiction, and on the promise of an empathetic fictional device.

But the impact of such works remains to be seen. Brecht [10] underlines that catharsis prevents active critical reflection on the social conditions depicted in a work. Thus, because of the empathy it creates, doesn't *Bury me, my Love* make the reflection necessary for social and political changes more difficult to approach? Alternatively, to what extent is there a need to create empathy for Syrian migrants, i.e. to what extent is empathy necessary for the reader to be able to reflect on social and political changes?

**Examples of Smartfictions**

***Ana Ana The Game***

- (app store) https://apps.apple.com/fr/app/ana-the-game/id1202981332
- (play store) https://play.google.com/store/apps/details?id=com.plug_in_digital.anathegame

***Another Lost Phone: Laura's story***

- (app store) https://apps.apple.com/fr/app/another-lost-phone/id1267197755
- (play store) https://play.google.com/store/apps/details?id=com.accidentalqueens.anotherlostphone

***Enterre-moi, mon amour/Bury me, my Love***

- (app store) https://apps.apple.com/fr/app/enterre-moi-mon-amour/id1281473147
- (play store) https://play.google.com/store/apps/details?id=com.plug_in_digital.emma

***Lifeline***

- (app store) https://apps.apple.com/fr/app/lifeline/id982354972#?platform=iphone
- (play store) https://play.google.com/store/apps/details?id=com.threeminutegames.lifeline.google

***Memento M***

- (app store) https://apps.apple.com/us/app/memento-m/id1533799527
- (play store) https://play.google.com/store/apps/details?id=com.glaznev.detective5

***Seven – Endgame***

- (app store) https://apps.apple.com/fr/app/seven-endgame/id1476673731
- (play store) https://play.google.com/store/apps/details?id=air.de.sponsorads.endgame

***Simulacra***

- (app store) https://apps.apple.com/fr/app/simulacra/id1252035454
- (play store) https://play.google.com/store/apps/details?id=com.kaigan.simulacra

***Somewhere: The Vault Papers***

- (app store) https://apps.apple.com/fr/app/somewhere-the-vault-papers/id1340903844
- (play store) https://play.google.com/store/apps/details?id=com.tanuki.somewhere

## References

1. Picard, M.: La smartfiction: une fiction interactive à lire, un rôle à incarner ou une partie à jouer sur son smartphone? PhD Dissertation. Université de technologie de Compiègne, Compiègne (2022)
2. Ricœur, P.: Time and Narrative, vol. 1. University of Chicago Press, Chicago (1985)

3. Bachimont, B.: Le sens de la technique : le numérique et le calcul. Editions Les Belles Lettres, Paris (2010)
4. Lavocat, F.: Fait et fiction. Pour une frontière. Seuil, Paris (2016)
5. Pavel, T.: Fictional Worlds. Harvard University Press, Cambridge (1986)
6. Koenitz, H.: Understanding Interactive Digital Narrative: Immersive Expressions for a Complex Time. Taylor & Francis Ltd., Boca Raton (2023)
7. Parrott, S., Dillman, F., Northup, T.: A test of interactive narrative as a tool against prejudice. Howard J. Commun. **28**, 374–389 (2017)
8. Rouse, R.: Against the instrumentalization of empathy: immersive technologies and social change. In: Fisher, J.A. (ed.) Augmented and Mixed Reality for Communities, pp. 3–19. FL, Boca Raton (2021)
9. Schaeffer, J.-M.: Pourquoi la fiction ? Seuil, Paris (1999)
10. Brecht, B.: Schriften zum Theater. Suhrkamp, Berlin (1963)

# Traversing Boundaries When Translating a Literary IDN into Several Languages: A Case Study

Serge Bouchardon[1(✉)] and Nohelia Meza[2]

[1] Université de Technologie de Compiègne, Compiègne, France
serge.bouchardon@utc.fr

[2] Benemérita Universidad Autónoma de Puebla, Puebla, Mexico

**Abstract.** *Déprise* is an interactive digital narrative that was initially published online in 2010 (http://deprise.fr or http://lossofgrasp.com). Over time, this literary interactive narrative was translated from its original French version French into English (2010), Italian (2011), Spanish (2013) and Portuguese (2016), and more recently into Arabic, Chinese, German, Hungarian, Polish and Russian (2020). Every translation led to an intercultural and transcreative process (Portela, Pold & Mencia, 2018) involving the translators and the author. We asked the English, Italian, Spanish, and Portuguese translators of the work for feedback on the translation process via interviews. In this paper, we employ the written exchanges with the translators to explore and question the modes of collaboration between author and translator as well as the significance of translating specific dimensions of literary IDNs. Additionally, we briefly discuss some future research trajectories on translating IDNs: the role of indirect translation (Gambier, 1994), the cultural dimension of the works, and translation as reinvented memory.

**Keywords:** Translation · multilingualism · translinguistic · transcreation

## 1 Introduction

At ICIDS conferences, the issue of translating an IDN was primarily addressed as a form of translation between media (for example "adaptation of stories as a translation between media, such as literature and film", [1]), but rarely as translation into several languages. This paper presents an overview of the different experiences in translating the literary interactive digital narrative *Déprise* [2][1]. Our objective was to comprehend the various strategies that the process involved. In order to do so, we have asked the English, Italian, Spanish, and Portuguese translators of the work for feedback on the translation process: Valerie Bouchardon (*Loss of Grasp*, 2010), Giovanna di Rosario (*Perdersi*, 2011), Martha Asunción Alonso (*Perderse*, 2013), and Diogo Marques (*Perda de controlo*,

[1] For further reference: http://deprise.fr or http://lossofgrasp.com. For video capture of the interactions: https://youtu.be/nd6_b158qOs.



L. Holloway-Attaway and J. T. Murray (Eds.): ICIDS 2023, LNCS 14384, pp. 14–27, 2023.
https://doi.org/10.1007/978-3-031-47658-7_2

2016). Drawing upon the written exchanges with the translators, we discuss the following points: 1) modes of collaboration between author and translator (programming strategy between translator and author; the translator's digital literacy and familiarity with digital literary works; the translator's visibility); 2) the significance of translating specific dimensions (code migration, semiotic forms and gestures, embedded voices). Additionally, we briefly discuss some future research trajectories concerning the translation of IDNs (the role of indirect translation (Gambier, 1994), the cultural dimension of the works, translation as reinvented memory). Lastly, following the four facets of translating digital literary works as identified by María Mencía, Søren Pold, and Manuel Portela's [3] – 1) translinguistic; 2) transcoding; 3) transmedial; 4) transcreation – we explore whether such facets are found in the translator's experiences with *Déprise*.

## 2 A Case Study: *Déprise/Loss of Grasp*

### 2.1 General Aspects of the Digital Narrative

*Déprise* [2] (henceforth referred to *DP*) is an online literary interactive narrative. The English version of the work (*Loss of Grasp)* won the New Media Writing Prize in 2011. This work is part of the *ELMCIP Anthology of European Electronic Literature* [4] and the *Electronic Literature Collection volume 4* [5]. *DP* consists of six scenes that portray the mindscapes of a man who gradually loses grasp of his life. In scene 1, the protagonist contemplates his life and experiences a stormy moment, a *loss of grasp*; in scene 2, he meets his future wife on a date; in scene 3, he reads his wife's twofold love/breakup letter; in scene 4, he reads his son's poignant text; in scene 5, he experiences an internal struggle which culminates in a complete *loss of grasp*; and in scene 6, he decides to confront the situation to take control of his life again. With each scene, the reader is challenged to decipher the relationship between the computer's interfacial imaginaries and her/his own self. The work was originally programmed in Flash in 2010 and migrated to HTML/JavaScript in 2018. Though this paper is based on the English, Italian, Spanish, and Portuguese Flash versions of the work, it is important to note that the Arabic, Chinese, German, Hungarian, Polish and Russian versions were published in January 2020 (see Fig. 1) and were exclusively developed in JavaScript.

### 2.2 The Interview Process

The initial interviews and exchanges were conducted during the same years as the individual translations, involving Valerie Bouchardon (*Loss of Grasp*, 2010), Giovanna di Rosario (*Perdersi*, 2011), Martha Asunción Alonso (*Perderse*, 2013), and Diogo Marques (*Perda de controlo*, 2016); subsequently the translators were recontacted in 2020. All correspondence occurred through email and the questionnaires were written in French and English. The languages of communication between the author and the translators were as follows: V. Bouchardon (French), di Rosario (French/English), Alonso (French), Marques (English). Multilingualism was part of the process from the outset. For instance, Diogo Marques, responsible for the Portuguese translation, used the English version as the source text and compared certain aspects of his translation with the French original

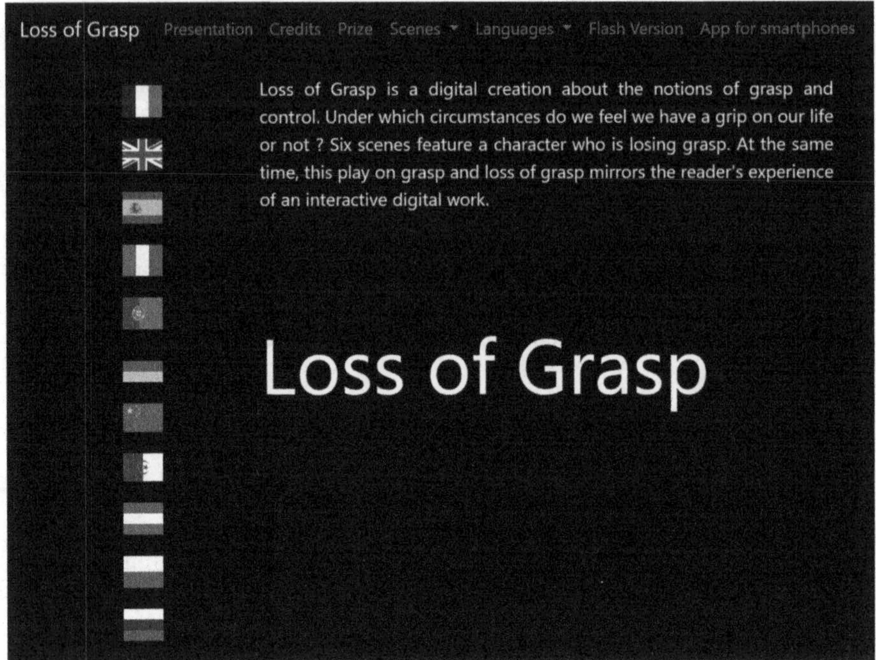


**Fig. 1.** Homepage of Déprise/Loss of Grasp.

as well as the Spanish and Italian versions, but communicated with the author in English. Undoubtedly, the exchanges between the author and the translators led to an intercultural and multilingual dialogue, inviting to traversing linguistic and cultural boundaries.

## 3 Different Forms of Collaboration

### 3.1 Between Text and Code

In digital works, "code" can create a certain distance between the translator and the author. The extent of collaboration between the author and the translator impacts the author's task of programming the "translated text". Consider for example the importance of semiotic manipulation when recreating similar literary effects in the different versions of a work. In the case of *DP*, most of the translators sent the linguistic text to the author without subsequent involvement in the development of the code adaptations of their respective versions.

In the course of the interview, V. Bouchardon (*Loss of Grasp*, 2010) expressed the following: "I preferred to work with the code file. I needed to see the coding context to better understand the interplay between the code and what appears on the screen." This statement raises the question of the structural opacity of any computer program, the question of the mediation of computation between the code and the representation on screen. Di Rosario (*Perdersi*, 2011) had a similar thought when dealing with the reproduction of the rhetorical figures of the text:

*My primary concern has always been to reproduce "the movements" of the original text in my translation. It's not just a linguistic challenge, of course, when I think of Déprise and all its "rhetorical figures", I still wonder if I really managed to render them all in Italian. My aim was to preserve the "invisible" digital text, and I am not thinking, in this case, about the code but about what the code allows the writer and the reader to do.*

These two examples highlight the particularity of literary IDNs in delineating the boundaries between code, author and translator; how does the "code distance" between the author and the translator affect the programming of the digital work into different versions? Following the interviews, we observed a pattern: once the linguistic content was sent to the author, programmed into the new version, and shared as a trial version between author and translator, the translators would frequently request modifications to their versions after reading and interacting with their version of the work. We noticed that particularly reading time (on the screen), interaction and manipulation challenges played an essential role in the translation test version process[2].

### 3.2 The Translator's Digital Literacy and Familiarity with Digital Works

The first critical approach to the translation of *DP* into a different language (Italian version) was made by di Rosario and Borràs [6]. The researchers pointed out that the role of the translator in the digital era is changing "as not only does s/he need to translate words, but also images and movements, and sometimes s/he is also required to have the technical competence to do it." By "technical competence", we refer not only to the translator's digital literacy (i.e. computer skills) but also to a certain level of familiarity with digital works. During the interviews, di Rosario, Alonso, and Marques answered that *DP* was the first digital work they had ever translated[3]; and specifically, for Alonso (*Perderse*, 2013), she had never heard of digital works before and therefore translating *DP* was a completely new experience for her.

In response to this, Marques asks: "Should digital literary works of art be translated by non-specialists of digital literature?" One way to answer Marques' interrogation is to consider the example of Alonso (Spanish version), who is not a specialist of digital literature, but who managed to translate the work through email communication with the author. However, Alonso's translation primarily centered on working with the linguistic content and phonetics, and not with the code file as was the case for V. Bouchardon, di Rosario, and Marques himself. Considering that Marques and di Rosario are digital literature researchers, that V. Bouchardon is an ESL teacher and Alonso is a translator,

[2] In a subsequent study, it will be relevant to go further in highlighting the key differences that the translation of IDNs has with other forms of media translation over time. In particular, it could be interesting to look at the intricacies of diverse genres affecting the translator's task, such as those involved in translating a print novel and timeline media and/or video and live-AI-rendered content.

[3] V. Bouchardon had already translated other works by the author, "Les douze travaux de l'internaute" (2008) and "Toucher" (2009), di Rosario and Marques will later translate, "Opacité" (2012) and "Détrace" (2016).

we can further ponder how the translator's professional background influences the translation of the source digital text? Is there a specific digital literacy for the translator of digital literature?

Recording voices (scenes 1, 2 and 4) as part of the translation process is specific to *DP*. This involves translating the transcript, identifying a voice actor/actress, asking them to read and record the translated transcript and send it to both the translator and author. For example, while working on the Portuguese version, Marques said that "he needed to find three people to voice the text and to ensure access to recording equipment"; similarly, di Rosario noted that there is also a very basic technical problem to keep in mind: "in order to translate digital works, you need several technical tools specifically for the recording"[4]. V. Bouchardon, on the other hand, employed the same software (Audacity) for recording herself as she uses with her students, thereby circumventing the need to learn a new tool. As we can observe, the level of technical integration into the different translation methodologies fluctuates depending on the professional background of the translator and on the extent of the collaboration between author and translator. Sometimes, the translators found it necessary to acquire a new set of skills depending on the challenges they encountered; for instance, we can notice that translating and recording new audio content into other languages was underlined by Marques and di Rosario as an important step in their translation methodology. This aspect presented not only technical complexities but also posed challenges related to voice performance, as will be elaborated upon in Sect. 4.3, "sound and meaning".

### 3.3 The Visible and the Invisible

In their article titled "Renderings: Translating Literary Works in the Digital Age", Marecki and Montfort [7] discuss how the role of the translator changes when translating digital literature in comparison with traditional works:

> *In traditional works, the translator is often invisible, a background figure, sometimes subtly credited or even not mentioned at all. In the case of digital works, the translator becomes visible, an ambassador of the work, often explaining its mechanism and the translation process.*

The interviews reveal the translators as active and versatile figures when it comes to working on digital literature. They are able to ask questions, speak to the author about stylistic matters, develop their own methodologies, acquire new digital literacy skills (if needed), and experience the act of translation through new modes of aesthetic and literary communication (such as interacting with and manipulating their linguistic text, in contrast with print literature). There is a dialogue, an exchange of ideas and at times an involvement in the coding process. Translators are recognized (as evidenced in the work's credits) and have a voice and role in the creative process.

[4] It is important to mention that V. Bouchardon and Marques used their own voices in the English and Portuguese versions. This is an example of transcreation in translation as they performed their linguistic translation by recording their voice and making it part of the digital work. This fact underlines the idea of the translator as a collaborator-mediator, one that is present not only through his/her words (linguistic text) but also through the presence of his/her voice (audio).

Moreover, visibility and invisibility in translating digital literature can be explored in a different way if we go back to the idea of the invisible digital text existing beyond the screen, and its visible linguistic translation. As di Rosario explains when sharing her translation experiences:

> *In a certain sense I find that the linguistic translation is "visible", i.e. one can overlook the connotation of a word or its nuances, yet easily refer back to the original text, to at least check the original word (the word is present and fixed on the page). In digital literature, things get more complicated, because obviously one can translate the linguistic content correctly, and at the same time, part of the meaning of the work – that is also created by other movements, by manipulations, etc. – can be forfeited.*

Di Rosario emphasizes once again the importance of interaction and manipulation of the work to evaluate the aesthetic effects of the linguistic text beyond the screen. It seems that within the translation process, there is certainly a negotiation between the visible and invisible text and its aesthetic outcome. For his part, Marques [8] highlights the ideas of transparency, translucency, and intersemiotic aspects when translating digital works:

> *It is interesting to note that the idea of transparency and translucency in digital interfaces that is being propelled by digital technology industries, can be compared to the idea of transparency and translucency in the context of translation. Namely when it comes to translating something that stops being exclusively discursive in order to become multimodal and involve multisensory perception.*

Certainly, intersemiotic translation is specific to digital literature where visual, auditory and other sensory channels play an important role in the construction of meaning of the works. Marques' and di Rosario's observations indicate that their concerns as translators are directly related to the competencies that they already have as digital literature readers and researchers (how do we read digital literature?).The fact that di Rosario mentions "digital rhetorical figures" shows a specific aspect of the concealed dynamics of literariness within a work of digital literature. On the other hand, Marques' reflections on the complexity of multisensory perception (e.g. App version) bring to the forefront the intersemiotic choices (e.g. shifts of time, context, and texture of semiotic resources), Bouchardon and himself had to make during the process of collaborative translation.

## 4 Translating the Specific Dimensions of Digital Literature

### 4.1 From Flash to JavaScript

*DP* is one of the many digital works that have encountered the challenge of programming software obsolescence. Flash, the original software in which the French, English, Italian, Spanish, and Portuguese versions were developed, stopped running in December 2020. In a bid to adapt the work to the current technological challenges, the author migrated these four versions to JavaScript in 2018. The process of loss and gain in translation was reflected on the "screen disturbances" from one piece of software to another. Certain "iconic features" of the Flash version were lost, while other "aesthetics aspects" were improved in the JavaScript version. It is important to note that this paper does not address the "re-adaptions" of the linguistic text, such as the transition from the English Flash version to the English JavaScript version; however, we are aware that a "revised translation process" is needed for the previously published versions of the work that have been recently re-programmed due to software obsolescence (Figs. 2 and 3).

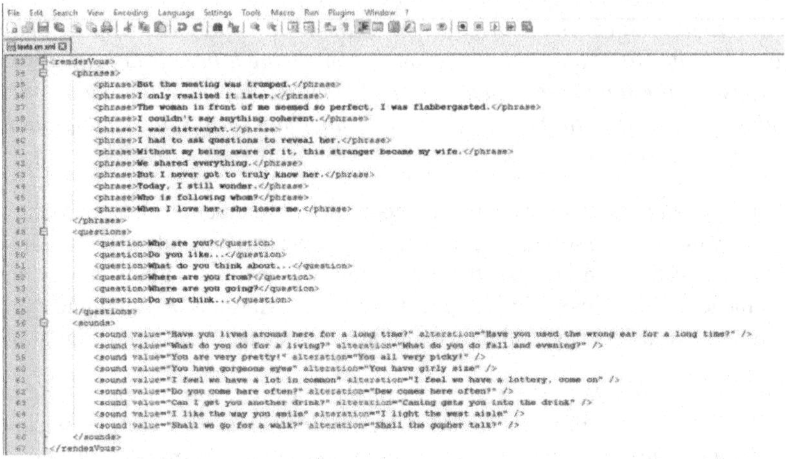

```xml
<rendezVous>
    <phrases>
        <phrase>But the meeting was trumped.</phrase>
        <phrase>I only realized it later.</phrase>
        <phrase>The woman in front of me seemed so perfect, I was flabbergasted.</phrase>
        <phrase>I couldn't say anything coherent.</phrase>
        <phrase>I was distraught.</phrase>
        <phrase>I had to ask questions to reveal her.</phrase>
        <phrase>Without my being aware of it, this stranger became my wife.</phrase>
        <phrase>We shared everything.</phrase>
        <phrase>But I never got to truly know her.</phrase>
        <phrase>Today, I still wonder.</phrase>
        <phrase>Who is following whom?</phrase>
        <phrase>When I love her, she loses me.</phrase>
    </phrases>
    <questions>
        <question>Who are you?</question>
        <question>Do you like...</question>
        <question>What do you think about...</question>
        <question>Where are you from?</question>
        <question>Where are you going?</question>
        <question>Do you think...</question>
    </questions>
    <sounds>
        <sound value="Have you lived around here for a long time?" alteration="Have you used the wrong ear for a long time?" />
        <sound value="What do you do for a living?" alteration="What do you do fall and evening?" />
        <sound value="You are very pretty!" alteration="You all very picky!" />
        <sound value="You have gorgeous eyes" alteration="You have girly size" />
        <sound value="I feel we have a lot in common" alteration="I feel we have a lottery, come on" />
        <sound value="Do you come here often?" alteration="Dew comes here often?" />
        <sound value="Can I get you another drink?" alteration="Caning gets you into the drink" />
        <sound value="I like the way you smile" alteration="I light the west aisle" />
        <sound value="Shall we go for a walk?" alteration="Shall the gopher talk?" />
    </sounds>
</rendezVous>
```


**Fig. 2.** Example of XML code for the scene 2 of Loss of Grasp (for the Flash version in 2010).

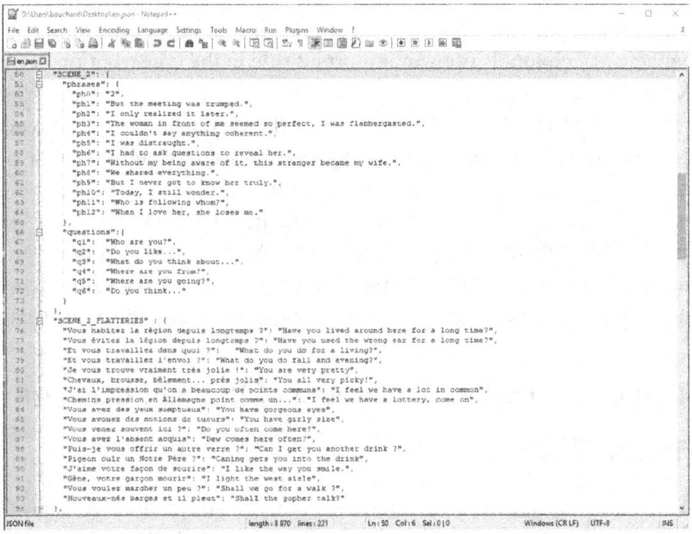

```json
"SCENE_2": {
  "phrases": {
    "ph0": "2",
    "ph1": "But the meeting was trumped.",
    "ph2": "I only realized it later.",
    "ph3": "The woman in front of me seemed so perfect, I was flabbergasted.",
    "ph4": "I couldn't say anything coherent.",
    "ph5": "I was distraught.",
    "ph6": "I had to ask questions to reveal her.",
    "ph7": "Without my being aware of it, this stranger became my wife.",
    "ph8": "We shared everything.",
    "ph9": "But I never got to know her truly.",
    "ph10": "Today, I still wonder.",
    "ph11": "Who is following whom?",
    "ph12": "When I love her, she loses me."
  },
  "questions":{
    "q1":  "Who are you?",
    "q2":  "Do you like...",
    "q3":  "What do you think about...",
    "q4":  "Where are you from?",
    "q5":  "Where are you going?",
    "q6":  "Do you think..."
  }
},
"SCENE_2_FLATTERIES" : {
  "Vous habitez la région depuis longtemps ?": "Have you lived around here for a long time?",
  "Vous évitez la légion depuis longtemps ?": "Have you used the wrong ear for a long time?",
  "Et vous travaillez dans quoi ?":   "What do you do for a living?",
  "Et vous travaillez l'envoi ?": "What do you do fall and evening?",
  "Je vous trouve vraiment trés jolie !": "You are very pretty",
  "Chevaux, brousse, bêlement... près jolis": "You all very picky!",
  "J'ai l'impression qu'on a beaucoup de points communs": "I feel we have a lot in common",
  "Chemins pression en Allemagne point comme un...": "I feel we have a lottery, come on",
  "Vous avez des yeux somptueux": "You have gorgeous eyes",
  "Vous avouez des notions de tueurs": "You have girly size",
  "Vous venez souvent ici ?": "Do you often come here?",
  "Vous avez l'absent acquis": "Dew comes here often?",
  "Puis-je vous offrir un autre verre ?": "Can I get you another drink ?",
  "Pigeon ouïr un Notre Père ?": "Caning gets you into the drink",
  "J'aime votre façon de sourire": "I like the way you smile.",
  "Gêne, votre garçon mourir": "I light the west aisle",
  "Vous voulez marcher un peu ?": "Shall we go for a walk ?",
  "Nouveaux-nés barges et il pleut": "Shall the gopher talk?"
},
```


**Fig. 3.** Example of JSON file for the scene 2 of Loss of Grasp (for the smartphone App version in 2018).

With this in mind, it can be argued that *DP* undertook a true process of transcoding (moving from Flash to JavaScript) and transmediation (transitioning from PC to an App for smartphones and tablets). Rethinking the scenes with a tactile dimension (given the absence of mouse pointer on smartphones) implied a challenging transcreation task for both the author and the translators. The translation between machine -readable codes has had an effect on the visual – and audio – glitch effect apparent in the JavaScript versions. For example, scene 1 (the protagonist's stormy moment, complete *loss of grasp*) is rendered differently with JavaScript in both the web-based and the App version causing the speed of semiotic displacement to decrease (Fig. 4). Similar examples include the interaction with the love/breakup letter written by the protagonist's wife in scene 3 wherein the act of reading the text aligns more cohesively with upward and downward motions (JavaScript) compared to the right-to-left approach (Flash). Additionally, the appearance of the individual phrases in scene 6 is perceived as slower and less graspable in the JavaScript rendition than in Flash. It seems that the "compositional principle" [9] of the work could not be expressed in the same way with the shift from Flash to JavaScript.

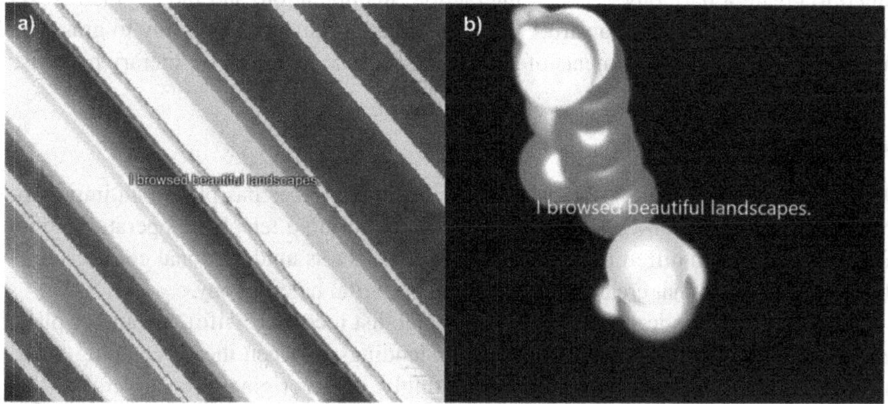


**Fig. 4.** a) Excerpt from scene1 (Flash version); b) Excerpt from scene1 (JavaScript web-based version).

## 4.2 Semiotic Forms and Gestures

The interplay of semiotic resources (words, images, audio, gestures, etc.) plays an important role in digital literature translation practices. Can we truly achieve intersemiotic cohesion in the translation of certain works of digital literature? For example, when recreating similar literary effects (i.e. figures of speech and rhetorical figures) in the different versions of the piece. In *DP* such literary and rhetorical effects are possible thanks to "figures of manipulation" (meaning gestural manipulation). These figures rely on a gap between the reader's expectations while manipulating the text and the result on the screen [10]. Considering this, we argue that the translatability of the literary effect of the figures of manipulation calls for a careful intersemiotic translation in all the current target languages (English, Italian, Spanish, Portuguese).

For example, in scene 2 (the rendez-vous when the protagonist meets his wife), a question mark appears on the screen, waiting for the reader to explore its functionality. A few seconds later, the reader understands that s/he needs to click on the question mark for a series of questions to randomly appear on the screen: *"Who are you?", "Do you like...", "What do you think about...", "Where are you from?", "Where are you going?", "Do you think..."* (Fig. 5a). Following Mencía, Pold, and Portela (2018), this is a key moment for the translation of the piece at different levels: 1) translinguistic: insofar as the translators had to translate the different versions of the linguistic text from the source language to the different target languages (Fig. 5b, 5c, 5d); 2) transcoding: insofar as the author had to reproduce this effect on the five new JavaScript versions as well as on the App (migrating platforms); 3) transmediation: insofar as the translators and the author had to integrate certain semiotic modalities into the App version (e.g. multilingual visual narration of the woman); 4) transcreation: insofar as the author and translators had to reproduce the literariness and translatability of the "figures of manipulation" (interaction and manipulation) that unveil the image of the woman's character. The translation process aimed to create a harmony between interaction, manipulation, and the linguistic texts in different languages that construct the same image. The aim is not only to grasp the meaning of the aesthetic elements of expression but also to search for literary patterns.

### 4.3 Sound and Meaning

*DP* is a polyphonic creation. Translating the different voices has played an important role in the translation process. The voices of the narrator, a telephone operator and an adolescent appear in different scenes. These voices act as unidirectional conversations at different rhythms that create an atmosphere of digital heterophony.

In scene 2 (the rendez-vous when the protagonist meets his wife), the author plays with what he calls "alterations" or misunderstandings between the voice being heard and what actually appears on screen. Interestingly, in the original French version, this effect was created accidentally. That is, the original idea was to use a speech recognition software programme to generate these alterations or misunderstandings.

a. *Vous habitez la région depuis longtemps ? (Vous évitez la légion depuis longtemps*
b. *Et vous travaillez dans quoi ? (Et vous travaillez l'envoi ?)*
c. *J'ai l'impression qu'on a beaucoup de point communs (J'ai la pression et la pinte en commun)*
d. *Je vous trouve vraiment très jolie ! (Chevaux, brousse, bêlement... prés jolis)*
e. *J'aime votre façon de sourire (Gêne, votre face a des soupirs)*
f. *Vous voulez marcher un peu ? (Nouveau-nés barges et il pleut)*

Except for V. Bouchardon, the translators were not aware of the use of speech recognition software programme to generate these alterations, and therefore tried to reproduce this effect in the English, Italian, Spanish and Portuguese versions. The stylistic challenge was experienced differently by each of them, di Rosario (*Perdersi*, 2011) explains:

> Another complicated part was what Bouchardon called the "alteration": in fact, in one scene there are some sentences that will be changed. I left some of the meanings, especially in the main sentences, but I played with the sound of the

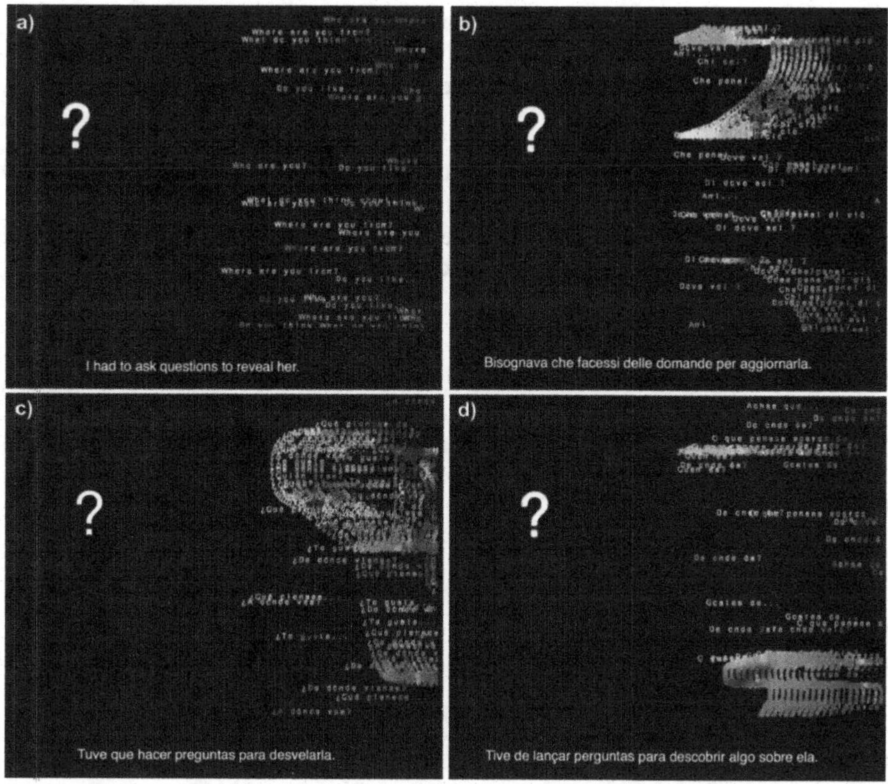


**Fig. 5.** Déprise, Flash version, scene 2 target languages: a) English, b) Italian, c) Spanish, d) Portuguese.

words in the "alteration", like Bouchardon did in the French version so the meaning of some sentences is totally different.

For her part, Alonso (*Perderse*, 2013) notes:

When I had to translate *Déprise*, I worked on the alterations in order to obtain the same effects of surprise as in French. For that, I played quite freely on phonetics. I consider this aspect (the recreation of rhythms and sounds) to be the main challenge of any translation. This seems to me to be of major importance in the case of a digital piece, directly appealing to all the senses of the reader[5].

In his experience, Marques (*Perda de controlo*, 2016) comments:

[5] It is important to underline that the Spanish translator (Alonso) communicated with the author in French, « Quand j'avais eu à traduire Déprise, j'avais travaillé les altérations dans le but d'obtenir les mêmes effets de surprise qu'en français. Pour cela, j'avais joué assez librement sur la phonétique. Je considère que cet aspect (la recréation des rythmes et des sonorités) constitue le principal défi de toute traduction. Cela me semble revêtir une importance majeure dans le cas d'une œuvre numérique, faisant directement appel à tous les sens du récepteur ».

> I found particularly challenging to "transcode" into Portuguese that specific French humour present in all of Serge's interactive fictions. For instance, in the case of cultural transfers, such as thorny idiomatic expressions and the added difficulty in translating homophonic words.

For V. Bouchardon, the experience was a little different. The translation of this part was the result of an ongoing discussion with her husband (the author). Moreover, as an ESL teacher, V. Bouchardon is used to her students confusing sounds and words in English. She relied on her teaching experience to render the "alterations".

**Translation examples scene 2**

**French (original):**

"J'aime votre façon de sourire"
(Gêne, votre face a des soupirs);

**English:**

"I like the way you smile".
(I light the west aisle);

**Italian:**

"Mi piace il tuo modo di sorridere"
(So il tuo ruolo nell'uccidere);

**Spanish:**

"Me encanta tu sonrisa"
(Andar por la cornisa);

**Portuguese:**

"Gosto da maneira como sorris"
(Gosto da bandeira como só ris)

Translating the dichotomy of meaning and sound is one of the greatest challenges in the translation of scene 2. The translators' imagination and stylistic strategies proved a true process of transcreation, considering that the original version was made with a speech recognition software programme. Certainly, the linguistic and phonetic exercise triggered the following questions: how to translate cultural humour in a work of digital literature? How do different cultures interpret *DP*? The fact that *DP* continues to be translated into different languages gives it a "prismatic translation" effect [11]. On the one hand, the voices on scene 2 belong to different cultural contexts (France, Spain, Italy, Portugal) and individuals; and on the other hand, random cultural elements were used in the translations to fit each individual context. Moreover, these translations show the inextricable connection between multilingualism and multiculturalism as a product and as a challenge of translation.

## 5 Future Trajectories

### 5.1 The Role of Indirect Translation

The French (original) and English versions of *DP* were released simultaneously in 2010. In the interviews, the translators expressed that for some of them the source language alternated between the French and the English version. Therefore, there are two things to consider: 1) the translator's knowledge of other languages, 2) the existing translations at the date of a new version. We know for a fact that the source text used by V. Bouchardon was the French version (2010). In the case of di Rosario (2011) and Alonso (2013), they also worked with the French version (2010) but had the possibility to make aesthetic and linguistic comparisons with the English version (2010); whereas, Marques' (2016) source text was the English version, but he had the linguistic competencies to read the original French version, and make comparisons with the Spanish and Italian versions. The interconnections among the source and target languages open the possibility to speak of a process of indirect translation in digital literature, namely a translation of a translation [12].

As we can observe, V. Bouchardon's English version (*Loss of Grasp*, 2010) stands as a referent considering that English acts as a language of reference and encounter between translators (*lingua franca*). With this in mind, we can ask, up to what extent has V. Bouchardon's English translation influenced other versions of *DP*? Which would be considered as the source text: *Déprise* (2010) or *Loss of Grasp* (2010), or maybe both? What is the visibility and *literary impact* of indirect translations in the future versions of *DP*? In a future critical approach, we will certainly investigate the methodological possibilities of indirect translation in literary IDNs (borrowings, comparisons, dissimilarities), taking as a case study the six new versions of *DP* (Arabic, Chinese, German, Hungarian, Polish and Russian).

### 5.2 The Cultural Dimension

*DP* contains passages strictly related to Western culture. For instance, in scene 3, the reading from left to right of the love/break up letter in comparison to reading from right to left in the Arabic version; also in scene 3, the inclusion of Georges Bizet's Carmen as background music; in scene 4, the concept of "hero" expressed by the protagonist's son; also in scene 4 the mention of the word Zoïle (a Greek critic); to name but a few examples. The adaptation to the different versions of such aesthetic and poetic effects raise the following questions: how do we substitute or compensate for such cultural aspects in the target culture? How do we deal with cultural transferences when translating works of digital literature? In the example of the love/breakup letter in the Arabic version, we find that the double meaning and visual effect of the linguistic text is relevant to the meaning of the work, but not culturally consistent with the target language. A similar thing happens with Bizet's Carmen where the Opera plays an important role in the construction of the literary atmosphere of the scene – as the protagonist reads the letter, but it might not be suitable for the different contexts of the translations; or the translation of the word (persona) "Zoïle" into the different languages.

In her article, "Digital cultures: A view from French studies and literature" [13], Erika Fülöp expresses a desire to "counter the stereotype of a homogenous global culture in the Digital Age", insisting on the fact that digital literature preserves the traces of pre-digital cultures. Fülöp's reasoning is closely related to the translation of literary digital creations today. Should the role of the translator (into English, for example) be to dilute cultural references so that an English-speaking audience may *identify* with the work, or on the contrary to reproduce any traces of cultural specificity, thus emphasizing the cultural diversity of the productions of digital literature more than their international dimension [14]? If so, is cultural diversity expressed uniquely through the linguistic dimension of digital literature? What about the relation and equilibrium between digital aesthetics and cultural transferences?

### 5.3 The Digital: A Reinvented Memory

If we consider translations of literary IDNs as archives of cultural and technological elements: computer software that stores ways of expression of a specific digital software period (Flash obsolescence and perhaps in the near future, JavaScript), cultural translation of idiomatic expressions, cultural adaptations of the fine arts; a link could be made between translation and preservation. The added value of digital technology is not where one expects. The digital medium is not a natural preservation medium but on the contrary it is hell for preservation. But digital technology makes us enter another universe which is a universe of *reinvented* and not stored memory [15].

From an anthropological point of view, this model of memory is more valuable and more authentic than the model of printed media which is a memory of storage (the book that one stores on a bookshelf just like the memory that one would store in a case of one's brain). Indeed, cognitive sciences teach us that memory does not function on the model of storage and conservation. Preserving is thus permanently reinventing the content – just like translating. The issue is to have an accurate and faithful invention, a reconstruction in which the changes are explicit and commented upon. On a similar level, translation highlights the digital age as a move from a model of stored memory to a model of continuous *reinvented* memory. Thus, from this point of view, considering the interplay of intersemiotic forms in literary IDNs (words, images, audio, gestures) and keeping in mind Reynolds' proposition of "prismatic translation" [11], literary IDNs can be regarded as a good laboratory to experiment with translation in the digital age.

## 6 Conclusion

The insights drawn from the interviews underscore that translation processes generate a creative tension that interweaves media, semiotic forms, programmed writing, aesthetic experience, and cultural aspects. These translation processes – spanning the translinguistic, transcoding, transmedial and transcreative dimensions (Mencía, Pold and Portela, 2018) – prove to be ways of traversing boundaries and barriers.

Culture is present within literary IDNs in a plethora of forms; therefore, translation can act as a vehicle for the dissemination of cultural works, reaching diverse audiences. Interviewing translators yields a comprehensive perspective of the different processes and methodologies used when translating a literary IDN, particularly when the goal is to cover more than one target language. The growing number of literary IDNs, characterized by a diversity of genres and technological apparatus, will not only shape the evolution of translation methodologies, but will also help to redesign research trajectories within the field itself.

## References

1. Spierling, U., Hoffmann, S.: Exploring narrative interpretation and adaptation for interactive story creation. In: Interactive Storytelling, ICIDS 2010, Edinburgh, UK, 1–3 November 2010, Proceedings, pp. 50–61 (2010)
2. Bouchardon, S., Volckaert, V.: Déprise/Loss of Grasp. http://deprise.fr or http://lossofgrasp.com (2010, Flash version), (2018, HTML/JavaScript version)
3. Mencía, M., Pold, S., Portela, M.: Electronic literature translation: translation as process, experience and mediation. Electronic Book Review (2018). http://electronicbookreview.com/essay/electronic-literature-translation-translation-as-process-experience-and-mediation/. Accessed 3 June 2023
4. Engberg, M., Memmott, T., Prater, D.: ELMCIP Anthology of European Electronic Literature (2012). https://anthology.elmcip.net/. Accessed 3 June 2023
5. Inman Berens, K., Murray, J.T., Lyle, S., Rui, T., Zamora, M.: Electronic Literature Collection, vol. 4 (2022). https://collection.eliterature.org/4/,2022. Accessed 3 June 2023
6. Di Rosario, G., Borràs, L.: Translating digital literature: two experiences and a reflection. Texto Dig. **8**(1), 138–162 (2012). https://doi.org/10.5007/1807-9288.2012v8n1p138. Accessed 3 June 2023
7. Marecki, P., Montfort, N.: Renderings: translating literary works in the digital age. Digital Schol. Human. **32**(suppl_1), 84–91 (2017). https://doi.org/10.1093/llc/fqx010. Accessed 3 June 2023
8. Marques, D.: Reading digits: haptic reading processes in the experience of digital literary works. PhD Thesis, Portugal, Universidade de Coimbra (2018). https://estudogeral.sib.uc.pt/handle/10316/81171?mode=simple. Accessed 3 June 2023
9. Cayley, J.: Translation as process. In: Mitchell, C., Raley, R. (eds.) Amodern 8, Translation-Machination (2018). http://amodern.net/issues/amodern-8-translation-machination/. Accessed 3 June 2023
10. Bouchardon, S.: Figures of gestural manipulation in digital fictions. In: Bell, A., Ensslin, A., Rustad, H. (eds.) Analyzing Digital Fiction, pp. 159–175. Routledge, London (2014)
11. Reynolds, M.: Translation: A Very Short Introduction. Oxford University Press, United Kingdom (2016)
12. Gambier, Y.: La retraduction, retour et détour", Meta : journal des traducteurs/Meta: Transl. J. **39**(3), 413–417 (1984). https://doi.org/10.7202/002799ar. Accessed 3 June 2023
13. Fülöp, E.: Digital cultures: a view from French studies and literature. Explor. Media Ecol. **17**(3), 271–277 (2018). https://doi.org/10.1386/eme.17.3.271_1. Accessed 3 June 2023
14. Bouchardon, S.: Mind the gap! 10 gaps for Digital Literature?. Electronic Book Review (2019). http://electronicbookreview.com/essay/mind-the-gap-10-gaps-for-digital-literature/. Accessed 3 June 2023
15. Bouchardon, S., Bachimont, B.: Preservation of digital literature: from stored memory to reinvented memory. Cibertextualidades **5**, 184–202 (2013). http://cibertextualidades.ufp.edu.pt/numero-5-2013/electronic-publishing-models-for-experimental-literature. Accessed 3 June 2023

# The Ethical Colonizer? Grand Strategy Games, Colonization, and New Ways of Engaging Moral Choices

Mia Consalvo[1], Andrew Phelps[2](✉), Lindsay D. Grace[3], and Roger Altizer[4]

[1] Concordia University, Montreal, QC, Canada
[2] American University, Washington, DC, USA
andymphelps@gmail.com
[3] University of Miami, Miami, FL, USA
[4] University of Utah, Salt Lake City, UT, USA

**Abstract.** This work explores the relationship of "4x" games rules, the historical narratives they offer, and player choice. Such games offer an ability for players to alter the accepted form and format of history by playing through alternate scenarios based on their choices as key countries, governments, and political groups. However, these choices are limited by the game's governing mechanics, which prescribe the historical geopolitical status of the countries they portray, shaping in-game propensities for accruing specific resources, production of products, and shipping with specific partners.

Using the game *Victoria 3* as an initial case study, we explore a 'successful' play, although complicated by socioeconomic concerns, of playing as "Belgium" in an initial campaign, and then a contrasting experience playing as "Cambodia" under the same system. The resulting successes and failures offer useful perspective; we examine not just the failure of rules-systems as they pertain to historically based interpretations and the co-creation of narrative regarding such, but also touch on the role that these systems have in representing the differing capabilities of various positions/nations within the game. Ultimately, the player can draw their own conclusions on the concept of colonialism, but games such as *Victoria 3* have much to say on the capabilities of these systems to construct narratives based on player choice, where the interpretation of that narrative is significant to the evaluation of larger economic and governmental concerns.

**Keywords:** Grand strategy games · Ethics · Moral dilemmas · 4x games · Interactive digital narratives

## 1 Introduction

Scholars have studied many videogames for their inclusion of ethical dilemmas and morality-based choices. Titles as diverse as *Papers, Please; Skyrim; Life is Strange* and those in the *Mass Effect, Witcher*; and *Fallout* series have come under scrutiny for the ways that their storylines, game mechanics, and representations all interweave to produce worlds where choices matter to players, and where - at least sometimes -


L. Holloway-Attaway and J. T. Murray (Eds.): ICIDS 2023, LNCS 14384, pp. 28–37, 2023.
https://doi.org/10.1007/978-3-031-47658-7_3

there are no easy or correct answers to the quandaries presented. Research on these games and in this area is diverse and ongoing [5, 9–12, 15, 16, 18]. Miguel Sicart's work is foundational here, pointing to the possibilities of designing games with "wicked problems" for players to enjoy [11]. Zagal likewise argues for greater study of "ethically notable games" that create novel strategies for engaging players [17]. Likewise, scholars such as Consalvo and Phelps have analyzed games such as *Night in the Woods* to better understand how such games makes arguments procedurally, denying player agency as a way to make moral statements [4]. Other research has investigated how players perceive such games, including their use of mechanics such as "morality meters," and how the ability to customize characters/avatars can/cannot be helpful [3].

At the same time, grand strategy or "4x" (shorthand for "explore, expand, exploit, exterminate") games have also been studied, but often with a different focus. Much of that work has involved the possibilities for using such games to teach history as well as political and social systems [14], along with concerns about how such games accurately (or not) present culture and historical places [2]. Increasingly however, games such as those in the *Civilization, Europa Universalis, Victoria,* and *Hearts of Iron* franchises have been rightfully critiqued for the ways they continue the colonialist project, framing most advances in civilization as coming from the west, and reusing tropes springing from colonization and colonialism without careful thought or nuanced representation. Critiques from scholars such as Souvik Mukherjee examine how Orientalism is expressed in games such as *Civilization,* and how the spatiality built into such games via the activity of "filling in the map" or taking over more countries or territories and then controlling it enacts or replays elements of colonialist projects [8]. Likewise, Sybille Lammes has written about how such games both contain nostalgia for certain elements of the past, as well as offering the possibility for playing with history, and potentially re-envisioning it as well as our futures [7].

Yet those varied critiques have not yet been combined for more substantive investigations of how 4x games offer players potential ethical dilemmas to examine. Hartmut Koenitz argues interactive digital narratives offer "representations of complexity that foster systemic thinking by facilitating an understanding of multiplicity, interconnectedness, and long-term effects" [6]. Additionally, scholars including Eliane Bettocchi et al. have argued for rethinking the design criteria and possibilities of IDNs to go beyond the Eurocentric foundations of game design to better include non-Western creators as well as designs and ideas for both pedagogical as well as ludological ends [1, 13].

Grand strategy games do just this – players are not simply presented with binary choices isolated in time and space – instead they allow players to build and shape systems, seeing how different choices can play out over years, decades, and even centuries. The story of the game is interpreted by what the player has built. Such games' interactive systems can convey not only the results of player agency, but also population pushback, rebellion, and even failure. All this can be done through more and less "accurate" versions of history as well as through fantasy and science fiction versions of similar systems. What better way to play with and explore the complexities of the real past, or potential pasts or imagined futures, and the ethics of advancement within those eras, than with games such as *Victoria 3 (V3)* that offer deep simulation of the political, economic, and social systems of particular historical periods?

This analysis is part of a larger project engaged in a comparative analysis of several 4x games that present possible ethical dilemmas to players via their various systems, narratives, and representations. Here, however, we confine ourselves to the Paradox Interactive game *Victoria 3,* released in 2022. As with most such games, players of *Victoria 3* can easily amass hundreds of hours of gameplay, as the game offers the ability to play as one of dozens of countries and lets the player take very different approaches to achieving 'victory.' Gameplay starts in the year 1836, with a fairly accurate snapshot in place of technological, social, and geopolitical developments for different countries across the globe. The objective is to play through 1936 – a 100-year time span, and achieve either pre-set objectives, or the player's own. Players can also engage in modding the game as well as in competing against other players, although this paper only examines the single-player vanilla version (without mods) of the game. Even within those limits there are still too many options for a full analysis of every option, choice, or narrative available to the player. This paper highlights two different playthroughs and a subset of choices offered, one as Belgium and one as Cambodia. To do so the lead researcher engaged in approximately 40 h of gameplay, which included initial familiarization with the game itself, a full playthrough of the Belgium campaign (as seen in Fig. 1), and approximately 10 h of playthrough as Cambodia. The Cambodia playthrough was halted when numerous "fail states" were encountered and enough difference was perceived between that country and Belgium to begin analysis. Notes were taken during gameplay, and screenshots of significant events captured. Initial impressions were shared with the team, who collaborated in writing the analysis and bringing in relevant theory to the project. With respect to researcher positionality, all four authors come from North America, and bring a Western perspective to their game experience. Further research on this topic should be conducted by Asian, European, African or other scholars to assess

**Fig. 1.** Starter campaigns to learn gameplay

their own reactions and understandings of the game as well as potential mods that might challenge Western, colonialist frameworks.

Even this limited accounting however demonstrates our central argument – that such grand strategy games both succeed and fail in interesting ways to have the player engage with a variety of moral dilemmas, and craft their own narrative of how history might have turned out in specific geographic locales. They therefore merit further study as IDNs with important implications.

## 2 Playing as Belgium

In *V3*, Belgium is first offered to the player as a tutorial country – one of four options given for learning to play the game. Due to their complex nature, tutorials for grand strategy games are a necessity, particularly for new players. Tutorial campaigns offer the player clear objectives to achieve (e.g. build a factory, enact a new law, expand the bureaucracy), they have active tooltips and explainers that communicate not simply *how* to do something but also *why* it is a good idea (see Fig. 1). The countries in tutorial campaigns are also fairly stable, either economically and/or politically.

Starting a game of *V3* feels a bit like flipping open a history book to a random page. A certain government is in power, particular laws are in place, and specific technologies have already been developed. This isn't random however- as the game starts in 1836, there is no women's suffrage yet, for example, but technologies like the printing press are widespread. The game offers the player a number of objectives of increasing complexity to achieve, which the player can choose to fulfill or ignore. Those tasks give the player concrete goals to achieve as they learn how to play the game, unlocking more advanced objectives, or the player can move the country in their own desired direction. As part of the tutorial campaign, the player also learns how to acquire the goods they need to build new businesses, factories, and state run offices. At first such items come from their own natural resources (such as lumber mills) and then via trade with other countries for things not grown or produced locally.

Inevitably, as with our own playthrough, the focus turns from an inward focus to an outward focus. In our playthrough, the sticking point (no pun) was rubber. Belgium's textile mills, motor industries, electrics industries, barracks and conscription centers increasingly needed rubber for steady production, the tooltips explained. But the only place to source rubber was from rubber plantations, something not found locally in Belgium. Instead, rubber came from plantations in places like Congo, Brazil, and Cambodia. Yet direct trade with those places wasn't possible in the game's historical setting. For one, Belgium was part of a trade group led by Great Britain and couldn't trade on its own, and for another, most of the rubber coming from plantations elsewhere was not independently produced but was the result of colonies controlled by other European nations. So, at first, Belgium decided to acquire rubber via trade with Great Britain. But that was only a short term solution, it turned out. Even Great Britain had a perpetual shortage of rubber, leading us to the question of whether or not to colonize a locale with rubber and control production on their own.

At this point, if the game were a narrative adventure, the player would likely be offered a choice of whether or not to colonize and/or control a specific country that produced rubber, in order to enhance their own economy. Yet *V3* sets conditions up very differently. The game doesn't explicitly ask if one can "become a benevolent colonizer" or even a fair trading partner. The interactivity set up through a strategy game is far more complex, leading the player to have to consider many more steps to achieve their goals, and possibly consider the ramifications of those choices.

Because of the game's fairly accurate historical period, most of the geographic locations that produce rubber are not available to become trading partners on their own, as they can be Unincorporated States or not open to trading with others. Instead, one must either forgo rubber (and all associated forward development) or go the route of colonization. Yet it still isn't as simple as "colonize/not colonize." As Belgium, the player begins with the starting condition of "No Colonial Affairs," where the country's laws do not allow for such activity. To even consider the possibility of engaging in colonization, the player must also research the technology of "Colonization" if it isn't already unlocked ("luckily" for Belgium it is unlocked). They player must also research "Quinine" if they wish to colonize areas where there is a high prevalence of Malaria.

*V3* offers two paths other than No Colonial Affairs: Colonial Resettlement and Colonial Exploitation. The game characterizes each option slightly differently – in Colonial Resettlement, "colonies are established to provide land to settlers from the country's incorporated states" while in Colonial Exploitation, "colonies are established to exploit the area for their natural resources and cheap labor." In practice, both involve moving one's population to regions they were never invited to, setting up camp, and pushing out the locals, although the Exploitation option does so at a faster pace. Notably, Quinine research is a necessity to help keep not only the player's Belgian settlers healthy but also to give to native occupants. However, as the game explains, it is only the settlers that get the medicine. If settlements scale up too rapidly, "Native Uprisings" can occur, forcing the country into war. However, given the relative technological inferiority of neighboring countries in Africa and Southeast Asia, this isn't much of a problem (from the perspective of the game-as-system). The only *real* challenge is getting to the "good spots" in Africa, Asia and elsewhere before other colonizing European nations do so. Those "good spots" are resource rich environments that further the player's goals.

## 3 What Ethical Dilemmas Does the Player Engage with as Belgium?

Although there are plenty of 'micro-choices' in *V3* that allow the player to engage in ethical reflection (should they prioritize production and disregard worker safety, or slow production and ensure the populate is safe and therefore happier), major choices in *V3* aren't often presented explicitly as "choices" – i.e., with two or three alternatives offered at once for the player to choose between. Instead, decisions such as whether or not to colonize, or abolish child labor, are presented via more complex systems- most often the laws and policies that the country has in place. For example, the player-as-Belgium must engage the political system to change its laws to allow for even the possibility of colonization. To do this they must manage the political parties in power who have the ability to act upon, or stymie and delay, those laws. And if no political party in power favors such a law, it cannot be introduced. Once it is tabled for discussion, further events can occur that might speed up, stall, or destroy its chances.

For example, when trying to pass a law to allow for "Colonial Resettlement," which takes many weeks of debate in the government, a "No Colonial Affairs" movement began in our population, which spawned micro-events such as one where the populace was concerned that "cheap colonial labour" would be utilized, thereby making their own jobs obsolete. Another micro-event can occur titled "the ethics of exploitation" (see Fig. 2) stating that "the government's attempt to pass the Colonial Resettlement law has brought the ethics of colonialism to the forefront of public debate." The player further learns that some are objecting because "we have no right to interfere, control, or exploit. They say we bring 'civilization'; we bring misery and oppression; we rig the entire social economic structures of the colonies to serve our selfish needs."

Through these micro-events as well as the larger event of trying to engage in Colonialism, *V3* attempts to portray some of the issues associated with colonization. The player can then determine – should they reassure the populace they will not lose their jobs, should they slow down plans for establishing colonies and potentially lose lucrative sites to other nations – how much or how little to engage? While these are not actual people being displaced or exploited, the historical reflection being offered does allow the player to think through the politics and the ethics of such systems in ways that more limited choice-based games cannot.

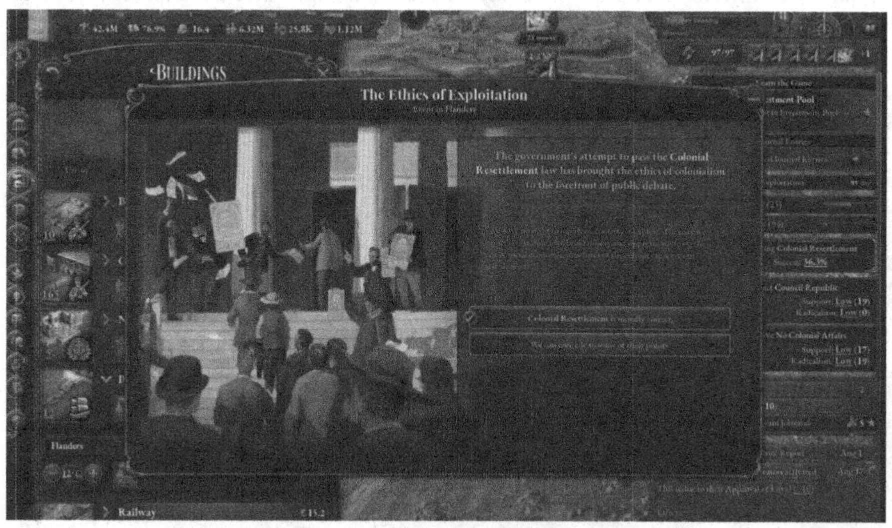


**Fig. 2.** The Ethics of Exploitation

Of course, even in *V3* the player cannot truly opt out of the colonialist system, although that too can be part of the moral argument to be made. Players can delay or slow colonization efforts, 'concede' some points to the protesters, and promise to tread carefully. But no real options are offered as a way to bypass this exploitative system. By doing this, the game acknowledges the real history that has occurred, but attempts to interject a variety of ethical and moral frameworks for the player to consider. Further, given that the player cannot opt out entirely (unless they stop playing), they must eventually concede their own complicity in propping up and perpetuating such systems. Of course, not all players will care, and/or will dismiss the scenarios as 'just a game,' but the complexity offered, and the lack of an easy way out, at least offer the possibility for ethical reflection on how such systems have played out in the actual past.

## 4 Playing as Cambodia (Aka Hard Mode)

Another way to think through moral dilemmas via 4x games would be to try and play as the colonized, or the smaller, "less strategic" countries. In *V3* however some places are unplayable – the player cannot start as an Unincorporated State, which leaves out certain areas on the map. Yet there are still plenty of regions that offer countries available for play, although they can be orders of magnitude more difficult to succeed with.

For example, Cambodia is a playable country, but does not appear in any of the tutorial campaigns that offer greater help and/or an easier onboarding to success. Choosing Cambodia, the game seems to suggest, assumes that the player is experienced, and/or does not wish for extra or focused guidance while playing. Yet such help and guidance are actually needed in this situation far more than in Belgium – when gameplay starts in 1836 the country is impoverished and only a minor player in regional (let alone international) affairs. It doesn't have any of the advantages that Belgium enjoys, and many more disadvantages.

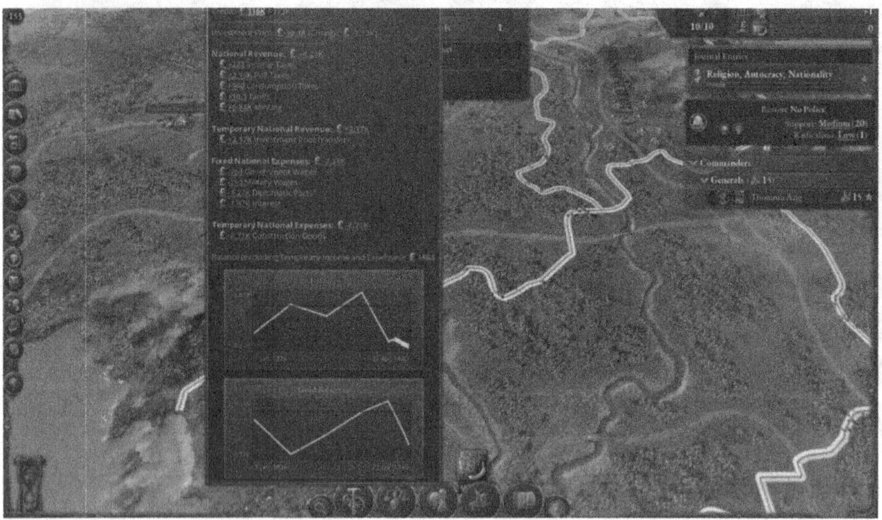

**Fig. 3.** Cambodia's economy, quickly sliding into debt

In the game Cambodia starts off resource poor. The player can start to build out its infrastructure, but if they aren't careful, they will quickly go into debt (as illustrated in Fig. 3), which is exactly what we did. We needed more industry to make money, but it costs money and time to build that industry, and we did not have the money.

Being relatively inexperienced players, we also brought our success at building in Belgium to Cambodia, not carefully thinking through the much smaller income and cash reserves the nation had. Perhaps predictably, production stalled, and the cash reserves ran dry. Looking for places to earn more cash or save money, we scrutinized the country's expenditures. We decided to levy import taxes on foreign goods, and to start imposing consumption taxes on certain goods. Certainly, alcohol and silk could be taxed, although we balked at taxing food staples. We also slashed the wages of our government workers, even as the game told us that our bureaucracy was insufficient to collect the taxes actually owed. Yet still we had to balance those forces to avoid a popular rebellion, and (further) impoverishment. Even this was not enough. Next, we tried declaring bankruptcy to get rid of our debt and start over, but this only meant a penalty to future production for the next several years. The hole was only getting deeper.

Even more careful examination of our cash outflows found that we were engaged in providing regular "Tribute" to Vietnam. We asked to leave the agreement – they refused. We threatened war, they ignored us. We attacked, they responded, and we lost. Then we were stuck paying the Tribute along with War Reparations. Finally, a flood hit our capitol city, causing further damage and distress (see Fig. 4). This was *V3* on Hardcore Mode. There was no thriving – only a sort of basic survival persisted.

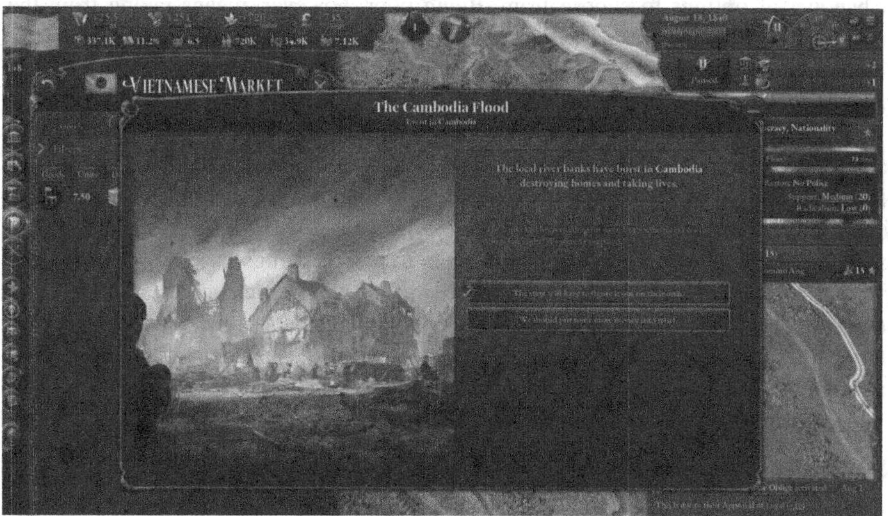


**Fig. 4.** A flood takes what's left of our hopes (and money).

## 5 The Privilege of Choice: Discussion and Conclusion

Most of the literature studying moral dilemmas in games points to how they offer choices to players, either narratively or sometimes through gameplay mechanics. Yet what stands out most about the Cambodia campaign was its distinct *lack* of choices. Certainly, the player-leader could try to shuffle different political parties in and out of power, although the parties with platforms they wanted to enact were so far out of favor it would have been nearly impossible to make any real reforms. More distressingly, the economy was in such bad shape there was almost nothing we players could do – no choices to make – to improve things. Production illustrates that well. Whereas when playing as Belgium we could queue up a dozen (or dozens by the end) construction projects, and let them progress, in Cambodia, we could choose *one* and then hit the fast forward time button to get it to finish. Playing as Cambodia involved a lot of waiting and wasted time. Whereas, with Belgium, we were constantly pausing to make different choices and decisions, with Cambodia, pausing did not matter. The country, Cambodia, was so underdeveloped, so cash poor, and so on the edge, that time was the only currency that mattered. Yet even if the country's development could be "fast forwarded," during that same time, other countries were getting ahead, and moving forward, technologically, culturally, economically, and socially.

Even the micro-events or choices the game presented to Cambodia seemed designed to insult or offend – there was no way we could afford to "put money into relief" for flood victims – there was no money available to spare. In that way the choice was largely a non-choice, only reinforcing how precarious Cambodia's position was. Through those events, the game demonstrated in ways others could not how few choices poor nations have compared to rich ones. Being rich is fun, the game suggests, as it involves a platter or banquet of options to choose from. Being poor, however, means taking from the poor to make them poorer, in the hopes of one day extracting oneself from obligations. Solutions to get out of poverty (bankruptcy, war) don't fix the problems – they often make them worse, and in punitive ways.

On its own, a Cambodia campaign would never make for interesting or enlightening gameplay. But by juxtaposing countries like Belgium and Cambodia, the game invites players to grapple with the complexities of history, and the conclusion that there aren't simple or easy answers to complex problems. *Victoria 3* is not a perfect game, but its interactivity and choice systems invite players to pull at strings, to play with time and space, to see how varied world history is, as well as why some choices are made, and others are discarded. Of course, *Victoria 3* is only one game – more study is needed on other games in this genre, to see how they combine ideologies, mechanics, choices, and narratives, to offer players sophisticated ways to tell intricate stories.

## References

1. Bettocchi, E., Klimick, C., Perani, L.: Can the subaltern game design? In: Proceedings of the 2020 Digital Games Research Association Conference (2020). http://www.digra.org/wp-content/uploads/digital-library/DiGRA_2020_paper_376.pdf
2. Chapman, A.: Digital Games as History: How Videogames Represent the Past and Offer Access to Historical Practice. Routledge (2016)
3. Consalvo, M., Busch, T., Jong, C.: Playing a better me: how players rehearse their ethos via moral choices. Games Culture 1555412016677449 (2016)
4. Consalvo, M., Phelps, A.: Getting through a tough day (again): what possum springs says about mental health and social class. Am. J. Play **12**, 338–362 (2020)
5. Formosa, P., Ryan, M., Staines, D.: Papers, please and the systemic approach to engaging ethical expertise in videogames. Ethics Inf. Technol. 1–15 (n.d.)

6. Koenitz, H.: Understanding Interactive Digital Narrative: Immersive Expressions for a Complex Time. Routledge, Abingdon, Oxon; New York, NY (2023)
7. Lammes, S.: Destabilizing playgrounds: cartographical interfaces, mutability, risk and play. In: Cermak-Sassenrath, D. (ed.) Playful Disruption of Digital Media. GMSE, pp. 87–97. Springer, Singapore (2018). https://doi.org/10.1007/978-981-10-1891-6_6
8. Mukherjee, S.: Videogames and post colonialism: an introduction. In: Videogames and Post Colonialism, pp. 1–28. Springer, Cham (2017). https://doi.org/10.1007/978-3-319-54822-7_1
9. Nay, J.L., Zagal, J.P.: Meaning without consequence: virtue ethics and inconsequential choices in games. In: Proceedings of the 12th International Conference on the Foundations of Digital Games (FDG '17), pp. 14:1–14:8. ACM, New York (2017). https://doi.org/10.1145/3102071.3102073
10. Schrier, K.: An Investigation of Ethical Thinking in Role-Playing Video Games: A Case Study of "Fable III" (Ed.D.). Teachers College, Columbia University, New York (2011)
11. Sicart, M.: Beyond Choices: The Design of Ethical Gameplay. The MIT Press, Cambridge (2013)
12. Sicart, M.: The Ethics of Computer Games. MIT Press (2011)
13. Silva, C., Reyes, M.C., Koenitz, H.: Towards a decolonial framework for IDN. In: Vosmeer, M., Holloway-Attaway, L. (eds.) Interactive Storytelling: 15th International Conference on Interactive Digital Storytelling, ICIDS 2022, Santa Cruz, CA, USA, December 4–7, 2022, Proceedings, pp. 193–205. Springer, Cham (2022). https://doi.org/10.1007/978-3-031-22298-6_12
14. Squire, K.D.: Replaying History: Learning World History Through Playing "Civilization III" (Ph.D.). Indiana University, Indiana (2004)
15. Staines, D., Consalvo, M., Stangeby, A., Pedraça, S.: State of play: video games and moral engagement. J. Gaming Virtual Worlds **11**, 271–288 (2019). https://doi.org/10.1386/jgvw.11.3.271_1
16. Zagal, J.: The Videogame Ethics Reader. Cognella, San Diego (2011)
17. Zagal, J.P.: Ethically notable videogames: moral dilemmas and gameplay. In: Proceedings of DiGRA 2009. Presented at the Digital Games Research Association Conference, West London, UK (2009)
18. Zanescu, A.: Counter-Balkanism in The Witcher & Gwent: A Historical Reinvention Beyond the Balkan Paradigm (masters). Concordia University (2018)

# Gaming the System: Case Study in Investigative Journalism and Playful Interactive Narrative Design to Explain Systemic Bias in Immigration Policy

Lindsay D. Grace(✉)

University of Miami, Coral Gables, FL 33146, USA
L.Grace@Miami.edu

**Abstract.** Drawing from the theoretical underpinnings of prior work in interactive narratives to explain complexity, playable explanations, and newsgames this work aims to expand the impact and accessibility of comprehensive investigate journalism to a wide audience of North, Central and South Americans. The goal was to apply the benefits of ludic interactive narratives to explain the complexities and systemic biases in the United States immigration system for differing immigration scenarios between 2017–2021. The game combines elements of documentary games, persuasive play, and the fundamentals of interactive narrative to provide a playful explanation of explicit and implicit policy. It is, in short, an interactive system about a system. This interpretation of the system was derived not from a top-down view of the system, but by the reverse engineered understanding informed by two years of investigative journalism research informed by the data in both the Panama Papers and Paradise Papers. This paper articulates the development process, release, and subsequent observations from an experienced engaged by more than 45,000 players. This case study is understood as the first ever playful interactive based on the Panama Papers and Paradise Papers investigations.

**Keywords:** Playful Interactive Narrative · Investigative Journalism · Panama Papers · Paradise Papers · Immigration and Borders

## 1 Introduction

In an increasingly complex world, the propensity for interactive narrative to explore and explain seems evident. In some contexts, complexity is the result of a delicate balance of systems upon systems, such as balancing homeostasis in the natural world of an organism or the balance of environmental factors that govern the earth's weather. In other cases, complexity is an act of obscuring rules, to mask biases in systems or otherwise hide a truth. The potential of interactive narratives is that they can expose these and other factors of a system, simply by modeling them and offering these models as playful experiences from which such character can be interpreted. In the least, such narratives provide an opportunity to explore complexity in a way that supports examination across


L. Holloway-Attaway and J. T. Murray (Eds.): ICIDS 2023, LNCS 14384, pp. 38–49, 2023.
https://doi.org/10.1007/978-3-031-47658-7_4

a wide audience [11]. Where the legal language of a government policy, for example, may not be easily understood by an audience untrained in law, the narrative version of the system can make the system's relationships apparent and explorable. This work applies interactive narrative to a complex system, leaning heavily on Koenitiz's notion that interactive narrative can help users interpret complexity [19].

The primary aim of this work is to provide case study in playful interactive narrative to explore the complexity of a large-scale system, involving multiple federal governments, local governments, and international agreements. It offers an interactive narrative modeled from the 2017–2021 foreign immigration and fiscal policies that manage the porosity of the United States borders. This model is derived from a multi-year investigative reporting project first launched in response to the Panama Papers [16] and Paradise Papers [1]. Its complexity is a product of law, finance and the prior lack of a single resource explaining the intersection of these. It is further complicated by nuances that are more apparent through case study, than the apparent systems reveal.

The Panama Papers (also less commonly known as the Mossack Fonseca papers) refers to the more than 11 million documents leaked to the German newspaper, Süddeutsche Zeitung outlining attorney-client privileged financial information about offshore accounts. This leak resulted in an investigative journalism initiative involving over 100 media organizations across more than 80 countries. The historical moment and resulting research culminated in a global data journalism effort, which outlined global injustice and income inequality ensnaring political figures in fraud allegations and revealing the systems that protect financial assets for a wealthy few. The Paradise Papers refers to a similar information exposure. In contrast, the Paradise Papers were not leaked by a single source and have resulted in litigation involving corporations and media organizations. In general, the Paradise Papers offered more data, but the Panama Papers resulted in more legal action. In both cases, these data collections exposed the legal, illegal, and gray areas of wealth transfer, management, and multinational government policies. They provided the real-world case studies to illustrate the nuance and complexity of the global systems shaping migration of people and wealth.

The method used to turn this data into understanding, was investigative journalism. As a practice, it is a form of journalism requiring deep investigation for months or even years of researching and report preparation. This form of journalism has been remarkably effective at identifying large-scale crime and systemic problems in political systems [7]. Its purpose is to report the truth as contrasted with perception, in much the way a regulatory body or other watchdog might research, identify, and announce such discrepancies. In the context of the reporting for both the Panama Papers and Paradise Papers, the clear challenge is that the subjects work between regulatory bodies. The ambiguities of these analogously international waters mean there is little regulation and oversight between them. In this case, investigative reporting functioned across geo-political borders, through the International Consortium of Investigative Journalism (https://www.icij.org/), in the absence of a regulatory body. It is one of the many reasons these reports are unique and important to an increasingly complex world whose borders can be crossed digitally [1].

In the spirit of this pioneering first at the apex of international collaboration, technological innovation through data journalism and disclosure to a wide audience, the team behind this work aimed to create an experience that demonstrates the complexity unveiled through the investigative reporting from Panama Papers and the Paradise Papers. The work applies the investigative research of pioneering Hispanic journalist, Romina Ruiz Goiriena, a member of the project team and one of the 300 or more journalist involved in the collaborative investigation of both data sources. It aims to make the previously non-transparent relationship of US immigration policy, wealth, and immigration more transparent via the outcome of investigative journalism.

As such, this project represents the first known game produced from investigative journalism on the Panama Papers or Paradise Papers. It is also understood to be the first such playful experience designed on the topic. The case study may prove useful in informing future work that seeks to combine investigate journalism to playful interactive narratives. The aim is to tell the story of a complex system, revealing their nuance and supporting journalism's aim to reveal truth. The work was conducting in paralleled to a 3-part reporting series published by the English language newspaper Miami Herald and the Spanish language news source El Nuevo Herald by the collaborating journalist. The resulting interactive narrative, which accompanied the series is archived at https://gamingthesystem.journalismgames.com/ and https://juegodelsistema.journalismgames.com/ to support future research.

## 2 Playful Interactive Design Process

While those familiar with early work in digital news games would be tempted to reference early work in newsgames [1, 3] and the work of Gonzalo Frasca [10], this particularly work is aligned less with that research than with the notion of playable explanations and narrative infographics. The relatively recent design practices of creating digital play extend the more generalizable elements of captology [9] with the rhetorical potential of ludic interactive experiences. While a potential outcome of this work, the aim was to work less toward the political cartoon concept of newsgames [21] and more toward playable models or parables [6] and infographics [8] with narratives. Work in this domain includes Parable of the Polygons [17], The Evolution of Trust [5], How Does an Autonomous Car Work? [20] and others [11].

To remain true to the aims of journalism, this work does not strive to provide fictionalized elements or rhetorically based game mechanics. It is at best aligned with Bogost's et al.'s notion of reportage games [4], although it extends them by turning an investigative journalism derived understanding of a system into a digital tool that allows any player the ability to explore that system. In this way the effort is more akin to efforts in playable explanations, as described by Nicky Case [5] and Ciccoricco [6].

The work was designed with a model-first approach. This model was built using months of data driven analysis and the team's reporter outlined collection of if-then-else cases by which individuals were successful and unsuccessful in emigrating from their countries into the United States. The investigative journalists focused on the patterns, revealed in the data, for those seeking citizenship in the United States from countries in Central and South America.

The resulting research found sharp contrast between two groups - asylum seekers and wealthy emigres. The research revealed clear paths for each in policy and contrasted those with practice. These dichotomies were demonstrated, through data, as further amplified when each group joined the US population. Most notably, the investigative journalist identified a systemic bias that seems to ignore the source of certain types of income beyond specific wealth minimums. This revelation of kleptocratic emigration was the focus of much of the reporting research.

Based on these investigative reporting findings, an interactive narrative was designed to demonstrate two archetypal routes for immigration. The original model on which the design was based is shown in Fig. 1. These rough notes on the gates that typically determined success or failure for a given population in the immigration process informed the design of the final game. They were created from investigative journalism research from the aforementioned leaked documents and augmented with personal interviews.

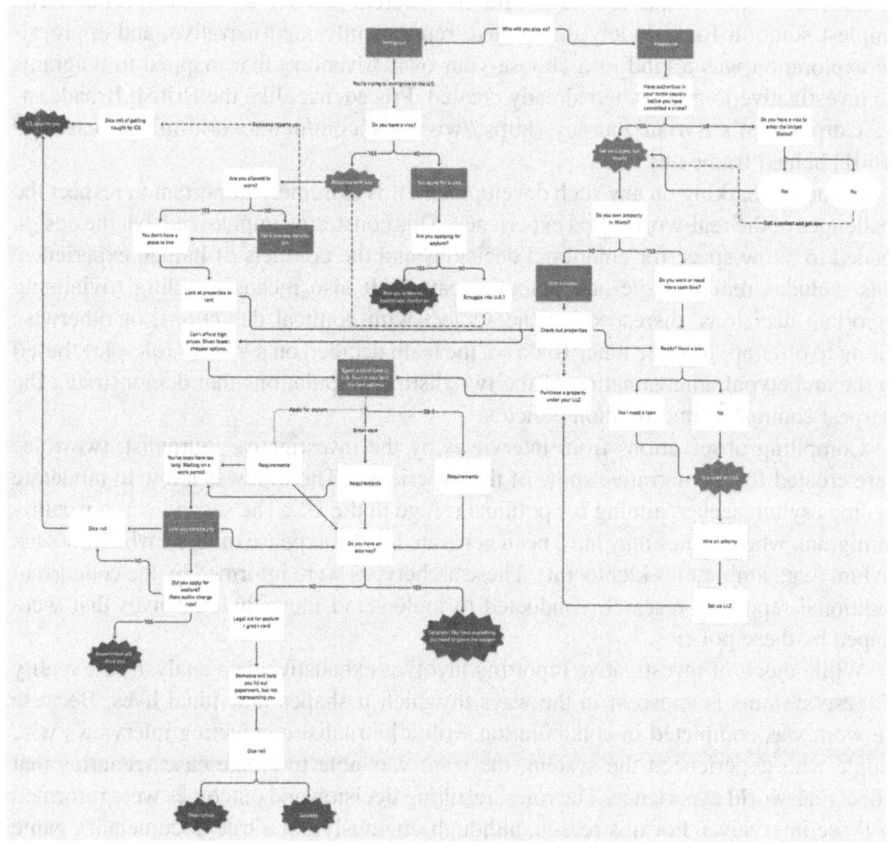


**Fig. 1.** The original decision tree forming the logical paths for the immigration narrative.

After referring to examples provided through repositories of newsgames [15] the project's lead, a single game designer and a single investigative journalist paired to producing a playful interaction. The aim was to make these findings more easily understood by a wider audience and augment the traditional news reporting. Beyond the assumed appeal of playful interactions, the core motivation for a ludic experience comes from players' willingness to try and try again. As explained in Doing Things with Games: Social Impact through Play [14], the notion is that players are willing to work through problems they might not otherwise engage when framed as playful experiences. A core design assumption that leads to these decisions was that the maze of policy, situation, timing, and opportunity that results in success or failure in the immigration system is best understood through repeated attempts. Games and play, propelled by a narrative, were assumed to be a good way to encourage people to try more than once to succeed.

Multiple game concepts solutions were considered for implementation including an action focused role-playing game and an analog board game. To determine the optimal solution, a list of possible game solutions was created and roughly sketched. The final solution was subsequently aimed to impart the system through narrative that encouraged its audience to engage and reengage with the different paths to success and failure. The simplest solution for a widely distributed, reporter-informed narrative, and appropriate exploration was a kind of a choose-your-own-adventure that mapped to diagrams the investigative journalist had already created. Precedence, like the British Broadcasting Corporation's Syrian Journey (https://www.bbc.com/news/world-middle-east-32057601) helped frame this work.

Before embarking on any such development, it is extremely important to respect the challenges of the real-world lived experience. This constraint emphasized that the design needed to allow space for emotional decisions and the conflicts of human experience. This includes real struggle and potential payoff. It also means avoiding trivializing important decisions, disrespecting the subject with comical depictions, or otherwise failing to offer appropriate tone. To do so, the team decided on a kind of role-play, based on the archetypal amalgamation of the two distinct populations that demonstrated the sharpest contrast in immigration policy.

Compiling observations from interviews by the investigative journalist, two roles were created for the narrative spine of the experience. The first was a low to moderate income asylum seeker, aiming for political refuge in the US. The second was a wealthy immigrant, who's riches may have been generated at the expense of those who now seek asylum (e.g., ambiguous kleptocrat). These archetypes were informed by the concurrent traditional reporting research conducted to understand the individual lives that were shaped by these policies.

While much of investigative reporting involves exhaustive data analysis, the reality of these systems is apparent in the ways in which it shapes individual lives. Because the work was completed in collaboration with a journalist conducting interviews with people who experienced the system, the team was able to create case scenarios that reflect real-world experience. The roles, resulting decision and outcomes were informed by those interviews. For this reason, although obviously not a true documentary game [2] (also referred to as docu-game or docugame) it is informed by documentary research involving archival content [13].

The final design reflects the character archetypes, financial, political, and legal systems employed between 2017–2019. It seeks to explain the then contemporary US Immigration system as informed by the period the Panama Papers and Paradise Papers reveal. The resulting playable system aimed to illustrate the injustice of recent US policies for immigration, particularly in the politics of those seeking asylum versus those that may have created the need for others to seek asylum. It was also designed to demonstrate the systems that exacerbate immense economic disparity between people in urban centers in the US. It attempts to reveal the biases in US immigration policy that support foreign kleptocracy by creating systems that are less than critical of wealthy foreign nationals during this period. It uses a basic narrative to provide an archetypal set of case studies, based on journalist research, of five groups of immigrant populations: wealthy kleptocrats; wealthy politically linked expatriates, middle and lower socio-economic status asylum seekers; legal immigrants; illegal immigrants.

## 3 Implementation

The project was designed to be released in conjunction with a multi-part traditional journalism news series. The total production timeline for the project was three months, largely constrained by the publication date for the final, non-interactive reporting project and the need to disseminate information about contemporary policies quickly. Prior work in producing games at the pace of news [12] helped frame the technical implementation and set expectations for such an experiment.

Given the limited budget, the game was produced as a prototype between a single game designer and one investigative journalist. The initial prototype was implemented in a single week, by first mapping simple decisions to the previously demonstrated decision tree. In the first prototype, players were asked basic questions without a narrative overlay. The first prototype was more like a quiz, asking players questions like *whether they'd like to apply for asylum* or *create a limited liability company (LLC) in the US*. This first prototype was designed simply to assure that the logical consequences of the experience mapped appropriately to the journalist's model.

Once all logical relationships were confirmed to be accurate, the narrative layer was added in much the way a game might move from abstract visual elements (e.g., circles and squares) to higher quality final art (e.g., sprites or 3D models). Questions like "*would you like to form a Limited Liability Corporation*", became, "*your lawyer suggests creating an LLC, would you like to do so?*" Later iterations add more narrative elements (e.g., character, setting, etc.), with a friend character suggesting a player speak with a lawyer and then that lawyer offering the suggestion for a cost. Elements of traditional storytelling, like setting, were also added both with meaningful (.i.e., narrative shaping) and meaningless choices (i.e., non-consequential). Players could choose specific neighborhoods in which to live which has the meaningful choice of shaping their monthly budget but does not shape the player's chances of being deported. The meaning or meaninglessness of these choices was adjusted to shape the narrative and remain true to the original model.

This process, which involved several prototype iterations, allowed for accurate representation, and re-representation of the journalist's report while adding narrative elements that support player understanding. These additions included adding specific locations, financial costs for process, calculations, and others. Variables such as the player's chosen name and inventory management like the amount of money the player has in the bank were also added in subsequent iterations. These variables added some of the most depth to the experience. As an example, on essential decision for an asylum seeker who already works in the United States would be to go to work or not. The variable of a work visit has the probability of losing the job or being caught by immigration agents for working illegally while seeking citizenship. The probability for positive and negative outcomes for the player are never explicitly outlined for the player. Instead, like life, they learn from the experience. Practically, each visit to work is calculated as a 1:7 chance of being caught without a work visa for a player who elects to go to work and does not have a work visa. The player on this path would typically need to go to work at least 7 times to earn enough to afford the legal support to continue their asylum application. Hence a kind of procedural catch-22 occurs, as it is highly likely an asylum seeker without a work visa will be caught before they earn enough to complete their application for asylum.

Iteratively, each protype was first evaluated for fidelity to the model, then for engagement. The final prototype iteration involved adding images to illustrate the situations at each decision point. To do so and to remain within budget, creative commons photography was manipulated using Adobe Photoshop filters to apply a graphic novel aesthetic.

Before release, the project's prototypes, which were created using Twine 2.6 and Adobe Photoshop filters, were subject to several editorial reviews by the collaborating journalist and the supporting media organizations. The final release was an iteration on the prototypes, applying both the aesthetic stylistic conventions of the publishing newspaper and revision to the images by the media organization's artist. Like other such projects, the team size scaled as the project's scope scaled. The project's prototyping phases were conducted by a mere 2-person collaboration. The final product, including translation, accessibility standardization, visual standardization, and editing were the result of a part-time team exceeding 10 news professionals (Fig. 2).

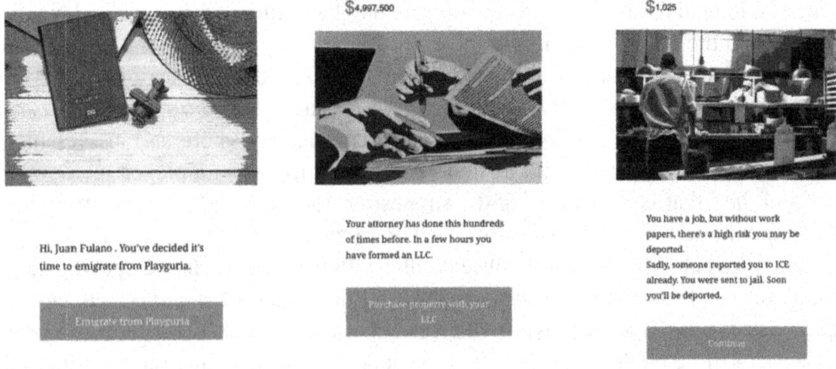


**Fig. 2.** The final version of the experience as a screenshot on desktop and mobile view, in three panels. First is the starting screen for both player roles, the second is a panel from the kleptocratic role play and the 3rd is from the asylum seeker with visa path (no work permit).

By design, the game incorporates a variety of real-world data sources to substantiate examples in the game. These were typically offered as more information boxes or in the context of warnings for pivotal decisions. These were designed to invite the player toward long-tail investigations, like the work of an investigative journalist. The sources provided for this data were produced by bipartisan and non-profit organizations about immigration. They were directly linked so that players could follow them to the original source (Fig. 3).

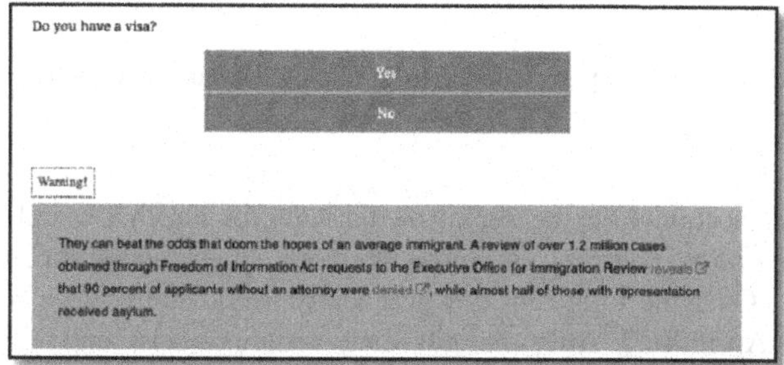


**Fig. 3.** Details for more information and external data source sidebars.

Likewise, because it is a playable system, based on real world data it was important to expose data sources within the narrative. This included links to journalism and official announcements with explanations about important policy changes and the way that they have shaped the player's choices.

## 4 Reception

The web-based experiences were offered for mobile and desktop browsers via MiamiHerald.com and its Spanish language equivalent. It was embedded with each article published by the Miami Herald and El Nuevo Herald on their respective website for this investigative reporting project. It was also shared via news outlets alongside the multipart investigative journalism piece of the same name and related press. English and Spanish language versions were publicly available. Translation was completed by the investigative journalist. Data on user sessions was tracked using embedded standard web analytics, provided through the site's internet hosting service. Given the large number of players and their geographic diversity it was decided pretest and posttest surveys would diminish appeal and complicate the experience.

Between its October 19, 2021, launch and January 1, 2022, the game received 47, 321 individual players. Peak interest, coincided with the three publications of the news report, but a steady expected decline followed. October 2021 was the highest player activity with 44,212 monthly players. November saw 906, December 245 and a mere 116 by the end of January 2022. Player interest, like news topics, declined sharply in a short time (Fig. 4).

The Spanish language version aggregated the most players, 45,420 players, while the English language had 1901 players between launch, October 19, 2020, and January 1st, 2021. Traffic to the game started spiking the day after launch, changing from primary sources, the newspaper's websites, to secondary sources and social media thereafter. Incoming traffic switched from the original links, to shared content, primarily

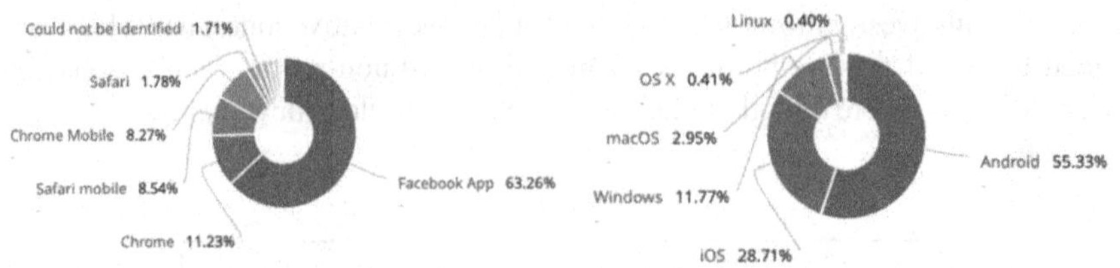


**Fig. 4.** Charts indicating where players came from to play the game and the operating systems they used to play.

through personal accounts on the social media sites for Facebook and Twitter. The project employed no marketing to promote the work, so any social media spread was entirely organic. Over the long run, however, daily traffic settled to a regular 20–25 players through April 2022. After that day daily visits are between 0–10 across both languages and remain so with brief spikes of 30–50 players into the year 2023.

The mean for each player session was 3 min per game session. The median was 6. This may indicate that some players failed to succeed, failed to read all statements, read less carefully on subsequent tries, or were satisficing some solutions. The longest player profiles exceeded 10–15-min play sessions, which at scale may also be anything from incomplete sessions that were no longer continued (e.g., left a browser window open but stopped playing the game) to the more optimistic further investigations and conversations that may have slowed player performance.

Players visited from 29 countries in total, with the largest share from networks in Mexico (63%), the USA (25%), Colombia (3%) and Guatemala (2.5%). The top 10 countries by number of players are listed in Table 1.

**Table 1.** Top 10 player populations by country.

| Mexico | 32,001 | 70.22% |
|---|---|---|
| Colombia | 5,790 | 12.71% |
| United States of America | 5,484 | 12.03% |
| Canada | 459 | 1.01% |
| Guatemala | 194 | 0.43% |
| Spain | 193 | 0.42% |
| Germany | 173 | 0.38% |
| France | 105 | 0.23% |
| Ecuador | 102 | 0.22% |
| Australia | 99 | 0.22% |

The technographic data on players matches global patterns for contemporary distribution of mobile platforms and social media preference. Hence, as might be expected, the game's largest single audience came from mobile users on Android devices 55%.

Shared via the Facebook app (distinct from Facebook.com website) exceeded 63%. No Twitter shares were recorded directly from the Twitter application, although a small portion were shared via various web browsers.

## 5 Conclusion

The success in implementation is largely notable for scale. For a low budget project, focusing on a very specific topic, more than 45,000 play session in a single month is a respectable engagement. This is further emphasized by the amount of time each player spent and in the voluntarily social media spread that occurred organically. From these perspectives there is success in the project's ability to meet its goals.

While by design the aim was objective reporting of the model derived from data via investigative journalism, it did prove very difficult to avoid editorial tone while also offering an engaging narrative. The element of tone, and perhaps the structure of playful experiences in which the obstacle is a policy, necessitated some editorial tone. This is where playable models, or playable explanations or the notion of reportage games is complicated by the reality of implementation. In concept, keeping interactive narrative's objective through data informed models should be relatively simply. In practice, the narrative frame itself, may inadvertently introduce biases, just as any system might. While the creators of the project endeavored to offer a playable model, that playable model is of course subject to the ways in which the problem is framed. In this case, the problem is a system, and the players are allowed to explore that system as any of a myriad of people most affected by it. This is clearly not a practical situation, as few people can choose their lot in life, but this experiment was never designed to be a simulation. It was instead designed to investigate the practicality of converting an investigative journalist's interpreted model of a system reverse engineered from the data that system created. For this reason, it is hoped that such a case study is useful for further work.

From the perspective of persuasive play, the game's system itself obscures the statistical (and sometimes random) probabilities of a given path. Instead, players see only choice and its circumstance, via a simple web-playable chose your own adventure. Players can easily win with ill-gotten wealth but will struggle to succeed otherwise. This truth, derived from the data collected, and resulting model, may help identify structural inequality. In the least it's hoped that such work provides evidence of a process for blending interactive narrative with investigative journalism and reporting and its potential.

Further reflection on the process and potential pitfalls of this work is complicated by the myriad of stakeholders, legal concerns, and sensitives that arise from designing experiences about such topics. It should be sufficient to acknowledge that such work is often subject to an extensive editorial process that while common to quality journalism, may work counter to the efforts of game designers to produce timely newsgames. This is an important tension that exists across the common intersection of quality, rigor, and timeliness. Such work is often subject to the tongue-in-check expression - good, cheap, and fast, choose two. In the context of newsgames, this is further complicated by the structures of journalistic publication, which are appropriately risk-averse, and rigor focused. The culture of game making is sometimes at odds with this when facing the threat of technological atrophy and the challenges of rigorously examining an interactive system.

Since these tensions exists in simple projects involving the basic if/then structure of Twine games, the future for such work is complicated. As an example, generative artificial intelligence derived systems, for which interactive system interrogation becomes much more complex may present too great an obstacle to warrant their implementation in newsgames. Instead, perhaps, as has been done routinely in independent games community, the experimentation and exposition of such systems may remain an independent endeavor employed in the context of art and creative practice. In so doing, such work may flourish or fail without the edifice of journalistic structure and the power of news institutions.

**Acknowledgements.** This work was created with support from the University of Miami's School of Communication and University of Florida's Brechner Center for Freedom of Information. The Gaming the System series was produced by the Miami Herald and el Nuevo Herald in partnership with the Fund for Investigative Journalism and the National Association for Hispanic Journalists. Romina Ruiz-Goiriena initiated the project, lead the project concept and reporting and was essential to the project's success. The content of the game and this publication are solely the responsibility of the authors and does not necessarily represent the official views of the supporters.

## References

1. Berglez, P., Gearing, A.: The panama and paradise papers. The rise of a global fourth estate. Int. J. Commun. **12**, 20 (2018)
2. Bogost, I, Poremba, C.: Can games get real? A closer look at 'documentary' digital games. In: Computer Games as a Sociocultural Phenomenon: Games Without Frontiers War Without Tears, pp. 12–21 (2008)
3. Bogost, I.: Curiosity journalism, or the first decades of newsgames. Convergence **26**(3), 572–576 (2020)
4. Bogost, I., Ferrari, S., Schweizer, B.: Newsgames: Journalism at Play. Mit Press (2012)
5. Case, N.: The Evolution of Trust. https://ncase.me/trust/. Accessed 12 Apr 2023
6. Ciccoricco, D.: How to play a parable. Storyworlds: J. Narrat. Stud. **10**(1–2), 21–46 (2018)
7. De Burgh, H.: Investigative Journalism. Routledge (2008)
8. Diakopoulos, N., Kivran-Swaine, F., Naaman, M.: Playable data: characterizing the design space of game-y infographics. In: Proceedings of the SIGCHI Conference on Human Factors in Computing Systems, pp. 1717–1726, (2011)
9. Fogg, B.J.: Persuasive computers: perspectives and research directions. In: Proceedings of the SIGCHI Conference on Human Factors in Computing Systems (1998)
10. Frasca, G.: Videogames of the oppressed: critical thinking, education, tolerance, and other trivial issues. In: First Person: New Media as Story, Performance, and Game, pp. 85–94 (2004)
11. Gómez-García, S., de la Hera Conde-Pumpido, T.: Newsgames: the use of digital games by mass-media outlets to convey journalistic messages. Games Culture **18**(4), 449–474 (2023)
12. Grace, L.D.: Newsjam: making games at the pace of news. In: Proceedings of the International Conference on Game Jams, Hackathons, and Game Creation Events, pp. 17–20 (2018)
13. Grace, L.: Gamifying archives, a study of docugames as a preservation medium. In: 2011 16th International Conference on Computer Games (CGAMES), pp. 172–176. IEEE (2011)
14. Grace, L.D.: Doing Things with Games: Social Impact Through Play. CRC Press (2019)

15. Grace, L., Haung, K.: State of Newsgames 2020: Snapshot Analysis of Interactives, Toy and Games in Journalism and Allied Industries. JournalismGames.com, Miami (2020)
16. Graves, D., Shabbir, N.: Gauging the global impacts of the 'panama papers' three years later. Reuters Inst. Study Journalism (2019)
17. Hart, V., Case, N.: Parable of the Polygons. https://ncase.me/polygons/. Accessed 2 May 2023
18. Koenitz, H., Barbara, J., Palosaari Eladhari, M.: Interactive digital narratives (IDN) as representations of complexity: lineage, opportunities and future work. In: Interactive Storytelling: 14th International Conference on Interactive Digital Storytelling, ICIDS 2021, Tallinn, 7–10 December 2021, Proceedings 14. Springer, Cham (2021)
19. Koenitz, H.: Understanding Interactive Digital Narrative: Immersive Expressions for a Complex Time. Taylor & Francis (2023)
20. Shin, Y. Alcanta, C., Steckelberg, A.: The Washington Post, How Does an Autonomous Car Work? https://www.washingtonpost.com/graphics/2019/business/how-does-an-autonomous-car-work/. Accessed 5 June 2023
21. Treanor, M., Mateas, M.: Newsgames-procedural rhetoric meets political cartoons. In: DiGRA Conference (2009)

# Fostering Interdisciplinary Learning for Elementary Students Through Developing Interactive Digital Stories

Anisha Gupta[1](✉), Andy Smith[1](✉), Jessica Vandenberg[1], Rasha ElSayed[2], Kimkinyona Fox[2], James Minogue[1], Aleata Hubbard Cheuoua[2], Kevin Oliver[1], Cathy Ringstaff[2], and Bradford Mott[1]

[1] North Carolina State University, Raleigh, NC 27695, USA
{agupta44,pmsmith4,jvanden2,jminogu,kmoliver,bwmott}@ncsu.edu

[2] WestEd, San Francisco, CA 94107, USA
{relsaye,kfox,ahubbar,cringst}@wested.org

**Abstract.** Recent years have seen growing awareness of the potential digital storytelling brings to creating engaging K-12 learning experiences. By fostering students' interdisciplinary knowledge and skills, digital storytelling holds great promise for realizing positive impacts on student learning in language arts as well as STEM subjects. In parallel, researchers and practitioners increasingly acknowledge the importance of computational thinking in supporting K-12 students' problem solving across subjects and grade levels, including science and elementary school. Integrating the unique affordances of digital storytelling and computational thinking offers significant potential; however, careful attention must be given to ensure students and teachers are properly supported and not overwhelmed. In this paper, we present our work on a narrative-centered learning environment that engages upper elementary students (ages 9 to 11) in computational thinking and physical science through the creation of interactive science narratives. Leveraging log data from a pilot study with 28 students using the learning environment, we analyze the narrative programs students created across multiple dimensions to better understand the nature of the resulting narratives. Furthermore, we examine automating this analysis using artificial intelligence techniques to support real-time adaptive feedback. Results indicate that the learning environment enabled students to create interactive digital stories demonstrating their understanding of physical science, computational thinking, and narrative concepts, while the automated assessment techniques showed promise for enabling real-time feedback and support.

**Keywords:** Digital storytelling · narrative-centered learning · block-based programming


L. Holloway-Attaway and J. T. Murray (Eds.): ICIDS 2023, LNCS 14384, pp. 50–67, 2023.
https://doi.org/10.1007/978-3-031-47658-7_5

## 1 Introduction

Digital storytelling, which seeks to combine traditional storytelling with digital tools, has received growing recognition as an effective tool for enabling learning in K-12 classrooms [24,29]. Digital storytelling activities can take many forms, though generally focus on students creating a narrative, documentary, or interactive story around a topic [24,29,32]. Studies have shown digital storytelling to be an effective tool in subjects outside of language arts, promoting exploration of science phenomena [8,9], as well as enhancing critical thinking and motivation [28]. However, the benefits from digital storytelling-based interventions are not uniform across all students, highlighting the need for more effective support for both students and teachers.

An additional hurdle for utilizing digital storytelling activities in the classroom is the need to overcome a perceived lack of alignment with curricular requirements beyond use in language arts. Notably, there is growing emphasis on computational thinking and science at the elementary level, and teachers who already face dwindling instructional time may view storytelling as a sub-optimal form of teaching [30]. However, there is a growing body of research showing the synergies of the storytelling process, where students create, refine, and present a story, with critical aspects of computational thinking and science [16,21]. Additionally, with a growing focus on STEM education, many teachers also see the value in integrating language arts skills across multiple disciplines. Given these factors, there is an opportunity for tools and systems supporting storytelling activities if they can be designed to support learning while not overwhelming students and teachers.

INFUSECS is a narrative-centered learning environment designed to engage upper elementary students (ages 9 to 11) in deep, meaningful physical science and computational thinking learning through the creation of interactive science narratives. In INFUSECS, students use a block-based programming interface that enable the creation of narrative programs that drive a virtual stage for storytelling. This interface features a palette of specialized blocks that can be dragged and dropped to form an interactive script—complete with dialogue, scene changes, character entrances and exits, and branching—in the style of a "choose your own adventure." By engaging with this hands-on, narrative design tool, students not only visualize but also play out their interactive stories, bringing concepts and competencies in physical science and computer science to life. This design builds on best practices for creating block-based programming environments suitable for young learners [10,31].

This paper reports on an analysis of the interactive narratives students created in a pilot study using INFUSECS. Specifically, we investigate the following two research questions as we look to better support students' interdisciplinary learning:

***RQ1:*** *In what ways are students able to use block-based narrative programming to create interactive narratives, when evaluated from a multidimensional perspective?*

> ***RQ2:*** *Do AI-driven automated assessment techniques enable accurate evaluation of student created interactive narratives across multiple dimensions?*

To answer these questions, we use data collected in a pilot study with upper elementary grade students using InfuseCS. Results show students produced a range of stories, exhibiting a variety of storytelling, physical science, and computational thinking concepts. Furthermore, automated assessment techniques were capable of accurately evaluating student stories across multiple dimensions (i.e., storytelling, physical science, and computational thinking), although less accurately than human evaluators. Additional inspection of results from the automated assessment models reveals potential areas of improvement, as well as insights to consider for other learning environments looking to analyze interactive narratives created by upper elementary students.

## 2 Related Work

Narrative offers a promising tool for engaging students in meaningful problem solving. Narrative not only provides a unique modality to understand the world around us [3] but also to communicate our conceptual understandings to others [2]. In the context of education, digital storytelling activities, in which students create their own narratives, have shown great promise in leveraging narrative to enhance science learning [25], and improve cognitive measures such as visual memory and writing skills [27]. Positive outcomes have also been demonstrated on affective measures such as student engagement and motivation [29], as well as 21st century skills such as argumentation and cooperation [18].

The benefits of digital storytelling interventions are not uniform and depend heavily on the ability of students to construct narratives with the provided tools and resources. This has led to a wide range of research into the design and support of digital storytelling interventions for students across a variety of age ranges. Rao et al. [23] found that priming students, via emotional stimuli or by having the students display varied facial gestures, resulted in statistically richer stories. Relatedly, Chu et al. [5] found that students' storytelling was enhanced through creative, imaginative enactment. Franklin et al., [7], sought to leverage the similarities between storytelling and computational thinking using a modified version of the Scratch environment. Students created animated stories involving 2D movement of sprites, as well as using user inputs to trigger events such as audio clips. The Storytelling Alice system allowed middle school students to manipulate 3D characters and scenery to create stories and motivate students, particularly female students, to learn computer programming [13–15]. Evaluations of these systems tend to focus heavily on interest toward computing and demonstration of computational thinking skills rather than evaluating or supporting storytelling. Other systems have investigated using block-based programming in a tangible, sticker-based block language used as part of an interactive storybook [11], and as a method for introducing computational thinking strategies into English language learning [21]. This work extends these efforts by collecting a corpus of student created interactive science narratives represented as block-based narrative programs and applying automated assessment techniques to evaluate the narratives from a multidimensional perspective.

AI techniques, such as natural language processing, have been explored for automating the evaluation of student generated text within the context of interactive learning environments in a range of applications. Carpenter et al. [4] explored machine learning models for automatically analyzing student reflections written during game-based learning, and found pre-trained ELMo embeddings to be the best representation for improving predictive performance of the models. Park et al. [20] introduced a framework for automating the detection of disruptive talk within in-game chat in the context of collaborative game-based learning, finding that models using pre-trained BERT embeddings performed the best. Ke et al.'s [12] survey on advances in automated essay grading explores recent work for grading longer text responses. These works point to the potential of natural language processing techniques for automatically assessing student created narrative programs.

## 3 The INFUSECS Learning Environment

INFUSECS is a narrative-centered learning environment designed to promote engaging computationally-rich science learning for students in upper elementary school, while developing proficiency in digital storytelling and computational thinking. Using INFUSECS, students solve physical science problems and develop interactive science narratives reflecting on their problem-solving experiences. These interactive science narratives are driven by programs students create using a block-based programming language to bring their storyworld to life on a virtual stage (Fig. 1).

INFUSECS features an overarching backstory about a group of explorers stranded by a tropical storm on a remote Pacific island. Students work to develop solutions to problems the explorers encounter on the island. INFUSECS consists of two main components: *Science Explorer* and *Narrative Designer*. The Science Explorer presents students with problem-solving activities they can select from and permits them to interact with characters and tools in the virtual environment to learn about different types of energy and energy conversions. The science content area, and exercises were designed to align with US science standards for this age group. After completing their science investigation students progress to using the Narrative Designer, which incorporates a block-based programming interface, to create a short interactive science narrative related to the problem-solving prompt and science concepts they explored.

### 3.1 Science Explorer

Narrative serves an exceptional tool for structuring problem-solving scenarios that can engage students in science investigations. Using the Science Explorer,

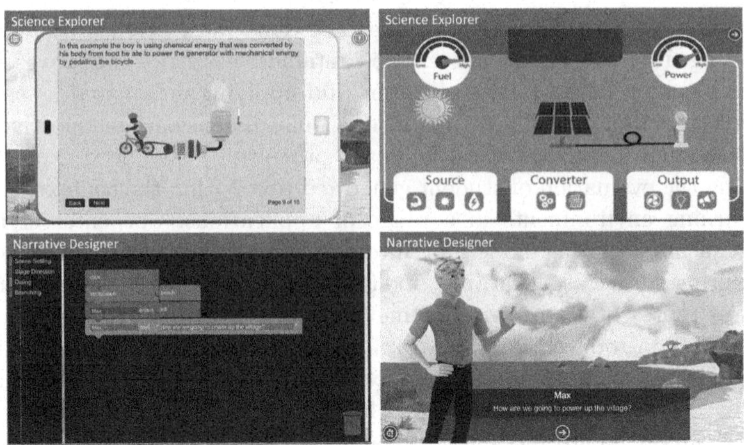


**Fig. 1.** InfuseCS narrative-centered learning environment.

students select scenarios to explore that center around disciplinary core ideas in physical science, such as developing a solution for powering up their makeshift village on the island. The Science Explorer allows students to identify relevant facts, pose hypotheses, research knowledge gaps, and conduct simulation-based investigations as they work toward their solution.

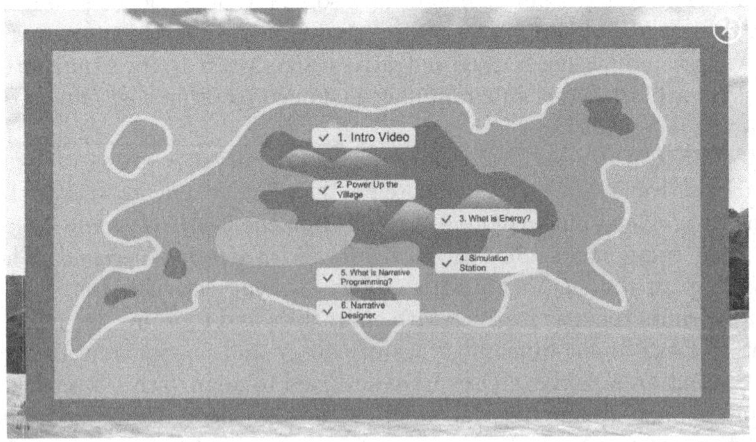


**Fig. 2.** Map of locations students can visit on the island.

After viewing the backstory, which appears as an animated sequence, students are presented with a map of the island denoting various locations they can visit in order to gather knowledge necessary for helping the explorers with the problem-solving scenario (Fig. 2). The first location introduces students to the explorers stranded on the island, as well as introduces them to some of the science equipment they were able to salvage from their ship. The next locations continue to introduce students to different characters, as well as presents students with interactive media content around types of energy and energy conversion. INFUSECS supports a variety of interactive multimedia content, including workbooks containing text, images, and videos, as well as interactive simulation activities demonstrating scientific phenomena. After developing a solution to the problem, students gain access to the final two locations on the map that serve as a transition to the Narrative Designer component of INFUSECS. Students are first introduced to the narrative blocks they can utilize to create their narrative programs and then presented with an overview of the block-based narrative programming interface, including details on how to iteratively develop and test their interactive narratives.

### 3.2 Narrative Designer

INFUSECS's Narrative Designer enables students to develop interactive science narratives through an easy-to-use, drag-and-drop interface based around block-based programming (Fig. 3). It allows students to incrementally develop, elaborate, and refine their stories in a rapid creative cycle, while supporting testing of their stories through its interactive visualization engine. It provides students access to characters, props, and scenery to populate their storyworlds.

**Fig. 3.** Iterative narrative program development.

The block-based programming interface of INFUSECS utilizes four types of custom blocks which are designed to enable key aspects of storytelling (Fig. 4). This includes setting the location of the scene, arranging characters, enabling dialogue between characters, and supporting branching stories. Since INFUSECS targets upper elementary students (ages 9–11), the custom narrative blocks are designed utilizing best practices from previous research in this age range [6,7]. These best practices include limiting the programs to a single thread of execution and avoiding event-driven programming. This is accomplished by providing students with a start block, and only executing blocks connected to it. To further limit the potential for syntactic errors, each category of narrative block utilizes a distinct color to leverage visual affordances, and argument blocks are typed so that only the correct type of argument can be used (e.g., blocks denoting locations can only be used with the scene setting block). The blocks also limit the set of characters and locations students can use. To help scaffold students in creating their narrative programs, an initial starter story is provided to encourage students to modify and customize the program rather than being a purely generative activity. There are four block categories available to students: *Dialogue* blocks, *Stage Direction* blocks, the *Ask Audience* block, and *Scene* blocks.

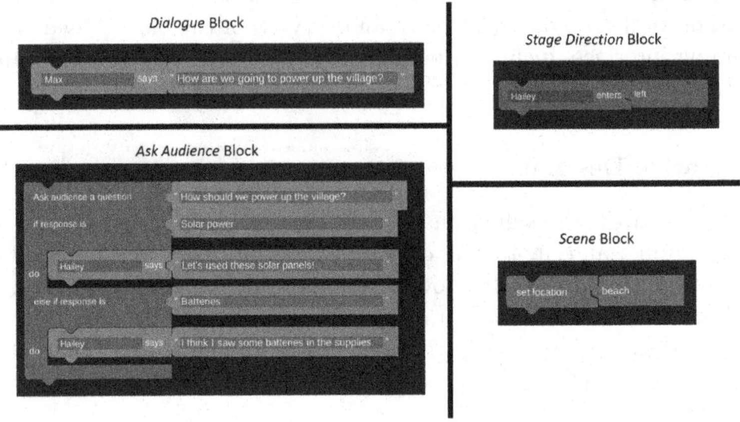


**Fig. 4.** Custom narrative blocks.

The most used blocks in student narratives are *Dialogue* blocks and *Stage Direction* blocks. *Dialogue* blocks generate lines of character dialog through the combination of a Character block and a Text block. The Character block contains a dropdown list of characters that have been previously introduced to the student earlier in the activity, as well as a Narrator option. *Stage Direction* blocks enable students to place and remove characters from the scene. *Stage Direction* blocks consist of an Enter block that places a character in a scene at a specific position (left, center, right), or an Exit block that removes the defined character from the scene. Like the *Dialogue* blocks, characters are selected via a dropdown menu.

The *Ask Audience* block allows students to incorporate branching into their narratives. Modeled after an If-Then-Else block, the *Ask Audience* block requires students to define three parameters. First, they must define the prompt that will be presented to the viewer of the story. The next two parameters represent the two choices that will be presented as options. Under each choice of the *Ask Audience* block is space for students to add additional blocks defining what will occur if the user chooses that branch.

The final category is *Scene* blocks, which allow students to set the location where the events in the narrative take place. Location blocks are chosen from a predefined set to fit with the remote island scenario of the activity, and to align with art assets for the visualization engine described below.

When first entering the narrative programming interface, students are presented with a starter story that uses at least one of each type of block. This story was designed to be runnable, so that students can experiment with the visualization controls early in the process of developing their story. At any point in the narrative programming process, students can press the run button to play their story (Fig. 3). This is accomplished by first converting the block-based representation into Ink script (https://www.inklestudios.com/ink/), a narrative scripting language developed primarily for game applications. Ink script representations of each block are defined using Google's Blockly framework, with a server taking the XML representation of the block program and returning an Ink script. The Ink script is passed to the visualization engine, which presents the animated story using Unity assets. The visualization pauses after each dialog utterance to give the audience time to read, and advances when a button is pressed. When the end of the Ink script is reached, the student returns to the narrative programming interface where they can continue to iterate and revise their story until they are satisfied. Students are encouraged to incorporate the science concepts they explored earlier using the Science Explorer into their stories as they reflect on their problem solving.

## 4 Pilot Study

A pilot study was conducted using InfuseCS to better understand its capabilities for supporting upper elementary students' interdisciplinary learning. The pilot study consisted of three data collections in Spring 2022. The first two data collections occurred in two traditional classroom settings in the western United States. Participants in these data collections included 57 fourth grade students, ages 9 to 11, and the classroom teachers facilitated the learning experience with InfuseCS in their classrooms. The two teachers had previously attended 8 h of professional development during which they were introduced to InfuseCS and were guided through best practices regarding how to teach the physical science and computational thinking content as well as suggested pacing. The third data collection took place in a summer camp context in the southeastern United States. Participants in this data collection included 26 rising third through fifth grade students. The research team led this implementation during a single day of the students' 5-day computer science-focused camp. Due to challenges with conducting in-person research due to the COVID-19 pandemic only a subset of the students completed all of the study activities. In the analysis presented in this paper, we include data from the 28 students who completed all of the study activities. Informed parental consent and student assent was obtained from all participants under a human subjects approved protocol for the pilot study.

The research team suggested four 45-minute sessions for the classroom implementations, whereas all sessions for the summer camp group were condensed into a single day (approximately 4 h total). The implementation flow for both the classroom and camp studies included a brief introduction, completion of a short pre-survey on prior experience with coding and computing, engaging with InfuseCS during which students learned the science content, completing a paper narrative planning worksheet, and finally creating their block-based narrative program within InfuseCS.

## 5 Results

Students' narrative programming began with an initial starter story (as previously discussed), which provided a runnable narrative program that demonstrated all of the available blocks. Of the 28 students, across both contexts, 3 students interacted with the narrative programming interface, but did not change or add to any of the starter story blocks. Student stories ranged from a minimum of 0 self-selected blocks to a maximum of 59 ($M$ = 15.0, $SD$ = 14.4), with the bulk of the blocks appearing in the student-created narratives being *Stage Direction* ($M$ = 5.4, $SD$ = 7.3) and *Dialogue* ($M$ = 6.3, $SD$ = 6.8) blocks. Students changed locations in their stories using *Scene* blocks approximately 2 times ($M$ = 2.3, $SD$ = 2.0), with the *Ask Audience* block being used least often ($M$ = 1.0, $SD$ = 0.8). Students used roughly 2 to 3 characters in their stories ($M$ = 2.8, $SD$ = 1.36) and ran them approximately 32 times each to visualize their stories ($M$ = 31.6, $SD$ = 30.0).

> ***RQ1:*** *In what ways are students able to use block-based narrative programming to create interactive narratives, when evaluated from a multidimensional perspective?*

To investigate RQ1, we evaluated the students' stories across three dimensions: story structure, science concepts, and computational thinking. For this evaluation, we created a 3-level rubric with evaluative criteria (Table 1). These categories were of interest because InfuseCS aims to support interdisciplinary learning, namely writing in language arts, science knowledge construction and use, and computational thinking (CT) skills and practices. The 0 to 2 rating scale was selected for ease of scoring, indicating minimal to sufficient demonstration of the skills under consideration. The criteria for determining story structure ratings included students' stories, however simple and brief, containing a recognizable beginning, middle, and end. Science concept usage was assessed according to students' use of science concepts and terminology included in InfuseCS's Science Explorer. The criteria for rating computational thinking included both the number and correct usage of blocks.

Two researchers trained on a portion of data, not used in the final analysis, resolving misunderstandings, and further refining the rubric. Both researchers independently rated the 28 student stories, then computed kappa for each category [17]. The Story Structure category achieved moderate agreement with a kappa of .71 and the Science Concept and Computational Thinking categories achieved strong agreement with kappas of .84 and .83, respectively. We calculated averages for each category: Story Structure ($M$ = 1.3, $SD$ = 0.77), Science

**Table 1.** Narrative evaluation rubric.

| | Story Structure | Science Concepts | Computational Thinking |
|---|---|---|---|
| 0 | No modifications to the starter story, or additions are nonsensical (e.g., "fjioau") | No inclusion of science concepts from the Science Explorer | Two or fewer block types are used |
| 1 | Modification of the starter story, but story is incomplete | Science concepts included, but are used inaccurately | 3 to 4 block types are included, but misused |
| 2 | Story is complete and logical | Science concepts included and used accurately | All blocks are used correctly |

Concepts ($M = 1.1$, $SD = 0.8$), and Computational Thinking ($M = 1.2$, $SD = 0.79$). Across all 28 stories, students earned an average score of 3.7 ($SD = 1.87$) out of a possible 6 points. Figure 5 shows the distribution of story ratings when summing the scores for all three categories.

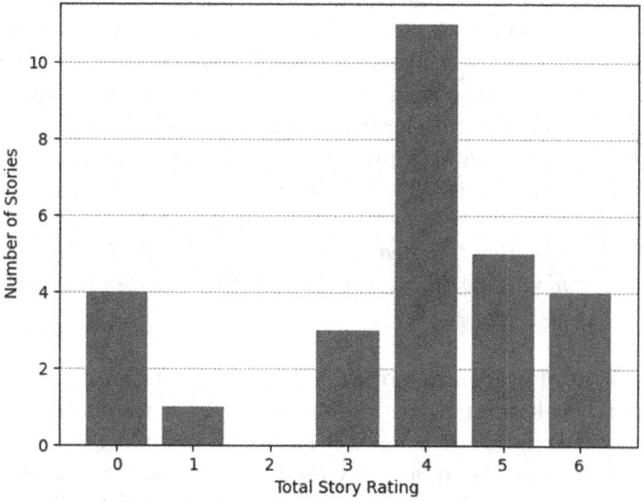


**Fig. 5.** Distribution of story ratings.

Overall, students performed roughly equally across the 3 areas, showing promise in their ability to integrate the different disciplinary concepts. When looking at the distribution of story ratings, it is notable that no students had a total score of 2, and only 1 student scored a 1. This indicates a significant gap between the low scoring students and the next grouping of students. More investigation is needed to determine if this gap is due to motivational factors, or perhaps a lack of comfort or understanding with the task. Fifty percent of the student stories (14) received a total rating between 3 and 4 points, and predominantly consisted of stories demonstrating varying levels of incorporation of science concepts ($SD = 0.50$), computational thinking ($SD = 0.62$), and story structure ($SD = 0.75$), with only one story scoring equally across all three dimensions of evaluation. Although most of these students demonstrated proficiency in one or two evaluation aspects, their stories require substantial improvement across other dimensions.

To support students in identifying weaknesses within their stories and improving the specific aspects necessary to achieve a higher rating within classroom time constraints, real-time feedback highlighting the areas requiring more attention could prove beneficial. By automating the assessment of stories in each evaluation dimension, students could receive such feedback, or alternatively, teachers could be prompted to guide students who require assistance. In fact, providing feedback across multiple criteria of overall story creation serves the purpose of offering students a rubric, which has been demonstrated to effectively support their learning and academic performance in traditional learning environments [1]. However, due to the creative and open-ended nature of the activity, students might inadvertently overlook the rubric designed to evaluate their stories. Hence, it becomes invaluable to have real-time feedback that not only addresses adherence to all the rubric criteria but also provides an automated assessment of the quality with which they fulfill each individual item on the rubric. Human evaluation of students' stories is both time consuming and labor intensive. Moreover, not all educators have the expertise or training to appropriately evaluate students' stories across all three dimensions [19]. Automating the evaluation of stories can help provide real-time feedback to students, while relieving the workload associated with manual scoring.

> ***RQ2:*** *Do AI-driven automated assessment techniques enable accurate evaluation of student created interactive narratives across multiple dimensions?*

Manual evaluation of students' stories can help us with post-hoc evaluations. However, manual evaluation of natural language text is resource intensive, both in terms of time and effort, and is not well suited for providing real-time feedback for students to improve the quality of their stories. Automated evaluation of student generated narratives across the different dimensions discussed above could be used to drive adaptive feedback in the block-based narrative interface. For instance, if the narrative's science rating is detected to be low, a feedback mechanism could prompt students to integrate appropriate science concepts in their stories. Alternatively, a teacher could be notified to provide assistance to the student. To automate each of the assessments in order to enable such real-time evaluation of student created interactive narratives, we investigated a set of AI-driven models. Given that the Story Structure and Science Concepts categories were largely based on the textual components of the narrative program, we first investigate natural language processing techniques for these categories.

Each student narrative program was converted into a string by concatenating all of the *Dialogue* blocks that the student utilized in their story, as well as parameters from any *Ask Audience* blocks. The resulting string representing the student story was then passed through a text normalization pipeline. A content knowledge-specific system dictionary was generated by extracting all of the text from the Science Explorer that introduced relevant science concepts to the students. Punctuation was removed from the text and the remaining text was split into words and added to the dictionary. Stop words were then removed from the dictionary, followed by lemmatization of the remaining words. Each student story was preprocessed similarly-removing punctuation, splitting text into words, removing stop words, and lemmatizing words that exist in NLTK's English vocabulary. The preprocessed words in the student story are then spell corrected to a word from the system dictionary if they are within a Levenshtein distance of 3. If they do not resemble any word from the system dictionary, they are not altered or removed from the story. The preprocessed words are then concatenated with space delimiters to reconstruct the story.

We generated a bag of words (BoW) feature representation for the stories using a similar process-punctuation was removed, the text was split into words, stop words were removed, and the remaining words were lemmatized. A bag of words feature vector was constructed with an entry for each word in the system dictionary. If a word in the story was found within a Levenshtein edit distance of 3 to a word in the system dictionary, the value in the bag of words feature vector for that word was set to 1. The bag of words feature vector was complemented with word count as an additional feature for each story to construct a baseline feature representation. While the BoW approach provides a straightforward method for identifying keywords and basic features, it is limited in its ability to capture local context and syntax. To address this limitation, we also incorporated advanced language models in our study, including Bidirectional Encoder Representations from Transformers (BERT) and Embeddings from Language Models (ELMo), both of which are pre-trained on large corpora and can effectively capture semantic nuances by understanding the context and relationships between words. These models were selected for their ability to provide a richer feature representation than BoW models alone.

We generated a dataset consisting of the most completed versions of the students' stories, determined by the saved version with the highest number of blocks used. The results for automated science and story ratings were then calculated using pre-trained versions of BERT (uncased distilBERT [26]) and ELMo embeddings [22], both with and without spelling correction applied to the stories. Alongside the BoW and word embeddings techniques, we investigated the impact of augmenting the dataset by subsampling each story by incrementally building the story one block at a time, and adding it to the training dataset with the human annotated rating for the completed story as the corresponding label. Using the resulting training dataset, a support vector machine was trained on the word embedding features to predict the story rating and science rating for the stories. Baseline results were obtained by training another support vector machine on the bag of words features.

Given the limited size of our dataset, we evaluated the support vector machine using leave-one-out cross validation. Accuracy and Cohen's kappa scores are listed for story rating prediction in Table 2, and for science rating prediction in Table 3. From Table 2, we observe the best results for story rating were achieved using BERT embeddings without subsampling, with accuracy 78.57% and Cohen's kappa of 65, indicating very high agreement with human scores. From Table 3, we observe the best results for science rating were achieved using ELMo embeddings with subsampling, with accuracy 57.14% and Cohen's kappa of 34.12, indicating fair agreement with human ratings. For both story and science rating predictions, we observe that the best performing baseline bag of word-based models are outperformed by the best performing word embedding-based models.

**Table 2.** Predictive performance for automated story rating.

| Subsampled | Representation | Accuracy | $\kappa$ | Acc. with spell correction | $\kappa$ with spell correction |
|---|---|---|---|---|---|
| No | ELMo | 57.14% | 28.51 | 57.14% | 28.51 |
| No | BERT | **78.57%** | **65.00** | 75.00% | 59.59 |
| Yes | ELMo | 64.00% | 39.13 | 64.00% | 39.13 |
| Yes | BERT | 67.86% | 44.62 | 68.00% | 44.62 |
| No | BoW | – | – | 46.00% | 12.5 |
| Yes | BoW | – | – | 57.00% | 24.49 |

**Table 3.** Predictive performance for automated science rating.

| Subsampled | Representation | Accuracy | $\kappa$ | Acc. with spell correction | $\kappa$ with spell correction |
|---|---|---|---|---|---|
| No | ELMo | 50.00% | 22.99 | 50.00% | 23.14 |
| No | BERT | 46.43% | 17.65 | 50.00% | 22.99 |
| Yes | ELMo | **57.14%** | **34.12** | 54.00% | 28.49 |
| Yes | BERT | 46.00% | 17.16 | 50.00% | 22.53 |
| No | BoW | – | – | 50.00% | 21.60 |
| Yes | BoW | – | – | 32.14% | −0.08 |

To automate Computational Thinking rating for students' stories, we use a feature vector consisting of the number of *Scene*, *Dialogue*, and *Ask Audience* blocks as input features to a logistic regression model with human-annotated Computational Thinking scores as target labels for prediction. A prediction accuracy of 62.96% was achieved.

## 6 Discussion and Limitations

InfuseCS enabled students to produce a wide range of interactive narratives, ranging from 2 to over 30 lines of dialogue. As the target of the system is inherently interdisciplinary, the multidimensional rubric we developed allows us to better understand what aspects students struggle with, and where and how different types of support could be incorporated into the intervention. Overall, students performed roughly equal across the three concept areas, showing promise in their ability to integrate storytelling, science, and computational thinking concepts. Furthermore, automated assessment techniques demonstrated potential for predicting computational thinking, science, and story ratings of narrative programs created by elementary school students. Predictions from the models could be used to provide pedagogical support to students based on their predicted scores.

We achieved the best results for predicting story ratings using BERT embeddings on complete versions of students' stories. For science rating prediction, we obtained the best results using ELMo embeddings by training on subsampled stories. Training on subsampled stories did not improve the accuracy of story rating predictions. A possible explanation for this is that incomplete subsampled stories with rating labels corresponding to complete stories might be misleading for the model during training.

Preprocessing the stories through spell correction based on vocabulary used in the learning environment improves the predictive accuracy for science ratings by 4% for models trained on BERT embeddings, and have negative or no effect on the models trained on ELMo embeddings. We also see the best model performance using ELMo embeddings without spellcheck. This might indicate that ELMo embeddings are inherently better at handling misspelled words as compared to BERT embeddings. The spellcheck with respect to vocabulary used in the learning environment is also not reliable in some cases. For instance, while the spellcheck was able to correct "soral" to "solar", "recourses" to "resource", and "energey" to "energy", it incorrectly changed names of characters like "max" and "mia" to "fan" and "oil", since they are not recognized words in the English dictionary and are within a Levenshtein distance of 3 of vocabulary used in the learning environment.

The distinction between the human scoring rubric for computational thinking ratings 1 and 2 is based on correct usage of the block parameters for each block type. Blocks for which students left the required parameters blank or filled them in with text that did not reflect their purpose (such as conditions for Ask Audience blocks) were considered to be incorrectly used. Since a representation of block parameters were not included as input features for the automated computational thinking evaluation, this could have led to stories with computational thinking rating of 1 being mislabeled as a rating of 2.

One of the main limitations of our work is that the results are evaluated on a dataset consisting of only 28 students. With a larger and more diverse dataset, we would have the opportunity to expand and refine our set of rubrics for evaluating student-created stories. This would allow us to go beyond the basic elements of narrative structure, such as assessing whether the story has a beginning, middle, and end, to include more robust and nuanced evaluation metrics, such as rubrics that measure the "interestingness" or "creativity" of the stories. Additional data would also help us better train and evaluate our automated scoring models. Moreover, we concatenated the dialogue blocks from the block-based narrative programs to construct stories in text format that are used for model training and evaluation. Some of the structure of the program is lost in this process, losing information of who said what in the story, if-then logic in Ask Audience blocks, and stage directions. Preserving such information from the stories might help improve predictive performance of our automated scoring models.

## 7 Conclusion and Future Work

Digital storytelling continues to show great potential for improving student learning across a wide range of ages and subject areas. It offers promise as an effective way of embedding computational thinking into existing subjects such as language arts and science. However, we need to better understand how to best utilize these activities in different learning contexts in a way most beneficial to all students. This includes more sophisticated methods for evaluating students' narratives, as well as supporting their creation.

In this work, we have presented an analysis of student stories created using the InfuseCS narrative-centered learning environment. InfuseCS engages students in science explorations and enables them to create interactive narratives using a structured, block-based programming interface. Data from 28 students who participated in a pilot study using InfuseCS was analyzed to better understand the nature of the narratives students created. The narrative programs showed that InfuseCS enabled students to create narratives demonstrating understanding of concepts focused on storytelling, science, and computational thinking. However, not all students were able to produce narratives of high quality. While most stories received high scores in one or two evaluation dimensions, they exhibited a notable deficiency in some aspect of the evaluation, as determined by human scoring. In an effort to enable real-time support to students on which aspects of their story needs more attention, we investigated automated assessment techniques. The automated assessment of student stories showed promise across all three evaluation dimensions, though further refinements are necessary to reach human level accuracy.

Future studies should investigate the effectiveness of providing different supports driven by robust automated assessment techniques. There is also a need to develop and investigate expanded rubrics for student narrative programs, allowing for more granular analysis and targeted interventions across narrative systems. Follow-up studies featuring think-alouds and interviews with students should be conducted to allow for better interpretation of the choices students make in their stories along with their rationale. Additionally, future research should explore the utility of more advanced large language models for automated story assessment. While this study employed pre-trained BERT and ELMo embeddings, newer models such as GPT-4 offer potentially richer representations of text. These advanced language models could provide a more nuanced understanding of students' narrative programs. Finally, it will be important to work with teachers to develop tools to better enable them to support their students in generating the best narratives possible.

**Acknowledgements.** This research was supported by the National Science Foundation under Grants DRL-1921495 and DRL-1921503. Any opinions, findings, and conclusions expressed in this material are those of the authors and do not necessarily reflect the views of the National Science Foundation.

## References

1. Andrade, H., Du, Y.: Student perspectives on rubric-referenced assessment. Pract. Assess. Res. Eval. **10**(1), 3 (2005)
2. Avraamidou, L., Osborne, J.: The role of narrative in communicating science. Int. J. Sci. Educ. **31**(12), 1683–1707 (2009)
3. Bruner, J.S.: Acts of Meaning: Four Lectures on Mind and Culture, vol. 3. Harvard University Press, Cambridge (1990)
4. Carpenter, D., Cloude, E., Rowe, J., Azevedo, R., Lester, J.: Investigating student reflection during game-based learning in middle grades science. In: Proceedings of the 11th International Learning Analytics and Knowledge Conference, pp. 280–291 (2021)
5. Chu, S.L., Quek, F., Tanenbaum, T.J.: *Performative Authoring:* nurturing storytelling in children through imaginative enactment. In: Koenitz, H., Sezen, T.I., Ferri, G., Haahr, M., Sezen, D., Çatak, G. (eds.) ICIDS 2013. LNCS, vol. 8230, pp. 144–155. Springer, Cham (2013). https://doi.org/10.1007/978-3-319-02756-2_18
6. Dwyer, H., Hill, C., Hansen, A., Iveland, A., Franklin, D., Harlow, D.: Fourth grade students reading block-based programs: predictions, visual cues, and affordances. In: Proceedings of the 2015 ACM Conference on International Computing Education Research, pp. 111–119 (2015)
7. Franklin, D., et al.: Using upper-elementary student performance to understand conceptual sequencing in a blocks-based curriculum. In: Proceedings of the 2017 ACM SIGCSE Technical Symposium on Computer Science Education, pp. 231–236 (2017)
8. Henriksen, D.: Full STEAM ahead: creativity in excellent STEM teaching practices. STEAM J. **1**(2), 15 (2014)
9. Henriksen, D., Mishra, P., Fisser, P.: Infusing creativity and technology in 21st century education: a systemic view for change. J. Educ. Technol. Soc. **19**(3), 27–37 (2016)
10. Hill, C., Dwyer, H.A., Martinez, T., Harlow, D., Franklin, D.: Floors and flexibility: designing a programming environment for 4th–6th grade classrooms. In: Proceedings of the 2015 ACM SIGCSE Technical Symposium on Computer Science Education, pp. 546–551 (2015)
11. Horn, M.S., AlSulaiman, S., Koh, J.: Translating Roberto to Omar: computational literacy, stickerbooks, and cultural forms. In: Proceedings of the 12th International Conference on Interaction Design and Children, pp. 120–127 (2013)
12. Ke, Z., Ng, V.: Automated essay scoring: a survey of the state of the art. In: Proceedings of the International Joint Conference on Artificial Intelligence, vol. 19, pp. 6300–6308 (2019)

13. Kelleher, C.: Supporting storytelling in a programming environment for middle school children. In: Iurgel, I.A., Zagalo, N., Petta, P. (eds.) ICIDS 2009. LNCS, vol. 5915, pp. 1–4. Springer, Heidelberg (2009). https://doi.org/10.1007/978-3-642-10643-9_1
14. Kelleher, C., Pausch, R.: Using storytelling to motivate programming. Commun. ACM **50**(7), 58–64 (2007)
15. Kelleher, C., Pausch, R., Kiesler, S.: Storytelling Alice motivates middle school girls to learn computer programming. In: Proceedings of the SIGCHI Conference on Human Factors in Computing Systems, pp. 1455–1464 (2007)
16. Lee, I., Martin, F., Apone, K.: Integrating computational thinking across the K-8 curriculum. ACM Inroads **5**(4), 64–71 (2014)
17. McHugh, M.L.: Interrater reliability: the kappa statistic. Biochemia medica **22**(3), 276–282 (2012)
18. Niemi, H., Multisilta, J.: Digital storytelling promoting twenty-first century skills and student engagement. Technol. Pedagog. Educ. **25**(4), 451–468 (2016)
19. Paiva, J.C., Leal, J.P., Figueira, Á.: Automated assessment in computer science education: a state-of-the-art review. ACM Trans. Comput. Educ. (TOCE) **22**(3), 1–40 (2022)
20. Park, K., et al.: Disruptive talk detection in multi-party dialogue within collaborative learning environments with a regularized user-aware network. In: Proceedings of the 23rd Annual Meeting of the Special Interest Group on Discourse and Dialogue, pp. 490–499 (2022)
21. Parsazadeh, N., Cheng, P.Y., Wu, T.T., Huang, Y.M.: Integrating computational thinking concept into digital storytelling to improve learners' motivation and performance. J. Educ. Comput. Res. **59**(3), 470–495 (2021)
22. Peters, M.E., Neumann, M., Zettlemoyer, L., Yih, W.T.: Dissecting contextual word embeddings: architecture and representation. arXiv preprint arXiv:1808.08949 (2018)
23. Rao, N., Chu, S.L., Faris, R.W., Ospina, D.: The effects of interactive emotional priming on storytelling: an exploratory study. In: Cardona-Rivera, R.E., Sullivan, A., Young, R.M. (eds.) ICIDS 2019. LNCS, vol. 11869, pp. 395–404. Springer, Cham (2019). https://doi.org/10.1007/978-3-030-33894-7_42
24. Robin, B.R.: Digital storytelling: a powerful technology tool for the 21st century classroom. Theory Pract. **47**(3), 220–228 (2008)
25. Robin, B.R.: The power of digital storytelling to support teaching and learning. Digit. Educ. Rev. **30**, 17–29 (2016)
26. Sanh, V., Debut, L., Chaumond, J., Wolf, T.: DistilBERT, a distilled version of BERT: smaller, faster, cheaper and lighter. arXiv preprint arXiv:1910.01108 (2019)
27. Sarıca, H.Ç., Usluel, Y.K.: The effect of digital storytelling on visual memory and writing skills. Comput. Educ. **94**, 298–309 (2016)
28. Shahid, M., Khan, M.R.: Use of digital storytelling in classrooms and beyond. J. Educ. Technol. Syst. **51**(1), 63–77 (2022)
29. Smeda, N., Dakich, E., Sharda, N.: The effectiveness of digital storytelling in the classrooms: a comprehensive study. Smart Learn. Environ. **1**, 1–21 (2014)
30. Tan, M., Lee, S.S., Hung, D.W.: Digital storytelling and the nature of knowledge. Educ. Inf. Technol. **19**, 623–635 (2014)

31. Weintrop, D., Hansen, A.K., Harlow, D.B., Franklin, D.: Starting from scratch: outcomes of early computer science learning experiences and implications for what comes next. In: Proceedings of the 2018 ACM Conference on International Computing Education Research, pp. 142–150 (2018)
32. Yang, Y.T.C., Wu, W.C.I.: Digital storytelling for enhancing student academic achievement, critical thinking, and learning motivation: a year-long experimental study. Comput. Educ. **59**(2), 339–352 (2012)

# Merging Archaeological Site Recreation and Museum Exhibition

Vincenzo Lombardo(✉), Vittorio Lauro, Vittorio Murtas, and Srushti Goud

Dipartimento di Informatica and CIRMA, Università di Torino, Turin, Italy
{vincenzo.lombardo,vittorio.lauro,vittorio.murtas,srushti.goud}@unito.it

**Abstract.** Archaeological projects require a great amount of work in the representation and storage of digital data about the excavation of the archaeological site, the information about the encountered findings, and the analyses carried out by the laboratories and the consequent interpretations of the facts. However, though archaeological databases are of primary importance for retracing the interpretation processes and identifying the supporting elements, they often remain a pure archive, with no more accesses after the excavation activities; often, disciplinary experts work in isolation, and usually relying on scientific literature that rarely includes a friendly access to the datasets. A well-known presentation setting in archaeology is to exhibit results through virtual reality. Virtual reality yields the recreation of the remote site in a geospatial layout as well as the reproduction the diachronic phases of the excavation and the encounter of findings.

This paper presents BeA-ViR, an application for virtual archaeology that is devoted to traversing boundaries and borders on multicultural dimensions (Japan-Europe), multi-targeted audiences (general audiences and multi-disciplinary scholars), and multiple platforms (desktop, CAVE, and web). It relies on a comprehensive database that merges archaeological and archaeometric knowledge about the site and the findings.

**Keywords:** Archaeology · Virtual reality · Traversing borders

## 1 Introduction

Archaeological projects produce such a large amount of digital information that some researcher stated that "excavation is digitization" [27]. Data have been increasing with the advent of archaeometry, which includes the activities of measurement and interpretation carried out by hard scientists, and imaging, where photogrammetry and laser scanning implement the documentation of the archaeological sites before, during, and after the destructive processes of the excavation (see, e.g., [24,36]). Also, the *digital twins* that result from the digitization of the encountered artifacts contribute to morphological research as well as to conservation, restoration, and communication processes [2]. All these data


L. Holloway-Attaway and J. T. Murray (Eds.): ICIDS 2023, LNCS 14384, pp. 68–84, 2023.
https://doi.org/10.1007/978-3-031-47658-7_6

are collected, curated and recorded in suitable databases [13,16]. These datasets are then available online through public repositories, such as the Digital Archaeological Record[1] and the Archaeology Data Service[2], for quantitative analyses that yield novel interpretations (see, e.g., [29]) and for dissemination purposes in exhibitions (see, e.g., [3]).

For both research and dissemination, a relevant role is played by virtual reality, that exploits the abundance of 3D models elaborated from the photographic documentation of excavation and artifacts. *Virtual* or *digital archaeology*, a collective term for the use of digital technology to investigate and communicate about the past, uses interactive multimedia, immersive environments, and three-dimensional modeling to recreate and visualize sites and artifacts [26] (see [23] for a recent review). VR applications for archaeology can provide explorations of the sites, by providing access to the metadata concerning sizes, distances, materials, or chronology, and representing the different excavation campaigns in different sub-environments distributed along some diachronic scale [16]. In other, more spectacular applications, famous sites are exposed to the general public, to enjoy reconstructions of buildings and life in the ancient site, providing a suitable storytelling that illustrates the available up to date interpretations about the community who have been historically living the site (e.g., [20]). In general, there has been a vast debate on what is storytelling for archaeology, sometimes oscillating between technical scientific writing and creative historical narratives (i.e., fictional narratives based on archaeological record and anthropological theory). The goal is to identify a multiplicity of writing formulas, ranging from academic conformity with the past to "better ways to connect our [i.e., archaeologists'] interests with the public interest so we might have empathy for people in the past as well" [33, p. 171].

Archaeological projects can last decades, while excavation campaigns follow one another, accumulating digital data and metadata, long before an interpretative model recognized and shared by the scientific community can be elaborated. The database is updated while the excavation activities and the laboratory analyses go on and it also happens that exhibitions are organized to engage the interested human communities with the project. These communities are the depository of the values that motivate the conservation of the archaeological site [34]. In these cases, an updatable virtual environment is a viable solution for informing the communities and keeping alive the digital materials, which suffer obsolescence and inaccessibility [14]. The virtual environment must merge the conventions for the exhibition of the archaeological site (reconstruction of known parts, hypotheses to be reported, and artist inventions to be marked) with the conventions of the museums for the exhibition of artifacts, with information extracted from the database and exhibited together with items from related sites. Both conventions assume an interactive narrative approach for organizing materials and engage public in the exploration of archaeological matters.

[1] http://www.tdar.org/, visited on 15 September 2023.

[2] http://archaeologydataservice.ac.uk/, visited on 15 September 2023.

This paper presents a VR application, called BeA-ViR, that merges the reconstruction of the archaeological site updated to what archaeologists know at some point of the project and the exhibition of the encountered artifacts, together with the information stored in the database. BeArchaeo (Beyond Archaeology[3]) is a digital-born project that records data throughout the entire process of excavation, interpretation, and presentation of findings from a Japanese Kofun, a late 6th-century mounded tomb located in Soja City, Okayama Prefecture, Japan. A semantic database[4] contains comprehensive information on all excavation and analytical activities being carried out. The virtual application has been employed in three physical exhibitions (in Japan and Italy) that illustrate the methodological project.

The paper is organized as follows. In the next section, we describe the related work in the use of virtual reality for archaeology and museum exhibitions. Then, we illustrate the design and implementation of the BeA-ViR application, with some preliminary evaluation after the public exhibitions in Japan and Europe.

## 2 Related Work

Building an application for the exhibition of an ongoing archaeological project in virtual reality relies on a number of approaches from different fields, namely archaeological reporting methods, virtual reality systems, and virtual museum practices.

Archaeology has always been linked to the data collected during the excavation activities and to their cataloging, management and interpretation [11], and data collection has received a specific attention in Japan ("Japan may be the biggest producer of archaeological data in the world") [32, p. 1]. This aspect is due to the nature of the archaeological excavation, which is configured as a specific experience that is 1) unrepeatable and destructive (so, collected data are the only reference to the original site), 2) often distant (because taking place far from the research laboratories), and 3) with limited access (as only some researchers have access to the excavation area) [4]. The wide use of surface survey instruments (photogrammetry and laser scanner), underground survey (resistive georadars and dynamics), topographic mapping (kinetic and static GIS) and various types of archaeometric analyses have added much technicality to data reporting, then increased with networking infrastructures, bringing a necessity of workflow, data management and collaborative research [10]. With reference to 3D models, there have been proposals for the integration of 3D contents with solutions for their visualization into the overall archaeological reporting process. For example, the Interactive Reporting System (IRS) is a web-based tool that relies on 3D web information for the generation of digital interactive reports of excavations [6].

[3] https://www.bearchaeo.com/, 15 September 2023.

[4] https://bearchaeo.unito.it/omeka-s/s/bearchaeo-resources-site/page/welcome, 15 September 2023.

3D models are useful for communication when integrated into a virtual reality system, with several examples for archaeology. In fact, virtual archaeology is the current logical end of a long path of visualization techniques aimed at filling the gap given by the remoteness of the sites and the limited use of the findings, together with the sketches of interpretation hypotheses [28]. The virtual recreation of sites and artifacts represents a fundamental branch of archaeology and the entire lifecycle of acquisition, processing, data analysis, archiving and dissemination has become integrated [17]. There also are many examples of archaeological research through virtual reality systems. For example, in Japan, Masuda et al. proved the hypothesis of the use of natural light to illuminate the Fugoppe cave, where prehistoric inhabitants carved fascinating engravings [21]. More recently, Elaine A. Sullivan could "peel away the layers of history" at the necropolis of Saqqara, in Egypt, to reveal the changes in the sight lines, skylines, and vistas at different periods [31]. At the crossroad of database documentation and virtual reality visualization is the pioneering Çatalhöyük project, investigating on a Neolithic settlement in Turkey. A number of VR tools, in a few decades, have provided a virtualization of the layer-by-layer excavation, leveraging on 3D GIS data, digital collaborative systems (so-called tele-immersion) and data curation. The study of the spatial and layout data has shifted from the usual 2D mapping to a 3D archive, including the mapping of strata on their XYZ position in the virtual excavation volume [7].

Finally, for our project, we mention the approaches to the virtual exhibitions. For ongoing archaeological projects, this is a peculiar case. Artifacts are still under study and cannot be physically exhibited; moreover, if they undergo invasive archaeometric studies (which, e.g., analyze one section or a sample of it) the digital twin is the only item that is actually the same as the encountered fragment; finally, virtual exhibitions are useful to compare the site artifacts with artifacts belonging to other museums or other sites. Virtual museum idea and technology exist since the early 90's, implemented with various technologies, from precomputed video with decompression, to CD-based multimedia, to more and more realistic interactive 3D graphics [22]. A virtual museum uses information and communication technologies to provide visitors with interactive exhibits, education, and access to historical and cultural information, including (though not always) the presentation of the museum collections through 3D representations of artifacts [30]. The Virtual Museum Transitional Network [9] has provided the terminology and an initial classification system of virtual museums reflecting administrative, descriptive, technical, and use issues. More recent approaches aim at a three-valued classifications, namely content-centric, communication-centric, and collaboration-centric virtual museums (surveyed in [1]), addressing, respectively, content and surroundings, with navigation elements, knowledge transfer and learning linked to objects, and web platforms with shared workspaces and participatory approaches. For example, a hypertext based on geo-referenced archaeological artifacts belongs to the last two categories and has been realized in the project presented here.

Virtual museums can refer single items as well as multiple item collections. Related to archaeology are approaches that implement some format of exploratory or environmental storytelling for the access to the reconstruction sites as well as exhibits. While multiple item exhibitions, together with multiple sites, are commonly available, more typical of the archaeological field are the reconstructions of the sites and single item exhibitions. We report two examples here. Christou et al. [5] have been among the first to propose a reconstruction of a Greek temple in a CAVE setting, with photographs and ground plans used to create an artistic reconstruction for the purpose of engaging visitor. As a single item exhibition, the virtual regain of the destroyed 38 m Eastern Buddha figure of the Giant Buddhas in Bamiyan, Afghanistan (destroyed in 2001), integrated into the model of the scanned niche [35]. The virtual model has been the results of several scientific explorations, including an all-season photographic survey of cave structures around the vicinity of the Giant Buddhas, carried out by Japanese missions in the 1960s and 1970s.

## 3 System Design for Ongoing Archaeological Project

Two major notions of the archaeological interpretation concern geo-spatial extents and time intervals related to some site. Archaeology analyzes sites and unearthed findings to form chronological schemes and georeferenced layouts that can purposefully support the reconstruction of the past society. Actually, time as a concept appeared relatively late in archaeology, while space is the fundamental concept that supports research also before the fieldwork starts [8, Chapter 6]. In an ongoing archaeological project, it is required to provide access to partial interpretations, that may only address mere technical issues (e.g., some pottery shard is of a non-calcareous material) as well as inform the general public of the current understanding, including both historical background facts (e.g., hypothesis that the provenance of some materials is from some area, because of the comparison with other known artifacts) and the virtual exhibition of the main findings (to engage the community with what is tangibly going on). So, the relation of the current site and the related encountered findings with other sites and findings of the area is relevant for both the researchers and the public, giving relevance to geospatial context.

The BeArchaeo project addresses ongoing activities, excavations of a Kofun burial mound and the archaeological/archaeometric analyses of the findings from the Kofun as well as from other sites of the same area and nearby prefectures provided by local museums. Kofuns are megalithic tombs or burial mounds of the protohistory of Japan (3rd to 7th century CE). They name the Kofun period of Japan (proto-)history. Some of them are famous for their distinctive keyhole-shape and some are inscribed on the UNESCO World Heritage List; their shape can also be circular or rectangular, with several sizes, to a few meters to hundreds of meters, depending of social status of the buried individual. The Tobiotsuka Kofun, excavated in the BeArchaeo project, has a circular shape, with a diameter of 30 m.

In this phase, while the excavations are not completed yet and about 200 findings have been unearthed and are being analyzed (mostly pottery shards and some metal weapon fragments, such as arrowheads), the system design has to account for an engaging narration of current status of the project, relying on a geospatial layout for the involved sites and to exhibit the current findings, with related findings from other sites, in a museum setting. The goal is to provide an organization of the materials and knowledge that can engage both the researchers and the general public, by adopting an environmental storytelling, that realizes an immersive narrative experience by evoking pre-existing narrative associations [12], namely the visit to an archaeological site and to a museum, respectively. Interactive overlays and information panels provide basic narration units, while getting close to objects allow to discover its major facts and possibly going deep into the results of the archaeometric measurements and the partial interpretations. The flow chart in Fig. 1 illustrates the hierarchical structure: from a main exhibition hall, which reports a geospatial layout connecting real geographic positions of the sites and their diachronic arrangement, the user can access the site reconstruction of the excavated Kofun (site complex exhibition) that consists of the current site, which in turn gives access to the reconstruction of the historical site and a focus on the burial chamber; the reconstruction of the current site given also access to the related virtual museum, with the exhibition of the major unearthed findings with the current interpretations; the current site also includes the excavation records, namely a visualization of the trenches. The related sites and findings are:

- another related Kofun (2), where the reconstruction only addresses the burial chamber (for comparison with the excavated Kofun);
- virtual museums related to multiple-finding exhibitions coming from related sites, including a rough reconstruction of the site (current and historical structure);
- virtual museums related to single-finding exhibitions displaying outstanding pieces, connected for bringing related religious or symbolic values to the excavated Kofun.

This flow chart of information is implemented as a VR application, that traverses many boundaries and borders.

## 4 The Virtual Reality Application

The general architecture of the VR application (Fig. 2) relies on a representation of the archaeological and archaeometric knowledge encoded in a database. The database contains both the descriptions for the general public and scientific data with the corresponding interpretations, addressed by scholars of several disciplines. The VR application relies on these database descriptions, that have been encoded by scientists (after the designer guidance) in the database and the digitally scanned sites and artifacts. The latter are displayed in different environments, as summed up in the flow chart above, with descriptions uploaded

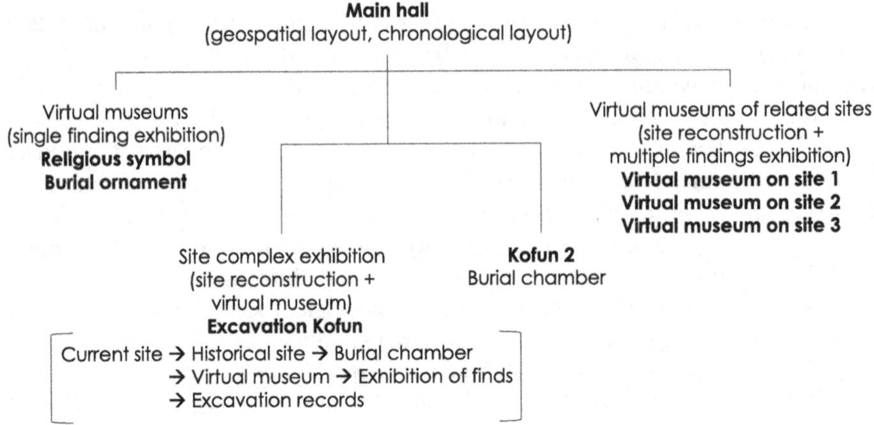


**Fig. 1.** Flow chart of the BeA-ViR system. Accessible VR environments are in boldface.

from the database. The system is deployed on three platforms, namely a CAVE application, a desktop installation, and the web browser plugin (bottom left, bottom right, bottom middle, respectively, in the figure). It is also possible to explore the database content only, with a simple web interface.

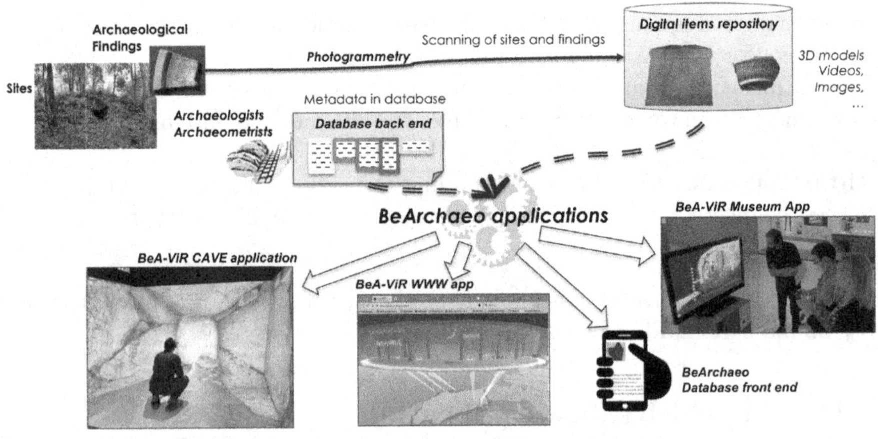


**Fig. 2.** Software architecture of the BeA-ViR system.

### 4.1 Traversing Boundaries and Borders

The BeA-ViR application addresses a number of issues of traversing boundaries and borders. The first is the multi-cultural context of the project. Given its international character and since the installation is displayed both in Japanese and European museums as well as on the web, the application has to reconcile general and specific aspects of Japanese culture. The general aspects concern the geography of the involved Japanese regions and the chronological proto-historic periods of Japan; also, narrative texts have to include introductory notes about Japanese proto-historic features (such as the megalithic mounded tombs). The specific aspects include a focus on the interested local areas of Okayama and Shimane prefectures in Japan (which are significant for the Japanese public, but generally unknown to Europeans), as well as the cultural exchange processes between these areas during the Kofun period. The latter issue was also a key objective of the archaeological/archaeometric investigation: in fact, the travel and trade of materials between communities is one of the interpretation keys for the evolution of civilizations.

Related to this issue are also the multi-lingual features of the application and the multidisciplinary approach to archaeometric investigation: on the one hand, the database of excavations and artifacts includes notes in both English and Japanese, and the text is arranged accordingly to provide a layout of both descriptions; on the other hand, the knowledge representation has to accomodate all the several scientific disciplines contributing to the enterprise (e.g., chemistry, physics, archaeomagnetism - see [19]). In Fig. 3, we can see the multi-lingual naming of proto-historical periods as well as their mapping onto western calendar indications, and the multi-character-set of sites, connected to the general geographic map of Japan, with a mark of the interested region in West Japan (for local visitors).

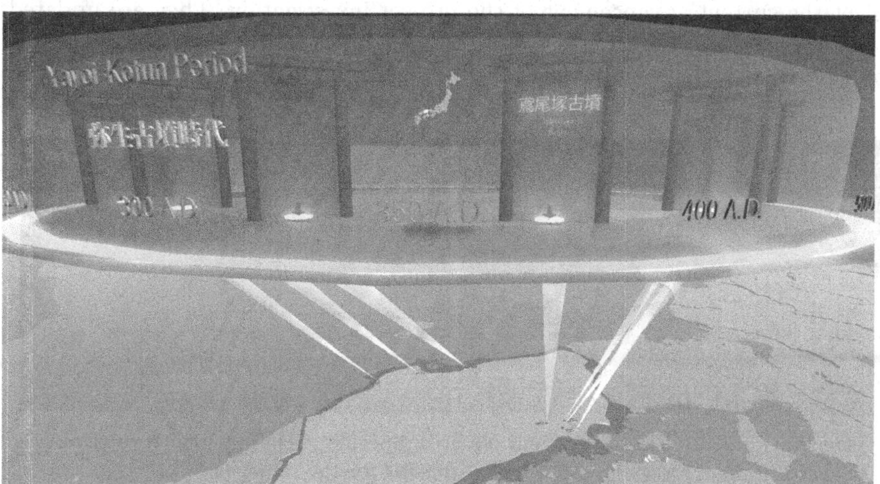


**Fig. 3.** Main Hall and connection with the geographical region (Color figure online)

The second issue of traversing boundaries is on the characterization of the target audience, which could be the general public, on the one hand, and multidisciplinary scholars, on the other. General public is interested in the major facts about the excavations and findings, especially in this ongoing phase, with attention to methodological issues (e.g., how a finding is analyzed and what are the current hypotheses) and the path to the complete picture (if the composition of the finding is non-calcareous, possibly its provenance is the Kibi area. Scholars are instead interested in accessing the current test results (e.g., images of sections of a pottery shard from the electronic microscope) or comparing the test results of different techniques (e.g., comparing the elemental compositions of two samples). The multi-user experience is implemented by providing both levels in the underlying descriptive database entries. Narrative, wide, and easy-to-understand descriptions for the general public; specific data, including images of the artifacts from Optical and Scanning Electron Microscopy and PLM (Polarized light microscopy), X-Ray fluorescence analysis reports and tomography data, directed to scholars.

Interpretations are associated to appropriate items or a combination of them, reported as a complex item in the database. The interaction metaphor used to distinguish the activation of the two different displays, that is of the visualization of the two descriptive entries, relies on the proximity of the user navigation. In Fig. 4, we can see the general and specific descriptions, respectively, for a pottery shard. If the visitor stays at some distance (Fig. 4a), the system displays a panel with a general description of the finding; if the visitor gets much closer (Fig. 4b), the system creates a virtual room with many panels reporting the individual archaeometric investigations on the same finding (in the example case in the figure, two scanned images from sections of the same shard are reported, with the respective descriptions). Panel texts are directly uploaded from the database and reflect the current advancement of the project investigation. They are updated as the project develops, always respecting the directives for their use in the VR application.

(a) General audience description for a pottery shard.

(b) Specific archaeometric investigations results for the same shard.

**Fig. 4.** General and specific descriptions for a finding.

The third issue of traversing borders is the technical deployment of the application, that can be CAVE, desktop, and web (see Fig. 2). Though it mainly origins as a technical issue, it has relevant implications on immersion and interaction. The objective is to ease the dissemination, because diverse institutions could be interested in diverse communication formats, and the collaboration between the disciplinary scholars, who may be using different communication modalities and hopefully receive, across versions, a consistent and seamless experience. The application design addresses the three technical deployments. Aesthetics, color, and functionalities are consistent across platforms to create a cohesive experience. The entrance to a virtual room (being it a site reconstruction or a museum exhibition) is realized through a collision with a specific object (step onto a footboard): this metaphor is very immediate for the CAVE environment and is transposed to the desktop and the web implementation; also, it could be employed for future implementations, such as mobile or HMD (traversing further borders). All the technical platforms provide controls for first-person displacement and aerial exploration by soaring or jumping, before falling with gravity. Users who do not want to perform a free exploration can be lead through a "guided tour", which stops at predefined points of interest in the exhibitions.

### 4.2 The BeA-ViR Virtual Reality Environment

The VR environment that implements these traversals relies on realistic models, for site reconstructions and artifact exhibition, and abstract structures in space, for the virtual museum exhibition. The realistic models exploit the photogrammetry acquisitions that are realized for the digital documentation of the excavation process [15]; the abstract structures are realized as floating horizontal discs, bearing gates to the virtual rooms. The information about what are the geographic locations identified by the gates is expressed by depicting light cones between a map point and the gate. The opening environment (called Main Hall, Fig. 3) is a double-encircled disc, spatially located above the Japan region that is of relevance for the project: the inner circle implements the geospatial dimension (with the gates), the exterior circle represents the chronological dimension. Red gates implement the controls for accessing the individual environments mentioned in the flow chart. When the user approaches the external circle, a semi-transparent wall appears, between them and the gates, reporting a timeline of Japanese historical periods and their mapping to western periods: for example, in Fig. 3, the Yayoi-Kofun transition period centers on year 300 A.D. This timeline wall lets users explore the sites (or sub-environments) by using a chorological indexing. While moving around the wall to follow the timeline, gates appear/disappear depending on the existence of the corresponding site in some era. Only the gates that port to sites that were active in the traversed era are represented and accessible on the inner surface.

The Main Hall controls the access to the environments through the red gates (or torii). The users can move freely, via gamepad or mouse and keyboard, depending on the implementation platform. The footboards with a downward arrow invite to step onto for accessing the specific environment. The accessible environments split into site reconstructions and virtual exhibitions of findings (cf. the flow chart). Site reconstructions (Fig. 5) are explorable 3D models that address both the current status (a) and the archaeological interpretation of the site at historical periods (b). There also are extra artificial structures, marked with unnatural colors, to display interpretive features of the reconstruction (see, e.g., the blue catwalk in Fig. 5b, to highlight the passageway to the burial chamber). Again footboards allow the switch between the representations and the return to the Main Hall.

Virtual museums can be multiple finding exhibitions and single finding exhibitions (Fig. 6). Contrasting with site reconstructions, these are nocturnal environments, with the floating disc posited onto the geographical location. Multiple finding exhibitions (Fig. 6a) host a site reconstruction (current status alternated with archaeological interpretation), encircled by the main findings from that site. The user can travel around the disc and inspect every finding with its story and possibly going deep into its archaeological and archaeometric investigations, data, and interpretation hypotheses. Single finding exhibitions (Fig. 6b) position the finding at the center of the disc. The display of the finding is alternated with the display of the site where it has been encountered. All the switches (between finding and environment and between current site and archaeological interpretation) are performed through footboards.

(a) Current status.

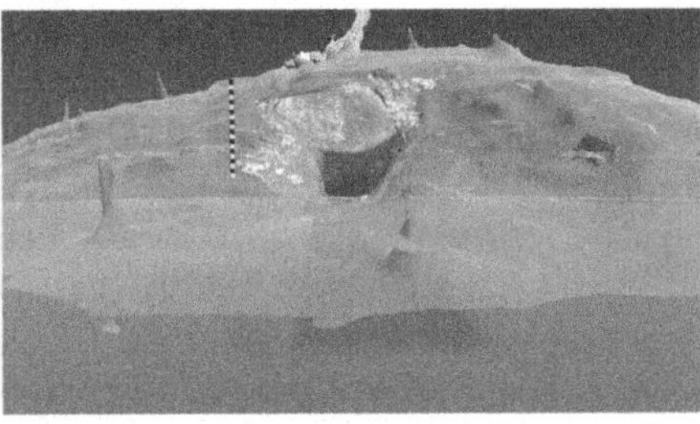

(b) Archaeological interpretation.

**Fig. 5.** Navigable Kofun site reconstruction.

(a) Virtual museum for multiple item exhibition.

(b) Virtual museum for single item exhibition (notice height measure on the left).

**Fig. 6.** Environments in the VR application.

### 4.3 Implementation of the VR Application

BeA-ViR has been implemented with Unity in a modular way, so that it could be easily deployed on the three platforms: desktop, web browser, and CAVE. All deployments share the same 3D and 2D assets (with very limited customizations). Starting with the design phase, a domain model and a class diagram were created with UML. This UML schema has driven the implementation and all refinements (which are still ongoing, along with the project). The implementation follows the design and narrative choices as it involves the creation of the three layouts of environments and their associated functions. The main 3D assets are archaeological findings and structures photoscanned through an acquisition pipeline created within the project [15].

Some variants as well as optimization techniques were applied for adapting the application to platforms and improving performance. The desktop version, designed for museum installations, comes with advanced graphics, such as realistic lighting, shadows, and high-definition models and textures. It requires a powerful computer to run smoothly. The WebGL version for the browser has required an optimization (polygon decimation, texture compression, baked lights and some removed shaders), for a smooth execution on the variety of devices and browsers. The highly performative CAVE version did not require optimization on graphics, but a particular coding for the synchronization of the four computers (one per wall) on a local network, with scripts exclusively running on the server process (the front wall of the CAVE) and some functions assigned to the client processes (the other walls).

The presentation of several character sets in the multi-lingual environment, specifically Western and Japanese character sets, was an intriguing problem. An extensive search for a character font has selected the Noto Sans Japanese[5], for the correct display of all characters (including hiragana, katakana, and kanji - a large subset) in the GUIs of the three versions.

Informational panels built after an access to the database entries (set up in Omeka-S CMS to enable a semantic representation [18,19]). through a Unity implementation of the database Omeka-S API[6]. The library, in particular, enables users to get the metadata for the exhibited objects and to display custom vocabularies for the archaeometric information addressed to scholars. The implementation currently allows the data to be read only, but it is expected that, in the future, the code will be expanded to also guarantee write options. This could allow multi-disciplinary scholars to work on and annotate details about specific fields in the database, sharing and disseminating knowledge to future users of the application.

---

[5] https://fonts.google.com/noto/specimen/Noto+Sans+JP.

[6] https://github.com/RenderHeads/UnityPlugin-OmekaAPI, GPL-3.0 License, the same as BeA-ViR.

### 4.4 Preliminary Evaluation

At the three public installations of the project, we carried out evaluations of the prototype through the submission of questionnaires (see details in [25]). Evaluations were based on a Likert scale (1-Bad to 5-Great), addressing the overall usability of the system, the effectiveness of the control system, the clarity of design, the archaeological information provided. We also carried out some qualitative observations to assess the overall user experience. 19 people participated to a first evaluation on the desktop application, distributed into 5 age groups (2/12–17, 3/18–24, 5/25–33, 4/34–45, 4/46–60); then, other 7 users, again aged 12 to 60, with various cultural backgrounds, tested the web browser version. The second group also included 3 multi-disciplinary scholars (from the archaeological/archaeometric team), who are, together with the general audience, a target of the project.

About the general public, the results showed that the application and archaeological information were generally well accepted (3.6 average, with 0.9 of standard deviation). However, since a large number of users struggled with gamepad controls (2.5 avg), we developed the "guided tour" functionality, which enables users to see artifacts through virtual jumps, skipping the exploration phase. About the behavioral difference between general public and scholars, we also measured the exploration time of each type of environment (site reconstruction, single finding exhibition and multiple finding exhibition), the display duration for each finding, and the rate of pressing the controls. Both groups have appreciated the overall experience as well as the archaeological information received (both over 4, on the Likert scale). General public did not get the timeline behavior and found hard to coordinate virtual first-person motion (2 and 2.5, respectively). Introducing tooltips were suggested to reduce the likelihood of accidental impacts with item interaction. Experts generally appreciated the system interaction but have required the improvement of the archaeometric information. For example, they appreciated the microscope photos of the artifacts, but proposed to add information about the stratigraphic unit for each finding, to increase the knowledge network and improve the interpretation process. In the case of the 3D reconstructions, they suggested showing the reconstruction stages in a diachronic setting.

Some expert was impressed by the merging of fine 3D representations with detailed archaeometric data, usually kept distinct in projects. In general, unsurprisingly, experts looked for more information than general audiences: on average, the experts pressed the information button a double number of times (38 VS. 19, in a 15-minute session) with respect to the general public, who were usually more focused on the aesthetic/graphic content of the application. Finally, users could correctly recognize the 3-tier environment (site reconstruction, multiple finding exhibition, single finding exhibition), demonstrating the average clarity of the content organization. Users have spent on average more time in multiple finding exhibitions and less time in site reconstruction and single finding exhibitions, which likely need the delivery of more information or some highlighted feature.

## 5 Conclusions

This paper has presented a virtual reality application for the exhibition of archaeological projects, which merges the reconstruction of the sites and the exhibition of findings in virtual museums, employing interactive 3D graphics in a unified design. The application design takes into account the chronological and the geospatial dimensions, which are common in archaeology. A modular implementation has allowed an easy porting on various devices and platforms. The application, which is applied to the hard case of ongoing archaeological projects, exploits the database entries, set up for the recording of the excavation process and the documentation of findings, guiding researchers in the insertion of appropriate descriptions for the narrative development associated to item entries in the database.

We aim at improving the application for deploying archaeological exhibition of ongoing projects, while contributing to scholars' research via an easy access to database entries, improving the connections. A future virtual museum editor could rely on the application modular structure, to enable curators and scholar to adapt their content to the environment structure.

The case study has been a joint project Europe-Japan on a Kofun burial mound, excavated in Japan, with the encountered findings. Exploiting the virtual reality application, such findings are also related to other sites and findings in neighbor areas. The project is ongoing, with interpretations sometimes including mere hypotheses and incomplete archaeometric data. A preliminary evaluation has been carried out to understand the user reception of an application that merges different uses for the experts and the general public.

The BeA-ViR application traverses boundaries and borders in several dimensions. The virtual environment addresses multi-cultural and multi-lingual issues, related to the Japanese-European public presentations and the deployment in Japanese-English at the same time. It also addresses general public and multidisciplinary scholars at the same time, introducing a proximity metaphor to let interested people explore the knowledge and hypotheses in depth. Finally, it addresses a multi-platform deployment, with issues related to graphic and interaction designs, in order to ensure a seamless experience across platforms (desktop, CAVE, and web browser).

**Acknowledgements.** The BeArchaeo project has been funded by the European Union's Horizon 2020 research and innovation programme, under the Marie Skłodowska-Curie, Grant Agreement No. 823826. The content of this paper represents the views of the authors only and is their sole responsibility; it cannot be considered to reflect the views of the European Commission and/or the Consumers, Health, Agriculture and Food Executive Agency or any other body of the European Union. The European Commission and the Agency do not accept any responsibility for use that may be made of the information it contains.

## References

1. Baloian, N., Biella, D., Luther, W., Pino, J.A., Sacher, D.: Designing, realizing, running, and evaluating virtual museum: a survey on innovative concepts and technologies. JUCS - J. Univ. Comput. Sci. **27**(12), 1275–1299 (2021). https://doi.org/10.3897/jucs.77153
2. Barsanti, S.G., Caruso, G., Micoli, L.L., Rodriguez, M.C., Guidi, G.: 3D visualization of cultural heritage artefacts with virtual reality devices. In: The International Archives of the Photogrammetry, Remote Sensing and Spatial Information Sciences, 25th International CIPA Symposium, vol. XL-5/W7 (2015)
3. Cassidy, B., Sim, G., Robinson, D.W., Gandy, D.: A virtual reality platform for analyzing remote archaeological sites. Interact. Comput. **31**, 167–176 (2019)
4. Carandini, A., Caciagli, R.: Storie dalla terra: manuale dello scavo archeologico. De Donato (1981)
5. Christou, C., Angus, C., Loscos, C., Dettori, A., Roussou, M.: A versatile large-scale multimodal VR system for cultural heritage visualization. In: Proceedings of ACM Symposium on Virtual Reality Software and Technology, pp. 133–140. ACM (2006)
6. Derudas, P., Dell'Unto, N., Callieri, M., Apel, J.: Sharing archaeological knowledge: the interactive reporting system. J. Field Archaeol. **46**(5), 303–315 (2021)
7. Forte, M., Dell'Unto, N., Lercari, N.: Digital çatalhöyük: a cyber-archaeological approach. In: Hodder, I., Tsoraki, C. (eds.) Communities at Work: The Making of Çatalhöyük, vol. Çatalhöyük Research Project Series No. 15, pp. 89–102. British Institute at Ankara, Monograph 55, London (2021)
8. Gamble, C.: Archaeology, The Basics. Routledge, Digitizing Sponsor Kahle/Austin Foundation, Distributed by the Internet Archive edn. (2007)
9. Giannoulis, G., et al.: Terminology, definitions and types for virtual museums. Technical report, V-MUST net (2014). http://www.v-must.net/sites/default/files/D21c2014
10. Gupta, N.: Preparing Archaeological Data for Spatial Analysis, pp. 17–40, January 2020. https://doi.org/10.4324/9781351243858-2
11. Hodder, I., Orton, C.: Spatial Analysis in Archaeology. New Studies in Archaeology. Cambridge University Press, Cambridge (1976)
12. Jenkins, H.: Game Design as a Narrative Architecture. Henry Jenkins Blog (2004)
13. Karatas, T., Lombardo, V.: A multiple perspective account of digital curation for cultural heritage: tasks, disciplines and institutions. In: Kuflik, T., Torre, I., Burke, R., Gena, C. (eds.) Adjunct Publication of the 28th ACM Conference on User Modeling, Adaptation and Personalization, UMAP 2020, Genoa, Italy, 12–18 July 2020, pp. 325–332. ACM (2020). https://doi.org/10.1145/3386392.3399277
14. Kintigh, K.: America's archaeology data keeps disappearing even though the law says the government is supposed to preserve it. The Conversation (2018)
15. Lauro, V., Lombardo, V.: The cataloging and conservation of digital survey in archaeology: a photogrammetry protocol in the context of digital data curation. Heritage **6**(3), 3113–3136 (2023). https://doi.org/10.3390/heritage6030166
16. Lercari, N., Shiferaw, E., Forte, M., Kopper, R.: Immersive visualization and curation of archaeological heritage data: çatalhöyük and the digit app. J. Archaeol. Method Theory (2017). https://doi.org/10.1007/s10816-017-9340-4
17. Levy, T.E.: On-site digital archaeology 3.0 and cyber-archaeology: into the future of the past - new developments, delivery and the creation of a data avalanche. In: Cyber-Archaeology, pp. 135–153. Archaeopress, Oxford (2010)

18. Lombardo, V., Damiano, R., Karatas, T., Mattutino, C.: Linking ontological classes and archaeological forms. In: Pan, J.Z., et al. (eds.) ISWC 2020. LNCS, vol. 12507, pp. 700–715. Springer, Cham (2020). https://doi.org/10.1007/978-3-030-62466-8_43
19. Lombardo, V., Karatas, T., Gulmini, M., Guidorzi, L., Angelici, D.: Transdisciplinary approach to archaeological investigations in a semantic web perspective. Semant. Web J. **14**(2), 361–383 (2023)
20. Manuelian, P.D.: Giza 3D: digital archaeology and scholarly access to the Giza pyramids: the Giza project at Harvard university. In: Proceedings of DigitalHeritage 2013 (Digital Heritage International Congress), vol. 2, pp. 727–734. Institute of Electrical and Electronics Engineers, Marseille, France, 28 October–1 November 2013 (2013)
21. Masuda, T., Yamada, Y., Kuchitsu, N., Ikeuchi, K.: Sunlight illumination simulation for archaeological investigation-case study of the Fugoppe cave-. In: VSMM 2004 : Proceedings of the Tenth International Conference on Virtual Systems and Multimedia, p. 850(10), 17–19 November 2004, Softopia Japan, Ogaki City, Japan (2004)
22. Miller, G., et al.: The virtual museum: interactive 3D navigation of a multimedia database. J. Vis. Comput. Anim. **3**, 183–197 (1992)
23. Morgan, C.: Current digital archaeology. Ann. Rev. Anthropol. **51**, 213–231 (2022)
24. Motz, C., Carrier, S.: Paperless recording at the Sangro valley project. In: Earl, G., et al. (eds.) Archaeology in the Digital Era, pp. 25–30. Amsterdam University Press (2013). https://www.cambridge.org/core/books/abs/archaeology-in-the-digital-era/paperless-recording-at-the-sangro-valley-project/0786382AF0ACBD65E74E1872EF382850
25. Murtas, V., Lauro, V., Lombardo, V.: Virtual archaeology in a multi-platform and multi-lingual setting. In: Adjunct Proceedings of the 31st ACM Conference on User Modeling, Adaptation and Personalization (UMAP 2023 Adjunct). Association for Computing Machinery (2023). https://doi.org/10.1145/35633593596664
26. Reilly, P., Rahtz, S.P.Q.: Archaeology and the Information Age: A Global Perspective. One World Archaeology. Routledge, London (1992)
27. Roosevelt, C.H., Cobb, P., Moss, E., Olson, B.R., Ünlüsoy, S.: Excavation is destruction digitization: advances in archaeological practice. J. Field Archaeol. **40**(3), 325–346 (2015). https://doi.org/10.1179/2042458215Y.0000000004
28. Sanders, D.H.: Virtual heritage: researching and visualizing the past in 3D. J. East. Mediterr. Archaeol. Heritage Stud. **2**, 30–47 (2014)
29. Silva, F., Linden, M.V.: Amplitude of travelling front as inferred from $^{1}$4C predicts levels of genetic admixture among European early farmers. Sci. Rep. **7**(1), 2045–2322 (2017). https://doi.org/10.1038/s41598-017-12318-2
30. Skalska-Cimer, B., Kadłuczka, A.: Virtual museum. Museum of the future? Tech. Trans. **119**, e2022004 (2022). https://doi.org/10.37705/TechTrans/e2022004
31. Sullivan, E.A.: Constructing the Sacred Visibility and Ritual Landscape at the Egyptian Necropolis of Saqqara. A Stanford Digital Project. Stanford University Press, Stanford (2020). https://constructingthesacred.org, ISBN: 9781503603332
32. Takata, Y., Yanase, P.: The production, preservation and dissemination of archaeological data in Japan. Internet Archaeology, vol. 58 (2021). https://doi.org/10.11141/ia.58.11
33. Thomas, J.T.: The archaeologist as writer. In: Dyke, R.M.V., Bernbeck, R. (eds.) Subjects and Narratives in Archaeology, pp. 169–188. University Press of Colorado (2015)

34. de la Torre, M.: Values and heritage conservation. Heritage Soc. **6**(2), 155–166 (2013)
35. Toubekisa, G., et al.: Preservation and management of the UNESCO world heritage site of Bamiyan: laser scan documentation and virtual reconstruction of the destroyed buddha figures and the archaeological remains. In: ISPRS Annals of the Photogrammetry, Remote Sensing and Spatial Information Sciences, vol. IV-2/W2. 26th International CIPA Symposium 2017, 28 August–1 September 2017, Ottawa, Canada (2017)
36. Trimmis, K.: Paperless mapping and cave archaeology: a review on the application of DistoX survey method in archaeological cave sites. J. Archaeol. Sci. Rep. **18**, 399–407 (2018). https://www.sciencedirect.com/science/article/pii/S2352409X1730768X, https://doi.org/10.1016/jjasrep201801022

# Teaching Interactive Digital Narrative Through Found Photography

Conor McKeown(✉) and Ellie MacDonald

University of Stirling, Stirling, UK
cpmmckeown@gmail.com, e.m.hopkins1@stir.ac.uk

**Abstract.** One challenge teaching the creation of interactive digital narratives to humanities students is engaging with programming/scripting. For students without any familiarity of code, even simple(r) tools (game engines) like Twine and Unity can present major challenges. Fortunately, it has been suggested that found objects can enhance the classroom experience of learning in unfamiliar ways: found objects allow students to anchor their new experiences to the everyday. This paper recounts the experience of creating a class – called 'Introduction to Digital Storytelling' – with the aim of giving students freedom to create interactive digital narratives through game engines while grounding their experience in the theory and practice of 'found photography'. We present the background and findings gathered after the course's first year. We believe found objects and Found Photography in particular, have the potential to ease some of the challenges of STEM skill acquisition, enabling students' digital creative practices.

**Keywords:** Interactive Digital Narrative · Found Photography · Unity · Twine · Pedagogy

## 1 Introduction

A recurring challenge noted by academics teaching STEM or STEM adjacent subjects is the difficulty of teaching programming to students without any prior experience [1, 2]. This is exactly the kind of difficulty an educator must expect when aiming to teach Interactive Digital Narrative design to those completing degrees within the humanities [3].

A range of solutions to this problem have been suggested but one that interested the authors of this paper, and the creators of our university's first 'digital storytelling' class, is the implementation of found object art and particularly 'found photography' understood in this article as a "celebration of the mundane" that is at once a "an ultimate denial of authorship" but also an "act of inclusion" [4]. Found photographs allow artists, scholars and – in this case – students, to make strange the familiar and put to work otherwise neglected objects. Putting the inspiration found from others' experimental teaching strategies into practice, the authors designed a curriculum that required students to build digital narratives (using Unity, Twine or similar game creation tools) based around found photographs. Guiding by example, the authors also built their own game


L. Holloway-Attaway and J. T. Murray (Eds.): ICIDS 2023, LNCS 14384, pp. 85–95, 2023.
https://doi.org/10.1007/978-3-031-47658-7_7

in the Unity game engine utilizing found photographs sourced from a "charity shop" (thrift-store), otherwise destined to be thrown away as landfill waste. On balance, student reactions were very positive, listing only a few concerns that can be covered in the future of the course. The authors of this paper suggest that using found objects is an easily practicable way of making the challenging task of teaching and learning complex interactive digital narrative tools like Twine and Unity much more approachable as they allow students (and staff) a chance to work with something familiar in a new way, limiting the emotional toll of engaging with new skills while adding depth to the otherwise mundane.

## 2 The Difficulties of Teaching IDN to Humanities Students

A challenge identified with teaching STEM subjects in schools is the persistent belief in students and educators that one can be (or not be) 'good at math' [1, p. 226]. While Ulises Eligio's in-depth study of the *Emotions in Mathematical Thinking* suggests many and varied possible reasons for this binary thinking (not limited to the social implications of math-clubs, the anxiety of learning about infinity and more) the established links between Math skills and success in connected STEM subjects means that many students approach topics like programming with trepidation. Research has uncovered connections between student confidence in STEM subjects like Physics and the parents' attitudes to similar subjects in the home [5]. These complex emotional/psychological connections are just as present and complex in the teaching and learning of computer science [2]. Salguero et al. have found connections to 'many areas of their lives' including personal obligations, lack of sense of belonging, in-class confusion, and lack of confidence [3, p. 319].

Given the current state of teaching STEM related subjects, teaching game development or even engaging with elements of interactive digital storytelling in its broadest forms, is likely to cause heightened levels of stress among students when it begins to resemble computer programming and mathematics. Kenton Howard Taylor and Rachel Donley's account of using Ink (scripting language) to teach interaction design notes this problem specifically: they write, 'Ink is relatively easy to learn, but this point in the scaffolding assignment sequence is also where students usually start to struggle since it requires them to write code' [3, p. 70]. Recent publications suggest an awareness of the more general stress that can be caused when attempting to teach interactive digital storytelling through the use of game engines: for instance, Brendan Keogh and Benjamin Nicoll's monograph on the Unity game engine notes that one great strength of the engine is its ease of use suggesting the difficulties of the alternative (programming an engine from scratch) [6]. Similarly, Thompson has suggested that a strength of the Twine platform is its accessibility given its text-based nature [7]. Beyond using game engines Nick Montfort's book on teaching creative programming to humanities students also notes the difficulties and challenges therein; that it can be 'difficulttounderstandthe bigger picture, hard to discernhow to usefully work with data and how togain comfort with programming, while dealing with the more advanced topics that are covered in introductory programming courses. Thatis, it can be hard to seethe forest for thebinary trees' [8, p. 12]. While these difficulties are partly due to students lacking familiarity, another difficulty is more challenging to overcome. Salguero's study of the drop-out and failure rates of programming heavy introductory courses [2] and Bennedsen & Caspersen's repeated studies on similar material [9] suggests that programming is simply a highly challenging skill to acquire[1].

Reading between the lines of these studies it's possible to put a picture together of the current state of play: for a complex variety of reasons that we are only beginning to unravel, students find STEM subjects challenging to engage with. Computer Science is one of these subjects, and it is the programming element of these courses that can be particularly challenging. For humanities students, engaging with emerging creative practice and interactive digital storytelling teaching, these problems are significant.

Of course, I am not the first researcher to have thought of this or considered some possible recourse. A tremendous inspiration on this course's construction was the paper by Danielle Wayne Dravenstadt whose writing on choice-based teaching with found objects provided a clear structure around which to build our teaching strategy [10]. Dravenstadt found that 'exploration of found materials prompts students to consider the use of artmaking materials with more care and curiosity' [10, p. 10]. Although our class was not of a similar genre to Dravenstadt's art classroom for younger learners, we felt there would still be tremendous potential for crossover. Similarly, ideas from art therapy suggested that 'using found objects can create a space for integrating and meaning making in the face of rupture' [11].

A challenge persisted as we were already stretching the limits of our knowledge by aiming to deliver an interactive digital narrative class to students from radically different backgrounds. Opening the class up to a range of found objects seemed to be opening too many possible doors. As such, we looked to Karen Cross' ideas about found *photography* or 'appropriations of the snapshot'. Although not simply an extension of readymade and found object art, there were enough similarities, we felt, to feel that we were acting in good faith by assuming that found photographs would have similar effects to those noted in found object studies. Beyond this, however, Cross notes that when we use found photographs we 'involve a range of scenarios of meaning-making, which are underpinned and developed according to a particular dynamic of object-relating that is both personal, cultural and often entangled within institutional challenges' [4]. Found photography then seemed like an excellent possible way to enable students to bring something into an IDN classroom that could push them to consider materials with care and curiosity, providing a space for meaning-making but also to entangle this practice into institutional challenges. I will return to this later in the paper to explicitly convey the unique advantage of found photography as it relates to IDN teaching, but for now, it is enough to say that the possibilities outlined by Howard and Donley noted above, getting students telling stories through another medium before resorting to coding, helped us to bridge disciplinary gaps.

[1] Although Bennedsen and Caspersen note that a 28% failure rate in computer science courses is 'not alarmingly high', it's difficult to translate this to different standards of higher education throughout the world. An almost 1/3 failure rate in UK HE would definitely raise some eyebrows.

## 3 Leading by Example: Teaching IDN Through Found Photography

Taking the lead from some of the excellent work noted above on using found objects and found photography in classes teaching IDN, we put this idea into practice through the design of our curriculum this year. Our 67 students were all from humanities and none declared any significant prior knowledge of programming. They participated in eleven taught weeks with the first six weeks taking place in more traditional classroom settings, the latter 6 in a computer workshop. In the first week students were introduced to selected works we felt were characteristic of fundamental narratology and narrative design with an emphasis on work that was primarily visual art, such as photobooks. In week two, the students were informed they had three intervening weeks to begin searching for and gathering photographs in much the same manner as suggested by Bat Or: the objects were to function as "fragmented and affect-loaded memories that need to be recognised and rejoined" [11]. Students were not only to touch, to explore and play with the photographs, but to allow themselves to give these objects entirely new meanings. These could be pictures they had previously taken themselves, or pictures they found (online or offline) as in an example we shared with them (which we will discuss shortly). They were told this collection would guide the project work to come. The aim was for students to begin reflecting on otherwise discarded media and begin to consider the stories these photographs might tell. In week 3 students were given some readings on photography basics such as composition and the basics of how cameras work, but it was stressed that the collection of pictures they gathered would be remediated by the end of the project – as such, the photographs would not be judged based on typical thoughts of aesthetic values, but – rather – viewed as part of a more holistic transformative project.

Weeks 4 and 5 were dedicated to workshopping the photograph collections students presented thus far (informed as well by the canon of post-structuralist scholarship and emerging works on new materialism in photography). When collections seemed too intentionally curated or to be telling an obvious story, they were instructed to turn their minds to the mundane (drawing on Stone and Or's work). To give just one example of this workshopping progress, a student had curated – or perhaps created – a collection of near commercial quality photographs of themselves and friends at a music festival. It was clear their intention was to showcase their well-developed sense of taste. However, this didn't work well within the parameters of the course – few stories could emerge organically from the photographs without clashing with the one that already existed. Reacting to this feedback they collected a series of almost unrelated photographs from stock images and began to construct a narrative to be realized interactively.

From week 6 the course shifted towards work on Interactive Narrative Design. Long, workshop style classes in front of computers familiar in computer science departments. Students were given guided, step-by-step instructions on how to use software packages (first two sessions on Twine, then two sessions on Unity) before a final class that was dedicated to troubleshooting and going over submission (this final class proved to be invaluable for reasons we'll discuss below).

### 3.1 Leading by Example

To make sure students knew exactly what was expected of them, it was decided that the best way forward was to make our own interactive digital narrative game that students could use as a guide and inspiration. Using our joint experience of having worked with professional found photography and the Unity game engine,[2] we put together a short game that combines elements of hidden-object/escape-the-room games with found photography. Planning for the game began in December of 2022 and the game was released to students in March 2023.

The game took inspiration from the found photos it sought to remediate: a series of pictures that had been abandoned and sold as scrap in a thrift store in Glasgow. The pictures show a relatively elderly couple on a trip to the USA in what appears to be the 1970's or early 1980's. The couple, presumably now deceased, were completely unknown to the owner of the shop where the photographs were purchased. As such, we had absolutely no knowledge of the story behind the pictures. The pictures were purchased as negatives, meticulously cleaned, digitized using a flatbed scanner at a high DPI.

One striking image [Fig. 1] from the collection was a hotel room in which a woman stands alone, looking directly at the photographer (presumably, the man that often appears within the photos). This image served as the inspiration for the main game world we would create. An initial draft version of the game was composed using Twine before using Blender and the Unity 2021.3 Long Term Support build, to devise our game. A digital version of the hotel room from the photograph became the main space for interaction, allowing players to track down a series of objects and the attached memories to escape the hotel room [Fig. 2]. The game begins with a slideshow of these photos playing rapidly across the screen and a voiceover in an old man's voice, cryptically hinting at the nature of time, memories and truth. After that, players are thrown into the hotel, and must collect objects within, whereupon they are shown another photograph and a voiceover plays, adding layers to the story we're choosing to tell, through voiceovers.

This simple game mechanic – find an object, hear an audio log – is something that has worked well for games like *Dear Esther* and other 'walking simulators'; however, we felt it was important to provide students with something slightly more engaging experience, true to the spirit of IDN. What's more, drawing on recent criticism of games like *Gone Home* who use the linear logic of collecting audio logs and progressing towards a point of simple truth, it was important to not be so connected to a singular narrative [12]. As such, while students could collect the objects and hear our imagined version of the lives that the people within had lived, we also made the point at which the students could leave the room optional. Importantly, none of the narrative elements connected to these endings were designed to feel any more 'good' or 'bad' than the others [13], in spite of the additional ergodic effort required to collect some over others. Instead, we were aiming to provide all players with a satisfying if somewhat obtuse experience of just one interpretation of the photographs.

On balance, the game worked to our objectives as it helped to give students a clear example of what's possible for IDN using a game engine like Unity but also achievable

[2] References to our own credentials intentionally omitted for anonymity.

**Fig. 1.** The picture from the collection as it appears within the game, floating back and forth, illuminated from behind.

within a short timeframe. What's more, because of the use of the photographs, there was always a central anchor point around which the narrative was built. This also meant that we could collaborate on a project while having very different skillsets.

The work between us was always an act of remediating found photographs into a new and engaging digital narrative – as such, the benefits theorized by Dravenstadt were apparent to us as well as our students. The found objects became as much about our lived experience as they were about the "true" story they may possibly have been connected to. A further strength of the game was that because we had created it ourselves from scratch, there were no questions we couldn't answer about it. If students wanted to know how to achieve *x* effect from the game, we could tell them. By comparison, using examples created by other people, the best we can do is guess.

### 3.2 Student Work and Implications

Standout submissions allow us to see the impact that found photographs had on their ability to work. A personal favorite of mine, though not one that received a particularly high grade, used pictures from the student's own phone to tell a branching science fiction story. Images of completely mundane places (the student's dorm room [Fig. 3], their bathroom mirror) and things (and empty pizza box, an inexpensive tripod [Fig. 4]) were recontextualized in a comical and engaging way. Using photoshop, they doctored a photo taken to resell the tripod on a marketplace website, into an adventure with multiverse exploration [Fig. 4].

**Fig. 2.** The hotel room, reimagine in the Unity Game engine making extensive use of lighting and filters to make simple shapes look interesting.

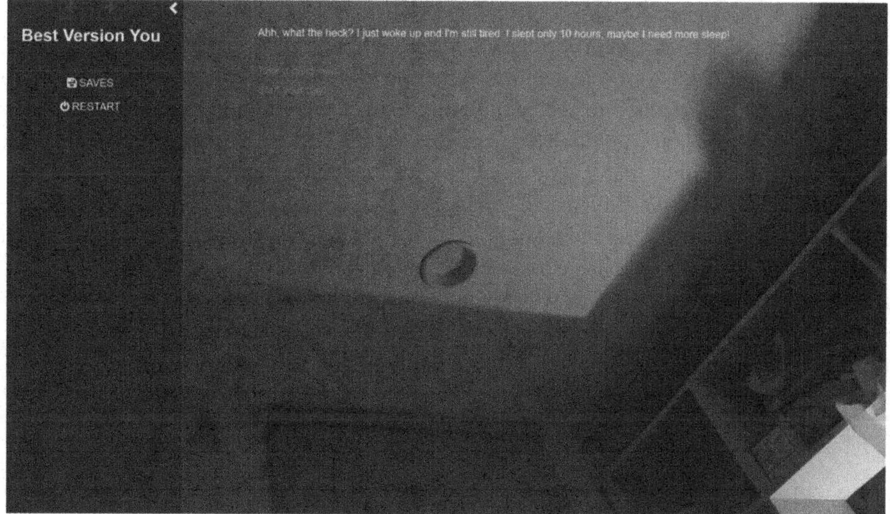


**Fig. 3.** A picture taken to test the student's new phone becomes the setting of a science fiction story.

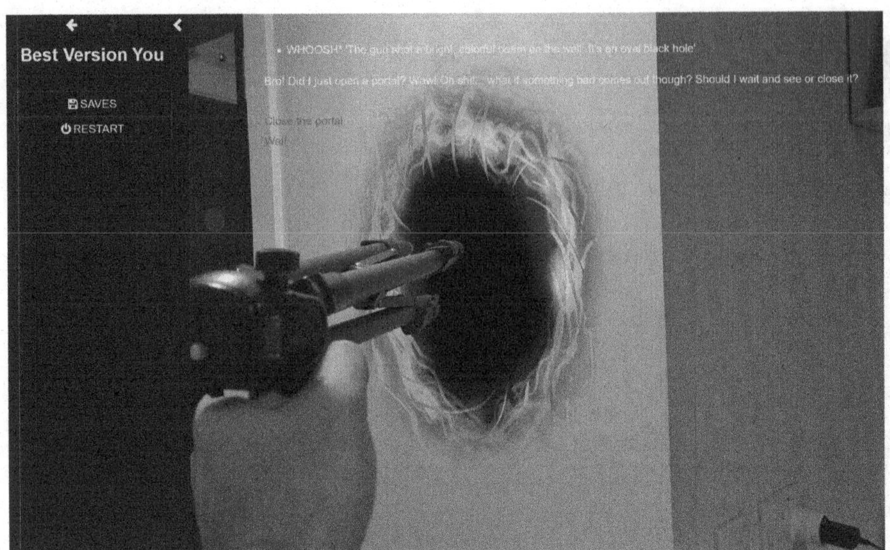


**Fig. 4.** A picture taken to help sell an old tripod becomes an adventure into another world.

While this student, and the other students involved had no prior knowledge or experience of programming, they found their tasks of telling an engaging story using pre-existing assets to be straightforward and manageable. In a large part this was due to their connection to the materials they were using. Twine's reliance on either HTML, CSS and Javascript, or else its own proprietary scripting language no longer seemed daunting when the tasks at hand were clear in the students' minds. They were confidently able to imagine what they wanted to see because the images were familiar to them and they already had examples they could draw from that we understood intimately.

Contrary to the idea that Twine could be a "limited system" that "might not be representative of the possibility space" [14], using found photographs opened up myriad new horizons for constructing IDN. Students were not lead or limited by their knowledge of tools, or the abilities of their instructors to open their minds to the potential of tools, but rather by the extent of their own imaginations to reconceptualize the photographs the found. Put another way, allowing themselves to be lead by found photographs, the students did the intellectual 'heavy lifting' in their imaginations. Their creations instead became a question of linking together visual elements in engaging ways, rather than first having to learn a tool and only then beginning to create.

### 3.3 Post-assessment Questionnaire

The success of the teaching was considered in several ways. Firstly, we took into consideration the class pass rate. Out of 67 students, there was a failure rate of just 4.4% and a non-completion rate of 10% with an average grade of 61% for completing students (though it should be noted that one submission was awarded a grade of 0% due to insurmountable technical difficulties with that submission and this unavoidably skewed our average). While it is somewhat circumstantial, this is a healthy rate of completion for a class at this level in the UK and indicates a strong overall impression if superficially.

To gather more detailed data on the success of the course we also asked the students to complete a short 40-question multiple choice questionnaire at the course's completion. Students were asked a simple series of questions including but not limited to: 'were staff on this module good at explaining things', 'have staff made the subject interesting', 'has this module been intellectually stimulating' and 'has this module challenged me to achieve my best work'? Questions were asked using a simple Likert scale and answers skewed positively to the left (positively) in our favour, with the exception of a question on organization and management which was more neutral. Space was given for students at the end of the questionnaire to allow students to comment openly about the module. Here, we were hoping that the found photography elements of the course would be mentioned but, sadly, no students made direct references to it.

Amplifying the quantitative data gathered at the end of the course, we also conducted interviews with several willing students in a casual and unstructured fashion as well. Some student feedback for the class was extremely positive with students noting 'this one class has changed my life' and that 'this has completely changed the way I think about education' (these students will have to remain anonymous given the nature of the consent they provided). Unfortunately, no student specifically mentioned found photography in their interviews either, and when asked about it, they didn't directly mention the qualities suggested by Stone and Or.

That the students didn't mention found photography wasn't unexpected. On the contrary, this was largely the point of including the found photographs within the course. The photographs gave students something familiar around which they could develop interactive digital narratives as in the example above. The purpose of the photographs was that they were to go unnoticed; to be points for inspiration that elevated the students, not important things in themselves. Returning to where we began with our understanding of found photographs as the 'mundane', the fact that students were unaware of their role in creation, rather, seems perfectly logical.

### 3.4 Pain Points and Room for Improvement

As mentioned, in future iterations of the course, it will be important for students to specifically answer questions about the importance of found photography in encountering STEM adjacent work like IDN. The current end of year survey did not prompt students specifically to speak on the topic. While we are wary of the influence asking this question might have on the students to colour their recollections, this is a necessary step considering that we received no specific feedback mentioning found photography so far.

Something that arose in delivering this kind of freeform interactive digital narrative focused teaching was that submitting a wide array of different types of work, while liberating for the students, can place a strain on current generation university infrastructure. At our university, staff submissions are handled using the popular 'Canvas' learning management system. This LMS is geared towards either word documents or fully standalone work, like a folder containing a Windows ".exe" application and its required files. Work students submitted via Twine was not as robust as either of these options and difficulties arose when student work was to be assessed by external staff without the necessary familiarity with Twine. Given the underlying HTML, CSS, Javascript guts of a Twine project and the current state of the Twine browser, sharing student projects often resulted in problems such as images not displaying correctly, sounds not working, etc.

While something that helped tremendously was building in a week for students just to submit their work, it is something that teachers interested in exploring this kind of path should be aware of. It is likely best to know who you will be working with to get student work marked, and to pool knowledge sufficiently to make sure students are treated fairly, even if their code results in a project that doesn't just run on a simple double click.

Another issue was that the switch from weeks 5 to 6, switching from ideation to practical implementation of ideas, several students actively resisted some of the ideas that were suggested to them. Primarily, the idea of 'textual worlds' [15] and procedural rhetoric [16]. In other words, the construction of agency through limitations of possible actions, and the communication of ideas through actions was resisted by students. Many found the ideas of agency difficult to comprehend and in some cases antithetical to their narrative ambitions: they wanted things to happen to their characters, and for their sense of right and wrong to be preserved, rather than for narratives to support player actions.

These shortcomings can and will be addressed in future versions of the course, initially by placing a greater emphasis on a wide array of narrative possibilities over the a canon of narrative theory.

## 4 Conclusion

Teaching IDN is challenging because of the crossover between it and STEM-centric subjects, especially when the students are from a humanities background. However, by looking to work produced in experimental classrooms, the work of art therapists and some theories of art and practice, it is possible to create a classroom environment that is enjoyable and supportive of student experiences but also that ensures the creation of high quality outputs in line with 21$^{st}$ century expectations of impact.

## References

1. Eligio, U.X. (ed.) Understanding emotions in mathematical thinking and learning. London, United Kingdom ; San Diego, CA, United States ; Cambridge, MA, United States ; Oxford, United Kingdom: Academic Press is an imprint of Elsevier (2017)
2. Salguero, A., Griswold, W.G., Alvarado, C., Porter, L.: Understanding sources of student struggle in early computer science courses. In: Proceedings of the 17th ACM Conference on International Computing Education Research, Virtual Event USA , pp. 319–333. ACM (Aug 202). https://doi.org/10.1145/3446871.3469755
3. Howard, K.T., Donley, R.: Using ink and interactive fiction to teach interactive design. In: Cardona-Rivera, R.E., Sullivan, A., Young, R.M. (eds.) Interactive Storytelling. LNCS, vol. 11869, pp. 68–72. Springer International Publishing, Cham (2019). https://doi.org/10.1007/978-3-030-33894-7_8
4. Cross, K.: The lost of found photography. Photographies **8**(1), 43–62 (2015). https://doi.org/10.1080/17540763.2014.974285

5. Hazari, Z., Tai, R.H., Sadler, P.M.: Gender differences in introductory university physics performance: the influence of high school physics preparation and affective factors. Sci. Educ. **91**(6), 847–876 (2007). https://doi.org/10.1002/sce.20223
6. Nicoll, B., Keogh, B.: The Unity game engine and the circuits of cultural software. In: Palgrave pivot, Cham, Switzerland. Palgrave Macmillan (2019)
7. Thompson, T.: Choose your own murder: non-linear narratives enhance student understanding in forensic science education. Forensic Sci. Int. Synergy **2**, 82–85 (2020). https://doi.org/10.1016/j.fsisyn.2020.01.009
8. Montfort, N.: Exploratory programming for the arts and humanities. The MIT Press, Cambridge, Massachusetts (2016)
9. Bennedsen, J., Caspersen, M.E.: Failure rates in introductory programming: 12 years later. ACM Inroads **10**(2), 30–36 (2019). https://doi.org/10.1145/3324888
10. Dravenstadt, D.W.: Learning to let go: motivating students through fluid teaching in a choice-based found object assemblage unit. Art Educ. **71**(5), 8–13 (2018). https://doi.org/10.1080/00043125.2018.1482158
11. Bat Or, M., Megides, O.: Found object/readymade art in the treatment of Trauma and Loss. J. Clin. Art Ther. **3**(1), 1–30 (2016)
12. Ruberg, B.: Straight paths through queer walking simulators: wandering on rails and speedrunning in gone home. Games Cult. **15**(6), 632–652 (2020). https://doi.org/10.1177/1555412019826746
13. Tancred, N., Vickery, N., Wyeth, P., Turkay, S.: Player choices, game endings and the design of moral Dilemmas in games. In: Proceedings of the 2018 Annual Symposium on Computer-Human Interaction in Play Companion Extended Abstracts, Melbourne VIC Australia, pp. 627–636. ACM (Oct 2018). https://doi.org/10.1145/3270316.3271525
14. Koenitz, H., Eladhari, M.P.: Challenges of IDN research and teaching. In: Cardona-Rivera, R.E., Sullivan, A., Young, R.M. (eds.) Interactive Storytelling. LNCS, vol. 11869, pp. 26–39. Springer International Publishing, Cham (2019). https://doi.org/10.1007/978-3-030-33894-7_4
15. Ryan, M.-L.: Narrative as virtual reality: immersion and interactivity in literature and electronic media, Transferred to digital print. 2001-[Im Kolophon: Milton Keynes: Lightning Source, 2010]. in Parallax. Baltimore, Md.: Johns Hopkins Univ. Press (2010)
16. Bogost, I.: Persuasive games: the expressive power of videogames. MIT Press, Cambridge, MA (2007)

# Late Breaking Works

# Figure of Speech Detection and Generation as a Service in IDN Authoring Support

Simon Akkerman(✉) and Frank Nack

INDElab, Informatics Institute, University of Amsterdam, Science Park 904, 1098 XH Amsterdam, The Netherlands
simonatshe@gmail.com, F.M.Nack@uva.nl

**Abstract.** IDN authoring is a complex and creative endeavour. This paper provides the basis for a collaborative text-based authoring tool to support the work with figures of speech, such as metaphors, similes and metonymies. Several models have been tested and BERT, as best performing, has been used for creating functions to predict a figure of speech and, using an embedding of the custom database, return figures of speeches that are closest to the input, and generating new figures of speech. The implemented functions were validated using writers active in different fields.

All the code, the databases and the models can be found in this GitHub: link to GitHub.

**Keywords:** Figures of speech · IDN Authoring Support · Machine learning

## 1 Introduction

IDN authoring on the level of meaning making is a creative human process that is done in collaboration with a system to establish potential narratives, where the creator imagines the narrative in multiple iterations, exploring many possible choices (presentation and interaction) and outcomes (protostory). The offered system support is service-oriented, i.e. supporting the finding or the creation of material [12,17].

Creating figurative language is an often difficult for authors, but relevant as figurative language can better portrayal the feeling of a concept or situation than literally describing the concept or situation [18,19]. The use of a diverse set of different, but overlapping, figures of speech has been proven to increase empathy with the concepts and situations for which the figure is a stand in [6]. It is valuable to create an automated support system either within the IDN authoring tool (see [17]) or provide a plugin for an existing text-based authoring tool like Twine (https://twinery.org/), to provide authors with means to create and diversify their use of figures of speech.

The research presented in this paper attempts to lay a basis for this kind of authoring support.


L. Holloway-Attaway and J. T. Murray (Eds.): ICIDS 2023, LNCS 14384, pp. 99–112, 2023.
https://doi.org/10.1007/978-3-031-47658-7_8

## 2 Related Work

### 2.1 Interactive Digital Narrative (IDN) Authoring

IDN authoring is a complicated endeavour that addresses content selection, mode of interaction, audience perception, and narrative generation. Whether the authoring process follows a rational (plan-driven) or action-centric (improvised and cyclic) model, the set of necessary stages the overall process follows is similar (see [10, pp. 327–340] [11, pp. 107–121] [25, pp. 62–73]. This paper considers in particular two phases in this process, where each process contributes to the system part of Koenitz's SPP model [12]:

1. Ideation, where the initial ideas about media production and an IDN intent are established.
2. Meaning Making, where a creator specifies the actual message(s) and themes to be conveyed to a particular audience for a particular designed context, resulting in processes where communication strategies in the form of articulation techniques are designed and related media assets are captured, generated or transformed.

As the different processes are interconnected and embedded in an overall iterative production methodology, sequences of analysis will be performed frequently [17].

### 2.2 Figurative Language

A substantial amount of theory has already been written on the definition of differing figures of speech (see [8,13,18,19]).
The most compact definitions of figures of speech are provided in the Encyclopaedia Britannica (EB) [26], which differentiates between different classes:

- Figures of resemblance or relationship (simile and metaphor).
- Figures of emphasis or understatement (hyperbole and synecdoche).
- Figures of sound (onomatopoeia and alliteration).
- Verbal games and gymnastics (pun and anagram).
- Errors (malapropism and spoonerism).

### 2.3 Machine Learning and Figurative Language

Previous research conducted on the topic of figures of speech in relation to AI limits itself to the understanding of the metaphor [1,5,18], but not classifying the different forms of this figurative language, of which metaphor is a very specific kind of figure.

Bizzoni and Ghanimifard [4] introduced a metaphor detection mechanism that is based on a bi-LSTM model and a structure based on recursive feed-forward concatenation. Their highest scoring model has a precision of 67.1%.

Prystawski et al. suggest that although models probabilistic models (such as GTP) models are designed for specific tasks, they can be tweaked to perform larger tasks such as in-context learning and metaphor handling [21].

Li [15] uses the second iteration of the generative pretrained model (GPT2) to generate metaphors, trained on 6.3k sentences, with an accuracy of 97.8%. Their model is able to generate metaphors with better readability and creativity compared to the baseline models, even in the situation where training data is insufficient.

## 3 Approach

The figures of speeches that are most suitable for this first part of the implementation of authoring services belong to the first and second category of the Encyclopaedia Britannica class schema [26], because the basis of these figures of speech reside in the domain of comparison between concepts and phenomena.

The focus of the classification system will be on Metaphor, Simile and Metonymy, because there are databases readily available (See Sect. 4: Data Allocation) to work with and alter, though in need of cleaning and classifying.

The basis of IDN authoring support in the form of a service is the recognition of different figures of speech with machine learning algorithms to support the analysis of material generated in the meaning making processes, and the generation of new metaphors as writer's aid during the ideation and meaning making process. This research adopts the broad framework of the EB and the logic markers of Ortneys classification method [18, pp. 49–51], defining the relations between concepts in the following logical notation:

- **Metaphor:** A metaphor is the expression of an understanding of one concept in terms of another concept, where there is some similarity or correlation between the two.
  Example: I'm an early bird, snow is a white blanket.
  Logic: A == B
- **Simile:** An expression that compares two, sometimes seemingly unlike phenomenon directly by using comparison words like; "like" and "as".
  Examples: This weather is like a shower.
  Logic: A == B IF "as" OR "like" in AB
- **Metonymy:** An expression where one word or sentence is replaced or substituted by another word or sentence that is similar or closely associated.
  Examples: Crown = royalty.
  Logic: A %= B

In the presented approach figures of speech are considered as a vehicle of meaning. Our approach is referenced in Fig. 1.

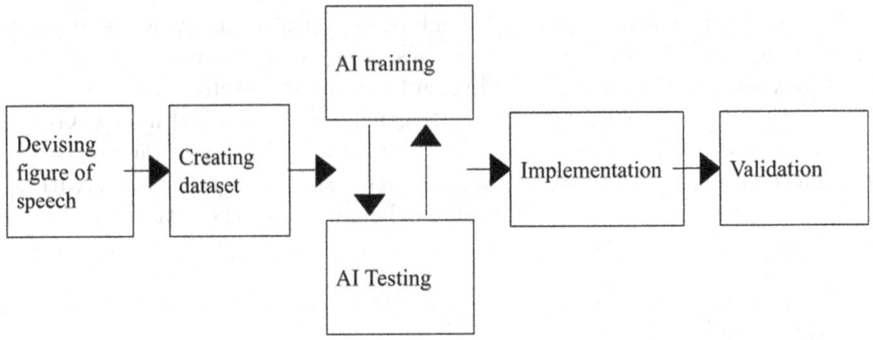


**Fig. 1.** Methodology pipeline

# 4 Data Allocation

## 4.1 Creating Annotations for the Data-Set

To create a dataset containing all the differing figures of speeches, we assigned a bare minimum of columns:

1. Figure, the original, unaltered, figure of speech
2. Meaning, the commonly accepted interpretation
3. Type, classification of the type

This research focuses on figures of speech from the English language, because they are readily obtainable.

## 4.2 The Use of Existing Data-Sets

The following existing data sets were used for the generation of the final data set:
**The UniMet Database:** The UniMet database [2] contains 26,702 metonymy instances of 189 languages across 24 metonymy patterns.
**Metaphor Dictionary by Grothe:** A website containing a database of metaphors created by Grothe [9].
**A Kaggle Project by Alwani:** A project created for the distinction between different figures of speech, containing different, separated, folders containing the different figures [27].
**Generic-KB Database by Bhakthavatsalam:** A data-base containing 3.5 million generic and therefore literal sentences, of which 100 thousand are classified as 'best' through their metric [3,24].

The above mentioned datasets have been altered and cleaned with the aim to create one, workable, data-set. Non-english texts have been extracted and redundant columns, 'country of origin' or 'theme', have been expunged.

In cases where different figures of speech are originally merged in one original dataset (i.e. Similie and Metaphor in the Grothe dataset) those have been separated in different files.

Regarding the neutral sentences, we took the 100000 best sentences that exist in the Generic-KB data-set, 50000 are randomly sampled and given the right column, meaning (in the case of neutral sentences the meaning is; "nothing") and type (neutral).

### 4.3 Final Data-Set

The combined data-set, of 85008 rows, contains 5177 metonymies, 24286 metaphors, 5540 similes and 50000 neutral sentences. The rows have the same columns and are ready to be used for training and fine-tuning.

The separate code for cleaning and filtering and the resulting databases can be found in the Github at the link provided.

## 5 Modelling

The classification of sentences into different figure of speech categories is a natural language processing problem. Therefore we use and fine-tune existing language models, of which BERT [23], developed by Google, and GPT [22], developed by OpenAI, are the most prominent examples.

### 5.1 Bidirectional Language Model

BERT is a deep bidirectional transformer for language understanding [23]. This deep learning neural network is the intuitive choice for its size and accuracy. As it is unknown if our dataset is sufficient enough to warrant the use of the original BERT, variations are also utilised, namely ALBERT and ELMo:

- AlBERT increases the model size, which is good for smaller data sets, but will lead to over-fitting on larger data-sets [14].
- ELMo has been proven to work on the understanding of contextual word recognition on smaller data-sets [20].

Because these neural network (BERT, AlBERT and ELMo) need only to be fine-tuned and do not need to be created from the ground up, the models are trained on five epochs with a 80/20 training/validation split.

**Table 1.** Model implementation results

| **Model** | Validation accuracy with neutral sentences | Validation accuracy without neutral sentences | Train accuracy with neutral sentences | Train accuracy without neutral sentences |
|---|---|---|---|---|
| **BERT** | 0.964 | 0.934 | 0.995 | 0.990 |
| **alBERT** | 0.898 | 0.867 | 0.958 | 0.942 |
| **ELMo** | 0.858 | 0.840 | 0.870 | 0.867 |

After having implemented the natural language processing modules, we measured the accuracy of each. The results are shown in Table 1. The calculation used the ReLu activation function, an 80/20 validation split and 5 epochs. BERT was the most accurate performing model, therefore a meta analysis was performed to gain insight on where it performed the best and the most poorly (see Fig. 2), where the colors indicate the number of figures classified. The exact percentages of these figures are shown in Table 2.

For the remaining classification work in the authoring pipeline (see Fig. 5) we use BERT.

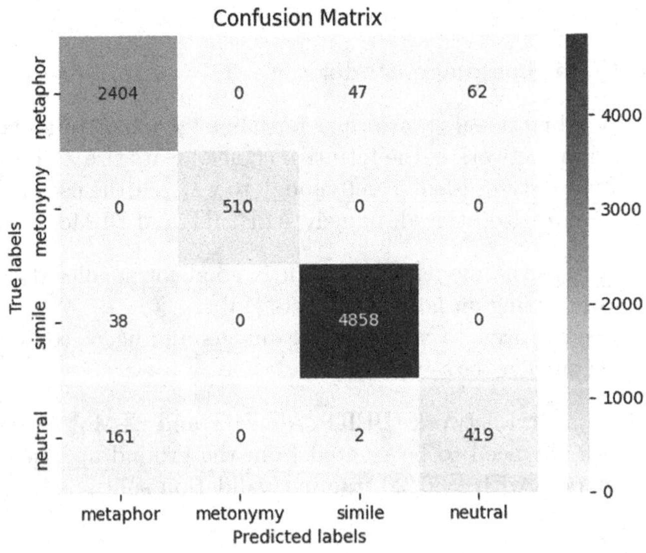


**Fig. 2.** Meta-analysis of the fine tuned BERT classification model. (Color figure online)

**Table 2.** BERT meta analysis percentages

| **Total** | Metaphors | Similes | Metonymies | Neutral sentence |
|---|---|---|---|---|
| **0.96** | 0.92 | 0.87 | 1 | 0.99 |

## 5.2 Autoregressive Language Model

As previous research has shown, GPT2 [22], when fine-tuned, can deliver sufficiently accurate results when generating novel metaphors [15]. A GPT2 model has been trained and fine-tuned on the created data-set, to be implemented into the system. GPT2 is used because it is easily accessible (unlike GPT3, GPT3.5 or GPT4) and can be retrained for future work on expanded and updated data-sets.

After fine-tuning on the created data-set and experimenting with different epochs on the GPT2 model, the most satisfactory results were found when the model was trained on 10 epochs, with a batch size of 50 and a learning rate of 2e-5.

Figure 3 shows a list of generated figures created by the fine-tuned GPT2 model when prompted with the sentence; "The day moves as the world turns."

```
1 = The day moves as the world turns to the moon, and the moons orbit around the sun is shifted to
2 = The day moves as the world turns to the sun, and the moon, and the stars, and the planets
3 = The day moves as the world turns on its head, and the sun sets, and the world turns on its
4 = The day moves as the world turns on its axis, and the world turns on its axis.
5 = The day moves as the world turns to the sun, and the sun is shining. The sun is shining,
6 = The day moves as the world turns to the future, and the world is going to be a lot more exciting
7 = The day moves as the world turns to the sun, and the moon begins to rise.
8 = The day moves as the world turns to the future, and the world turns to the past.
9 = The day moves as the world turns to the moon, and the sun sets, and the moon sets, and
10 = The day moves as the world turns on the lights and the sun sets, and the sun is shining brightly.
```

**Fig. 3.** Output of the trained and implemented GPT2 model with the prompt "the day moves as the world turns"

An example of the output when the input is: "The day moves as the world turns", is found in Fig. 4. Where the "ranking" column represents how close the sentence is to the input as determined by spatial distance cosine [7]. The "type" column is the classification in the original database and "figure" is the sentence that is returned.

| figures | type | ranking |
|---|---|---|
| Earth rotates once every day. | neutural | 0.655004 |
| Earth is round, day and night taking place si... | neutural | 0.644386 |
| Time is activity and events that take up the ... | neutural | 0.630468 |
| DAY means a calendar day. | neutural | 0.612714 |
| Today is only one day in all the days that wi... | metaphor | 0.609974 |
| Each day the world is born anew/For him who t... | metaphor | 0.603992 |
| Every day is Earth Day in the oil and gas ind... | neutural | 0.590162 |
| Energy transformations occur everywhere every... | neutural | 0.582234 |
| Night follows day, Just as moon follows sun. | neutural | 0.564188 |
| "June is the time for being in the world in n... | metaphor | 0.559607 |
| "A holiday gives one a chance to look backwar... | metaphor | 0.543003 |
| All other days have either disappeared into d... | metaphor | 0.542075 |
| All other days have either disappeared into d... | metaphor | 0.542075 |
| Dates have (part) daytimes. | neutural | 0.541289 |
| "As the world runs | simile | 0.530652 |
| "Politics as lived and practiced day by day | simile | 0.529752 |
| "When great causes are on the move in the world | simile | 0.517926 |
| Travel is measured in days. | neutural | 0.516052 |
| The day will happen whether or not you get up. | metaphor | 0.515943 |
| Tomorrows have (part) daylight. | neutural | 0.508963 |

**Fig. 4.** Example output of the system when given the sentence: "the day moves as the world turns"

## 6 Authoring Service

Once BERT has been established as the best performing classifier and GPT 2 as the figure of speech generator/variator, the service functions have been built that lay a first groundwork for a model that can be used for IDN authoring support.

As outlined in Fig. 5, a figure of speech authoring support service is considered as a set of services that can either help to analyse already written text to classify the existing figures of speech in it or the distribution of them over the text, or to generate new figures of speech based on a provided example. The different steps are outlined below:

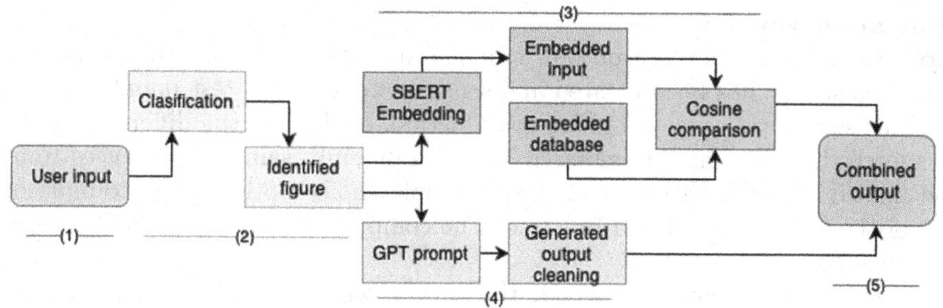


**Fig. 5.** Pipeline of user input to output

1. **Take in new figure of speech or texts:** The author inputs a newly created figure of speech into the system or a text from which they want a figure of speech to be made.
2. **Figure of speech identification:** The system takes the input, separates the sentences if needed and uses the created language model to return the corresponding classification with the highest percentage of confidence.
3. **Embedding:** *note that step 3 and 4 can happen simultaneously.* Using sentence embedding, the system embeds the given input by the user using SBERT [23]. The embedded input is compared with a separate data-set of embedded sentences. This data-set is pre-made, using SBERT, with the original database of sentences that the classification model was trained on (this embedded data-set can also be found in the GitHub). The comparison is done using spatial distance cosine [7], where A is the embedded input and B is the embedded sentence it is being compared with. The system then returns a list of similar figures ordered by their similarity, if the similarity-output from the spatial distance cosine formula is bigger than 0.5.
4. **GPT prompting:** The classified figure is put through the fine-tuned GPT2 model, after which it generates ten new variations on the given prompt and puts it in a numbered list.
5. **Combined output:** Finally the system combines both the cosine embedding result and the GPT generation result and returns them to the user.

# 7 Validation

## 7.1 Language Model Validation

To ensure that the created classification model is at least as accurate as humans or ChatGPT [16], a survey has been generated to test human figure of speech recognition, where the second test compares the results against ChatGPT (GPT 2 base) abilities.

**Human Survey Test**

**Approach:** To give insight on how humans can differentiate between figures of speech, a survey has been created and send out to a chosen test population.

This survey consists of a short introduction, explaining the different figures of speech discussed in this research and 50 randomly sampled sentences from the final data-set with corresponding multiple choice options. An example of one of the questions is found in Fig. 6. The complete survey can be found here: link to survey.

*The Pool of Subjects* to whom the survey has been delivered, is divided into the following categories: five writers (with at least a bachelors degree in a language major and who have completed at least one course in the subject of figurative language), ten data-scientists (with at least a bachelors in a computer science related field) and five others (with backgrounds in different fields like theoretical physics, pedagogic or psychology). The subjects who answered the survey were sourced from the authors personal network of contacts.

*The Analysis* The multiple choice answers are compared with the classification as given by the dataset (with answers being either right or wrong). Averaging the individual accuracy, gives a broad estimation on how well a test set of humans, both in total and in each group, can identify and classify figures. This score is compared with the score of the best performing language model.

**Findings:** The results of the human survey, categorised by group and in total are collected in Table 3.

It can be inferred that, overall, humans can differentiate between figures and neutral sentences fairly accurately. The ability to differentiate between different figures of speech, metaphor, simile and metonymy, is substantially worse. Note that the writers, who presumably have a better grasp of figurative language score 7% better than the total average. This demonstrates that the figure of speech is a complicated concept, even hard to handle for experts.

**The ChatGPT Test**

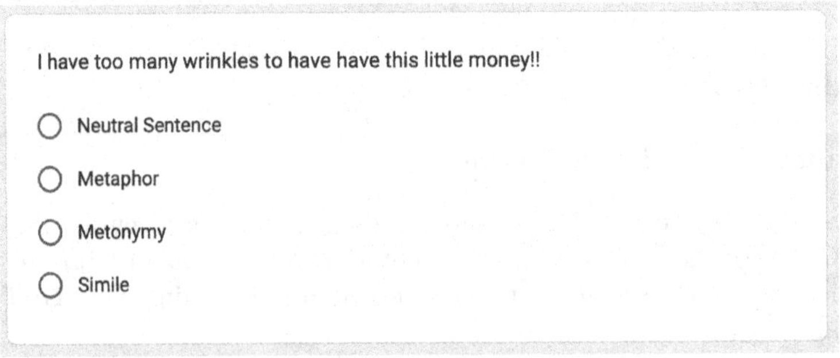

I have too many wrinkles to have have this little money!!

- ○ Neutral Sentence
- ○ Metaphor
- ○ Metonymy
- ○ Simile

**Fig. 6.** An example of one question and multiple choice answers of the survey

**Table 3.** Human survey results

| Group | Total | Metaphor | Simile | Metonymy | Neutral sentence |
|---|---|---|---|---|---|
| **Overall** | 0.61 | 0.33 | 0.31 | 0.27 | 0.81 |
| **Writers** | 0.68 | 0.41 | 0.33 | 0.40 | 0.88 |
| **Data science** | 0.56 | 0.28 | 0.28 | 0.20 | 0.76 |
| **Other** | 0.60 | 0.30 | 0.32 | 0.29 | 0.81 |
| **BERT** | 0.96 | 0.92 | 0.87 | 1 | 0.99 |

**Approach:** To gain insight on how well ChatGPT can differentiate between different figures of speech and neutral sentences, the same human test has been performed by ChatGPT in a similar way via prompting the following question:

*"*sentence*: is this a metaphor, metonymy, simile or neutral sentence?"*

**Findings:** The results are presented in Table 4. This table also contains the BERT model accuracy to show the comparison between the two modeling approaches.

It can be inferred that ChatGPT is not substantially better than humans on the recognition and differentiation between figures. However, it is more accurate on the differentiation between figures of speech and neutral sentences.

**Table 4.** ChatGPT survey results

| Model | Total | Metaphor | Simile | Metonymy | Neutral sentence |
|---|---|---|---|---|---|
| **Chat GPT** | 0.66 | 0.181 | 0.161 | 0 | 0.967 |
| **BERT** | 0.96 | 0.92 | 0.87 | 1 | 0.99 |

### 7.2 Service Validation

**Approach:** To verify if the services could be useful, five writers (the same five authors with a degree in a language major, two of which have experience with IDN authoring) were asked if, and how, they would use those services to support them.

**Findings:** The full transcripts of the interviews with the authors and more details about their different backgrounds can be found in the GitHub repository.

**Summary of the Feedback:** All writers stated that they could help them to create new figures of speech, variations on figures of speech or gain inspiration. They mentioned that this could take the form of, for example, variation on a theme, to more easily connect to the perspective of children or to help literature students learn in a more intuitive and interactive way. Thus, this approach, as viewed through the lens of IDN, could support authors in their 'meaning making' stages of narrative development. Two of the authors also mentioned that it could also be helpful as a tool for research and explicitly mentioned the embedding system. Thus, this system could support authors in the ideation stage of IDN development.

Overall everyone interviewed was looking forward to potentially using it.

## 8 Discussion

The results show that language classification models are an accurate identifier for figures of speech. However, as the results are not up to 100%, it still needs to be investigated if the current accuracy is perceived good enough by authors according to the task to be addressed or if the models still need improvement.

With respect to BERT, the biggest discrepancy in accuracy is between the neutral sentences and metaphors. However, the established approach is at 92% accuracy, still substantially better than both the human as well as the ChatGPT performance.

The GPT2 model works and gives variations on the metaphors given as prompts. The accuracy and useability of these variations are likely to improve as the database grows.

The sample size of the human survey with N(20) and the amount of authors (5) interviewed are sufficient enough to function for this proof of concept but should be expanded, for a more accurate view on how humans identify figures of speech.

## 9 Conclusion and Future Work

This paper delivers a first set of functions to create basic services that support authors in their use of figurative language. The models have sufficient accuracy to suffice as a proof of concept. Specifically, this paper provides the following contributions:

- A figures of speech dataset of accurately annotated figure of speech data classified as: 'metaphor', 'metonymy', 'simile' and 'neutral sentence', considered to be made open source.
- A model for the classification of existing and new figures of speech as well as neutral sentences with an accuracy of 96%
- An comparison system through embedding that can compare and return similar figures through the use of Spatial Distance Cosine.
- A fine-tuned GPT2 model that can generate new figures of speech as variation on the input figure.

Though the results show that authors can be automatically supported in figure of speech generation, labelling and maintenance, there are still open issues:

1. Creating an API for the created functions to be used in existing text-based authoring systems (like Twine).
2. Work on more complex figures of speech, such as analogy or synechdoch.

## References


1. Barnden, J.: Metaphor and Context: A Perspective from Artificial Intelligence, pp. 79–94. Palgrave Macmillan UK, London (2009). https://doi.org/10.1057/9780230594647_6
2. Batsuren, K., Enkhbold, E., Batbaatar, M.: UniMet: unified metaphor detection. GitHub repository (2022). https://github.com/kbatsuren/UniMet
3. Bhakthavatsalam, S., Anastasiades, C., Clark, P.: Genericskb: a knowledge base of generic statements. arXiv preprint arXiv:2005.00660 (2020)
4. Bizzoni, Y., Ghanimifard, M.: Bigrams and bilstms two neural networks for sequential metaphor detection. In: Proceedings of the Workshop on Figurative Language Processing, pp. 91–101 (2018)
5. Carbonell, J., Sánchez-Esguevillas, A., Carro, B.: The role of metaphors in the development of technologies, the case of the artificial intelligence. Futures **84**, 145–153 (2016). https://doi.org/10.1016/j.futures.2016.03.019. sI: Metaphors in FS
6. Chu, M., Meyer, A., Foulkes, L., Kita, S.: Individual differences in frequency and saliency of speech-accompanying gestures: the role of cognitive abilities and empathy. J. Exp. Psychol. Gen. **143**(2), 694–709 (2014). https://doi.org/10.1037/a0033861. Erratum in: J. Exp. Psychol. Gen. **143**(2), 709 (2014)
7. Chung, I., Kim, D., Kwak, N.I.: Maximizing cosine similarity between spatial features for unsupervised domain adaptation in semantic segmentation (2022). https://doi.org/10.1109/WACV51458.2022.00204
8. Garrett, J.: Aristotle on metaphor (2007)
9. Grothe, M.: Metaphors be with you. Dr. Mardy's Dictionary of Metaphorical Quotations. https://www.drmardy.com/metaphor/metaphorsbewithyou. Accessed 18 Apr 2023
10. Hardman, L., Obrenovic, Z., Nack, F., Kerherve, B., Piersol, K.: Canonical processes of semantically annotated media production. Multim. Syst. **14**(6), 327–340 (2008). https://doi.org/10.1007/s00530-008-0102-y
11. Koenitz, H.: Towards a Specific Theory of Interactive Digital Narrative, pp. 107–121. Routledge (2015)
12. Koenitz, H.: Understanding Interactive Digital Narrative - Immersive Expressions for a Complex Time. Routledge (2023)
13. Lakoff, G., Johnson, M.: Metaphors We Live by. University of Chicago Press (1980)
14. Lan, Z., Chen, M., Goodman, S., Gimpel, K., Sharma, P., Soricut, R.: Albert: a lite bert for self-supervised learning of language representations. arXiv preprint arXiv:1909.11942 (2019)
15. Li, Y., Lin, C., Guerin, F.: Nominal metaphor generation with multitask learning. In: Proceedings of the [Conference Name]. Department of Computer Science, University of Surrey, UK; Department of Computer Science, University of Sheffield, UK (August 2022)
16. Liu, Y., et al.: Summary of chatgpt/gpt-4 research and perspective towards the future of large language models (2023)
17. Nack, F.: IDN authoring - a design case. arXiv preprint arXiv:2306.13999 [cs.HC] (2023)
18. Ortony, A.: Metaphor and Thought, 2nd edn. Cambridge University Press (1993). https://doi.org/10.1017/CBO9781139173865
19. Ortony, A.: The Rule of Metaphor - The Creation of Meaning in Language, 1st edn. Routledge (2003)

20. Peters, M.E., et al.: Deep contextualized word representations. In: North American Chapter of the Association for Computational Linguistics. Association for Computational Linguistics, New Orleans (June 2018)
21. Prystawski, B., Thibodeau, P., Potts, C., Goodman, N.: Psychologically-informed chain-of-thought prompts for metaphor understanding in large language models (2023). https://escholarship.org/uc/item/2q01t47h
22. Radford, A., Wu, J., Child, R., Luan, D., Amodei, D., Sutskever, I.: Language models are unsupervised multitask learners (2019)
23. Reimers, N., Gurevych, I.: Sentence-bert: sentence embeddings using siamese bert-networks. In: Conference on Empirical Methods in Natural Language Processing (2019)
24. Bhakthavatsalam, S., Chloe Anastasiades, P.C.: Genericskb: a knowledge base of generic statements. Allen Institute for AI (2020)
25. Swartjes, I., Theune, M.: Iterative authoring using story generation feedback: debugging or co-creation? In: Iurgel, I.A., Zagalo, N., Petta, P. (eds.) ICIDS 2009. LNCS, vol. 5915, pp. 62–73. Springer, Heidelberg (2009). https://doi.org/10.1007/978-3-642-10643-9_10
26. The Editors of Encyclopaedia Britannica: Figure of Speech. Encyclopedia Britannica (2021). https://www.britannica.com/art/figure-of-speech. Accessed 2 June 2023
27. Alwani, V.: Kaggle dataset: figure of speech. Kaggle. https://www.kaggle.com/datasets/varchitalalwani/figure-of-speech. Accessed 2 June 2023

# ChatGPT as a Narrative Structure Interpreter

Alberto Alvarez(✉)

Game Lab, Malmö University, Malmö, Sweden
alberto.alvarez@mau.se

**Abstract.** Narrative structures define the skeleton of narratives and help at identifying common structures in stories, that then can be used to compare structures, define variations, and understand prototypical [structural] components. However, narrative structures are just one piece of the puzzle, their interpretation is what gives room to the stories seen in transmedia storytelling. In principle, a structure can be interpreted and developed with a myriad of stories, but requires some type of corpus to develop it further. Large language models such as ChatGPT could be employed for this task, if we are able to define a good narrative structure and give the tools to the algorithm to develop them further. For this paper, we use a narrative structure system called TropeTwist, which employs interconnected tropes as narrative structures, defining characters, conflicts, and plot devices in a relational graph, which gives raise to a set of trope micro- and meso-patterns. Using ChatGPT and through the web interface, we communicate all the possible elements to be used from TropeTwist and tasked ChatGPT to interpret them and generate stories. We describe our process and methodology to reach these interpretations, and present some of the generated stories based on a constructed narrative structure. Our results show the possibilities and limitations of using these systems and elaborate on future work to combine large language models for other tasks within narrative interpretation and generation.

**Keywords:** Narrative Structures · Large Language Models · ChatGPT · Games · Story Generation

## 1 Introduction

Narrative structures are fundamental to the definition of stories, and different authors have propose different ways to structure them based on the stories they analyze and the systems before them [5–7,21]. These structures define the design and configuration of stories, important elements within them and their relation, and key characteristic events. Barthes argues that these can be used to define how a story is to be developed [6], and could be used as an abstract representation.

Structures could be identified and be recurrent among stories, but interpreted in a plethora of ways; usually due to structures being more complex than just


L. Holloway-Attaway and J. T. Murray (Eds.): ICIDS 2023, LNCS 14384, pp. 113–121, 2023.
https://doi.org/10.1007/978-3-031-47658-7_9

a single element. For instance, the hero's journey is described in 17 stages [9] or Propp's analysis on the morphology of Russian folktale revealing 31 "narremes" [21]. This makes interpreting structures challenging. Some systems such as Szilas' ID Tension [26] or Scheherazade [12] consider elements of narrative structure in their design. However, most of these systems are, to some extent, complex since they need to represent and define many aspects of the story, making them richer. This is mainly done to simplify the interpretation process. For instance, the story beats in the narrative game Façade encoded a large amount of information (prerequisites, mandatory and optional inputs, actions, dialogues, and possible outputs) to facilitate their selection, concatenation, and final interpretation [17]. On the other hand, there are systems such as TropeTwist [2], that simplify the authoring process of the structure by not encoding as much information, but complexifies the interpretation step.

There are some advantages with these simplified systems such as more diversity at the interpretability step, faster development of structures, and simpler definitions, but interpreting these structures become a more complicated endeavor. A single narrative structure in TropeTwist can be interpreted in many ways, and its authors discuss that the ones presented in their paper are just a single interpretation - aligned with the structurally described game. Therefore, interpreting these [and other] type of narrative structures is a big challenge for narrative generation.

In this paper, we approach this challenge using large language models (LLM) and ChatGPT given its easy-to-use interface and the way we communicate the system rules. Given LLMs nature, varied outputs can be requested from the same prompt. We combine TropeTwist as narrative structure system and chatGPT as interpreter and generator. We present preliminary results from interfacing with chatGPT, analyze these qualitatively, discuss limitations and problems with using these type of models, and present our future work directions to foster ideation in the creative process.

## 2 Background

Propp [21] analyzed Russian folktales and their structure, which resulted in 31 steps; emphasizing that the arrangement of these structural steps gave meaning to the story discourse. Bremond [7] expanded Propp's analysis and proposed concepts and developed them into *sequences* as temporal and causal structures considering narrative possibilities resulting from choices. Contemporary to this, Barthes [6] proposed fundamental narrative unit to better assess and identify narrative structures. Baikadi and Cardona-Rivera [5] further discuss these fundamental units as *narremes*, encoding narrative state. TropeTwist [2], the system we use in this paper, use narrative structures with tropes [13,16] as the core way to define narrative in games and propose ways to generate them.

Furthermore, narrative, story, and quest generation have been tackled with different techniques such as planning algorithms [15,23,29] or grammars [4,11]. Lately, large language models and systems using these techniques such as GPT

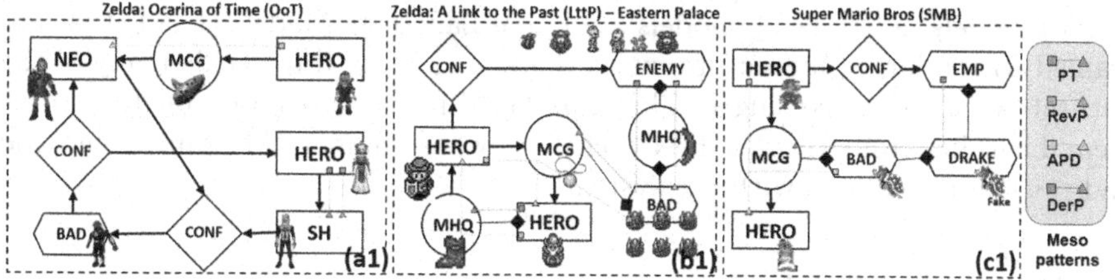


**Fig. 1.** Narrative structures of existing games created using TropeTwist and the set of available nodes. Adapted from [2].

and ChatGPT have been used for the generation of narrative and quests [24,28], and other type of content for games [25,27]. For instance, Chung et al. [10] explored the challenge of guiding narrative in GPT models, proposing a tool to sketch stories with GPT-3. Méndez and Gérvas preliminary evaluated the potential use of ChatGPT for story sifting and its limitations [18], which had a similar objective as the one in this paper; to preliminary evaluate ChatGPT capabilities for narrative interpretation.

## 3 TropeTwist and ChatGPT

TropeTwist and ChatGPT were combined to generate narrative structures and interpretation and stories, respectively.

### 3.1 TropeTwist

TropeTwist [2] is a narrative structure system that uses tropes as its base resource [13,14], and employs them as nodes and patterns, in a narrative structure graph. TropeTwist can be used to define generic and structural aspects of a story, leading to the identification of events, roles, and narrative elements. All of these are represented as nodes in an interconnected narrative graph. Nodes represent tropes (characters, conflicts, and plot devices) and can be connected to other nodes by means of three different connections: unidirectional edges ($\rightarrow$), denoting a relationship from a node to another node; bidirectional edges ($\leftrightarrow$), denoting a reflexive relationship between two nodes; and entailment edges ($\diamondsuit$–), denoting a node entails another. The authors developed three narrative structures depicting different games and situations shown in Fig. 1, which we use to experiment in this paper. TropeTwist's full definition, and how their graphs are composed, generated, and evaluated can be found in the original paper in more detail [2,3].

### 3.2 ChatGPT

ChatGPT is a system and chatbot developed by OpenAI in the end of 2022 that builts on top of the previously developed Generative Pre-trained Transformer

(GPT) models [8,22]. GPT models are Large Language Models (LLM) that are trained with a large amount of text data and can be used to tackle many of the natural language processing (NLP). ChatGPT training is based on Reinforcement Learning from Human Feedback [20], where human AI trainers provide and rank conversations with the system[1].

## 4 Process and Methodology

In this paper, TropeTwist is used to define narrative structures and ChatGPT (GPT version 3.5) to interpret them and generate a basic story. We defined the narrative structure of the general arc of Zelda: Ocarina of Time (ZOoT) [19] like in the original TropeTwist paper (shown in Fig. 1.a). This narrative structure graph was then used as a prompt for ChatGPT, and ChatGPT was tasked to interpret and generate a story.

TropeTwist system was adapted, compressed, and formalized as a chat prompt for ChatGPT. All possible tropes were given to ChatGPT along with their overarching category with a brief description of each adapted from Table 1 in the TropeTwist original paper [2] as well as the connections and their description. Then, the narrative structure to be interpreted was given to ChatGPT as a prompt. The following are the prompts used for ChatGPT:

> The following are the type of tropes that exist in the system. There doesn't need to be temporality within the system. Whenever you find one of these within "[]" you can replace it with the appropriate information:
> Heroes:
>
> - [HERO]: generic hero
> - [5MA]: 5 man band (5 heroes)
> - [NEO]: the chosen one
> - [SH]: super hero
>
> Enemies:
>
> - [ENEMY]: generic enemy
> - [EMP]: the empire is a collective enemy
> - [BAD]: Specfic enemy, which is the ultimate cause for all the bad.
> - [DRAKE]: the dragon is a type of enemy that can be anything and is the right hand of [BAD]
>
> Conflicts:
>
> - [CONF]: Non-specfic problem to overcome between characters
>
> Plot devices:
>
> - [PLD]: a feature or element that drives the plot forward
> - [CHK]: a plot device relevant to the story
> - [MCG]: A plot device with irrelevant nature to drive the story
> - [MHQ]: A plot device important to resolve a conflict

[1] https://openai.com/blog/chatgpt.

**Table 1.** Sample generated stories with ChatGPT using as narrative structure the one presented in Fig. 1.a.

---

In the peaceful kingdom of Elysia, a renowned hero named Leon ([HERO]1) stumbles upon an ancient artifact known as the Crystal of Destiny ([MCG]1). Intrigued by its mysterious powers, Leon embarks on a quest to unravel its secrets. Little does he know that the crystal holds the key to the emergence of a chosen one, Sophie ([NEO]1). As Sophie discovers her destiny, a conflict ([CONF]1) arises that threatens the tranquility of Elysia. A malevolent sorcerer, Lord Mortis ([BAD]1), seeks to unleash chaos and darkness upon the kingdom. Sophie finds herself entangled in this conflict, driven by her innate abilities and the weight of her newfound responsibility.

However, Lord Mortis is not content with a single conflict. He manipulates forces and orchestrates another crisis ([CONF]2), determined to crush Sophie's spirit and thwart her journey. Unbeknownst to him, this conflict also draws the attention of another hero, Emily ([HERO]2), who possesses extraordinary superhuman powers ([SH]1).

As Emily joins forces with Sophie, their combined strength and determination become a beacon of hope in the face of Lord Mortis's malevolence. Together, they confront their fears and insecurities, forging a powerful alliance to stand against the encroaching darkness.

The conflict ([CONF]1) intensifies as Sophie and Emily face Lord Mortis and his minions. United by their unwavering resolve, they navigate treacherous landscapes, engage in epic battles, and ultimately expose Lord Mortis's true intentions.

In a climactic showdown, Sophie's latent powers fully manifest, elevating her to a new level of strength and mastery. With Emily's support, she confronts Lord Mortis head-on, unleashing a wave of light and hope that banishes the darkness from Elysia. As the kingdom celebrates their victory, Sophie and Emily part ways, knowing that their bond and the triumph over evil will forever be etched in the annals of Elysian history. Sophie embraces her role as the chosen one, while Emily continues her journey as a beacon of justice and inspiration for those in need.

---

In a world plagued by darkness and oppression, a [HERO]1 emerges. Little do they know that their journey will lead them to uncover a hidden truth that will shape their destiny. The [HERO]1 encounters a mysterious plot device ([MCG]1) that holds the key to unlocking their true potential. As the [HERO]1 delves deeper into their quest, they begin to realize that they are more than just an ordinary hero. They are the [NEO]1, the chosen one destined to bring balance and restore peace to the land. This revelation sets them on a path of self-discovery and understanding their true purpose.

However, the path to fulfilling their destiny is not easy. The malevolent [BAD]1, the ultimate cause of all the chaos and suffering, becomes aware of the [NEO]1's existence. [BAD]1 sees the potential threat posed by the [NEO]1 and sets in motion a series of conflicts ([CONF]2) aimed at stopping them. Unbeknownst to [BAD]1, their actions inadvertently lead to an unexpected encounter. During a particularly intense [CONF]2, [HERO]2 reveals their true identity as [SH]1, a super-powered being capable of extraordinary feats. This revelation surprises both [BAD]1 and [HERO]2, creating a unique dynamic in the conflict.

Meanwhile, [NEO]1, driven by their newfound purpose, faces another conflict ([CONF]1) directly with [BAD]1. The clash between [NEO]1 and [BAD]1 intensifies as they challenge each other's beliefs and motivations. Each confrontation brings them closer to understanding the true nature of their entangled destinies.

Simultaneously, [SH]1, now aware of their own significance, embarks on a personal journey to reconcile their superpowers with their role as a hero. They encounter various obstacles and conflicts ([CONF]1) orchestrated by [BAD]1, ultimately leading to a final confrontation between [SH]1 and [BAD]1. The story reaches its climax as the intertwining conflicts and destinies of the [NEO]1, [HERO]2/[SH]1, and [BAD]1 converge. The resolution of these conflicts holds the key to the world's fate and the ultimate triumph of either darkness or light. The question remains: Will the [NEO]1 fulfill their prophecy and overcome [BAD]1, or will the forces of evil prevail?

---

The following are the type of connections that exist between tropes and nodes. They will be within “ ‘’ ” you can interpret them as you want: Connections:

- ‘->’: connection from an element towards an element
- ‘<->’: bidirectional connection between elements
- ‘<>-’: connection representing entail. A element entails another element.

  Finally, there might be more than one hero, enemy, conflict, and plot device named the same. I will write a number outside the “[]” to represent the same element.

## 5 ChatGPT as Interpreter

We evaluated ChatGPT possibility to be used as an interpreter of narrative structures and generate stories by evaluating qualitatively the interaction with the systems and its output. Following the process described in Sect. 4, we defined the narrative structure in Fig. 1.a as a prompt for ChatGPT. We used two prompts for ChatGPT, one where we asked ChatGPT to interpret, describe, and generate a story from the structure (sample shown in Table 1 row 1), and another with our interpretation, requesting ChatGPT to generate a story from it (sample shown in Table 1 row 2). The following is the prompt without our interpretation:

> Now, lets test this! The following is a narrative structure I designed (it will be in different lines but it all belong to the same structure). Please interpret the structure, describe it using the information above, and develop a story of around 200 words from it.
> [HERO]1 '->' [MCG]1 '->' [NEO]1
> [NEO]1 '->' [CONF]1 '->' [BAD]1
> [BAD]1 '->' [CONF]2 '->' [NEO]1
> [BAD]1 '->' [CONF]2 '->' [HERO]2
> [HERO]2 '->' [SH]1
> [SH]1 '->' [CONF]1 '->' [BAD]1

Our interpretation added the following paragraph:

> My interpretation of that narrative structure is the following:
> The [BAD]1 has a [CONF]2 with [HERO]2, but a plot twist is that [HERO]2 is actually [SH]1, and [SH]1 who has a [CONF]1 with [BAD]1. Simultaneously, [HERO]1 has as first objective to collect the [MCG]1 and that would mean that the [HERO]1 is the [NEO]1. Now, given the apparition of [NEO]1, [BAD]1 has a [CONF]2 with [NEO]1, and reciprocally, [NEO]1, has a [CONF]1 with [BAD]1.

We prompted ChatGPT multiple times with both prompts to interpret and generate stories resulting in slightly different stories but with a similar interpretation. The structure might have been straightforward with the connections used and some parts could be seen as temporal and causal steps. For instance, [HERO]1 '->' [MCG]1 '->' [NEO]1, and the subsequent connection between [NEO]1 '->' [CONF]1 '->' [BAD]1, could be interpreted as the need of [HERO]1 to find [NEO]1 before any conflict with [BAD] to arise. However, when focusing on the game that the structure is based on, we see that these are not necessary.

The resulting stories proposed interesting arguments and developments yet not as diverse as expected. For instance, they all account for some artifact that needs to be acquired and inspected ([MCG]1) and with that the [HERO]1 will encounter and find [NEO]1. However, the use of the artifact and how NEO appears differs in the stories. The story remained similar when using our interpretation, but certain parts were adapted to it, such as [HERO]1 ending being [NEO]1 rather than finding them when investigating [MCG]1. Conflicts were interpreted as-is. Instead of seeing them as conceptual, the system interpreted as a particular event or series of challenges that needs to be overcame.

### 5.1 Limitations

TropeTwist has a small sample of categories and tropes, which limits the structures that can be defined. We did not give ChatGPT access to the possible patterns or tested the reflexive and entailment connections, which could give space to even more wide narrative interpretations. Further, we acknowledge that the challenges of using tropes could be amplified with LLM and ChatGPT given that these systems already encode many biases, and should be used with caution. Regarding creativity, tropes could be seen as something to avoid. Yet, we see their simple definition and connections, and possible wide range of interpretations as a strength when used adequately.

## 6 Conclusion and Future Work

We presented our process, methodology, and prompts for a preliminary exploration of using ChatGPT as a narrative interpreter and generator when provided a formal definition of a narrative structure with TropeTwist [2]. The samples presented in Table 1 are just some of the stories generated by one narrative structure depicting the overarching story arc of ZOoT.

We see the potential of LLMs and ChatGPT to receive a formalization of narrative structure systems and for them to interpret and generate stories, and even generate structures themselves. This could then allow to fully generate a story at different stages of the narrative (structure, interpretation, story). However, we see this combination between TropeTwist and ChatGPT as a mixed-initiative tool that can help the generation and production of stories, where a quick interaction loop would be necessary. As starting point, TropeTwist is already implemented in a mixed-initiative tool (Story Designer [3]) that interfaces between narrative and level design [1]. Our evaluation was qualitative and based on our expectations, which needs to be further supported with user studies and deeper analysis of the interaction. For instance, what are the parts that create more meaningful differences in the final story and how can we emphasize those are open questions. Understanding the value of these systems and their usability and user experience is a fundamental next step.

In general, while the system's output was not as diverse as expected, the slight differences in the generated stories create an interesting starting point for constructing a story or as a step in a refinement process.

## References

1. Alvarez, A., Dahlskog, S., Font, J., Togelius, J.: Empowering quality diversity in dungeon design with interactive constrained MAP-elites. In: 2019 IEEE Conference on Games (CoG) (2019)

2. Alvarez, A., Font, J.: TropeTwist: trope-based narrative structure generation. In: Proceedings of the 13th Workshop on Procedural Content Generation, FDG (2022)
3. Alvarez, A., Font, J., Togelius, J.: Story designer: towards a mixed-initiative tool to create narrative structures. In: Proceedings of the 17th International Conference on the Foundations of Digital Games (2022)
4. Alvarez, A., Grevillius, E., Olsson, E., Font, J.: Questgram [Qg]: toward a mixed-initiative quest generation tool. In: Proceedings of the 16th International Conference on the Foundations of Digital Games. FDG 2021, Association for Computing Machinery, New York (2021)
5. Baikadi, A., Cardona-Rivera, R.E.: Towards finding the fundamental unit of narrative: a proposal for the narreme. In: Proceedings of the Third Workshop on Computational Models of Narrative, pp. 42–44. European Language Resource Association (2012)
6. Barthes, R.: Introduction à l'analyse structurale des récits. Communications **8**(1), 1–27 (1966). https://doi.org/10.3406/comm.1966.1113
7. Bremond, C., Cancalon, E.D.: The logic of narrative possibilities. New Literary Hist. **11**(3), 387–411 (1980). https://doi.org/10.2307/468934, https://www.jstor.org/stable/468934?origin=crossref
8. Brown, T., et al.: Language models are few-shot learners. In: Larochelle, H., Ranzato, M., Hadsell, R., Balcan, M.F., Lin, H. (eds.) Advances in Neural Information Processing Systems, vol. 33, pp. 1877–1901. Curran Associates, Inc. (2020). https://proceedings.neurips.cc/paper_files/paper/2020/file/1457c0d6bfcb4967418bfb8ac142f64a-Paper.pdf
9. Campbell, J.: The Hero with a Thousand Faces, The Collected Works of Joseph Campbell. Pantheon Books (1949)
10. Chung, J.J.Y., Kim, W., Yoo, K.M., Lee, H., Adar, E., Chang, M.: TaleBrush: sketching stories with generative pretrained language models. In: Proceedings of the 2022 CHI Conference on Human Factors in Computing Systems. CHI 2022, Association for Computing Machinery, New York (2022). https://doi.org/10.1145/3491102.3501819, event-place: New Orleans, LA, USA
11. Doran, J., Parberry, I.: A prototype quest generator based on a structural analysis of quests from four MMORPGs. In: Proceedings of the 2nd International Workshop on Procedural Content Generation in Games. PCGames 2011, ACM, New York (2011). https://doi.org/10.1145/2000919.2000920, event-place: Bordeaux, France
12. Elson, D.: DramaBank: annotating agency in narrative discourse. In: Proceedings of the Eighth International Conference on Language Resources and Evaluation (LREC 2012), pp. 2813–2819. European Language Resources Association (ELRA), Istanbul, Turkey (2012). http://www.lrec-conf.org/proceedings/lrec2012/pdf/866_Paper.pdf
13. García-Sánchez, P., Velez-Estevez, A., Julián Merelo, J., Cobo, M.J.: The Simpsons did it: exploring the film trope space and its large scale structure. Plos One **16**(3), e0248881 (2021). https://doi.org/10.1371/journal.pone.0248881, https://dx.plos.org/10.1371/journal.pone.0248881
14. Harris, J.: Periodic Table of Storytelling (2016). https://jamesharris.design/periodic/
15. Horswill, I.: Generative text using classical nondeterminism. In: Proceedings of the EXAG Workshop at AIIDE, p. 7 (2020)
16. Horswill, I.D.: Dear leader's happy story time: a party game based on automated story generation. In: Proceedings of the 12th Artificial Intelligence and Interactive Digital Entertainment Conference, p. 7 (2016)

17. Mateas, M., Stern, A.: Integrating plot, character and natural language processing in the interactive drama Façade. In: Proceedings of the 1st International Conference on Technologies for Interactive Digital Storytelling and Entertainment (TIDSE-03), vol. 2 (2003)
18. Méndez, G., Gervás, P.: Using ChatGPT for story sifting in narrative generation. In: Proceedings of The 14th International Conference on Computational Creativity (2023)
19. Nintendo R&D4: The Legend of Zelda: Ocarina of Time (1998), game [N64]. Nintendo, Kyoto, Japan. Last played December (2016)
20. Ouyang, L., et al.: Training language models to follow instructions with human feedback. In: Koyejo, S., Mohamed, S., Agarwal, A., Belgrave, D., Cho, K., Oh, A. (eds.) Advances in Neural Information Processing Systems, vol. 35, pp. 27730–27744. Curran Associates, Inc. (2022). https://proceedings.neurips.cc/paper_files/paper/2022/file/b1efde53be364a73914f58805a001731-Paper-Conference.pdf
21. Propp, V.: Morphology of the Folktale: Second Edition. American Folklore Society Bibliographical and Special Series, University of Texas Press (1975). https://books.google.se/books?id=cyc7AQAAIAAJ
22. Radford, A., Narasimhan, K., Salimans, T., Sutskever, I.: Improving Language Understanding by Generative Pre-Training. Tech. rep., OpenAI (2018)
23. Riedl, M.O., Young, R.M.: Story planning as exploratory creativity: techniques for expanding the narrative search space. New Gener. Comput. **24**(3), 303–323 (2006). https://doi.org/10.1007/BF03037337
24. van Stegeren, J., Myundefinedliwiec, J.: Fine-tuning GPT-2 on annotated RPG quests for NPC dialogue generation. In: The 16th International Conference on the Foundations of Digital Games (FDG) 2021. FDG 2021, Association for Computing Machinery, New York (2021). https://doi.org/10.1145/3472538.3472595, event-place: Montreal, QC, Canada
25. Sudhakaran, S., González-Duque, M., Glanois, C., Freiberger, M., Najarro, E., Risi, S.: MarioGPT: open-ended text2level generation through large language models (2023). arxiv:2302.05981
26. Szilas, N.: IDtension : a narrative engine for interactive drama. In: 1st International Conference on Technologies for Interactive Digital Storytelling and Entertainment, p. 12 (2003). https://ci.nii.ac.jp/naid/10026187402/en/
27. Todd, G., Earle, S., Nasir, M.U., Green, M.C., Togelius, J.: Level generation through large language models. In: Proceedings of the 18th International Conference on the Foundations of Digital Games. FDG 2023, Association for Computing Machinery, New York (2023). https://doi.org/10.1145/3582437.3587211, event-place: Lisbon, Portugal
28. Värtinen, S., Hämäläinen, P., Guckelsberger, C.: Generating role-playing game quests with GPT language models. IEEE Trans. Games, 1–12 (2022). https://doi.org/10.1109/TG.2022.3228480
29. Young, R.M., Ware, S.G., Cassell, B.A., Robertson, J.: Plans and planning in narrative generation: a review of plan-based approaches to the generation of story, discourse and interactivity in narratives. Sprache und Datenverarbeitung, Spec. Issue Formal Comput. Models of Narrative **37**(1–2), 41–64 (2013)

# Curatorial Challenges of Exhibiting VR IDN's in Film Festival Formats

Ágnes Karolina Bakk[1(✉)] and András Szabó[2]

[1] Moholy-Nagy University of Art and Design, Zugligeti 9-25, Budapest 1121, Hungary
Bakk@mome.hu

[2] Code and Soda Ltd., Petőfi Sándor Str 5, Budapest 1052, Hungary

**Abstract.** This paper aims to present the current curatorial challenges of exhibiting or showcasing seated narrative VR experiences or installation-type free-roaming VR works, including VR IDNs that represent complexity. The observations primarily relate to exhibitions that take place in the framework of film festivals, and are partly based on personal curatorial experiences of the authors.

**Keywords:** VR · curating · IDN · film festival

## 1 About Curating for Film Festivals

### 1.1 Introduction

There is a question of whether we are still writing for screens or for spaces and whether this can have an effect on authorial practices [1], however in this paper we would like to draw attention to the practical issues related to both screenwriting practices (which focus on temporal-durational aspects of a production) and space writing practices (which focus on the spatial aspect of a production, which in some cases might make use of the physical space) and to the challenges that are faced when exhibiting these productions in temporary exhibition space.

Virtual reality uses two main categories of production (the 360° videos/cinematic VR, that can be captured with omnidirectional 360° cameras and rendered into a movie, and CGI content that can be produced by using game engines that can be rendered to create virtual worlds), and it is important to note that cinematic VR does not allow the representation of the viewer, while CGI-based virtual reality productions do, and they do allow the experiencer to move in the space or to have some level of agency. Many of the new types of stand-alone headsets (such as Meta Quest 1, Quest 2) contain gyroscopes and accelerometers, and they can even track the user's movement in real-time and can update the virtual image according to their perspective. Many productions that lately became widely available do not exploit the potential of the VR devices fully and rather rely on the traditional narrative capacities inherited from cinema, and this is also due to the current technological settings as well as the limited possibilities of exhibiting or promoting in online platforms. While in the case of cinematic VR we can observe a form of screenwriting practice, these productions are, while being "to a certain level


L. Holloway-Attaway and J. T. Murray (Eds.): ICIDS 2023, LNCS 14384, pp. 122–128, 2023.
https://doi.org/10.1007/978-3-031-47658-7_10

emotionally engaging, […] mostly seem to serve as an exercise into what the medium eventually will be able to contain" [2]. The interactive CGI formats could allow for more interactive artistic manifestations, but in the current productions, they still heavily rely on cinematic storytelling format – which currently prevents them from reaching a clearly crystallized institutional format yet.

### 1.2 VR as an Artistic Medium

In 1989 Jaron Lanier acknowledged the possibilities of VR in artistic practices. He mentions that "Virtual Reality is […] like having shared hallucinations, except that you can compose them like works of art; you can compose the external world in any way at all as an act of communication […]. When Virtual Reality sponges up good energy from the physical plane, then what you get in Virtual Reality is beautiful art, beautiful creativity, beautiful dreams to share, beautiful adventures" [3]. Installation art and cinematic artistic practices all embraced the VR technology. But presenting VR productions that have interactive digital narratives is rather challenging as the audience members have to experience the story in an exhibition format where the time-based art works require a more undisturbed attention. Graham and Cook [4] point out that "spectators find it difficult to direct their attention towards the entire (and often unknown) duration of a video artwork". This is also applicable to virtual reality formats.

While early VR works (such as Brenda Laurel's The Placeholder, or Char Davies' Osmose) heavily relied on the sense of embodiment of the viewer, more recent productions are putting less emphasis on how the viewer's body is interacting with the environment, rather emphasizing the importance and the impact of the story on the viewer. The more story-focused approach of VR productions also predestinated the form to be showcased in the frame of film festivals, this is mainly because the VR productions often use cinematic tools and they rely on traditional cinematic dramaturgy. This step might mean that the medium of VR reached a new level of maturity, which I will discuss in the next section.

### 1.3 Media Historical Traces and Parallels

Every medium manifests their medial characteristics more explicitly when they are in early phase. When developing the medium and continuously experimenting with it, artists can slowly arrive to its institutionalization phase. Some scholars such as Noël Burch [5] make a distinction between "primitive mode of representation" and the "institutional mode of representation" while some like André Gaudreault and Tom Gunning offer an alternative dichotomy between the "system of monstrative attractions" and the "system of narrative integration" [6, 7]. These distinctions refer to the characteristic of cinema which was more present in its early stage as an art form, a multisensorial staged experience that offered a special type of entertainment for the viewers, and distinguish between productions that rely more on the features of the medium and those that rely more on narrative aspects. 'Cinema of attraction', a term coined by Tom Gunning [8], is a useful term to adopt in the context of immersion's relation to film. Gunning defines cinema of attraction as an artform that "solicits a highly conscious awareness of the film image engaging the viewer's curiosity [9]." This is similar to what happened with the early artistic practices of virtual reality.

Rebecca Rouse [10] further developed the concept of cinema of attraction and applied it to new media under the term 'media of attraction'. The concept offers a framing for interactive works created by using virtual reality or augmented reality techniques. The qualities that such productions have are the following: being participatory, interdisciplinary, unassimilated (i.e. not yet institutionalized) and "seamed". Recently, VR began to overcome the phase of media of attraction and is gaining new and new venues of exhibition in cinema festival contexts, digital technology conferences, as well as in museums [11] but the technological challenges still remain to be an issue to some extent. The question of VR productions that are designed for various headset types represent a problem which requires curators to ask for technical riders before- hand. While due to the narrative boom—as mentioned before—many productions are designed for the most prevalent VR headset types, and the heavily interactive ones and those that have high quality graphical imagery require running on PC VR. In the case of the latter, many require a wire or suitably placed sensors in a spatially extend- ed setting (e.g. see Inarritu's production [12] or the recent production by Monika Maslon [13]). Jaller conceptualizes these as attraction windows, or story rooms or performances spaces, depending on the installation setting, but all of them have the same problem: the number of audiences usually has to be scaled down, a problem for which several festivals and exhibitors could not find the problem [14].

## 2 Installing the VR and the Body

In this paper the authors aim to present several issues that curators of such events have to face when conceptualizing and exhibiting IDN's as virtual reality productions. We will be using the term IDN referring to "narrative expressions in the digital medium that change due to input from an audience" [15]. As these all express a narrative that can be unfolded only in a time-based manner, they require different viewing practices compared to fine art exhibitions. Accordingly, the curators have to address this in their curatorial concept, and deal with the question of how the curated VR works fit the film festival and how do the works relate to gaming as well. Another important issue is addressing the sense of embodiment and also the effect this has on the viewer, along with the viewers' taxonomy that they apply to the viewed VR works. According to Gaudenzi: "[a]ny project that starts with an intention to document the "real" and does so by using digital interactive technology [is to be] considered an interactive documentary" [16]. In productions that aim to re-enact fact-based issues, the immersive nature of VR enhances the viewer's sense of presence, which in turn contributes to the audience perceiving the production as a documentary. This type of argumentation or categorization are also used by documentary film festivals that have a VR section or a talent development lab dedicated for interactive digital media creators (see e.g. Copenhagen-based CPH festival).These issues arise due to the fact that these productions are heavily narrative-driven and these present a challenge regarding how to showcase them in a manner that takes into consideration the time constraints and how to offer proper onboarding and off- boarding for the audience members (especially in the case of third-wave revival of VR) [17].

### 2.1 Sense of Embodiment

The early artistic work produced for installation settings of VR addressed the characteristic (and the promises of VR) by tackling the sense of embodiment that VR can offer as its unique feature. Creators experimented with the media specificities and affordances that interactive VR applications could offer, such as the sense of embodiment (SoE) [18]. The sense of self-representation required for SoE is characterized by:

1. The Sense of Self-Location, defined as "one's spatial experience of being inside a body" and which involves "the relationship between one's self and one's body", while presence is "the relationship between one's self and the environment" [18];
2. The Sense of Agency, defined as the feeling of having "global motor control, including the subjective experience of action, control, intention, motor selection and the conscious experience of will" [18];
3. The Sense of Body Ownership, defined as the feeling of the body as being the source of experienced sensations and "one's self-attribution of a body" [18].

These are all important features that early VR works heavily relied on when designing the productions.

## 3 Challenges of Curating and Exhibiting Artistic and Narrative VR Works

While VR and video games resemble each other in the way they align their users, the multi- sensorial capacity is unique for VR. Technologically advanced VR equipment have the potential to offer tactile feedback, and the illusion of proprioception and vestibular sensations, which, according to Raz brings the experiencer and the avatar "into an unprecedented perceptual proximity". As mentioned earlier, this also contributes to the strong documentary characteristic of VR. However, the original concept and the finished productions often differ from each other, and this is also a strong source of frustration for the creators [19], which makes them often aim at a more simpler con- cept in order to be able to foresee the exact output.

Raz states that "There is a growing agreement among filmmakers and critics that the future of this process critically depends on the extent to which VR artists will formulate effective stylistic strategies that exploit the unique potentials of their medium and avoid its pitfalls" [20]. While as Raz also quotes many filmmakers who acknowledge the very close relationship between the cinematic medium and VR, the possibilities of interactivity and agency are changing the author's control over the plot. According to Raz "non-narrative VR forms, which highlight the sensory aspects of the artistic experience, are apparently less affected by these constraints [i.e. forced cuts and perspective shifts.] VR storytelling may depend on the development of alter- native attention-grabbing devices".

Although there is already a considerable literature on how to exhibit virtual reality at museums and artistic exhibitions, there are not many studies about VR sections of film festivals, especially about how to exhibit VR productions that offer a cinematic experience.

Existing practices often provide space for narrative-based VR productions in such festival as Venice Biennale, SXSW, Tribeca Film Festival or Sundance, but lately in several European countries the documentary film festivals started to launch their own VR sections. In what follows, we would like to share our experiences with the issues and challenges that arose during one of these festivals of Vektor VR, organized in Budapest, Hungary.

### 3.1 Maintaining the Sense of Immersion, Both for Cinematic VR and Interactive VR

Productions created in the format of linear 360° videos offer fewer challenges: these require a seated position for the viewer, preferably on a revolving chair, and the headsets are required for offering a more effective isolation. Interactive productions are of several types: seated ones also require usually a revolving chair, but depending on if it is PC VR or standalone, they require further preparation.

When conceptualizing the curatorial selection, we can take into consideration several aspects of VR IDN's that can help us present the selection in a coherent way. Fisher, Vosmeer and Barbara's framework [21] offer a series of aspects and challenges for scripting VR, which also gives us, curators, a good idea regarding what to take into account about the aspects of the productions when selecting and exhibiting:

4. Scripting the body for VR IDN's means that writers (and curators) should be aware of the body's position and how is it possible to move within the story space [21]. When curating such works, it is important that the selection makers take these into consideration in regard of all of the works.
5. Embodiment and Movement: the Sense of Embodiment or identification with the avatar can create "temporary identity shifts"; in the cases that the interactor does not have an avatar, the identity shift can happen via identification with a character and taking that character's point of view [21]. When selecting the VR productions, it is important to outline the possible experience design and to assess how each production is in alignment with the rest of the selection.
6. Breaking the wall by acknowledging that the viewer is there [21]: it is important to present multiple perspectives and to script the interactor in a way that they know what is expected from them in terms of dramatic agency.
7. Guiding the interactors' gaze is similarly important, as it can also encourage reviewing, which can foster the sense of complexity that the viewers can have about the given VR IDN. This is also important to take into consideration when making the selection or installing the works, as this can also create a certain dialogue between the included VR productions.
8. Environmental storytelling aspects should also be considered when selecting the VR productions. Many of them include an "antechamber" where the interactors can have the chance to be primed to the narrative and to its environment. This is important also because it can prepare the interactor for identity shifts and possible interaction types.

## 4 Conclusions

In this paper we aimed at presenting the practical aspects of VR exhibitions that require attention from a curatorial viewpoint. It is important to note the conceptual framing of the selection, as it is required for presenting a thematically and experientially consistent production. We expect the presented issues to become more prominent and relevant as more and more festivals are aiming to have their own VR selection, and the discussion above can offer a framing for creating curatorial concepts.

## References

1. Reyes, M.C.: From screenwriting to space-writing. Disegno – a designkultúra folyóirata **6**(1), 86–103 (2022). https://doi.org/10.21096/disegno_2022_1mcr
2. Vosmeer, M., Roth, C.: Exploring narrative novelties in VR. In: Mitchell, A., Vosmeer, M. (eds.) ICIDS 2021. Lecture Notes in Computer Science, vol. 13138, pp. 435–444. Springer, Cham (2021). https://doi.org/10.1007/978-3-030-92300-6_44
3. Kevin, K., Barbara, S.A.H.: Virtual reality: an interview with Jaron Lanier. Whole Earth Rev. **64**, 108–120 (1989)
4. Graham B. & Cook S.: Rethinking Curating. Art after New Media. The MIT Press, Cambridge (2010)
5. Burch, N., Lane H.R.: Theory of Film Practice. Princeton University Press (1973)
6. Burch, N.: Un mode de représentation primitif? Iris **2**(1), 113–123 (1984)
7. Gaudreault, A., Gunning, T.: Early cinema as a challenge to film history. In: Strauven, W. (ed.) The Cinema of Attraction Reloaded. Amsterdam University Press, Amsterdam (2006)
8. Gunning, T.: The cinema of attraction: early film, its spectator and the avant-garde. In: Elsaesser, T., Barker, A. (eds.) Early Cinema: Space, Frame, Narrative, pp. 229–235. BFI, London (1986)
9. Gunning, T.: An aesthetic of astonishment: early film and the (in)credulous spectator. In: Braudy, L., Cohen, M. (eds.) Film Theory and Criticism, 7th edn. Oxford University Press, New York/Oxford (2009)
10. Rouse, R.: Media of attraction: A media archeology approach to panoramas, kinematography, mixed Reality and beyond. In: Nack, F., Gordon, A.S. (eds.) ICIDS 2016. LNCS, vol. 10045, pp. 97–107. Springer, Cham (2016). https://doi.org/10.1007/978-3-319-48279-8_9
11. Gifreu-Castells, A.: Approach to the curatorship of virtual reality exhibitions. In: Buckley, B., Conomos, J. (eds.) A Companion to Curation (2019). https://doi.org/10.1002/9781119206880.ch19
12. Innaritu, A.G.: Carne Y Arena. Cannes Film Festival (2017) Immersive Mixed-Reality Installation
13. Masłoń, M.: Control Negative. Dok Leipzig (2022) Virtual Reality Installation
14. Jaller, C.: Designing the exhibition modus of virtual experiences: virtual reality installations at film festivals. In: Brooks, A., Brooks, E.I., Jonathan, D. (eds.) ArtsIT 2020. LNICSSITE, vol. 367, pp. 45–63. Springer, Cham (2021). https://doi.org/10.1007/978-3-030-73426-8_3
15. Koenitz, H.: Understanding Interactive Digital Narrative: Immersive Expressions for a Complex Time. Taylor & Francis, London (2023)
16. Gaudenzi, S.: The living documentary: from representing reality to co-creating reality in digital interactive documentary. Ph.D. Thesis. London, UK: Goldsmiths - Centre for Cultural Studies, University of London (2023)
17. Belisle, B., Roquet, P.: Guest editors' introduction: virtual reality: immersion and empathy. J. Vis. Cult. **19**(1), 3 (2020). https://doi.org/10.1177/1470412920906258
18. Kilteni, K., Raphaela, G., Mel, S.: The sense of embodiment in virtual reality. Presence Teleoperators Virtual Environ. **21**(4), 373–387 (2012). https://doi.org/10.1162/pres_a_00124
19. Rouse, R., Engberg, M., JafariNaimi, N., Bolter, J.D.: $MR^X$: an interdisciplinary framework for mixed reality experience design and criticism. Digit. Creativity **26**(3–4), 175–181 (2015). https://doi.org/10.1080/14626268.2015.1100123

20. Raz, G.: Virtual reality as an emerging art medium and its immersive affordances. In: Carroll, N., Di Summa, L.T., Loht, S. (eds.) The Palgrave Handbook of the Philosophy of Film and Motion Pictures, pp. 995–1014. Springer, Cham (2019). https://doi.org/10.1007/978-3-030-19601-1_42
21. Fisher, J.A., Vosmeer, M., Barbara, J.: A new research agenda: writing for virtual reality interactive narratives. In: Vosmeer, M., Holloway-Attaway, L. (eds.) Interactive Storytelling, ICIDS 2022. LNCS, vol. 13762, pp. 673–683. Springer, Cham (2022). https://doi.org/10.1007/978-3-031-22298-6_43

# *What Really Happened Here?*

## Dealing with Uncertainty in the Book of Distance: A Critical Historiography Perspective

Jonathan Barbara[1,2](✉) and Mads Haahr[1]

[1] School of Computer Science and Statistics, Trinity College Dublin, Dublin, Ireland
{barbaraj,haahrm}@tcd.ie

[2] Saint Martin's Institute of Higher Education, Hamrun, Malta

**Abstract.** Uncertain cultural heritage presents a dilemma in its narrative representation. History seeks to push a grand narrative, at the expense of less convenient narratives. Critical historiographic approaches favor the consideration of multiple narratives as they focus on the mediation of history rather than arriving at a single truth. Virtual Reality Interactive Narratives, such as *The Book of Distance*, exemplify how uncertainty can be represented through re-enactment. In this late breaking work, we provide a close reading of *The Book of Distance* through the lens of critical historiography and suggest improvements for future similar experiences.

**Keywords:** Interactive Digital Narratives · Virtual Reality · History · Critical Historiography

## 1 Introduction

As we seek to make sense of different social cultures, and what makes them who they are, we often look at their past to cast light on current traditions, held beliefs, and way of life. Whilst many cultures trace their origins to places away from their current territories, as a result of migration, colonization, and expansion, others feel connected to cultural heritage still evident amongst their modern settlements despite hundreds of generations separating whichever culture raised such structures and their modern-day inhabitants. Such separations, whether geographical or temporal, introduce a memory loss that depends on primary or secondary historical sources to give witness to an event or behavior. For example, what we remember of our earliest childhood is heavily influenced by photos we have of that time.

A single or a group of coherent evidence that gives unequivocal witness, absence of evidence that gives no witness, or two or more conflicting forms of evidence: how do we handle the absence of, or the abundance of conflicting, evidence? Absence results in gaps that we as humans seek to fill in order to provide a complete picture. Over-abundance results in inconsistencies from which we as humans seek to identify one consistent story supported by a subset of evidence as being the legitimate one, influenced by the court of law's need to resolve disputes, forcing historians to come to a singular truth [1].


L. Holloway-Attaway and J. T. Murray (Eds.): ICIDS 2023, LNCS 14384, pp. 129–136, 2023.
https://doi.org/10.1007/978-3-031-47658-7_11

An alternative look at the interpretation of history is presented by Critical Historiography [2], which does not seek historical facts objectively, but rather presents the mediation of history as a participatory process engaging with the past's uncertainty [3].

This seems to suggest that interactive narratives, which have the interactor decide on which narrative path to take, can be a useful tool to explore uncertainty, particularly within historical narratives. Indeed, uncertainty has often featured in scholarly work on tangible cultural heritage (cf. [4]), but is also gaining a foothold in intangible cultural heritage – especially in scholarship dealing with memory [5].

In this short paper, we explore the role of uncertainty in interactive narratives that present a critical historiographic perspective. Specifically, we use Mann and Sprecher's model of quasi-tangible cultural heritage as a lens through which to carry out a close reading of *The Book of Distance*, a Virtual Reality (VR) interactive experience in which the Canadian narrator explores the uncertain history of his immigrant Japanese grandfather. We interpret the design decisions made in this experience in the light of this model to inform future designs of experiences that deal with historical uncertainty.

## 2 Uncertainty in History

The ideal of history as an objective scientific endeavor, as championed by Ranke [6], found opposition by philosophers Nietzsche [7] and Croce [8] who argued in favor of a subjective evaluation of history in terms of contemporary interpretation [9]. Through history's characterization as both a science and a narrative [1], it is argued that debates on historical truth will never resolve [10], and thus uncertainty remains a key element of history.

Indeed, both scientific and interpretive perspectives of history may suffer from a level of uncertainty: quantitative uncertainty in the former, qualitative uncertainty in the latter. In the case of tangible cultural heritage, evidence is primarily in the form of the structure itself, and uncertainty here refers to approximate quantitative measurement of its form's characteristics [4]. When a structure's original form may not be reflected in its current state, such as the Sphinx of Giza, or no longer existent, such as the Colossus of Rhodes, one relies on accounts written or depicted by contemporaries to determine or deduce its original form.

The activities held around tangible cultural heritage, such as events and rituals, usage and skills, are much harder to discern because their description, limited by the vocabulary of text or the static nature of depiction, does not fully satisfy the need of observation. This lack of description, or, if present, the lack of sufficient detail to represent the behavior, or, on the other hand, the multitude of accounts that may contradict each other, lead to a level of uncertainty around intangible cultural heritage.

### 2.1 Dealing with Uncertainty

Curthoys lists four reasons as to why "historical evidence is insufficient for us to know the truth of the past, certainly the complete truth" [9]. There is either too little evidence, too much evidence, partial and selective historical records which introduce bias, and haphazard survival of evidence with the mundane surviving where the critical perishes [9].

It is informative to look at how Herodotus dealt with uncertainty in the fifth century BCE: in the face of multiple witness accounts about an event, he chose to narrate all of these contradictory accounts, such as in his iconic work titled *The Histories.* In doing so, Herodotus does not intend to portray the truth, but rather to present the claims (*logoi*) of contemporaries and leave the interpretation and judgement to the reader [10]. This is in contrast to Thucydides, who presented a single authoritative account in a dominant tone, and Bury, who declared that history is a science, no less and no more, leaving no space for artistic interpretation [1].

White and Barthes contribute to a critique of the narrative structure by claiming that historians use "a range of time-honored narrative techniques ... to endow unfamiliar events and situations with meanings" [11], and thus description becomes interpretation [12]. Structural anthropologist Levi-Strauss accuses historians of imposing structure and relationships on people and events of the past and achieving coherence by leaving out incompatible facts: "historical continuity is secured only by dint of fraudulent outlines" [13].

Thus, uncertainty is inherent in the recount of history, with storytellers seeking to present a coherent whole while presenting often contrasting factual evidence. This is where a different perspective to representing history comes useful: critical historiography.

## 3 Critical Historiography

With historians claiming to be seeking the objective single truth of the past, proponents of critical historiography seek to foreground the mediated representation of history rather than the recovery of objective historical facts [2, 3]. History is thus not seen as a "total fact" but is rather constructed from a number of narratives [3]. This challenges the idea that heritage is owned by an authoritarian figure who determines the "truth" but considers other perspectives.

Critical historiography is framed as an "active construction, animation and recombination process of historical events and the locale of history" and thus, critical historiography is said to engage "actively in the conflicts and uncertainty of the past and present" [3].

Post-structuralist Trouillot presents historiography as being "implicated by technologies of collection of documents, their structuring into narratives and how interfaces of their dissemination culminate in a historical infrastructure, not always visible but very impactful on how heritage is formulated" [14]. Interactive digital narratives are indeed interfaces of dissemination of structured narratives.

### 3.1 Quasi-Tangible Cultural Heritage Model

Unhappy with UNESCO's dichotomy between tangible and intangible cultural heritage, Mann and Sprecher present a quasi-tangible cultural heritage model that acknowledges the agency of the perceiver as an active part of cultural heritage [3]. This model follows a critical historiography approach that replaces the binary perspective with a continuum that blurs boundaries between the tangible and intangible, objectivity and subjectivity, fact and speculation [15]. The model considers three components: the historian, the spectator, and the place. The historian is the designer of the historical narrative, the spectator is the participant in the interaction with this narrative and the site is the location offering a "landscape narrative." Narratives are not pre-scribed but organized "on the ground," giving text a "spatial form." This reflects what in game academia is known as "environmental storytelling" and has already been applied to desktop archaeogaming in the past [16].

The model's methodology features three processes in a pipeline: data collection, computational methods and immersive generative storytelling. Data collection acquires its sources from direct and indirect, physical and narrative sources. Computational methods employ automated data labelling to create crosslinks. The third step combines physical and narrative data to render immersive scenes to the user interface. This model supports the generation of multiple narratives as per parameters given [3].

In keeping with the focus on "technologies of dissemination" [14], we now shift our focus onto VR. Already acknowledged as a medium for IDNs [17] and representing intangible cultural heritage [18], we now consider it as a medium of critical historiography.

## 4 VR as a Medium of Critical Historiography

Mann & Sprecher's work on the use of VR as a medium of critical historiography seeks to understand how VR can be used to question and undermine stable representations of sites and their histories, aided by the technology's "simple, faithful realism." They use VR as a tool with which to explore difficult pasts contextualised in their physical space, whilst offering "empathy and some reconciliation" [3].

VR, through its affordance for first-person perspective in a virtual environment, can offer a space for historical empathy, allowing the modern-day person to connect with characters from the past. Such "identification" (cf. [19]) can create meaning from intangible cultural heritage based on available evidence. However, limited evidence, compounded with the historian's present culture, risks creating an inherent bias in the historical inquiry [3] and interpretation [20]. Acknowledging such bias and its effect on historical interpretation is an important factor in establishing such a connection with our history [21].

Mann & Sprecher distinguish between being immersed in history and being immersed in historiography. While the former usually takes the form of historically based games following some grand narrative, being immersed in historiography means being immersed in the research setting, a "behind the scenes" view into the reconstruction of the heritage site [3].

VR brings together critical historiography's three elements: the VR interactor is the spectator witnessing the historical representation prepared by the historian as designer. Such representation is situated within a virtual space, often a digital twin of the physical site in question. Indeed, VR is not tied to a single site, unlike museum and site narratives that are physically bound to the place of heritage. VR can transcend boundaries and take the visitor across spaces designed around the experience – rather than experiences designed around the space. As Mann and Sprecher point out, this "offers the opportunity to approach the site, and the archive about the site, with no apparent prioritization between their material presence and their non-material discursive mediation" [3].

Mann and Sprecher present a number of projects that highlight the affordance of VR as "a medium to introduce a new participatory agency in the reading and writing of historical materials" [3]. They describe this as "re-enactment within a heritage context" [3], a reenactment of affective history that attempts to create affect in the VR interactor possibly leading to a "sympathetic identification with the past." However, for this to happen, re-enactment must remain open ended, and not prescribed, allowing for the representation of narratives that challenge the grand narrative [3]. A recent example of VR's support for multiple perspectives in the representation of history is the work of Waagen et al. [22].

## 5 Case Study: *The Book of Distance*

In this last section, we briefly report on a close reading of *The Book of Distance* [23], a VR IDN that has the interactor accompany Randall Okita, the narrator, discover his grandfather's personal history as he migrated from Japan to Canada prior to World War II, married and built a family business there before being taken to an internment camp as Canada feared enemy activity on its own soil when the War began. Whilst some merits of *The Book of Distance* as an IDN have been discussed elsewhere [24], we hereby wish to analyze the experience through the lens of critical historiography.

We first consider how does the experience fit into the quasi-tangible cultural heritage model of Mann and Sprecher? What aspects of its methodology can be seen in the experience?

Then we seek to address some questions that Mann and Sprecher make about the use of VR for critical historiography: "[W]hat does VR offer for critical historiography of sites, and what is at stake? Can we take advantage of the realistic illusionary capabilities of VR to teleport us in space and time while not losing touch with our role as critical thinkers? Does VR enable new modes of questioning the notion of facts?".

Yonezo's story is linked to a number of places: his home in Hiroshima, his journey into Canada, his new home, the internment camp to where he is forcibly taken, the chicken coop where his family were relocated to upon release, the farms upon which they worked, and the house he eventually bought from his hard-earned money. These geographically and chronologically distant sites are visited by the interactor as he follows Randall's narration of his investigation into this grandfather's uncertain history. This matches the model's three elements of spectator (interactor), historian (Randall), and site (all the places being visited).

As Yonezo barely spoke about his life, Randall had to piece evidence together to try and recreate his grandpa's life history. This evidence takes the form of photographs, digitized into interactable objects that can be handled and seen, including short descriptions on the back. Further evidence is in the form of letters that Yonezo had written, but more abundantly letters received from Canadian government departments as he had tried to learn more about his standing after his release from the internment camp. A third form of evidence is recordings of conversations Randall had with his father about granddad. This all fits within the model's first stage in the data pipeline: acquisition of 2D photos, recreation of 3D models from said photos, and reference to archives and literature. We have no knowledge as to whether computational methods were employed in the processing of this acquired data but the resultant VR narrative fits well into the third and last stage of the data pipeline. This narrative however does not change shape according to any parameters: it is a linear narrative as Randall only considers one hypothetical path full of questions.

In answering VR's offering for critical historiography, we agree with Mann & Sprecher's notion of re-enactment: in *The Book of Distance* the interactor takes a virtual camera in his hand and snaps photos of scenes that are shown in the digitized photos; the interactor hammers a fencepost in its place to help construct Yonezo's house, picks up their strawberries from the fields and hands them out on their table. The re-enactment serves to create a connection with the protagonist. But re-enactment is not limited to actions that help Yonezo. The interactor also re-enacts Yonezo's imprisonment as they activate a lever, which fences Yonezo inside an internment camp. The handling of photos and the listening to Randall's conversations with his father are all actions that happened in Randall's time, not Yonezo's. This ambiguous identification of the interactor as they teleport across space and time helps us to keep in touch with our role as critical thinkers. Our "home" in this experience is Randall's virtual office, giving us access to the evidence he has collected and serving as a hub to the different locations travelled by Yonezo. This gives us a "behind the scenes" perspective as Randall sews the different narratives together in order to create a coherent whole to satisfy his quest for exploring his grandfather's closely-guarded past. We are thus immersed in historiography, and we join the narrator in questioning his grandpa's silent narrative and seeking to fill it in with his investigations.

## 6 Conclusion

VR interactive narratives may not fit the needs of the historian seeking to push a grand narrative, but through their affordance of interaction and multiperspectivity, they present a suitable medium for critical historiography. Taking *The Book of Distance* as an example, we have seen how the constant shifting from one place to another, the re-enactment of the grandfather's life episodes, the narrator's studio acting as our hub, the access to digitized photographs, letters, and telephone conversations, all fit within a model for quasi-tangible cultural heritage reported in the literature. Uncertainty is embraced and built upon having the narrator ask questions while the interactor re-enacts, reflecting upon these questions. The shortcomings of this IDN in respect of this model are its linear narrative as a result of a prescribed narrative.

Future IDN experiences that seek to present a critical historiographic perspective of past events should seek to employ intelligent systems that unfold the narrative according to the interactor's choices, as per Koenitz' System-Process-Product model [25]. A knowledge base of historical data can provide the system with narrative potential that results through the interaction process. Repeat sessions expose the interactor to different potential narratives, with the outcome being not the identification of the "true" narrative, but embracing the uncertainty of the particular historical event.

## References


1. Curthoys, A., Docker, J.: The boundaries of history and fiction. In: The Sage Handbook of Historical Theory, pp. 202–220 (2013). https://doi.org/10.4135/9781446247563
2. Jarzombek, M.: A prolegomena to critical historiography. J. Arch. Educ. **52**, 197–206 (1999). https://doi.org/10.1111/j.1531-314X.1999.tb00272.x
3. Mann, E., Sprecher, A.: VR as critical historiography. In: Difficult Heritage and Immersive Experiences, pp. 80–103. Taylor & Francis (2022)
4. Pritchard, D., et al.: Study on quality in 3D digitisation of tangible cultural heritage. In: Proceedings of the Joint International Event 9th ARQUEOLÓGICA, vol. 2, pp. 1–7. https://doi.org/10.2759/581678
5. Wallen, L., Docherty-Hughes, J.R.: Uncertainty as affective state and critical engagement strategy in museum and heritage site settings. Glob. Perspect. **4**, 73071 (2023). https://doi.org/10.1525/gp.2023.73071
6. von Ranke, L., Dennis, G., Armstrong, E.: History of the Latin and Teutonic Nations (1494 to 1514) (1824)
7. Nietzsche, F.W.: On the uses and disadvantages of history for life (1983). https://doi.org/10.1017/CBO9780511812101.007
8. Croce, B.: History: Its Theory and Practice (Trns. D. Ainslee, New York) (1921)
9. Curthoys, A., et al.: Historians and disputes over uncertainty. Uncertainty and Risk: Multidisciplinary Perspectives (2009)
10. Curthoys, A.: Is History Fiction? ReadHowYouWant.com (2010)
11. White, H.: The historical text as literary artifact. In: The History and Narrative Reader, vol. 1, p. 223 (2001)
12. Barthes, R.: The discourse of history. In: Poetique, pp. 13–21 (1982)
13. Levi-Strauss, C.: The savage mind (1966). https://doi.org/10.1093/sf/45.4.608
14. Trouillot, M.-R.: Silencing the Past: Power and the Production of History. Beacon Press, Boston (2015)
15. Ekbia, H.R.: Digital artifacts as quasi-objects: qualification, mediation, and materiality. J. Am. Soc. Inform. Sci. Technol. **60**, 2554–2566 (2009). https://doi.org/10.1002/asi.21189
16. Livingstone, D., Louchart, S.J.-J., Jeffrey, S.: Archaeological storytelling in games (2016)
17. Fisher, J.A.: Epistemic rhetoric in virtual reality interactive factual narratives. Front. Virtual Reality. **3**, 845489 (2022)
18. Barbara, J.: Re-live history: an immersive virtual reality learning experience of prehistoric intangible cultural heritage. Front. Educ. **7**, 1032108 (2022). https://doi.org/10.3389/feduc.2022.1032108
19. Cohen, J.: Defining identification: a theoretical look at the identification of audiences with media characters. Mass Commun. Soc. **4**, 245–264 (2001). https://doi.org/10.1207/S15327825MCS0403_01
20. Stroud, K.: A neolithic world view lost in translation: the case of the Tarxien temples. J. Skyscape Archaeol. **5**, 191–209 (2019)
21. VanSledright, B.: Thinking historically. J. Curric. Stud. **41**, 433–438 (2009). https://doi.org/10.1080/00220270802688161
22. Waagen, J., Lanjouw, T., de Kleijn, M.: A virtual place of memory: virtual reality as a method for communicating conflicted heritage at Camp Westerbork. Herit. Mem. Confl. **3**, 87–93 (2023)
23. Oppenheim, D., Okita, R.L.: The book of distance: personal storytelling in VR. In: ACM SIGGRAPH 2020 Immersive Pavilion, pp. 1–2. ACM, Virtual Event USA (2020). https://doi.org/10.1145/3388536.3407896

24. Barbara, J., Haahr, M.: *Who Am I that Acts?* the use of voice in virtual reality interactive narratives. In: Mitchell, A., Vosmeer, M. (eds.) ICIDS 2021. LNCS, vol. 13138, pp. 3–12. Springer, Cham (2021). https://doi.org/10.1007/978-3-030-92300-6_1
25. Koenitz, H.: Understanding Interactive Digital Narrative: Immersive Expressions for a Complex Time. Taylor & Francis, Milton Park (2023)

# A Theory-of-mind Game for the Early Detection of Frontotemporal Dementia

Mark Bekooy, Dan Dan Berendsen, Martin Dierikx, Rolf Piepenbrink, Jan-Willem van Rhenen, and Rafael Bidarra(✉)

Delft University of Technology, Delft, The Netherlands
R.Bidarra@tudelft.nl

**Abstract.** People with behavioural variant frontotemporal dementia (bvFTD) struggle with social interactions and the recognition of emotions. Currently, questionnaires with pen and paper are used to diagnose people with bvFTD. In these questionnaires, people are asked to identify faux pas scenarios based on a short text. However, these questionnaires cannot convey enough emotion or realism for the test to be effective in recognizing early stages of bvFTD. We created Tommy's Quest, a serious game to support bvFTD detection. Based on the Theory of Mind, the game gently leads players to consider what the in-game characters are thinking, as this is often challenging for people with bvFTD. Tommy's Quest gives players an immersive feeling while answering the same type of questions as in the questionnaires currently used. However, the questions in the game are incorporated into a story which makes them less obvious. Moreover, the scenarios feel more real because they feature characters with emotions. The game generates a report based on the answers and choices of the player, to help researchers in their bvFTD diagnosis. An upcoming clinical study will be instrumental in assessing the potential of Tommy's Quest to help clinicians improve the diagnosis of bvFTD.

**Keywords:** Serious games · Interactive narrative · Dialogue-based games · Behavioural variant frontotemporal dementia · Faux pas

## 1 Introduction

Behavioural variant frontotemporal dementia (bvFTD) is one of the leading cognitive disorders caused by neurodegeneration, in patients under 65 years of age. This cognitive disorder progressively impairs specific cognitive processes, and changes a patients' behaviour, social conduct and emotional processing, without them recognizing that their response to a social interaction is inappropriate. Diagnosis of this disorder is currently complex, consisting of an extensive trajectory of cognitive functions, history taking, clinical observations and the tracking of behavioural and psychological symptoms over extended periods [10]. An important part of this testing trajectory is the measurement of patients' Theory of Mind (ToM) abilities, to infer the mental state of others. ToM abilities are one of the most important markers of bvFTD, as they are the first to regress.


L. Holloway-Attaway and J. T. Murray (Eds.): ICIDS 2023, LNCS 14384, pp. 137–145, 2023.
https://doi.org/10.1007/978-3-031-47658-7_12

Currently, ToM abilities are tested by means of paper surveys taken under the guidance of a clinician, but these are less than ideal for accurate diagnosis, as they lack audio-visual elements and immersiveness. Game technologies can likely create new opportunities for clinical neuropsychology, integrating both elements [10].

We created Tommy's Quest, a serious game aimed at empowering neuropsychology researchers in the early diagnosis of patients who are assumed to have bvFTD. This is achieved by having the patients play through an interactive narrative with scenarios that portray typical everyday social situations. The players' responses to in-game questions are aggregated in a report, to aid researchers in their diagnosis.

## 2 Related Work

We describe related work on bvFTD and ToM. Furthermore, we briefly describe other games somehow based on ToM.

### 2.1 Theory of Mind

Theory of Mind (ToM) is the ability to impute mental states to others (encompassing many areas such as beliefs, desires, knowledge, emotions and intent) [12]. Originally coined in 1978 by Premack and Woodruff in order to research whether chimpanzees possess this ability, the term later gained traction in the field of developmental psychology when it was shown that most children under the age of five lack this ability, and is therefore developed later in life [16]. Further research also proved this ability to be lacking in individuals with certain disorders, such as autism spectrum disorder (ASD) [2], schizophrenia [14] and clinical depression [15]. Among bvFTD patients, abilities related to ToM are often impaired [11,13].

Humans with ToM (abilities) make use of three underlying mechanisms in order to infer the mental states of others [3]: *inferring actions of others*, *shared-world knowledge* and *perceiving social cues*. The first mechanism is used in order to perform false belief tasks, such as the Sally-Anne test [2] and is not necessarily lacking in bvFTD patients. However, the other two are mechanisms in which bvFTD patients are deficient.

*Shared-world knowledge* is tested by means of story-driven tasks testing intent, emotion and social awareness. Stories often involve an interaction between two or more people, in which a situation is created that is slightly out of the ordinary. For instance, stories can contain one party telling a (white) lie, being ironic, telling a joke or misreading a social situation [9]. These stories are called *faux-pas* stories and are currently used to diagnose the ToM of bvFTD patients via a questionnaire [6,8].

bvFTD patients usually also lack in *perceiving social cues*. Research into this ToM mechanism is characterised by participants performing tasks such as emotional recognition of others, or gaze detection [11]. Currently, tests like these are not used for the diagnosis of bvFTD patients, because they are more difficult to employ. However, current faux-pas (paper) tests for diagnosis mostly lack visual or audio elements. Patients who are in the early stages of bvFTD will not be lacking severely in ToM-like abilities and will therefore often be able to perform sufficiently in these pen-and-paper tests. We pose that a game-like setting is able to more accurately convey the complexities and subtleties of social interactions.

### 2.2 Theory of Mind in Games

Recognizing complexities and subtleties in social interactions requires ToM. There exist games that also require ToM to play optimally which are mostly entertainment games. One example of these games is *Hanabi*. *Hanabi* is a cooperative card game where players cannot see their own cards but only the ones from other players. By giving clues to others about their cards, the players are tasked to play their cards in a certain order. However, since the clues that are allowed do not cover the full information about the cards, ToM is needed to attain the necessary knowledge to win the game [1]. Players can do certain actions or intentionally not give certain clues which gives information in itself. So, the players should consider what others are thinking to get the most successful outcome. Because of this, *Hanabi* is a model environment for the development of artificial intelligence that possesses ToM-like abilities, for instance, using reinforcement learning [4,7].

Other examples of entertainment games centred around ToM are the games *Among Us* and *Town of Salem*. In these games, one or multiple traitors exist among the players and the non-traitors have to identify the players who are traitors. All players can perform actions and come together in social interactions. For players (traitors or non-traitors) to succeed, they will have to use ToM to either pick out suspicious players or blend in successfully.

### 2.3 Serious Games for Diagnosing Neurodegenerative Disorders

To the best of our knowledge, there have been no games proposed to aid in the diagnosis of bvFTD. However, there are serious games that aid in the diagnosis of other neurodegenerative disorders, e.g. collecting player's data implicitly. A good example of such a game is *Sea Hero Quest* [5], which aims at identifying Alzheimer's disease by looking at the spatial navigation of the players. The collected data in this game, logging the time and distance taken to navigate through the levels, is only visible to the researchers.

## 3 Game Design

Our design philosophy revolves around three core concepts: *realism*, *subtlety* and *simplicity*. We argue that, by adhering to these key concepts, the main goal of

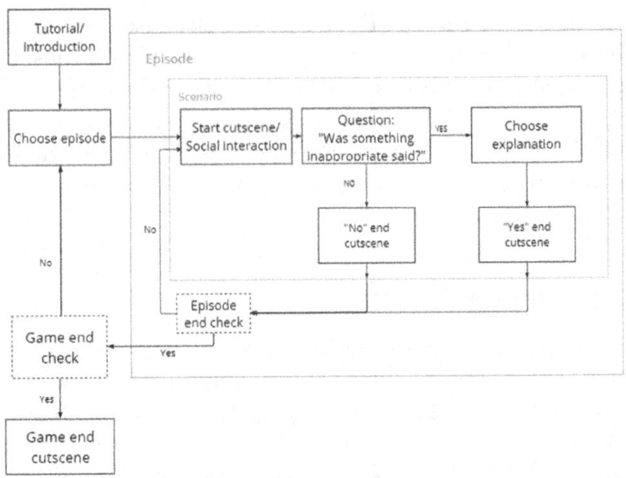


**Fig. 1.** The game loop

Tommy's Quest can be achieved: aid clinicians assess whether the player shows signs of bvFTD through faux-pas scenarios.

*Realism* refers to the scenarios in the storyline, which resemble everyday situations. In addition, the characters in Tommy's Quest are also realistic, resembling normal humans with different emotions, postures and facial expressions.

The core concept of *subtlety* mainly concerns how the faux-pas situations are incorporated and what the role of the player is. For the player of Tommy's Quest, the scenarios do not have the main focus: they are just present, providing the game setting that subtly exposes the player to each faux-pas situation. Regarding the player's role, the faux pas is never directly aimed at the player, as observing situations between two other actors is necessary to test ToM. However, the player is still engaged with the game, assuming an observing role.

Finally, *simplicity* leads Tommy's Quest to have as few distractions from the main goal as possible: the player is not burdened with complex irrelevant cognitive tasks. This also applies to the game mechanics and storyline, which are both kept simple to make Tommy's Quest accessible for all players.

### 3.1 Game Loop

The game loop of Tommy's Quest (see Fig. 1) consists of an introduction, a middle section containing several episodes, and finally the game ending. In the introduction (see Fig. 2a), the player is introduced to the main character, Tommy, and the storyline. Also, the mechanics of clicking through the dialogue and choosing answers is introduced to the player.

After the introduction, the game enters the main game loop where the player can choose a location (episode) to go to. At this location, the player plays through

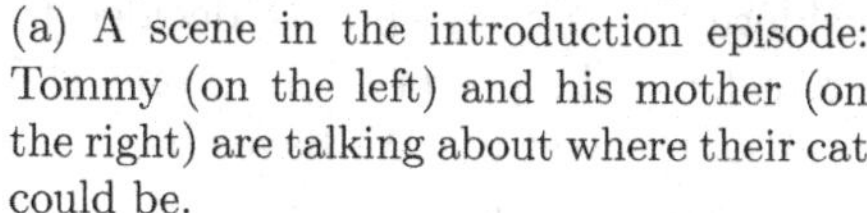

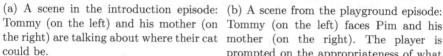

(a) A scene in the introduction episode: Tommy (on the left) and his mother (on the right) are talking about where their cat could be.

(b) A scene from the playground episode: Tommy (on the left) faces Pim and his mother (on the right). The player is prompted on the appropriateness of what she just said. Either answer leads to a different scene.

**Fig. 2.** In-game footage of example scenarios.

multiple scenarios. During each scenario, the player is presented with a short dialogue following the storyline and is asked a couple of multiple-choice questions. The answers chosen cause the player to go to a different location or scenario.

After a few scenarios, the player is done with the episode and can choose to go to one of the remaining locations. When all locations have been visited, the player is taken to the final episode, where the story finishes and the last few questions are asked. The two dashed-line boxes in Fig. 1 represent control checks run in the background, and they are transparent to the player.

### 3.2 Story

In Tommy's Quest, the player follows an intriguing story. The story revolves around a boy named Tommy, who has lost his cat. In order to find his cat, Tommy goes on an adventure around the neighbourhood. During this adventure, he interacts with other people in order to find his cat. The locations where Tommy goes are the local supermarket, a playground at the nearby park, the school, and Tommy's neighbours. These locations have been chosen as they are common locations and most recognizable in everyday life. This allows the game to feel more natural and closer to everyday life. At the end of the story, Tommy finds his cat, creating a sense of happiness and accomplishment for the player.

The story is not fully linear as the player can choose where Tommy goes during the game. These decisions lead to slightly different scenarios, but these will always lead to some anchor points that are played no matter what the player chooses. This way, the player has a sense of freedom of choice in a controlled manner. Also, the player always finds the cat at the end of the game. In other words, the player always gets to the same "happy ending", regardless of the answers given during gameplay, although with a somewhat different playthrough than that of another player.

The story in general is kept very shallow and simplistic by design, as the target audience for Tommy's Quest consists of people with a potential early-stage dementia. Therefore, players are not expected to remember a complex storyline in order to play the game. However, players are expected to remember details within each scenario. For this reason, game episodes can thus also be played in any order as they are designed to be independent of each other.

In Tommy's Quest, the player is immersed but is not a protagonist of in-game conversations. The player can thus observe the (faux-pas) scenarios and reflect on them without active participation. Considering this role, we have decided to use a main character, Tommy, that is different from the player of the game: the player will follow Tommy as he progresses through the story. We have chosen to approach the visual perspective of this game in this manner in order to consolidate two different challenges. On the one hand, the player assesses ToM-related situations between two different actors (none of them being the player). On the other hand, in order to make the game enjoyable and easy to follow for the player, the need arises for a consistent story in between different scenes, that at the same time is suitably shallow in scope to be easy to understand. By following a main character, every scene can be centred around this character, thus allowing for a consistent and progressive storyline.

### 3.3 Core Game Mechanics

To be able to play through the story, simple point-and-click mechanics were deemed the most suitable. Given our target audience's age range, between 18 and 65 with an emphasis on people aged over 40, it is fair to assume that the target audience possibly has limited gaming experience but at least knows how to operate a computer mouse. Thus no familiarity with keyboard or game controller inputs is assumed. For our purposes, the smaller and simpler the set of mechanics is, the better. Otherwise, players might end up focusing on understanding and learning complicated mechanics, rather than on the actual game.

To progress the story, the player is able to go from one scenario to another. Therefore, a set of navigation mechanics is required. Since no game experience is to be expected, this navigation is simple. Additionally, the player cannot deviate from the main storyline, hence their in-game freedom with regard to navigation is limited. Allowing players to wander around would likely introduce distractions and hamper the game's diagnosis goal. Exploring an open world is thus not an option. We found the most suitable option for navigation in Tommy's Quest is to click buttons to proceed in the game. When prompted with a multiple-choice question, options corresponding to each answer are shown; the story will not progress until the player has input a decision, as illustrated for example in Fig. 2b. During the dialogues, the player controls the pace by clicking to continue the dialogue. Clear prompts are displayed to indicate that the player can continue once they read the subtitles and are ready to move on.

Another game mechanic needed is the ability for the player to provide answers during and after observing scenarios. For instance, when the player is asked whether someone in the current scenario said something inappropriate, the player can choose either 'yes' or 'no'. Each option has some context of what the consequence of choosing that option will be, as illustrated in Fig. 2b. The selected answer leads the player to a different episode or scenario. Furthermore, upon a 'yes' answer, the player is asked to further explain their choice, by means of a multiple-choice question. The answers offered generally consist of (i) the correct option, (ii) an option that is sensible but not the intended answer, and (iii) one or more options that just do not make much sense. Only once an answer has been given, can the game continue.

Multiple choice has been selected for the player's explanation, as opposed to asking open questions such as done in the current pen-and-paper tests, for three main reasons: (i) requiring players' explanations for the diagnosis through open questions would break up the game flow too much; (ii) more importantly, given the constraints of the target audience, multiple choice is better suited to the diagnosis purposes, as it keeps the game mechanics simpler; we found that typing an answer to an open question would be too complicated and distracting for some; (iii) multiple-choice questions streamline diagnosis automation, since the answers do not have to be processed but rather just stored as is. So multiple choice keeps a natural game flow and allows for clear and easy diagnosis. A possible downside to multiple choice questions could be that none of the options offered corresponds exactly with the explanation that the player might come up with. However, this is mitigated by the diversity of options made available, covering sensible explanations, with which most of the players can identify with.

From a narrative perspective, the game mechanics is guiding the player through the story without judging them, thus ensuring, in a controlled fashion, that the player provides the data the researchers want to collect. Therefore, Tommy's Quest players are never punished, regardless of the answers they give.

### 3.4 Scores

With the player's answers, a score is calculated indicating how well the player masters ToM. Presently, a player can score a maximum of 18 points in total: six, for correctly identifying all non-faux-pas scenarios; the second six, for correctly identifying all faux-pas scenarios; and the final six points, for 'correctly explaining' why the faux-pas scenario is a faux pas (by choosing the correct multiple-choice option). This final score and the points per scenario are made available to the clinician, in a session log file.

## 4 Conclusion

Pen-and-paper tests currently used to assess whether a person shows signs of bvFTD, lack realism and immersion. This strongly reduces their accuracy and effectiveness. We have created Tommy's Quest, a serious game prototype that aids clinicians with this assessment. This serious game implements a novel combination of everyday scenarios and convincing visual and auditory elements.

Through a careful blend of simplicity, subtlety and realism, we have incorporated a variety of faux-pas scenarios immersed in everyday situations, kept the mechanics simple and held up the enjoyability to an acceptable extent. By numerous informal playtest sessions, Tommy's Quest was well received by (healthy) participants, who found its mechanics and controls simple to grasp, and its story, immersive and appealing.

A thorough clinical evaluation of Tommy's Quest is presently being designed, with the goal of evaluating the extent to which the game improves upon current pen-and-paper questionnaires. After ethical approval of the protocol, this assessment will be performed with potential bvFTD patients, under the guidance of expert clinicians, and its results will be presented in an upcoming publication and suitable venue. Nevertheless, the intense involvement and the expert advice of neuropsychologists throughout this project make us confident in the potential of Tommy's Quest in improving the diagnosis of bvFTD.

**Acknowledgments.** We thank Jackie Poos of the Erasmus University Medical Center for her support and guidance throughout this project.

## References

1. Bard, N.: The Hanabi challenge: a new frontier for AI research. Artif. Intell. **280**, 103216 (2020)
2. Baron-Cohen, S., Leslie, A.M., Frith, U.: Does the autistic child have a "theory of mind"? Cognition **21**(1), 37–46 (1985)
3. Byom, L.J., Mutlu, B.: Theory of mind: mechanisms, methods, and new directions. Front. Hum. Neurosci. **7**, 413 (2013)
4. Canaan, R., Gao, X., Chung, Y., Togelius, J., Nealen, A., Menzel, S.: Evaluating RL agents in Hanabi with unseen partners. In: AAAI 2020 Reinforcement Learning in Games Workshop (2020)
5. Coughlan, G., Coutrot, A., Khondoker, M., Minihane, A.M., Spiers, H., Hornberger, M.: Toward personalized cognitive diagnostics of at-genetic-risk Alzheimer's disease. Proc. Natl. Acad. Sci. **116**(19), 9285–9292 (2019)
6. Delbeuck, X., Pollet, M., Pasquier, F., Bombois, S., Moroni, C.: The clinical value of the faux pas test for diagnosing behavioral-variant frontotemporal dementia. J. Geriatr. Psychiatry Neurol. **35**(1), 62–65 (2022)
7. Fuchs, A., Walton, M., Chadwick, T., Lange, D.: Theory of mind for deep reinforcement learning in Hanabi. In: 33rd Conference on Neural Information Processing Systems (NeurIPS 2019) (2019). https://arxiv.org/abs/2101.09328
8. Giovagnoli, A.R., Bell, B., Erbetta, A., Paterlini, C., Bugiani, O.: Analyzing theory of mind impairment in patients with behavioral variant frontotemporal dementia. Neurol. Sci. **40**(9), 1893–1900 (2019)
9. Happé, F.G.: An advanced test of theory of mind: understanding of story characters' thoughts and feelings by able autistic, mentally handicapped, and normal children and adults. J. Autism Dev. Disord. **24**(2), 129–154 (1994)
10. Johnen, A., Bertoux, M.: Psychological and cognitive markers of behavioral variant frontotemporal dementia-a clinical neuropsychologist's view on diagnostic criteria and beyond. Front. Neurol. **10**, 594 (2019)

11. McDonald, S., Bornhofen, C., Shum, D., Long, E., Saunders, C., Neulinger, K.: Reliability and validity of the awareness of social inference test (tasit): a clinical test of social perception. Disabil. Rehabil. **28**(24), 1529–1542 (2006)
12. Premack, D., Woodruff, G.: Does the chimpanzee have a theory of mind? Behav. Brain Sci. **1**(4), 515–526 (1978)
13. Shany-Ur, T., et al.: Comprehension of insincere communication in neurodegenerative disease: lies, sarcasm, and theory of mind. Cortex **48**(10), 1329–1341 (2012)
14. Sprong, M., Schothorst, P., Vos, E., Hox, J., Van Engeland, H.: Theory of mind in schizophrenia: meta-analysis. Br. J. Psychiatry **191**(1), 5–13 (2007)
15. Wang, Y.G., Wang, Y.Q., Chen, S.I., Zhu, C.Y., Wang, K.: Theory of mind disability in major depression with or without psychotic symptoms: a componential view. Psychiatry Res. **161**(2), 153–161 (2008)
16. Wimmer, H., Perner, J.: Beliefs about beliefs: representation and constraining function of wrong beliefs in young children's understanding of deception. Cognition **13**(1), 103–128 (1983)

# Towards Procedural Generation of Narrative Puzzles for Open World Games

Sam Davern(✉) and Mads Haahr

Trinity College Dublin, University of Dublin, Dublin, Ireland
{daverns,haahrm}@tcd.ie

**Abstract.** Story Puzzle Heuristics for Interactive Narrative eXperiences (SPHINX) was developed as a system for generating narrative puzzles in adventure games. While SPHINX is capable of generating narrative puzzles for narrative games with a progressive structure, it cannot be applied to genres that adopt a progressive narrative structure with emergent components like open world video games. In this paper, we present the adaptations we will make to SPHINX to allow it to generate narrative puzzles in open world games that can act as optional side content. We argue that this can be achieved by creating a large database of puzzle items, actions, rules and goals; by altering when SPHINX generates puzzles; and by creating new item properties that remedy potential design issues that may arise. Some design implications are considered and avenues for further work are put forward.

**Keywords:** Procedural content generation · Puzzles · Open world · Video games · Interactive narrative · Authoring tools

## 1 Introduction

Story Puzzle Heuristics for Interactive Narrative eXperiences (SPHINX) was developed by de Kegel and Haahr [7] as a system for generating narrative puzzles in adventure games and as an alternative to other narrative puzzle generators such as the Puzzle Dice system [9]. It was then implemented in the short 2D point-and-click adventure game *Honey, I'm Home* by Morgan and Haahr [12] where players progressed through a linear sequence of areas by completing the narrative puzzle associated with each area. While this iteration of SPHINX increases the replayability of *Honey, I'm Home*, it does not allow players to complete narrative puzzles in an emergent way, as is often the case in popular open-world video games like *Elden Ring*, *The Legend of Zelda: Tears of the Kingdom*, and *The Witcher 3: Wild Hunt* where players can choose whether to complete puzzles and choose the order in which these puzzles are completed. We aim to build upon this first iteration of SPHINX, from here referred to as 'SPHINX 1' such that not only can it be applied to open world games but that it will allow for the presentation of emergent side narrative content in narrative progression games too [11].


L. Holloway-Attaway and J. T. Murray (Eds.): ICIDS 2023, LNCS 14384, pp. 146–154, 2023.
https://doi.org/10.1007/978-3-031-47658-7_13

## 2 Related Work

Work on narrative puzzle generation and, more broadly, quest generation describes novel systems that fulfil a similar purpose to SPHINX. For instance, the Puzzle-Dice system [9] adopts a similar approach to SPHINX in that it requires designers to create a database of items but only has a limited set of relationships that can exist between items. Work on using genetic algorithms and automated planning for quest generation [7] takes an interesting approach of assigning 'narrative tension' values to particular puzzle actions and uses these values to map generated puzzles to a three-act structure. The three-act structure begins with a tension of 0 that gradually increase until the resolution of the quest, where it returns quickly to 0. However, quests and narrative puzzles can often be quite short, making it difficult to evaluate how effectively they increase and decrease tension.

Ammanabrolu and colleagues [2] use Markov chains and neural language models to generate quests in text based adventure games; in their first generator, the probabilities of puzzle items following each other in a puzzle sequence are mapped on a Markov chain while in the second generator uses a neural language to generate a quest title, components and instructions. Regarding their first generator, the onus is on designers to decide how to weigh the probabilities between puzzle items using only domain knowledge which can be imprecise and difficult to tune. In the case of their second generator, the neural language model does not output puzzles in a format that could be used to instantiate puzzles in a non-text based game. A prototype generator developed by Doran and Parberry [8] has similar issues around compatibility with games that use 2D or 3D graphics. More recently, work has been conducted on incorporating generated pre-trained transformer (GPT) models into quest generation with authors stating that quests could often lack coherence [1] and varied widely in quality [17]. While both of the cited examples note that future GPT models may yield better results, limits user input as developers do not have the ability to alter the language model to better fit their project.

## 3 SPHINX 1

The SPHINX 1 [7] framework centers on an algorithm based on an extended context-free grammar that generates narrative puzzles from three main elements: items, rules, and areas. Items are game objects with specific types and properties, rules dictate how items and actions interact to result in a particular outcome, and areas represent individual sections of the game that each have an associated goal that must be achieved to reach the next area. Items can have string and bool properties that describe the function or purpose of an item, a descriptive string, a prefab and the option to set a specific spawn point. Puzzles are generated sequentially per area, working backwards from the area's associated goal to connect a chain of rules into a puzzle 'tree'. Rules are formatted using the following structure, starting from the goal on the left (Fig. 1):

$$itemType[properties_{0...n}]_{1...n} ::= action\ itemType[properties_{0...n}]_{1...n} \quad (1)$$

## 4 SPHINX 2

To allow for narrative puzzles to be presented to players in a dynamic and non-linear fashion in an open world game, we propose several key changes that we will make to SPHINX 1. SPHINX 1 was created by De Kegel and Haahr [7] in Unity and our update to this system will continue to use Unity (Fig. 2).

### 4.1 Puzzle Database

We aim to manually create a large database of items and rules that can map the relationships between many items and actions that are common across a wide array of open world games. Morgan and Haahr [12] implemented SPHINX 1 in a the adventure game *Honey, I'm Home*. A database of 60 items, 87 rules, and 4 areas (each of which have at least one pre-assigned goal) was created specifically for this game. This database is not only small but also has limited to no utility for use in other games. Should a designer wish to use SPHINX in their game, they would need to create the entire database of rules and items themselves, significantly increasing development time and costs. It is for this reason that we intend to include a large and comprehensive database of items, actions, goals and rules based on items, actions and goals that are commonly found in open world games in a variety of genres. Doing so creates a reusable library that designers can pull from and edit as they see fit. Naturally, games will still require bespoke items and rules that can only be used in a particular game but having a large database to work from affords designers the opportunity to spend more time on these items and rules without having to create ones that appear in many games already. This approach balances a focus on user input with the time and cost saving affordances of the database. For example, items in the base SPHINX database could include Box and Cat which could then be used in the rule:

$$Box[contains : Cat] :: = PutIn\ Cat\ Box \tag{2}$$

SPHINX 1 generates puzzles on a per-area basis where a form of backwards substitution creates a puzzle tree from a/the goal associated with an area. Each tree typically has at least two potential paths to the goal that the generator randomly picks from. By creating a limited but bespoke database of puzzle elements for a specific area, the onus is on the designers to essentially create a space of possible puzzles from which the generator chooses a canonical solution randomly for the current playthrough. SPHINX 1 includes the ability to increase the space of possible puzzle solutions by adding more items and rules, but doing so on a per-game basis is both costly and time consuming for designers. Not only will having a large reusable library of items and rules reduce workload and cost, but it will also drastically increase the number and complexity of puzzles that SPHINX 2 can generate.

The purpose of SPHINX 2 in an open world game is not to increase replayability as is the case with *Honey, I'm Home*, but to continually add more optional, emergent side narrative content for the player to engage with in a persistent world and to encourage exploration. In *Honey, I'm Home*, the world is essentially 'reset' at the beginning of each playthrough; items, characters and scenarios can be added and removed without impacting the narrative coherence of the game world. The advantage of each goal/area having a single canonical solution per playthrough in this case is that it is much easier to vary solutions for each playthrough without using up too many items in the database and ensuring that the same solution is less likely to be used in subsequent playthroughs. In contrast, using SPHINX in an open world game with a persistent world requires that many items, characters and locations remain consistent throughout a single playthrough to maintain narrative coherence. We do intend to include the provision for puzzle elements that are not constantly present in the world by allowing designers to associate a plot contrivance with an item in the form of dialogue or a description. However, doing this for every potential puzzle element, as would be required in SPHINX 1, reduces the credibility of the world and can hinder player immersion and should therefore be employed as sparingly as possible. Drastically increasing the size of the database alongside having puzzle elements present in the world be consistent throughout a playthrough allows the generator to create multiple canonical solutions to each puzzle, affording players a greater level of autonomy in how they approach solving them.

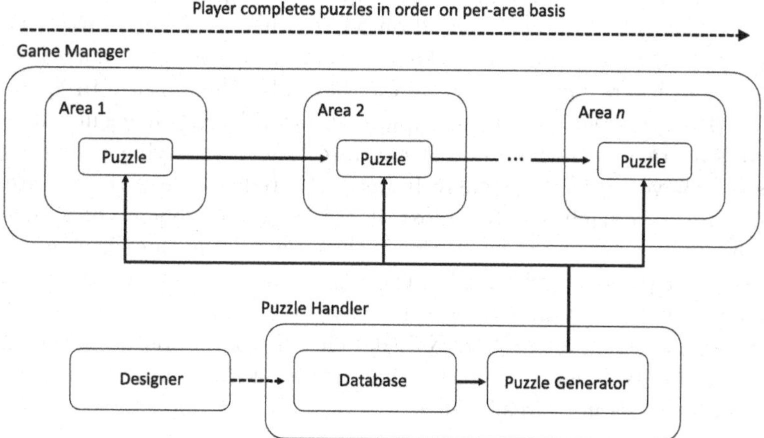


**Fig. 1.** Architecture of SPHINX 1 puzzle generation. The arrows point in the direction of the output from each component in the system. Solid arrows represent the direction of output within the system while dashed arrows represent input from outside the system.

### 4.2 Puzzle Generation

Secondly, we want to change the way in which SPHINX generates and instantiates puzzles such that it is no longer reliant on generating puzzles on a per-area basis. In *Honey, I'm Home*, progression to the next area (and by extension, progression through the narrative) is contingent on solving the current area's puzzle. In open world games, players can often explore most or all of the world from the beginning of the game with few barriers to progression. Instead of generating puzzles per area like SPHINX 1, we propose that SPHINX 2 will generate puzzles at run-time at set initiation points placed around the map by the designers. There will be a maximum number of active puzzles at one time, and they will be instantiated outside a set radius from the player character's location. Limiting the number of active puzzles prevents players from becoming overwhelmed and prevents the generator from endlessly generating puzzles while the player is engaging in another part of the game. Similarly, instantiating puzzles outside a particular radius from the player character, ideally outside of the player/camera's line of sight, allows necessary non-player characters (NPCs) or items to be instantiated at initiation points without players noticing. This prevents ludonarrative dissonance and helps maintain players' immersion in the game. The exact number of active puzzles and distance from the player at which they will be instantiated can vary based on the game but we aim to find a guideline range through user testing.

To allow designers to control for intricacy, it will be possible to restrict SPHINX 2 to generating puzzles where there is a minimum number of degrees of separation from the goal, e.g., it finds the shortest possible chain of items or actions needed to reach a goal (based on what is in the player's inventory) and also ensures that at least one more chain of items or actions can be used to reach a goal, giving players some agency in how they solve the puzzles. In open world games, it is possible for players to explore the world at their leisure and while this grants a great deal of agency, it can also hinder satisfying puzzle solving. Players who have explored extensively and collected a wide variety of items in their inventory are likely to have most of, if not all components of a generated puzzle already in their inventory. If this is the case, solving the puzzle would just require manipulating the relevant items in the player's inventory. To combat this and to make exploration and traversal necessary for puzzle solving, we propose incorporating a system into SPHINX 2 that checks what items are in the player's inventory and only generates puzzles that require a minimum number of items that the player does not already have.

### 4.3 New Properties

We will add the *singleton* bool property as a special case property to denote bespoke items that can only have a single instance at any one time. This provision also makes it easier for designers to include 'key items' or unique items that are relevant to the narrative of a specific game. Items can have a 'Long Description' associated with them in SPHINX 1 that adds a level of optional detail, should players desire it. In addition to this we will also allow for this description to act as dialogue for NPCs, should it be necessary for players to obtain a particular item from an NPC. It will also be possible to associate NPC dialogue with goals and initiation points.

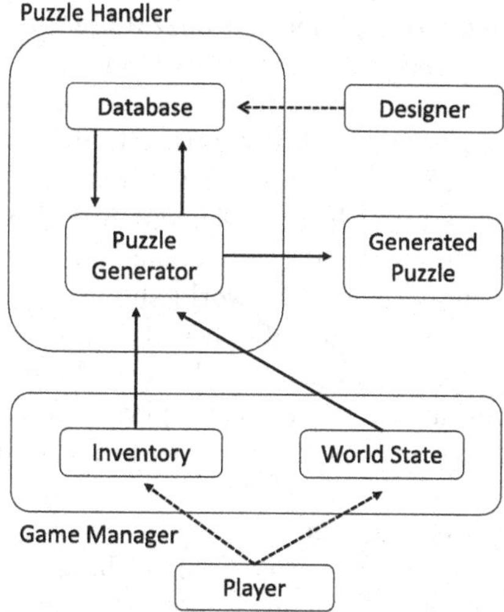


**Fig. 2.** Architecture of SPHINX 2 puzzle generation. The arrows point in the direction of the output from each component in the system. Solid arrows represent the direction of output within the system while dashed arrows represent input from outside the system.

### 4.4 Summary

In summary, the sequence of events in SPHINX 2 will be as follows:

1. The designer places puzzle initiation points throughout the game world.
2. The designer provides SPHINX with a list of rewards that can help players complete the main goal of the game.
3. The designer chooses what items and rules from the SPHINX database to include in their game and which to exclude, and adds any bespoke items or rules that can only be used in their game.
4. SPHINX, at runtime, checks what items are in the player's inventory and the current world state. The world state includes the number of active puzzles and initiation points within a pre-determined radius around the player.
5. If the conditions necessary to generate a puzzle are met, SPHINX picks a goal from its database, calculates a sequence of rules to reach a this goal and instantiates the puzzle at an initiation point.
6. The player follows the chain of rules to reach the goal and is rewarded.

## 5 Design Considerations

In addition to altering how SPHINX operates to allow for puzzle generation in open world games, the games themselves need to be designed with SPHINX in mind. One of the biggest hindrances to satisfying narrative puzzles in open world games is the amount of information navigation aids provide to players. For instance, if the components of a generated puzzle are located across the world, using maps or location markers that provide too much information make solving the puzzle trivial. If players are given the exact location of the item they need on a map, then they need only travel to it rather than intuit from the design of the open world where the item could be. For this reason, careful world design is important should a developer wish to implement SPHINX in their open world game. To ensure puzzles have narrative coherence and that their solutions can be intuited by players, the design of the world should lean on players' heuristic knowledge e.g., if a player needs to a loaf of bread as part of a puzzle, they should be able to buy one in a bakery; if they need a bucket, there should be one beside a well. Designing the world in such a way allows players to make educated guesses when solving puzzles and removes the need to provide too much information through navigation aids.

Once a system to procedurally generate narrative puzzles has been created, the challenge of making players want to complete these puzzles remains. Players must have significant intrinsic (where one is motivated by the satisfaction of completing a task) or extrinsic (where one is motivated by factors outside the task) motivation [15] to engage with puzzles that are ultimately optional. Andersen and colleagues [3] describe how secondary game objectives, like optional narrative puzzles, can harm players' experience of a game when these secondary objectives are not consistently useful in pursuing the main goal of the game. They also argue that 'secondary objectives that do not support the main goal require extensive testing to avoid negative consequences', significantly increasing workload and development costs. Therefore, rewarding players for completing optional narrative puzzles with game elements that facilitate them in completing the main goal of the game is very important should SPHINX 2 be implemented in an open world game with a progressive narrative structure. Rewards such as experience points for strengthening player characters, useful items like health potions, rare weapons or money, or optional world-building narrative content could all be used to encourage players to complete generated narrative puzzles.

It is also worth noting that meta-game rewards like achievements and trophies that do not serve the main goal of a game (such as those on Valve's Steam digital storefront and on Sony's Playstation and Microsoft's Xbox account services) have been shown to not only act as extrinsic rewards but to also act as intrinsic rewards that boost self-esteem and players' social status both online and offline [6]. In terms of applying this to generated narrative puzzles, it could be possible create achievements/trophies that can be earned by completing certain numbers of narrative puzzles in a single playthrough.

## 6 Conclusion and Further Work

The sections above have outlined the initial steps we will take to adapt SPHINX 1 for use in open world games with a progressive narrative structure. However, several user experience challenges remain when implementing the proposed SPHINX 2 in a game; namely players' interest in completing puzzles and the limited potential to create systems designed to aid players in completing these puzzles.

To address these user experience challenges, we intend to develop a gameplay demo of an open world game with SPHINX that incorporates the updates outlined above. Currently, we aim to create a simple world with a fantasy setting. Using this demo, we will conduct a series of user tests using player experience metrics like the *Game Experience Questionnaire* [10] or the *Ubisoft Player Experience Questionnaire* [4] to iteratively improve upon SPHINX in its new form.

Many games with human-authored puzzles have a wealth of online resources like walkthroughs and strategy guides that offer 'character information, back story, ...screen shots, ...hints and possibly "cheat codes" to help players advance quickly' [5] and solve difficult puzzles. Given the procedural nature of the puzzles SPHINX generates, creating walkthroughs of specific puzzles will not be possible. Therefore creating a 'narrative strategy guide' that compiles a game's SPHINX rules in plain language, reflecting the emergent nature of SPHINX puzzles [11], could be useful.

After the user experience challenges outlined above have been addressed, future work on SPHINX 2 could involve using player modelling data from scales such as the *Gamification User Types HEXAD Scale* [16] and *BrainHex* [13] to align narrative puzzles with player motivations. Similarly, SPHINX 2 could also be adapted to work in open worlds with procedurally generated terrain [14], similar to games like *Minecraft* and *No-Man's Sky*. Finally, we also aim to create an open-source SPHINX 2 Unity package that game developers can implement in their own games.

**Acknowledgments.** This work was conducted with the financial support of the Science Foundation Ireland (SFI) Centre for Research Training in Digitally-Enhanced Reality (d-real) under Grant No. 18/CRT/6224.

## References

1. Al-Nassar, S., Schaap, A., Zwart, M.V.D., Preuss, M., Gómez-Maureira, M.A.: QuestVille: procedural quest generation using NLP models. In: Proceedings of the 18th International Conference on the Foundations of Digital Games, pp. 1–4 (2023)
2. Ammanabrolu, P., Broniec, W., Mueller, A., Paul, J., Riedl, M.O.: Toward automated quest generation in text-adventure games. arXiv preprint arXiv:1909.06283 (2019)
3. Andersen, E., Liu, Y.E., Snider, R., Szeto, R., Cooper, S., Popović, Z.: On the harmfulness of secondary game objectives. In: Proceedings of the 6th International Conference on Foundations of Digital Games, pp. 30–37 (2011)
4. Azadvar, A., Canossa, A.: UPEQ: ubisoft perceived experience questionnaire: a self-determination evaluation tool for video games. In: Proceedings of the 13th International Conference on the Foundations of Digital Games, pp. 1–7 (2018)
5. Consalvo, M.: Zelda 64 and video game fans: a walkthrough of games, intertextuality, and narrative. Tele. New Media **4**(3), 321–334 (2003)
6. Cruz, C., Hanus, M.D., Fox, J.: The need to achieve: players' perceptions and uses of extrinsic meta-game reward systems for video game consoles. Comput. Hum. Behav. **71**, 516–524 (2017)

7. De Kegel, B., Haahr, M.: Towards procedural generation of narrative puzzles for adventure games. In: Cardona-Rivera, R.E., Sullivan, A., Young, R.M. (eds.) ICIDS 2019. LNCS, vol. 11869, pp. 241–249. Springer, Cham (2019). https://doi.org/10.1007/978-3-030-33894-7_25
8. Doran, J., Parberry, I.: A prototype quest generator based on a structural analysis of quests from four MMORPGS. In: Proceedings of the 2nd International Workshop on Procedural Content Generation in Games, pp. 1–8 (2011)
9. Fernández-Vara, C., Thomson, A.: Procedural generation of narrative puzzles in adventure games: the puzzle-dice system. In: Proceedings of the The Third Workshop on Procedural Content Generation in Games, pp. 1–6 (2012)
10. IJsselsteijn, W.A., De Kort, Y.A., Poels, K.: The game experience questionnaire (2013)
11. Juul, J.: Half-Real: Video Games Between Real Rules and Fictional Worlds. MIT press (2011)
12. Morgan, L., Haahr, M.: Honey, I'm Home: an adventure game with procedurally generated narrative puzzles. In: Bosser, A.-G., Millard, D.E., Hargood, C. (eds.) ICIDS 2020. LNCS, vol. 12497, pp. 335–338. Springer, Cham (2020). https://doi.org/10.1007/978-3-030-62516-0_30
13. Nacke, L.E., Bateman, C., Mandryk, R.L.: BrainHex: a neurobiological gamer typology survey. Entertainment Comput. **5**(1), 55–62 (2014)
14. Rose, T.J., Bakaoukas, A.G.: Algorithms and approaches for procedural terrain generation-a brief review of current techniques. In: 2016 8th International Conference on Games and Virtual Worlds for Serious Applications (VS-GAMES), pp. 1–2. IEEE (2016)
15. Ryan, R.M., Deci, E.L.: Intrinsic and extrinsic motivations: classic definitions and new directions. Contemp. Educ. Psychol. **25**(1), 54–67 (2000)
16. Tondello, G.F., Wehbe, R.R., Diamond, L., Busch, M., Marczewski, A., Nacke, L.E.: The gamification user types Hexad scale. In: Proceedings of the 2016 Annual Symposium on Computer-Human Interaction in Play, pp. 229–243 (2016)
17. Värtinen, S., Hämäläinen, P., Guckelsberger, C.: Generating role-playing game quests with GPT language models. IEEE Trans. Games, 1–12 (2022)

# Mind Stories: A Story Making Game - From Narrative Therapy to Interactive Narrative Therapy

Mirjam Palosaari Eladhari[1(✉)] and Hartmut Koenitz[2]

[1] Stockholm University, 106 91 Stockholm, Sweden
mirjam@dsv.su.se
[2] Södertörn University, Alfred Nobels allé 7, 141 89 Huddinge, Sweden
hartmut.koenitz@sh.se

**Abstract.** Narrative has been central to psychoanalysis from its inception. What has been explored less is the relationship between psychotherapy and interactive narrative. In particular, narrative therapy is a well-established practice in psychotherapy which shares central concerns with interactive narrative research and practice. In this paper, we explore the foundational role of narrative in psychotherapy and consider its interactive aspect. Then, we identify the overlap between interactive narratives and narrative therapy, and identify interactive narrative works which use this potential for therapeutic purposes. We also describe a concrete implementation, the board game Mind Stories, and introduce the concept of interactive narrative therapy.

**Keywords:** psychotherapy · narrative therapy · interactive narrative therapy · Mind Stories · story games · board games

## 1 Introduction

The use of interactive narratives for prosocial aims has been discussed before [11,30]. This includes applications in the field of health in general [17,22,28] and specifically in mental health [5,16]. In this paper, we discuss the concept of narrative therapy from the perspective of interactive narrative research, present the board game Mind Stories as a concrete exemplar of an 'interactive narrative for therapeutic purposes' (INTP) and introduce the concept of interactive narrative therapy. We are keenly aware that the topic of the conference is interactive digital storytelling, but we will argue for the relevance of both the design and the overarching concept in regard to both analog and digital interactive narratives and will consider digital examples throughout our paper.

### 1.1 Narrative and Therapy

Narratives have an important function for self-construction [25] and understanding of reality [6]. Equally, narrative plays an important role in psychotherapy,


L. Holloway-Attaway and J. T. Murray (Eds.): ICIDS 2023, LNCS 14384, pp. 155–167, 2023.
https://doi.org/10.1007/978-3-031-47658-7_14

whose origin with Sigmund Freud can be understood as a recognition of the therapeutic potential of narrative - put simply, Freud was convinced that the right narrative could heal patients. In that sense, psychoanalysis can be framed as the search for the 'healing narrative', as a form of interactive storytelling, in which the therapist guides the patient to a narrative that explains and ends the crisis. While subsequent developments in psychotherapy have de-emphasized the therapeutic potential of a single 'revelationary' narrative, the importance of narrative in general is widely recognized in psychology research and practice [1,2,20,21]. Narrative is still at the core of many therapeutic methods today, including contemporary variants of psychoanalysis and Cognitive Behavioral Therapy (CBT).

Indeed, narrative therapy is a well-established form of psychotherapy. In 1990, Michael White and David Epston published an influential volume, *Narrative means to therapeutic ends* [31], which is widely understood as the beginning of what is now referred to as Narrative Therapy. Alan Carr describes this approach as operationalizing Brunner's insight that narratives constitute reality and identity [6–8]. On this basis, as Carr explains, the therapeutic process becomes one of "re-authoring of personal narratives" with the ability to change "lives, problems, and identities" [10]. Carr further describes White's narrative therapy approach as comprised of the following steps:

- Adopt a collaborative co-authoring consultative position.
- Help clients view themselves as separate from their problems by externalizing the problem.
- Help clients pinpoint times in their lives when they were not oppressed by their problems by finding unique outcomes.
- Thicken clients descriptions of these unique outcomes by using landscape of action and landscape of consciousness questions.
- Link unique outcomes to other events in the past and extend the story into the future to form an alternative and preferred self-narrative in which the self is viewed as more powerful than the problem.
- Invite significant members of the persons social network to witness this new self-narrative.
- Document new knowledge and practices which support the new self-narrative using literary means.
- Let others who are trapped by similar oppressive narratives benefit from their new knowledge through bringing-it-back practices. [10]

What Carr describes here is a process of co-authoring a narrative where the therapist guides the client in a process in which they become the author of an improved version of their own 'life narrative'. This method has become popular in both psychotherapy practice and research. An edited collection of articles was published in 2004 as the "The Handbook of Narrative and Psychotherapy: Practice, theory and research" [2], there is a dedicated journal (International Journal of Narrative Therapy and Community Work), and a search on Google Scholar for the exact terms "narrative therapy" shows 1300 results for the year 2023 alone at the time of writing this article (August 2023). We can therefore describe Narrative Therapy (NT) as a thriving topic area in the broader field of psychotherapy.

### 1.2 Interactive Narrative and Therapy

From the perspective of interactive narrative research and practice, there is considerable overlap between the fields, including the understanding of narrative as malleable and dynamic [19,23], the emphasis on co-authorship [4,29], the client's empowered position as interactor/decision-maker [23] in their own narrative, a reflective position that considers both the narrative instantiated so far as well as the possibilities for interaction going forward (cf double/triple hermeneutic in the SPP model [18,27]), and finally the documentation of actions and consequences in the form of a narrative (cf. retellings [14] and subjective/objective product in the SPP model [18]).

Given these shared aspects, we see considerable potential for interactive narratives as tools for therapy and self-help, both in the form of Interactive Digital Narratives (IDNs) and Interactive Analog Narratives (IANs). IDNs are narratives realized in the digital computational medium, in which the interactor influences the progress and outcome. IANs share the role of the audience as interactor, but are realized with analog means, e.g. as a board game. When used in the service of therapy, we summarize them under the heading of 'interactive narrative for therapeutic purposes' (INTP). There is existing work in the ICIDS community which belongs to this category, for example the work by Brown and Chu [5] where patients can learn that they are in control of their own narrative and have the ability to change it. Another example is *Betwixt* [16], an IDN designed to teach mental resilience.

The authors will now demonstrate a concrete realization of the INTP potential by describing the board game Mind Stories.

## 2 Mind Stories Game

The Mind Stories game aims to help players by providing a safe space to recognize and address challenging situations and negative emotions. We often struggle to understand and cope with emotions, some of the most complex aspects in our lives. It can be difficult to express what burdens us, affects us negatively and weighs us down. Mind Stories provides tools to construct systemic representations of difficult emotions, situations and relationships, which are treated as 'shadows' within the play experience. The game enables players to express such 'shadows,' examine them together with others, and experiment with ways to address them.

Concretely, Mind Stories is a tabletop story game for 2–4 players. It is played in sessions, where each session revolves around one person's shadow, and takes about an hour. In the game, players unpack 'shadows' together. A shadow could for example be the fear of public speaking or the pain of exclusion. For each shadow, players define a scenario in which it appears, for example in a concrete situation at the workplace. The play is happening in three phases:

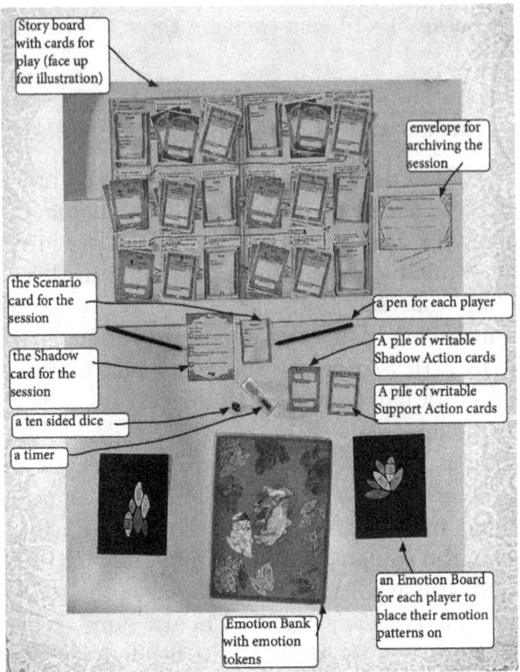


**Fig. 1.** Mind Stories Components at the beginning of a game session

1. **Set-up** of Shadows and Scenarios
2. **Playing** a session, where the Shadow acts towards the players, player support each other against it, and co-author events that push the story forward.
3. **Reflection**, by writing an epilogue, by reflecting on what could be useful to try in everyday life, and by giving other players tokens with personalised wishes and advice. A final act of reflection happens through archiving the personalized cards that represent the play session and are given to the person who defined the shadow.

### 2.1 Setup Phase

A session revolves around a particular shadow and the players' reactions to it. Figure 1 shows the components of the game at setup. In the beginning of game, each player defines a shadow's actions and utterances (See Fig. 3 and Fig. 2).

For each session, the group of players pick one of the players' shadows and imagine a scenario in which they face the shadow together. Players need to define the place, time and situation for the scenario as shown in Figs. 4 and 5.

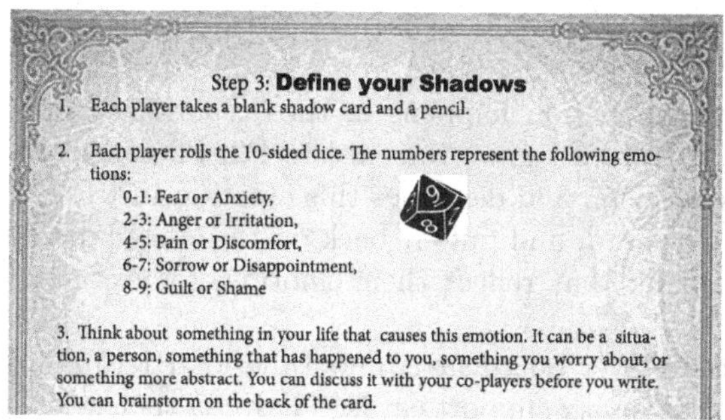


**Fig. 2.** Instruction for creating Shadow.

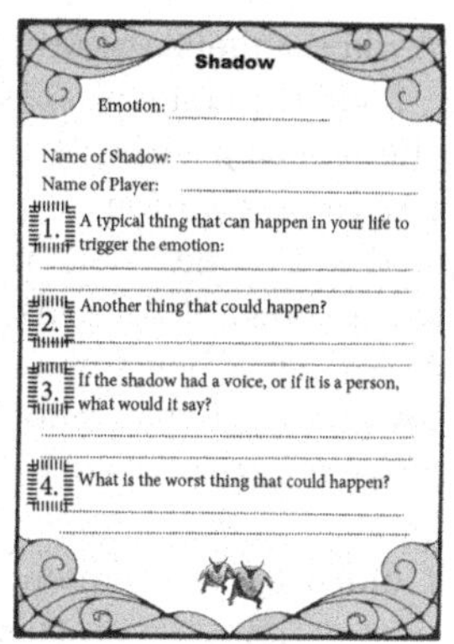


**Fig. 3.** Card for Shadow.

Step 4:
**Set Scenario**

1. Pick Shadow. Which players' Shadow will you play? If it doesn't matter, pick the Shadow of the youngest player.

2. Place. Together, think about an envionment that you are all familiar with where a scenario can happen where you "meet" the Shadow.
You could be on a trip toghether, it could at work, or at a social event or ceremony. If the Shadow was "born" in a certain situation you can use that, but magine that you and your co-players are in it together.

3. Time. The time can be in the past, or it could be something that could happen now.
You don't need to stay in the same place where the scenario starts - in your story you can go wherever your want.

Once you have decided on the place and the time - write it on your Scenario card. Do not worry about making it perfect. This is a starting point.

**Fig. 4.** Instruction for Scenario.

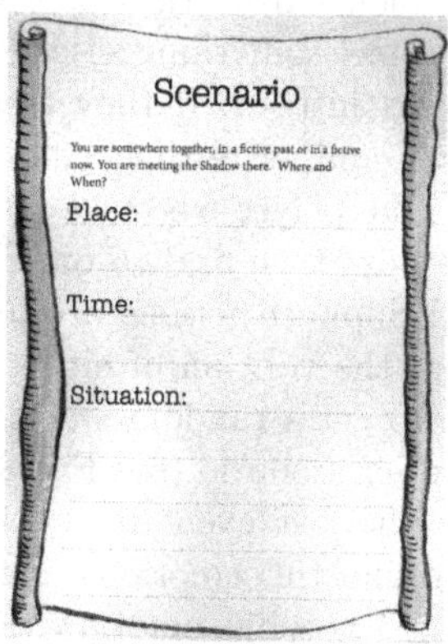


**Fig. 5.** Card for Scenario.

### 2.2 Play Phase

A story is created during play, guided by a story board that holds a sequence of cards to play (Fig. 9). These cards are the shadow's actions (see Fig. 6), players' support actions (see Fig. 7) and events in the story (see Fig. 8. Each player has an emotion board with tokens representing their feelings (Fig. 10). For each action that is directed toward a player, they reflect on their reaction, and pick a new emotion to add to their board - forming a colorful pattern representing their emotional state. By considering each other's reactions, players can experiment with different actions to learn to support each other better. They can also find new strategies for how to deal with shadows in real life.

A play sequence in Mind Stories with two players look like this: player 1 (P1), who made the shadow, picks up a shadow card from the story board. The action will be one that either P1 has written themselves at setup (ex. "a typical thing that triggers emotion x"), or it can be a shadow card from the deck (ex "guilt-tripped"). P1 then describes how this action happens in the scenario, as this action is directed towards player 2 (P2). P1 gives the card to P2. P2 considers how they feel when this happens to them, and describes this emotion to P1. P2 makes a note of that emotion on the card, and puts it back on the story board. P2 then takes a token from the bank that reflect their emotion, for example "guilt".

Guided by the sequence on the player board, it is now time for P1 to play support actions. To do this, P1 picks up six support cards. They can then select three of these to play. They can also choose to author their own support action, specific to the scenario. Let's assume that P1 picks the card "Express belief in co-players' ability". P1 tells P2 how they would express this, and makes a note on the card before giving the card to P2. P2 reads on the card that the intended effect of the card is to give them confidence. If that is indeed what "feels" appropriate, P2 notes this on the card, and takes an emotion token of confidence from the bank and adds it to the pattern on their emotion board. If they feel something else, for example joy or belonging, they take one of those tokens instead. If they feel something completely different, they take a blank token and write their emotion with their own words on it.

The player who was last targeted by the shadow will when be supported in the next turn and so on. This sequence is guided by the story board. Shadow- and Support actions are interspersed by events, things that just "happen", not from the volition of either players or the shadow. In the events, players roll a die to get a random emotion as a creative prompt for imagining what happens in their scenario (see Fig. 8).

The last event in a session is to write the "happy end". Together, players examine the emotion board of the player who defined the shadow (P1). P1 considers what emotion they wish to have more of, and tell the other players about it. The happy end event is then co-authored by all players with the purpose to entice this emotion.

### 2.3 Reflection Phase

The final phase of play is that of reflection. Players summarize their story in the form of a an epilogue. Before creating the epilogue, they look through the sequence of cards they have written on during play (see Fig. 11). In this phase they can also consider if some of the support actions they have defined themselves during play should go into the deck of support actions for general use. In this way, they can personalise their own copy of the Mind Stories game and also feed back knowledge gained during their play session - for example a support action created in a session could be helpful for someone else in a future session.

After writing the epilogue, players discuss what they have learned - what they want to remember and use in the future - how could they approach the "shadow"

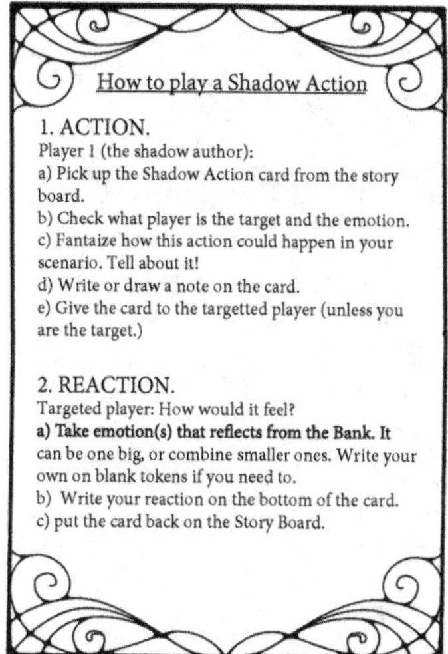

How to play a Shadow Action

1. ACTION.
Player 1 (the shadow author):
a) Pick up the Shadow Action card from the story board.
b) Check what player is the target and the emotion.
c) Fantaize how this action could happen in your scenario. Tell about it!
d) Write or draw a note on the card.
e) Give the card to the targetted player (unless you are the target.)

2. REACTION.
Targeted player: How would it feel?
**a) Take emotion(s) that reflects from the Bank. It** can be one big, or combine smaller ones. Write your own on blank tokens if you need to.
b) Write your reaction on the bottom of the card.
c) put the card back on the Story Board.

**Fig. 6.** Instruction for how to play a Shadow Action.

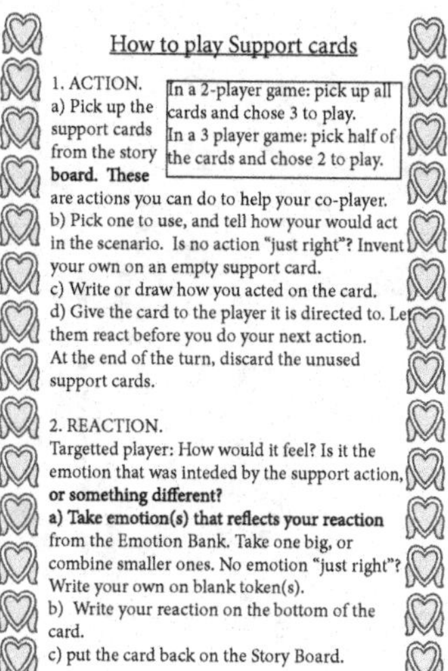

How to play Support cards

1. ACTION.
a) Pick up the support cards from the story **board. These** are actions you can do to help your co-player.

In a 2-player game: pick up all cards and chose 3 to play.
In a 3 player game: pick half of the cards and chose 2 to play.

b) Pick one to use, and tell how your would act in the scenario. Is no action "just right"? Invent your own on an empty support card.
c) Write or draw how you acted on the card.
d) Give the card to the player it is directed to. Let them react before you do your next action.
At the end of the turn, discard the unused support cards.

2. REACTION.
Targetted player: How would it feel? Is it the emotion that was inteded by the support action, **or something different?**
**a) Take emotion(s) that reflects your reaction** from the Emotion Bank. Take one big, or combine smaller ones. No emotion "just right"? Write your own on blank token(s).
b) Write your reaction on the bottom of the card.
c) put the card back on the Story Board.

**Fig. 7.** Instruction for how to play a Support Action.

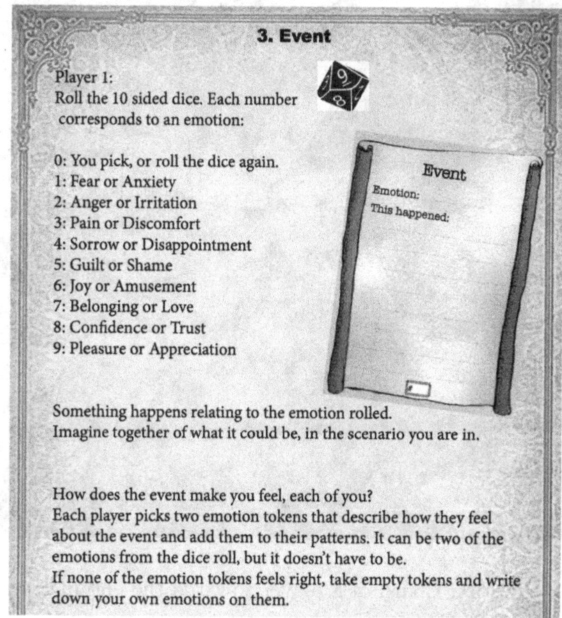

**3. Event**

Player 1:
Roll the 10 sided dice. Each number corresponds to an emotion:

0: You pick, or roll the dice again.
1: Fear or Anxiety
2: Anger or Irritation
3: Pain or Discomfort
4: Sorrow or Disappointment
5: Guilt or Shame
6: Joy or Amusement
7: Belonging or Love
8: Confidence or Trust
9: Pleasure or Appreciation



Something happens relating to the emotion rolled.
Imagine together of what it could be, in the scenario you are in.

How does the event make you feel, each of you?
Each player picks two emotion tokens that describe how they feel about the event and add them to their patterns. It can be two of the emotions from the dice roll, but it doesn't have to be.
If none of the emotion tokens feels right, take empty tokens and write down your own emotions on them.

**Fig. 8.** Instructions for co-authoring events

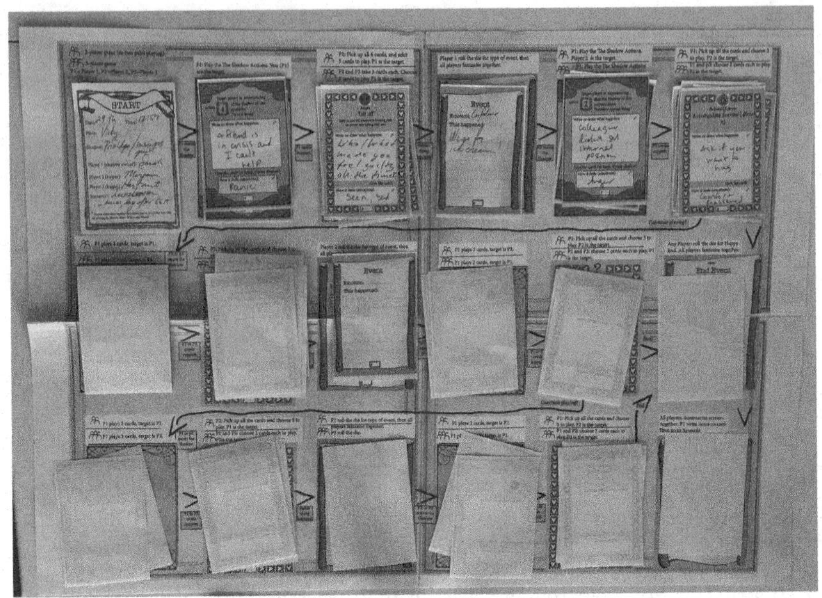


**Fig. 9.** Story Board during play

**Fig. 10.** Emotion Board of a player towards the end of a session

next time it appears in the everyday life? Then, players take a moment of silence to pick or write reward tokens for each other, considering what they wish for the other player or what they believe their co-player might need. Players keep these rewards as mementos of the session. The two tokens to the bottom left in Fig. 10 are examples.

The final action of the game is to archive the squence of cards played in an envelope and give to the player who has defined the shadow.

As the topics Mind Stories touches upon might be of sensitive personal nature, players are advised to be careful with sharing photos and telling others about the session. They should only share outside the play session with consent of the co-players. A benefit of the analogue format is that the play trace of a session can be kept private - the trace goes into a singular physical envelope rather than into a data cloud. The aim of this design choice is to enable players to verbalise issues that they might not otherwise feel comfortable to share.

**Fig. 11.** A sequence of cards from a play session.

## 2.4 Design Background and Motivations

The design of Mind Stories is inspired by what the designer (the first author) has learned from previous games they have made [13,15] and by other story games such as Microscope [26] and Fiasco [9]. The design is also informed by practicing therapists and psychoanalysts who have helped to play test the game. The choice of an analogue board game over a digital one was because a table-top framing is well suited for a game where people share their difficulties since it is happening in person, and in informal environments such as in homes. An earlier version of the game had a winning criteria: based on points, with the idea to exhaust the shadow's energy. Players used a resource-based mechanic gaining mental energy and using it to overcome the shadows together. However, this core mechanic seemed too far removed from the reality of actual emotional challenges. The current narrative-based version addresses this shortcoming.

Lessons learned from designing, play-testing, and playing the previous iteration have enabled the creation of the game described in this paper. Mind Stories is more focused on co-creative storytelling than on calculating how to achieve more desirable emotional states. Perhaps the most significant change is that Mind Stories focuses on players' actual emotional reactions rather than on numerical representations of emotions and associated game mechanics. This flexible system also solves the problem of the use of "basic" emotions in computational application. Research in the field of psychology that is often used in computational applications in the vein of affective computing [24] has identified a set of "basic" emotions that appeared to be common across cultures [12]. These findings come from observations of people's facial expressions. More recent research has found that even these supposedly "basic" emotions differ not only between cultures, but from group to group. We learn emotions as children, from those close to us [3]. The design of "Mind Stories" takes these findings into account by providing a set of emotions that has been proven to be useful in the designers' previous games, but most importantly by providing blank tokens for players to define their own emotions. This facilitates reflection on the player's actual emotions rather than on what they believe they are expected to feel.

## 3 Interactive Narrative Therapy

Adding the two strands followed in this paper, we see the advent of a new form of therapy which we term 'interactive narrative therapy.' This notion is based on the overlap between White and Epston's narrative therapy approach and central aspects of interactive narrative research, as well as the concreted realizations of the potential of 'interactive narrative for therapeutic purposes' (INTP) in previous works [5,16] and in Mind Stories.We define interactive narrative therapy as narrative therapy facilitated by IDN or IAN works and contrast it to narrative therapy in Fig. 12 (Table 1). While we do not propose that this approach can replace a human therapist, we see considerable potential for therapeutic progress through the engagement with such works. In addition, INTPs provide specific capabilities that can improve the therapeutic process. Initially, INTPs can aid a client to convey their own narrative with technical means such as writing and drawing prompts (digital or analog), natural language processing (NLP), text generation (e.g. via ChatGPT) or image generation (e.g. with stable diffusion). Then INTPs can make clients as interactors aware of their power to change the narrative through their own decisions. In addition, clients can try out different alternatives and revisit prior decisions through replay. Furthermore, INTPs can help identifying causal connections between choices and consequences. Finally, the resulting instantiated narrative object (digital/analog play trace) can be shared with significant members of the person's social network, preserved as an important memory object for the clients and be shared with other clients in similar situations. These qualities of interactive narrative therapy are already available in Mind Stories (see Fig. 12 (Table 1)). Future INTPs will be able to improve the implementation further and certainly will become even better tools for therapeutic purposes.

| Narrative Therapy | Interactive Narrative Therapy | Implementation in Mind Stories |
|---|---|---|
| Adopt a collaborative co-authoring consultative position. | The client as interactor co-authors their narrative experience with an IDN or IAN work. INTP help clients convey their own narratives with technical means (NLP, writing prompts/cards, drawing prompts/ cards, text generation and image generation) | Interactors are prompted to define individual challenges as 'shadows' and to co-author the scenarios they are explored in. |
| Help clients view themselves as separate from their problems by externalizing the problem. | The interactor position externalizes the problem. | Mind Stories externalize issues as 'shadows' and facilitates the exploration of ways to address them |
| Help clients pinpoint times in their lives when they were not oppressed by their problems by finding unique outcomes. | Prompts and survey questions help clients to pinpoint times in their lives when they were not oppressed by their problems and help in finding unique outcomes. | Interactors are prompted to create events and actions for each other that provide alternative outcomes for challenging situations. |
| Thicken clients descriptions of these unique outcomes by using landscape of action and landscape of consciousness questions. | Thicken clients' descriptions of these unique outcomes by using landscape of action and landscape of consciousness questions and transfer the results into the INTP. | Each action by a shadow or a co-player, and each event, helps flesh out the story with alternative perspectives. |
| Link unique outcomes to other events in the past and extend the story into the future to form an alternative and preferred self-narrative in which the self is viewed as more powerful than the problem. | Help clients link unique outcomes to other events in the past (e.g. by automatic key word generation and advanced search methods) and extend the story into the future using generative methods to form several alternatives and help select a preferred self-narrative in which the self is viewed as more powerful than the problem. | Mind Stories facilities the exploration of feelings created by actions and their accumulative consequences in three different ways. 1. Immediately in the actions and consequences of a game move, 2. in terms of emotions (manifest in the emotion board) and 3. In the overall progression and outcome (visible in the progression of the story board). |
| Invite significant members of the persons social network to witness this new self-narrative. | Invite significant members of the persons social network to witness this new self-narrative in the form of an instantiated INTP. | Significant members of the person's social network address issues in a systemic and playful way and witness the new self-narrative together while playing Mind Stories. |
| Document new knowledge and practices which support the new self-narrative using literary means. | Document new knowledge and practices which support the new self-narrative using technical means by identifying the actions that affected them. | By writing on the cards, and archiving the new knowledge after each completed play session, the new knowledge can be recalled by the interactor. |
| Let others who are trapped by similar oppressive narratives benefit from their new knowledge through bringing-it-back practices. | Let others who are trapped by similar oppressive narratives benefit from their new knowledge through bringing-it-back practices in the form of memories of successful approaches and replays. | New support cards created during play sessions are meant to be exchanged and thus can be used by other interactors in similar situations. |

**Fig. 12.** Table 1: Narrative Therapy [10] in comparison to Interactive Narrative Therapy and implementation in Mind Stories

## 4 Conclusion

In this paper, we have discussed the central role of narrative in psychotherapy and the specific overlap between White/Epston's narrative therapy approach and central aspects of interactive narrative research and practice. Furthermore, we discussed examples of IDN and IAN works which qualify as 'interactive narrative for therapeutic purposes' (INTP). Then, we have discussed the Mind Stories IAN board game as a concrete INTP exemplar in detail, both in terms of game play and in regard to the motivations guiding its design. On this basis we introduce the notion of 'interactive narrative therapy,' a therapeutic approach which applies interactive narratives to facilitate improved mental well-being. Mind Stories is an implementation of this approach and see considerable potential for interactive narrative therapy to improve personal mental health in the future. As a next step, we plan to conduct a full user study with Mind Stories to measure its effectiveness.

## References

1. Angus, L., Hardtke, K.: Narrative processes in psychotherapy. Can. Psychol. **35**(2), 190–203 (1994)
2. Angus, L., McLeod, J.: The Handbook of Narrative and Psychotherapy: Practice, Theory and Research. SAGE Publications Inc., Thousand Oaks (2004). https://doi.org/10.4135/9781412973496
3. Barrett, L.F.: The theory of constructed emotion: an active inference account of interoception and categorization. Soc. Cognit. Affect. Neurosci. **1**(12), 1–23 (2017)
4. Bolter, J.D.: Writing Space: The Computer, Hypertext, and the History of Writing. Lawrence Erlbaum Associates (1991)
5. Brown, S.A., Chu, S.L.: "You write your own story": design implications for an interactive narrative authoring tool to support reflection for mental health in college students. In: Mitchell, A., Vosmeer, M. (eds.) Interactive Storytelling: 14th International Conference on Interactive Digital Storytelling, ICIDS 2021, pp. 312–321. Springer, Cham (2021). https://doi.org/10.1007/978-3-030-92300-6_30
6. Bruner, J.: Life as narrative. Soc. Res. (1987). https://doi.org/10.2307/40970444
7. Bruner, J.: The narrative construction of reality. Crit. Inq. **18**(1), 1–21 (1991). https://doi.org/10.1086/448619
8. Bruner, J., Bruner, J.S.: Actual Minds. Possible Worlds. Harvard UP, Cambridge (1986)
9. Bully Pulpit Games: Fiasco. [analogue game] (2009)
10. Carr, A.: Michael White's narrative therapy. Contemp. Fam. Ther. **20**(4), 485–503 (1998)
11. Dubbelman, T., Roth, C., Koenitz, H.: Interactive digital narratives (IDN) for change. In: Rouse, R., Koenitz, H., Haahr, M. (eds.) ICIDS 2018. LNCS, vol. 11318, pp. 591–602. Springer, Cham (2018). https://doi.org/10.1007/978-3-030-04028-4_69
12. Ekman, P.: All emotions are basic. In: The Nature of Emotion. Oxford University Press (1994)
13. Eladhari, M.P.: Bleed in, bleed out - a design case in board game therapy. In: Proceedings of the 2018 DiGRA International Conference: The Game is the Message (DiGRA 2018), Turin (2018)

14. Eladhari, M.P.: Re-tellings: the fourth layer of narrative as an instrument for critique. In: Rouse, R., Koenitz, H., Haahr, M. (eds.) ICIDS 2018. LNCS, vol. 11318, pp. 65–78. Springer, Cham (2018). https://doi.org/10.1007/978-3-030-04028-4_5
15. Eladhari, M.: The pataphysic institute. In: Proceedings of the 6th AAAI Conference on Artificial Intelligence and Interactive Digital Entertainment (AIIDE 2010) (2010)
16. Harmon, S., Gale, H., Dermendzhiyska, E.: The magic of the in-between: mental resilience through interactive narrative. In: Mitchell, A., Vosmeer, M. (eds.) Interactive Storytelling: 14th International Conference on Interactive Digital Storytelling, ICIDS 2021, pp. 1–5. Springer, Cham (2021). https://doi.org/10.1007/978-3-030-92300-6_35
17. Kadastik, N., Bruni, L.E.: A transmedia narrative framework for pediatric hearing counseling. In: Mitchell, A., Vosmeer, M. (eds.) Interactive Storytelling: 14th International Conference on Interactive Digital Storytelling, ICIDS 2021, pp. 1–14. Springer, Cham (2021). https://doi.org/10.1007/978-3-030-92300-6_36
18. Koenitz, H.: Understanding interactive digital narrative: immersive expressions for a complex time. Routledge (2023). https://doi.org/10.4324/9781003106425
19. Laurel, B.: Toward the design of a computer-based interactive fantasy system (1986)
20. Lieblich, A.E., McAdams, D.P., Josselson, R.E.: Healing Plots: The Narrative Basis of Psychotherapy. American Psychological Association (2004)
21. McLeod, J.: Narrative and Psychotherapy. Sage (1997)
22. Mott, M., et al.: What's important to you, Max?: the influence of goals on engagement in an interactive narrative for adolescent health behavior change. In: Mitchell, A., Vosmeer, M. (eds.) ICIDS 2021. LNCS, vol. 13138, pp. 379–392. Springer, Cham (2021). https://doi.org/10.1007/978-3-030-92300-6_37
23. Murray, J.H.: Hamlet on the Holodeck. The Free Press (1997)
24. Picard, R.W.: Affective Computing. MIT Press (2000)
25. Ricoeur, P.: Narrative identity. Philosophy Today **35**(1), 73–81 (1991). https://doi.org/10.5840/philtoday199135136
26. Robbins, B.: Microscope - a fractal role-playing game of epic histories. Lame Mage Productions [Boardgame] (2011)
27. Roth, C., van Nuenen, T., Koenitz, H.: Ludonarrative hermeneutics: *a way out* and the narrative paradox. In: Rouse, R., Koenitz, H., Haahr, M. (eds.) ICIDS 2018. LNCS, vol. 11318, pp. 93–106. Springer, Cham (2018). https://doi.org/10.1007/978-3-030-04028-4_7
28. Si, M., Marsella, S., Miller, L.: Interactive stories for health interventions. In: Aylett, R., Lim, M.Y., Louchart, S., Petta, P., Riedl, M. (eds.) ICIDS 2010. LNCS, vol. 6432, pp. 291–292. Springer, Heidelberg (2010). https://doi.org/10.1007/978-3-642-16638-9_46
29. Suttie, N., Louchart, S., Aylett, R., Lim, T.: Theoretical considerations towards authoring emergent narrative. In: Koenitz, H., Sezen, T.I., Ferri, G., Haahr, M., Sezen, D., Çatak, G. (eds.) ICIDS 2013. LNCS, vol. 8230, pp. 205–216. Springer, Cham (2013). https://doi.org/10.1007/978-3-319-02756-2_25
30. van Enschot, R., Boogaard, I., Koenitz, H., Roth, C.: The potential of interactive digital narratives. Agency and multiple perspectives in *last Hijack interactive*. In: Cardona-Rivera, R.E., Sullivan, A., Young, R.M. (eds.) ICIDS 2019. LNCS, vol. 11869, pp. 158–169. Springer, Cham (2019). https://doi.org/10.1007/978-3-030-33894-7_17
31. White, M., Epston, D.: Narrative Means to Therapeutic Ends. WW Norton & Company (1990)

# Empathic Experiences of Visual Conditions with Virtual Reality

Georgi V. Georgiev[1(✉)], Vijayakumar Nanjappan[1], Iva Georgieva[2,3], and Zhengya Gong[1]

[1] Center for Ubiquitous Computing, University of Oulu, Oulu, Finland
{georgi.georgiev,vijayakumar.nanjappan,zhengya.gong}@oulu.fi
[2] Institute of Philosophy and Sociology, Bulgarian Academy of Sciences, Sofia, Bulgaria
[3] Institute for Advanced Study, Varna, Bulgaria

**Abstract.** When it comes to conditions related to vision, it can be challenging to foster empathy in designers toward affected users. However, utilizing Virtual Reality (VR) in an empathic design approach can help overcome these challenges and bridge the existing gaps. Previous research indicates that VR storytelling can be used to examine empathy; however, there is limited information regarding the application of this technique to color vision deficiency (CVD). In this study, we investigate whether a narrative and a game that simulates scenes as observed by individuals with CVD can induce cognitive and affective empathy. Moreover, we examine how this experience relates to performance and how it may contribute to identifying CVD-related issues. The participants were exposed to a normal vision condition and then a CVD condition while performing a color-based sorting task in a dedicated environment. The results indicate that neither cognitive nor affective empathy changed significantly before and after the experience. However, additional CVD-related problems were identified by the participants. Elaborating on this approach would give a greater insight into how to elicit empathic feelings by clarifying how a person with special needs, particularly CVD, experiences the world and how to design and improve such experiences.

**Keywords:** empathy · color vision deficiency · virtual environment · cognitive empathy · affective empathy · inclusive design

## 1 Introduction

Designers face a persistent challenge in accurately interpreting user needs and concerns. To address these, designers have developed deep empathy with their target users to understand their needs in their settings [20,23]. Research has argued that empathy has become an ideology in design rather than a principle suitable for some situations [13]. The correctness of this technique is questionable due to its inherent subjectivity and designers' subjectivity. Thus, designers need a research strategy that helps them understand and empathize with users.


L. Holloway-Attaway and J. T. Murray (Eds.): ICIDS 2023, LNCS 14384, pp. 168–180, 2023.
https://doi.org/10.1007/978-3-031-47658-7_15

Prior research suggested a Virtual Reality (VR)-based empathic design strategy that aims to employ VR as an "empathy machine" in an effort to alleviate this concern [14]. This tool may help users see the world from their perspective [15,16]. First-person immersive VR experiences can evoke empathy for unfamiliar populations [14] and reduce misconceptions and stereotyping [31], justifying this strategy. By immersing designers in a virtual environment (VE) that accurately simulates a target user's life scenario, designers can experience their world and gain valuable insights to create more efficient design solutions. Creating a narrative that explains the user experience and interprets the immersive scenario's goal in a novel way that enriches existing concepts may also help increase empathy and understanding of user perspectives.

This study investigates whether a virtual environment simulating a specific condition can help people empathize with it and identify its issues, needs, and concerns. A story and object sorting game were created to simulate red-green color vision deficiency (CVD) scenes, allowing non-CVD-affected people to experience CVD and empathize with it.

## 2 Virtual Storytelling for Empathy Generation

Empathy generation becomes increasingly important in design, especially for specific populations and complex needs. VR improves aging services workers' understanding of age-related health issues and empathy for older adults with vision loss [7]. In addition, VR simulations can potentially be used to evaluate the accessibility of new products or as teaching/empathy aids for conditions such as common visual impairments or specific visual field limitations [18]. In this way, the simulations improve the prosocial aspect of the design process and create participatory design products.

The immersive VR experiences demonstrated the potential to influence interpersonal emotions, particularly empathy, compared to lower immersive conditions [24]. VR experiences that let users put themselves in the shoes of others with specific experiences may help them understand and elaborate on their state. They can provide valuable output on how someone's condition is interpreted, transfer the experience of one group of users to another [10], and aid in comprehensive design techniques. Immersive VR uses storytelling to study empathy in marginalized and health conditions [6]. However, empathy VR has been questioned [1]. Furthermore, VR's effect on empathy-related feelings has been challenged [27]; specifically, immersive aspects might negatively influence empathic concerns [4]. VR has been seen as an effective perspective-taking machine rather than an empathy machine per se [2]. Nonetheless, in the area of design, specific conditions-simulating VR environments and setups are deemed necessary to promote empathy [3,22] to a required degree.

Color blindness, or color vision deficiency (CVD), is well-known but poorly understood. VR allows simulation of vision-affecting conditions in a highly immersive environment [18,29]. By presenting their challenges, VR can help users empathize with people with visual impairments like blurry vision, tunnel vision, and CVD. Narrative, character development, and interactive storytelling can make VR users feel for the characters and their struggles.

To understand empathy during exposure to a VR, we approach and measure two subcategories of empathy [9]. Our study measures Cognitive empathy (e.g., understanding how others feel) and Affective empathy (e.g., experiencing others' emotions) using the Affective and Cognitive Measure of Empathy (ACME) questionnaire [26]. Our approach focuses on the results of the gained empathy and potential implications of gained empathy for inclusive design rather than social expressions of empathy such as radical compassion [5]. VR's intended increase in empathic experiences may help designers better understand user experience. Prior studies suggest that VR is more effective at generating affective empathy than cognitive empathy [21], and improving attitudes toward certain social targets [28].

Previous studies on the VR-based empathetic design approaches suggest that virtual reality storytelling can be used to examine empathy; still, there is limited research on the application of this approach to color vision deficiency. Studies suggest that VR can be used to simulate the experience of color vision deficiency; however, these do not explicitly examine empathy for this condition [25,30]. An experiment involving CVD-simulated scenes in varying levels of detail revealed that objective and neutral experiences alone cannot elicit empathy [17]. VR operating designers will utilize task-irrelevant contextual information to address these issues. Overall, VR storytelling may be effective for studying empathy, but more research is needed for color vision deficiency. In this study, we use narrative for a general game-simulating scene rather than address all the elements in terms of interactive digital narratives, a category of digital media that affords audience interactivity, possibility spaces, and emergent narratives through the choices and actions of the interactors [19]. This type of narrative is set apart from linear narratives, creating new opportunities and challenges around ethics in their design and use [8,19].

Thus, we examine these research questions (RQ):

RQ 1: Can a narrative and a game that simulates scenes as seen by individuals with CVD elicit cognitive and affective empathy?
RQ 2: Does the performance in a game that simulates scenes as seen by individuals with CVD influence cognitive and affective empathy?
RQ 3: Can a narrative and a game that simulates scenes as seen by individuals with CVD contribute to identifying CVD-related issues?

## 3 Methodology

This study conceptualised a scenario utilising immersive VR to foster empathetic design approaches to the users. To achieve this, an interactive game with a storyline was developed to give users a simultaneous immersive VR experience in normal vision and CVD. The storyline of the game is to help Santa

Claus sort Christmas gift boxes delivered via a conveyor belt inside a traditional Finnish-style wooden log cabin (cottage) overseeing a sunset through the window. Participants started the game by sorting the gift boxes in normal vision mode using the VR controllers, followed by CVD mode. The forced alteration of the normal vision to red-green CVD halfway through their game is intended to elicit awareness to the users regarding the challenges faced by the CVD population.

## 4 User Study

### 4.1 Participants

Twenty participants (10 female, mean age = 27.2) volunteered to participate in this study. They were all students from a Finnish university and received a 10 Euro gift voucher as compensation for their time. A brief Ishihara CVD test conducted prior to the study revealed that none of the participants had significant color vision problems.

**Fig. 1.** Illustration of the VR game with a superimposed representation of the user in front of the conveyor belt between the two containers.

### 4.2 Immersive Virtual Environment

To enhance the virtual experience, we developed an authentic VE with topographic data from northern Finland (Fig. 1) to support the storytelling [12]. It is an approximately 10-minute interactive game where participants observe and interact with gift boxes in normal vision and CVD modes. The main interaction of the game takes place inside a wooden log cabin, overseeing a sunset through the window. It consists of a conveyor belt, three different colored (red, green, and blue) gift boxes, two sorting containers (one for each color, red and green), and a large collection box at the end of the conveyor belt for blue boxes. Only in the CVD mode, the colors of the entire virtual environment, including the gift boxes, containers, and the sunset change to represent the red-green color vision deficiency (deuteranopia). To render the VE in a CVD mode (Fig. 2), a transformation matrix was used to manipulate the scenes. This matrix is applied to the image's RGB values to render the scenes to present red-green CVD condition.

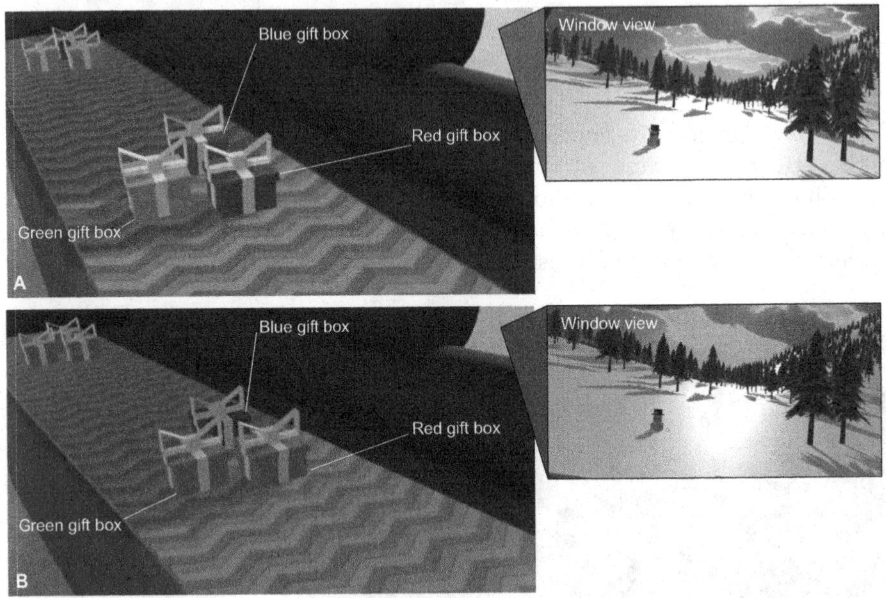


**Fig. 2.** Gift boxes and their sequence of arrival in the conveyor belt: normal vision (A) and CVD modes (B). (Color figure online)

### 4.3 Apparatus

We used a dedicated VR experiment lab space to conduct the user study. HTC Vive VR headset was used as a display device with Vive handheld controllers. The VR headset was connected to a VR-ready desktop running an NVidia graphics card. All participants were asked to stand in a pre-marked spot to perform interactions in the VR. A UVC disinfecting device was used to disinfect the headset and controllers before each user.

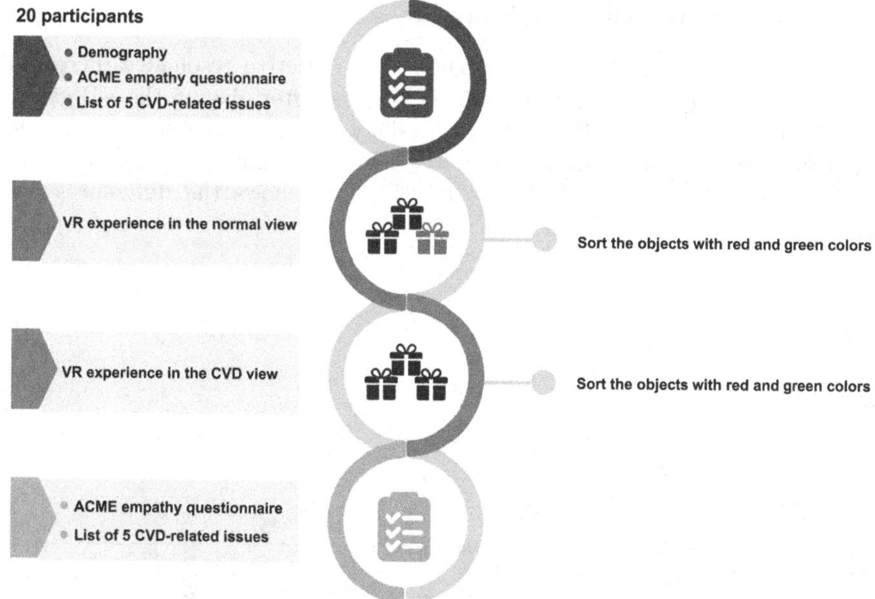


**Fig. 3.** Overview of the experiment procedure.

### 4.4 Procedure

The experiment consists of three stages. At first, all participants informed their consent before completing the demography and empathy (ACME) questionnaires and listed 5 CVD-related issues. They were asked to write down the CVD-related issues textually. In phase two, all participants were asked to wear the VR headset and given instructions on using the handheld controllers. Then, in a normal vision mode, participants were asked to pick gift boxes from the conveyor belt and place them in the large containers on both sides (see Fig. 3). They were tasked to sort the green gift boxes to the container on their left and the red ones to the container on their right side. The gift boxes appeared in a predefined random order while the speed of the conveyor belt gradually increased as the game progressed. After this, the game restarted in CVD mode, and participants continued the same task of sorting colored gift boxes into the containers. The entire VE was rendered in CVD mode. In both modes, the scores were displayed on a virtual heads-up display. Finally, the participants once again completed the empathy (ACME) questionnaire, followed by listing five CVD issues.

## 5 Results

Our results include empathy scores of the users before and after playing the VR game, the number of gift boxes missed in VR, and red-green CVD-related issues.

### 5.1 Cognitive and Affective Empathy

Although the mean of Cognitive empathy and Affective resonance increased (from 51.20 to 51.75 and 44.50 to 45.05) before and after playing the VR game, this increase was not significant as assessed by a paired samples t-test. The results for Cognitive empathy are $t(19) = -1.629$, $p = .299$, while for Affective resonance are $t(19) = -0.697$, $p = .495$. Figure 4 shows the differences per participant.

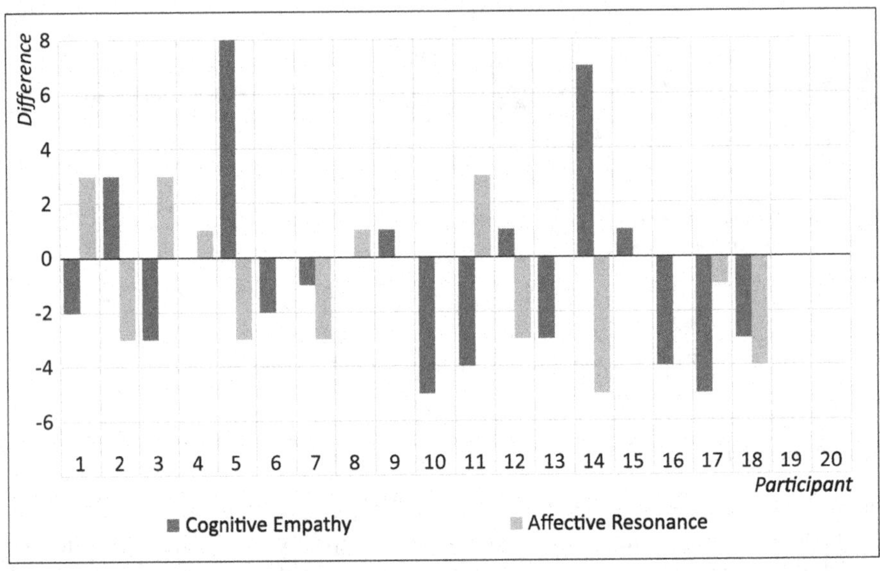


**Fig. 4.** Self-reported cognitive empathy and affective resonance before and after the VR game experience.

### 5.2 Number of Missed Gift Boxes

Figure 5 shows the number of red (A) and green (B) sorting misses per participant. The paired-samples t-test determined whether the mean difference between paired observations is statistically significant for missed, in other words, unsorted red gift boxes. Two outliers were found in a boxplot more than 1.5 box lengths from the edge. Inspection of their values revealed them to be extreme, and they were modified as less extreme (i.e., the next largest value instead) in the analysis. The difference scores of the number of missed red gift boxes for the normal vision and CVD modes were normally distributed, as assessed by Shapiro-Wilk's test ($p = .054$). Participants missed more red gift boxes in the CVD mode ($1 \pm 1.56$) than in the normal vision mode ($0.55 \pm 0.826$), with an increase of 0.45. Nevertheless, this increase was not statistically significant $t(20) = 1.28$, $p = .216$.

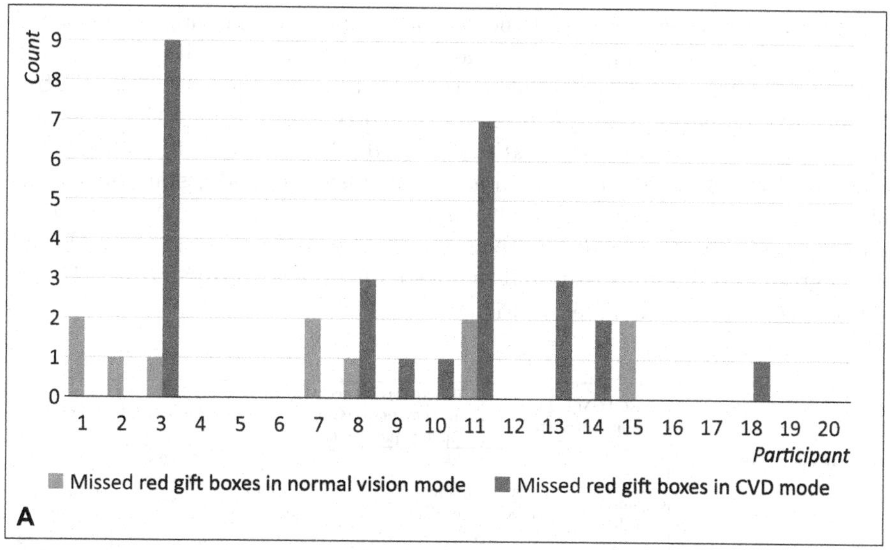


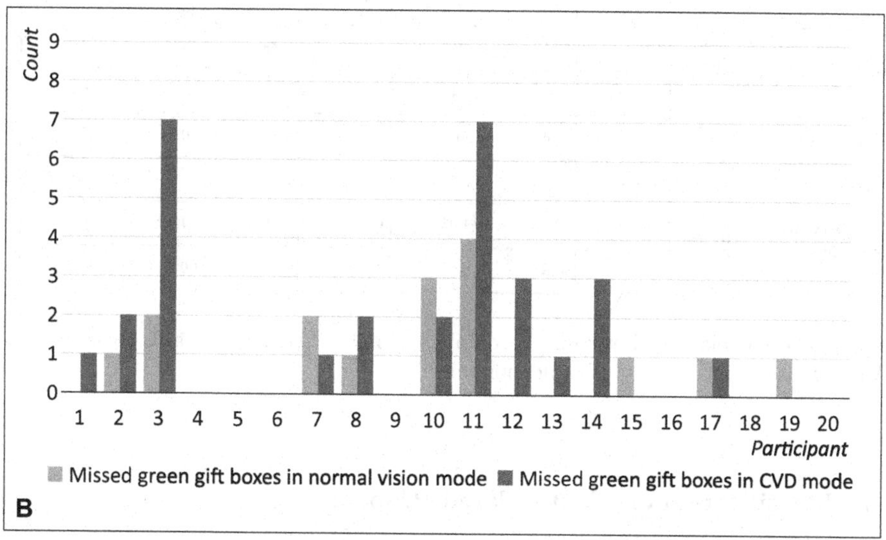


**Fig. 5.** Number of missed (unsorted) red (A) and green (B) gift boxes in normal vision and CVD modes. (Color figure online)

The number of unsorted green gift boxes had no outliers, as shown by a boxplot for values greater than 1.5 box lengths from the edge. The data is not normally distributed; therefore, the Wilcoxon signed-rank test was the nonparametric equivalent to the paired-sample t-test used in the analysis. There was an increase in CVD mode; however, this difference was not statistically significant, $z = -1.706$, $p = 0.088$.

Additional analyses examined the correlation between the number of object sorting misses in the CVD condition and participants' post-VR cognitive and affective empathy, as well as the differences between pre- and post-VR cognitive and affective empathy. Figure 6 presents the correlations among the variables, with statistically significant correlations indicated by bold font. In addition, the number of missed red gift boxes and green gift boxes showed a statistically significant correlation, as indicated by Kendall's tau-b coefficient of .489 ($p = .012$). Similarly, a significant positive correlation was observed between the number of missed green and red gift boxes and the overall missed gift boxes ($\tau_b = .743$ and .844, respectively), as depicted in Fig. 6.

| Kendall's tau_b | | Post-ACM Eempathy questionnaire | | Differences between pre- and post- ACM Empathy questionnaire | | Number of sorting misses objects | | |
|---|---|---|---|---|---|---|---|---|
| | | Cognitive empathy | Affective resonance empathy | Differences of cognitive empathy | Differences of affective resonance empathy | Number of sorting misses of red-colored objects | Number of sorting misses of green-colored objects | Total number of sorting misses objects |
| Number of sorting misses of red-colored objects | Correlation Coefficient | .175 | .094 | -.207 | .230 | 1.000 | **.489*** | **.743**** |
| | Sig. (2-tailed) | .336 | .604 | .264 | .233 | . | .012 | .000 |
| Number of sorting misses of green-colored objects | Correlation Coefficient | -.043 | -.049 | -.114 | .061 | **.489*** | 1.000 | **.848**** |
| | Sig. (2-tailed) | .809 | .782 | .532 | .747 | .012 | . | .000 |
| Total number of sorting misses objects | Correlation Coefficient | .012 | -.029 | -.139 | .071 | **.743**** | **.848**** | 1.000 |
| | Sig. (2-tailed) | .946 | .866 | .436 | .700 | .000 | .000 | . |

**Fig. 6.** The correlations between the number of missed (unsorted) gift boxes in the CVD condition and the ACME questionnaire.

## 5.3 Identification of CVD-Related Problems

Out of 20 study participants, 11 identified a maximum of 5 CVD-related issues pre- and post-VR. Four participants identified one more issue post-VR experience, and five identified two. On average, the identified issues were 3.37 for pre-VR and 4.11 for post-VR experience. A Wilcoxon signed-rank test was conducted to determine the effect of VR experience on the identified red-green CVD-related issues. There was a statistically significant increase in the identified issues $z = 2.739$, $p = .006$.

Cognitive empathy and affective resonance are two qualitative categories of CVD issues. The majority of participants worried about cognitive empathy issues, including traffic lights. About 50% of the participants indicated limited job prospects, especially in color-perceptual jobs. Several participants worried about mental health due to affective resonance, including sadness and bullying. As discussed in the following section, their descriptions became more detailed after CVD exposure.

## 6 Discussion

Although the quantitative data obtained from the questionnaire does not indicate a significant increase in empathic experiences before and after the VR game experience, an encouraging aspect of this experiment is that some participants reported their experiences of the CVD condition. These accounts provide an opportunity for further qualitative analysis to explore how participants' perceptions of CVD people changed, potentially yielding insights into strategies for enhancing both cognitive and affective empathy. In addition, they connected the CVD-related difficulties to other problems pertaining to specific conditions such as bullying, the possibility of good performance in tasks, and overall quality of life, with the potential to advance the field in terms of inclusive design.

In the case of issues related to cognitive empathy, for example, when they report that color distinguishing is important for some jobs, they realize CVD persons need to consider this and therefore imagine what kind of jobs there might be to match this condition. Providing such answers in the text helps the immersed users to rethink and reiterate the obstacles that might exist in front of CVD users. Moreover, the participants precisely understood the experience encountered by individuals with CVD, which might infer that their cognitive empathy increased. For instance, one participant conveyed that prior to experiencing CVD, they mistakenly thought that all colors as green for CVD people. However, after exposure to the CVD condition, he/she expressed a more accurate perception, describing their visual experience as predominantly consisting of shades of brown and grey.

Regarding the issues related to affective resonance, one participant listed several problems, including positive emotions, such as "cool" and "relax", before exposure to the CVD condition. However, she/he reported five problems that were all negative, such as "depression," "frustration," "bad emotions," "sadness," and "pressure" after exposure to the CVD condition. Furthermore, after exposure to the CVD condition, the participants reported the problems of individuals with CVD were more detailed. For instance, one participant reported that "they will have a hard time differentiating between fruits and food" before the experiment, and "it will be hard to see when food has gone bad, like apple or mushrooms have changed color" after exposure to the CVD condition. These might be potentially inferred because their affective resonances increased. The correct scores of gift box pickings were displayed on the interface, potentially motivating participants to enhance their engagement and effort in the subsequent CVD condition. As per prior research, it has been demonstrated that the utilization of leaderboards has a positive impact on the motivation of participants toward task engagement [11]. Moreover, the preliminary phase (normal view condition) allowed the participants to familiarize themselves with the experimental procedures, leading to improved performance in the CVD view condition.

Further emphasis on feedback in the game or post-experience narration in the form of retelling [8] can facilitate a critical understanding of the impact of the experience.

## 7 Conclusion

Interpreting how a CVD person sees the world and feels creates a different story from what the person might feel and be in the world. This point of view, even though it might show increased empathy, helps us to learn how to relate to people with special needs. The narrative behind these answers, such as "worry" or "pressure" shows the person answering to put themselves in the place of a CVD person and engage with the discourse about how would that feel. Expanding these answers into stories would give a greater insight into how to elicit empathic feelings by elaborating on how a person with special needs is in the world. By offering a shared experience, VR can enhance understanding and reduce stigma for vision-related conditions, making society more inclusive.

**Acknowledgments.** This work was supported by the European Union's Horizon 2020 research and innovation programme (Grant Number H2020-856998), and the Research Council of Finland (former Academy of Finland) 6G Flagship Programme (Grant Number: 346208). We appreciate the contribution of Santeri Harju and Lauri Klemettilä.

## References

1. Barbara, J., Koenitz, H., Bakk, Á.K.: The ethics of virtual reality interactive digital narratives in cultural heritage. In: Mitchell, A., Vosmeer, M. (eds.) Interactive Storytelling: 14th International Conference on Interactive Digital Storytelling, ICIDS 2021, Tallinn, Estonia, December 7–10, 2021, Proceedings, pp. 288–292. Springer, Cham (2021). https://doi.org/10.1007/978-3-030-92300-6_27
2. Barbot, B., Kaufman, J.C.: What makes immersive virtual reality the ultimate empathy machine? Discerning the underlying mechanisms of change. Comput. Hum. Behav. **111**, 106431 (2020). https://doi.org/10.1016/j.chb.2020.106431
3. Barhoush, Y., Georgiev, G.V., Loudon, B.: Empathy and idea generation: exploring the design of a virtual reality controller for rehabilitation purposes. In: Proceedings of the Sixth International Conference on Design Creativity (ICDC 2020), pp. 287–294, Oulu, Finland, The Design Society (2020). https://doi.org/10.35199/ICDC.2020.36
4. Barreda-Ángeles, M., Aleix-Guillaume, S., Pereda-Baños, A.: An "empathy machine" or a"just-for-the-fun-of-it" machine? effects of immersion in nonfiction 360-video stories on empathy and enjoyment. Cyberpsychol. Behav. Social Netw. **23**, 683–688 (2020). https://doi.org/10.1089/cyber.2019.0665
5. Bloom, P.: Against Empathy: The Case for Rational Compassion. Random House (2017)
6. Christofi, M., Hadjipanayi, C., Michael-Grigoriou, D.: The use of storytelling in virtual reality for studying empathy: a review. In: 2022 International Conference on Interactive Media, Smart Systems and Emerging Technologies (IMET), pp. 1–8 (2022). https://doi.org/10.1109/IMET54801.2022.9929546

7. Dyer, E., Swartzlander, B.J., Gugliucci, M.R.: Using virtual reality in medical education to teach empathy. J. Med. Libr. Assoc. **106**(4), 498–500 (2018). https://doi.org/10.5195/jmla.2018.518
8. Eladhari, M.P.: The story pile - representing story in the board game mind shadows. In: Rouse, R., Koenitz, H., Haahr, M. (eds.) Interactive Storytelling: 11th International Conference on Interactive Digital Storytelling, ICIDS 2018, Dublin, Ireland, December 5–8, 2018, Proceedings, pp. 280–284. Springer, Cham (2018). https://doi.org/10.1007/978-3-030-04028-4_30
9. Fisher, J.A.: Empathic actualities: toward a taxonomy of empathy in virtual reality. In: Nunes, N., Oakley, I., Nisi, V. (eds.) Interactive Storytelling, pp. 233–244. Springer, Cham (2017). https://doi.org/10.1007/978-3-319-71027-3_19
10. Georgieva, I., Georgiev, G.V.: Narrative self-recreation in virtual reality. Frontiers in Virtual Reality. **3**, 1–10 (2022). https://doi.org/10.3389/frvir.2022.854333
11. Halan, S., Rossen, B., Cendan, J., Lok, B.: High score! - motivation strategies for user participation in virtual human development. In: Allbeck, J., Badler, N., Bickmore, T., Pelachaud, C., Safonova, A. (eds.) Intelligent Virtual Agents, pp. 482–488. Springer, Berlin, Heidelberg (2010). https://doi.org/10.1007/978-3-642-15892-6_52
12. Harju, S., Klemettilä, L.: Empathic experiences of colour vision deficiency in virtual reality. http://urn.fi/URN:NBN:fi:oulu-202206233171 (2022)
13. Heylighen, A., Dong, A.: To empathise or not to empathise? Empathy and its limits in design. Des. Stud. **65**, 107–124 (2019). https://doi.org/10.1016/j.destud.2019.10.007
14. Herrera, F., Bailenson, J., Weisz, E., Ogle, E., Zaki, J.: Building long-term empathy: a large-scale comparison of traditional and virtual reality perspective-taking. PLoS ONE **13**, e0204494 (2018). https://doi.org/10.1371/journal.pone.0204494
15. Hu, X., Nanjappan, V., Georgiev, G.V.: Seeing from the users' eyes: an outlook to virtual-reality based empathic design research. Proc. Design Society **1**, 2601–2610 (2021). https://doi.org/10.1017/pds.2021.521
16. Hu, X., Nanjappan, V., Georgiev, G.V.: Bursting through the blocks in the human mind: enhancing creativity with extended reality technologies. Interactions **28**, 57–61 (2021). https://doi.org/10.1145/3460114
17. Hu, X., Casakin, H., Georgiev, G.V.: Bridging designer-user gap with a virtual reality-based empathic design approach: contextual information details. Proc. Design Society **3**, 797–806, Cambridge University Press (2023). https://doi.org/10.1017/pds.2023.80
18. Jones, P.R., Ometto, G.: Degraded reality: using VR/AR to simulate visual impairments. In: 2018 IEEE Workshop on Augmented and Virtual Realities for Good (VAR4Good), pp. 1–4 (2018). https://doi.org/10.1109/VAR4GOOD.2018.8576885
19. Koenitz, H., Barbara, J., Bakk, A.K.: An ethics framework for interactive digital narrative authoring. In: Hargood, C., Millard, D.E., Mitchell, A., Spierling, U. (eds.) The Authoring Problem: Challenges in Supporting Authoring for Interactive Digital Narratives, pp. 335–351. Springer, Cham (2022). https://doi.org/10.1007/978-3-031-05214-9_21
20. Koskinen, I.: Empathic design in methodic terms. In: Ilpo Koskinen, Katja Battarbee and Tuuli Mattelmäki (eds.) Empathic Design. User Experience for Product Design, pp. 59–68. IT Press (2003)
21. Martingano, A.J., Hererra, F., Konrath, S.: Virtual reality improves emotional but not cognitive empathy: a meta-analysis. Technol., Mind, Behav. **2**(1), 1–15 (2021). https://doi.org/10.1037/tmb0000034

22. McDonagh, D., Thomas, J.: Disability + relevant design: empathic design strategies supporting more effective new product design outcomes. Des. J. **13**(2), 180–198 (2010). https://doi.org/10.2752/175470710X12735884220899
23. Miyata, K., Yuizono, T., Nagai, Y., Kunifuji, S.: Human capital development through innovation design education. In: SIGGRAPH Asia 2017 Symposium on Education, Association for Computing Machinery, New York, NY, USA, pp. 1–8. (2017). https://doi.org/10.1145/3134368.3139219
24. Schutte, N.S., Stilinović, E.J.: Facilitating empathy through virtual reality. Motiv. Emot. **41**(6), 708–712 (2017). https://doi.org/10.1007/s11031-017-9641-7
25. Szczurowski, K., Smith, M.: Emulating perceptual experience of color vision deficiency with virtual reality. In: Craddock, G., et al. (eds.) Transforming our World Through Design, Diversity and Education, IOS Press (2018). https://doi.org/10.3233/978-1-61499-923-2-378
26. Vachon, D.D., Lynam, D.R.: Fixing the problem with empathy: development and validation of the affective and cognitive measure of empathy. Assessment **23**(2), 135–149 (2016). https://doi.org/10.1177/1073191114567941
27. van 't Riet, J., Meeuwes, A.C., van der Voorden, L., Jansz, J.: Investigating the effects of a persuasive digital game on immersion, identification, and willingness to help. Basic Appl. Social Psychol. **40**, 180–194 (2018). https://doi.org/10.1080/01973533.2018.1459301
28. Ventura, S., Badenes-Ribera, L., Herrero, R., Cebolla, A., Galiana, L., Baños, R.: Virtual reality as a medium to elicit empathy: a meta-analysis. Cyberpsychol. Behav. Soc. Netw. **23**, 667–676 (2020). https://doi.org/10.1089/cyber.2019.0681
29. Wang, Z., Liu, H., Pan, Y., Mousas, C.: Color blindness bartender: an embodied VR game experience. In: 2020 IEEE Conference on Virtual Reality and 3D User Interfaces Abstracts and Workshops (VRW), pp. 519–520 (2020). https://doi.org/10.1109/VRW50115.2020.00111
30. Yao, T., Yoo, S., Parker, C.: Evaluating virtual reality as a tool for empathic modelling of vision impairment: insights from a simulated public interactive display experience. In: Proceedings of the 33rd Australian Conference on Human-Computer Interaction, Association for Computing Machinery, New York, NY, USA, pp. 190–197 (2022). https://doi.org/10.1145/3520495.3520519
31. Yee, N., Bailenson, J.N.: Walk a mile in digital shoes: The impact of embodied perspective-taking on the reduction of negative stereotyping in immersive virtual environments. Proc. PRESENCE. **24**, 26 (2006)

# The Chronicles of ChatGPT: Generating and Evaluating Visual Novel Narratives on Climate Change Through ChatGPT

Mustafa Can Gursesli[1], Pittawat Taveekitworachai[2(✉)], Febri Abdullah[2], Mury F. Dewantoro[2], Antonio Lanata[1], Andrea Guazzini[3], Van Khôi Lê[4], Adrien Villars[4], and Ruck Thawonmas[5]

[1] Department of Information Engineering, Università degli Studi di Firenze, Florence, Italy
{mustafacan.gursesli,antonio.lanata}@unifi.it

[2] Graduate School of Information Science and Engineering, Ritsumeikan University, Kusatsu, Shiga, Japan
{gr0609fv,gr0634hi,gr0397fs,gr0450xi}@ed.ritsumei.ac.jp

[3] Department of Education, Literatures, Intercultural Studies, Languages and Psychology, Università degli Studi di Firenze, Florence, Italy
andrea.guazzini@unifi.it

[4] Graduate School of Engineering, ENSEIRB-MATMECA, Talence, France
{van_khoi.le,avillars}@bordeaux-inp.fr

[5] College of Information Science and Engineering, Ritsumeikan University, Kusatsu, Shiga, Japan
ruck@is.ritsumei.ac.jp

**Abstract.** This paper explores the potential of utilizing ChatGPT, a large language model (LLM), for generating and evaluating visual novel (VN) game stories in the context of global warming awareness through a VN game. The study involves generating two stories using ChatGPT, one with given global warming related keywords as an inspiration for ChatGPT along with a specified ending and another without, and evaluating them based on several linguistic criteria: coherence, inspiration, readability, word complexity, and narrative fluency. Results reveal that keywords-inspired story exhibit higher coherence, while the basic one demonstrate greater inspiration. The findings highlight the advantages of each story and emphasize the value of AI-driven narrative generation in creating engaging and informative experiences. Furthermore, the study introduces an innovative approach by employing ChatGPT as an evaluator for the story quality, by combining various prompt engineering techniques showcasing the diverse applications of LLMs in interactive storytelling. This work contributes to the growing field of LLM-based story generation and underscores the potential of AI-driven narratives in fostering awareness and engagement on critical issues like climate change.

**Keywords:** Global warming · climate change · visual novel · ChatGPT · narrative generation

M. C. Gursesli and P. Taveekitworachai—These authors contributed equally.


L. Holloway-Attaway and J. T. Murray (Eds.): ICIDS 2023, LNCS 14384, pp. 181–194, 2023.
https://doi.org/10.1007/978-3-031-47658-7_16

## 1 Introduction

Climate change is defined by United Nations as "long-term shifts in temperatures and weather patterns" [30]. While to some degree variations in atmospheric conditions occur in nature [4,51], human activities have managed to exacerbate this phenomenon to critical levels, being responsible for 1.1C° of global warming since 1800 [11]. Specifically, the human footprint in climate change can be found in the widespread consumption of fossil fuels that lead to an increase in greenhouse gases present in the atmosphere, which prevents solar heat from dispersing, thus increasing temperatures [18,30]. Several measures have been taken to tackle climate change issues, such as using video games as tools that have the potential to realize this enlightenment and intervention, due to their prevalence and the audiences they reach [15].

Serious games, a specific sub-type of video games that aim to increase knowledge and awareness while maintaining entertainment value for improved information retention and learning [12,21], have historically been used in various fields including training, military applications, interpersonal communication, and education [21]. As a subgroup of serious games, Games for Change (G4C) focus on influencing attitudes and promoting positive social and behavioral change [2] and have attracted the interest of developers, researchers, and non-profit organizations for their potential in climate change education [5,12,15,44]. These G4C include different game genres and themes designed to effectively engage players [3,28]. In particular, visual novels (VNs), a popular genre, have been extensively studied in G4C contexts, due to their ability to mediate messages while maintaining player motivation [8,9,29,47]. VNs, characterized by plot-driven narratives and player choices within text boxes [9], have a large community of players.

Among various means employed by serious games and G4C to create significant attitude changes, storytelling plays a crucial role [19,24,26]. Storytelling is the technique through which stories are developed and coherently exposed [6] and it manages to increase immersion, engagement, and motivation [21,26], also employing other technological vehicles (e.g.: virtual reality and augmented reality storytelling [22,49]). In the past decade, large language models (LLMs) have been used in many story generation studies and LLMs' AI has been shown to be successful [33,48,50]. However, despite recent interest in AI story generation [16,50], the studies on game stories and stories generated for G4C are highly limited. In this context, the contributions of our paper are as follows:

- Demonstrate a combination of prompt engineering techniques, i.e., zero-shot and generated knowledge promptings, for linguistic evaluation of generated visual novel game story.
- Propose a workflow utilizing various prompts for generating and evaluating a visual novel game story.
- Evaluate two global warming stories created by ChatGPT, one with given keywords and the other without any guidance, to ascertain which story has a higher level of coherence, inspiration, readability, word complexity, and narrative fluency.

The final objective involves taking the narrative produced by ChatGPT and integrating it into our work-in-progress VN game, as illustrated in Fig. 1.

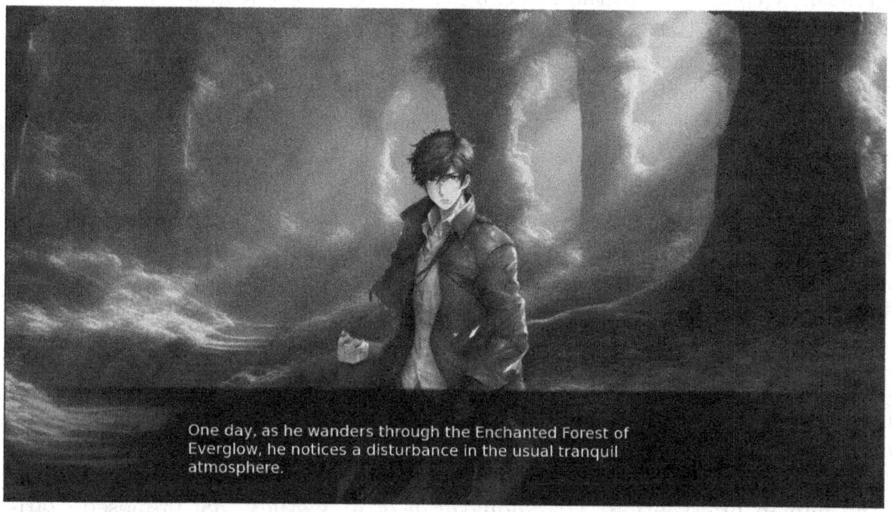

One day, as he wanders through the Enchanted Forest of Everglow, he notices a disturbance in the usual tranquil atmosphere.


**Fig. 1.** A screenshot of the visual novel titled **ICE Chronicles: Everglow's Crises**

## 2 Related Work

### 2.1 G4C, Storytelling, and VN

G4C defines video games as entertainment tools designed to influence individuals' behavior and attitudes in a positive change [2,27]. A study found that interactivity increases the effects of such games by providing better appreciation [37]. Moreover, games incorporating gameplay elements linked to the causes, as well as a simple story, have presented positive results [32]. G4C has the potential to serve educational objectives as well [17]. While it remains vital to increase adults' awareness, youth education is not something that can be neglected. Lastly, it is also known that using stories to reach players and change their attitudes is useful for serious games and G4C, since they are a good way to generate empathy [34,35].

Storytelling serves as a highly potent method for message conveyance, finding application across various advocacies. Climate change for instance, is among them [13,36]. By offering an interactive and immersive experience, emotions can be used in order to make the message more engaging. Especially, interactive storytelling finds application within games as well, making the story adaptive and thus augmenting player enjoyment [41].

VN is a game genre relaying on narrative and interactive storytelling where the story adapts based on player choices [8]. Furthermore, in contrast to conventional novels, VNs incorporate a diverse range of illustrations and images that significantly contribute to the player's overall experience [20]. For instance, the VN game titled *Cancer Sucks* [10] was able to provide empathy to the audience regarding breast cancer due to its storytelling. Therefore, in a similar fashion, using a VN to promote the risks of climate change can be effective.

Writing an engaging story can be difficult, yet, resources like LLMs are already used in such endeavors [1]. While not without its imperfections, such as maintaining narrative coherence, this study tries to address this concern by employing pre-generated places and characters. Additionally, the relatively concise length of the narrative minimizes this issue, making LLMs a good option to write satisfying story outcomes.

## 2.2 LLMs in Games

Recent studies have employed LLMs for game-related tasks like procedural content generation (PCG) [38,40,42]. PCG is an approach to automatically generate game content, including levels, quests, items, and story elements, with minimal to no human intervention [31]. Sudhakaran et al.'s study [38] proposed MarioGPT, a fine-tuned LLM that is capable of generating *Super Mario Bros.*' game levels. A study by Todd et al. [42] suggested that fine-tuned LLMs have the ability to generate novel and playable levels of *Sokoban.*

In contrast to Sudhakaran et al.'s [38] and Todd et al.'s studies [42] that employed fine-tuned LLMs, Taveekitworachai et al. [40] conducted a study to investigate optimal prompts for an instruction-tuned LLM, i.e., ChatGPT, to generate game contents. To achieve that, the study organized the $1^{st}$ ChatGPT4PCG competition, where participants are tasked with creating prompts for ChatGPT to generate Angry Birds-like structures that resemble English capitalized letters. To optimize the prompt for the PCG task, the participants are encouraged to leverage their creativity and prompt engineering skills.

Prompt engineering (PE) is an emerging field focused on developing and optimizing prompts for LLMs. A recent study [46] discerned six prompt pattern categories that function as reusable frameworks to accomplish specific tasks, e.g., tasks related to input semantics or formatting the output. In addition to prompt patterns, notable techniques have emerged to enhance LLMs' performance [7, 25,45]. Few-shot prompting [7,25] adds examples within the prompt—aiding contextual learning and performance improvement. Chain-of-thought prompting [45] guides models through reasoning using a few examples prior to conclusions.

Past studies demonstrated the usage of PE in narrative and storytelling [39, 48]. Yuan et al. [48] developed Wordcraft, a web application for collaborating with an LLM for the purpose of writing a story. Wordcraft demonstrated the usage of PE in creative writing and enhance the writers' co-writing experience. Swanson et al. [39] developed *Story Centaur*, a user interface to assist story writers with limited knowledge of PE in interacting with LLMs to generate stories. Story Centaur auto-generates prompts that enable few-shot prompting with a simplified interface for the writers.

Similar to Taveekitworachai et al.'s study [40], our study explores PE to generate game content. However, instead of generating game levels and solely targeting the game-related factor, we aim to generate VN's stories for G4C to foster awareness about global warming.

## 3 Methods

We generate and evaluate VN game stories using ChatGPT. An overview of the method is shown in Fig. 2. We provide detailed information about story generation, including the prompts used to interact with ChatGPT, in Sect. 3.1. In Sect. 3.2, we illustrate how we incorporate PE techniques for story evaluation based on selected criteria.

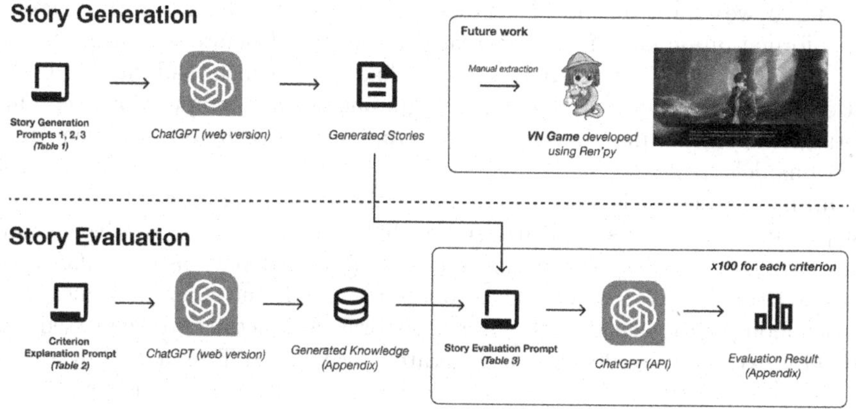


**Fig. 2.** An overview of the method used in the study: *Top*: The story generation process using ChatGPT and our final goal of extracting the generated story for a VN game. *Bottom*: The story evaluation process using ChatGPT along with the PE technique called 'generated knowledge' to evaluate the generated story based on selected criteria.

### 3.1 Story Generation with ChatGPT

We generate two stories using ChatGPT through the web interface[1], employing a series of prompts. While most of the prompts are the same, there is a slight difference in the initial prompt given to ChatGPT for their story generation. In the second story, we specifically ask ChatGPT to incorporate certain concepts related to climate change, the green environment, and terminology used by other studies in the field [14] to inspire the story generation.

[1] http://chat.openai.com.

The prompts are displayed in Table 1. We have chosen to use multiple prompts in the same context window to have ChatGPT generate the story chapter-by-chapter, ensuring greater coherence over time. Moreover, the subsequent parts of the story can build upon the previously generated content. This approach aligns well with the nature of our game, which consists of multiple routes where decisions made in earlier parts may impact the future story. Additionally, we explicitly instruct ChatGPT that our story will be divided into three chapters, reducing the chance of generating less relevant story content. Our inspiration for this approach comes from Wei et al.'s study [45], wherein they found that asking LLMs to work step-by-step improves the performance of the generated outcomes. This methodology also allows us to generate longer stories by introducing more chapters in the future.

To avoid significant deviations in characters, places, and story endings that may influence the emotions of our participants and impact our measures, we explicitly condition the prompts on characters and places. The ending is retrieved from the first generated story and provided during the second story generation. In doing so, we expect the model to utilize this information for generating a story. The information on characters and places is generated beforehand using ChatGPT[2]. Subsequently, the responses from ChatGPT, which contain this information, have been incorporated at the beginning of our prompt. Moreover, this information is also utilized for generating graphical assets by text-to-image generative models.

Our main objective is to promote awareness of global warming. Therefore, the first prompt of the series explicitly states that the story should revolve around global warming. Subsequent prompts are simpler and only ask ChatGPT to continue the story. We expect each response to include the story, dialogues, and choices, along with their effects. After the stories and details are generated, we manually extract the information generated by ChatGPT as a Ren'py script for the game, along with keywords and phrases used for generating character and background images. The full conversations, including the full prompts, the generated stories, and details, can be found at the following links: https://bit.ly/vn-story1 and https://bit.ly/vn-story2.

### 3.2 Story Evaluation with ChatGPT

Inspired by a study by Wang et al. [43] on using ChatGPT as a natural language generation evaluator and a study by Liu et al. [23] on improving LLM performance by first asking it to generate knowledge about the topics and incorporating that knowledge for the tasks, we develop similar prompts utilizing both ideas to evaluate generated stories in the following aspects: (1) coherence, (2) inspiration, (3) readability, (4) word complexity, and (5) narrative fluency. Our goal is to assess coherence in the generated stories to determine if the overall story progresses in the same direction, considering that the generated stories may contain branches. Additionally, we aim to evaluate whether ChatGPT draws

[2] The full conversation is available at https://bit.ly/chars-places.

**Table 1.** Prompts 1, 2, and 3 used to instruct ChatGPT to generate a game story for Chaps. 1, 2, and 3, respectively, where the bold part in Prompt 1 resides only when generating the second story.

| # | Prompt |
|---|---|
| 1 | Characters:<br>// Character details are omitted for brevity<br><br>Places:<br>// Place details are omitted for brevity<br><br>**Ending: The alliance, comprising beings from all walks of life, stands united against the dark force. Together, they muster the strength to face the malevolent adversaries, defending the Celestial Tower with the combined power of both realms.**<br><br>**The battle is fierce and intense, pushing them to their limits. However, through their unity, the alliance prevails, dispelling the dark force and restoring balance to the Celestial Tower.**<br><br>// Parts of the ending are omitted for brevity<br><br>**And so, the tale of Eamon and his companions became a legend, echoing through the ages as a reminder that even in the face of darkness, unity and compassion can heal the world and restore the balance between all living beings.**<br><br>Generate a fantasy game story about global warming. Generate it in Ren'py story format. Add choices when appropriate. Choices will only slightly affects dialogue but not the main story line. Also, generate the story affected by the choices.<br><br>Do not introduce new characters or locations aside from the ones already mentioned.<br><br>**Using the following concepts as an inspiration.**<br>**Concepts: greenhouse effect, ozone depletion, CO2 emissions, sea level rise, climate change, ice melting, air pollution**<br><br>This game contains three chapters. Generate the first chapter. |
| 2 | Continue the second chapter. |
| 3 | Continue the third chapter (final chapter). |

inspiration from the given words (those in bold) in Sect. 3.1 or not. For readability, word complexity, and narrative fluency, we want to assess general linguistic characteristics in the generated stories. The interactions are conducted via the web interface of ChatGPT. The prompts, source code, and results are available in Appendix.

We ask ChatGPT through OpenAI API using default sampling temperature to list and explain the factors contributing to the evaluation of the mentioned criteria, as shown in Table 2. After obtaining the generated knowledge, we incorporate it into the second prompt, shown in Table 3, where we provide ChatGPT with a story and ask it to evaluate the story based on those factors, assigning a maximum score of 10 for each factor. We also request ChatGPT to output the results in JSON format, making it easier for data extraction. All data are extracted as JSON files, and a script was used to summarize the results.

**Table 2.** A prompt used to interact with ChatGPT to obtain details and factors of the target criterion. The <|criterion|> is replaced with one of the criterion names: "coherence," "narrative fluency," "readability," and "word complexity." For inspiration, the <|criterion|> is replaced with "the use of specified concepts as inspiration", along with concepts in bold.

| **Criterion Explanation Prompt** |
|---|
| List and explain factors for evaluating the <\|criterion\|> of a visual novel game's story. |
| **Concepts: greenhouse effect, ozone depletion, CO2 emissions, sea level rise, climate change, ice melting, air pollution** |

## 4 Results and Discussions

This study evaluated two global warming stories generated by ChatGPT, one with given keywords along with the specified ending and the other without any keywords. The generated stories have different lengths, with the story containing words having a length of 2,736 words, and the one without words having 2,225 words when combining all branch content. This suggests that the generated stories without words may result in a higher word count. However, a more extensive experiment is required to confirm this hypothesis.

The story evaluation was based on the five aforementioned metrics. The factor was assigned a maximum score of 10, where 10 is the best and 0 is the worst. Each result from each factor in the story was an average score and standard deviation by performing 100 trials for each criterion of each story through the ChatGPT API. This approach allows us to ensure the reliability of the evaluation process, notwithstanding the stochastic nature of ChatGPT when utilizing the default sampling `temperature`. This approach ensures that the evaluation results are statistically robust and representative of the performance of ChatGPT in evaluating the stories. By conducting multiple trials, the study accounts for any variations or inconsistencies in the generated stories and stochasticity existed within the LLM.

**Table 3.** A prompt asked ChatGPT to evaluate a given story, based on the provided criterion details. Concepts in bold text are only given when we ask ChatGPT to evaluate the story against the "inspiration" criterion. The <|criterion_detail|> is replaced with its associated details generated by ChatGPT as shown in Appendix, while <|story|> is replaced with the generated story as mentioned in Sect. 3.1.

~~~~
Story Evaluation Prompt
Evaluate the following visual novel game story according to the specified criteria and assign a score
with a total of 10 for each criterion, where 10 is the best and 0 is the worst. Provide reasons for your
scores. Make sure to output it in a MarkDown code block, i.e., between ```json and ```.

Output format:
```json
{
"story_id": <|story_id|>,
"<|criteria|>: [{ "<factor_name>": <int score out of 10>, "reason": < reason for the given score > }]
} ```

Criteria:
<|criterion_detail|>

Concepts:
greenhouse effect, ozone depletion, CO2 emissions, sea level rise, climate change, ice
melting, air pollution

Story:
<|story|>
~~~~

The results of the study are presented in Table 4, which shows the average scores and standard deviations for the five different criteria for each story. Comparing the results of Stories 1 and 2, we can see that Story 2 has a higher coherence score, showing how effectively the story flows and how well the different parts of the story fit together. However, the word complexity score is much higher for Story 1, which means that it uses more complex vocabulary. The other three criteria have similar scores for both stories. This suggests that Story 2 is slightly better in terms of coherence, while Story 1 has more complex vocabulary. However, both stories are equally inspiring, fluent, and readable.

**Table 4.** The evaluation results of two global warming stories generated by ChatGPT, one with given keywords along with the specified ending and the other without any keywords, based on five factors

| | Coherence | Inspiration | Narrative fluency | Readability | Word complexity |
|---|---|---|---|---|---|
| Story 1 | 8.23 ± 0.09 | **7.38** ± 0.08 | **8.08** ± 0.00 | **7.95** ± 0.07 | **7.21** ± 0.07 |
| Story 2 | **8.25** ± 0.05 | 7.30 ± 0.10 | 7.89 ± 0.04 | 7.93 ± 0.00 | 5.48 ± 0.19 |

The table also presents the standard deviations, which exhibit notably low magnitudes. Specifically, Narrative Fluency in Story 1 and Readability in Story 2 both register values of 0. The low standard deviation in the evaluation scores of both stories suggests that ChatGPT consistently performs well in evaluating generated stories in this context. These findings demonstrate the potential of using LLMs like ChatGPT, when given appropriate prompts, for generating and evaluating stories related to climate change and creating effective structures for story writing in the context of a VN game. The study also emphasizes the importance of providing relevant prompts and guidance to enhance the coherence and overall quality of the generated stories.

The findings from the study reveal that both stories possess their own set of strengths and weaknesses, and the selection between them hinges on the individual reader's specific goals and preferences. Notably, the coherence score emerges as a pivotal metric in this investigation, as it gauges the logical and seamless progression of the narrative, a crucial element for capturing the reader's attention. Importantly, these results exhibit reliability and consistency, stemming from an extensive array of trials, thereby facilitating a comprehensive comparison between the two narratives and the identification of their respective strengths and weaknesses. It is worth highlighting that, in the eyes of ChatGPT, both stories are essentially comparable in terms of their linguistic attributes.

However, it is important to acknowledge a limitation in our study. While we thoroughly examined the scores and identified the strengths and weaknesses in the narratives, we did not fully explore how these objective measures align with people's personal preferences or the views of relevant experts on the generated stories. This aspect, which is crucial, was not addressed in this study. In future research, we will focus on this intriguing aspect, which involves understanding how readers' preferences match the specific strengths and weaknesses we identified in the stories. This should provide valuable insights into how the logical flow of a narrative interacts with individual readers' tastes. Such inquiries would also help us better understand how storytelling significantly influences readers and offers valuable guidance for authors looking to tailor their narratives for maximum reader engagement.

## 5 Conclusions

This study highlighted the potential of using ChatGPT for generating stories related to climate change and creating effective structures for story writing in the context of VN and G4C. We evaluated two global warming stories produced by ChatGPT, i.e., with and without climate-change-related keywords and a specified ending. The evaluation focused on coherence, inspiration, readability, word complexity, and narrative fluency of the stories. This study revealed strengths and weaknesses in both stories. While we assessed the narratives' strengths and weaknesses of the stories, the correlation between our evaluation metrics with the readers' preferences was not addressed. Future study should address this vital aspect to enhance the comprehension of how storytelling profoundly impacts readers, and to guide authors in improving stories that optimize readers' engagement.

# Appendix

## A. Generated Knowledge of Criteria

- Coherence: https://chat.openai.com/share/502ac82b-83c4-4874-874a-1a380f73196c
- Inspiration: https://chat.openai.com/share/ba7b7c33-866a-4f95-8253-38ce9ea6c60b
- Readability: https://chat.openai.com/share/18bc9653-f692-4ed9-9f3b-fcf345f0dfd0
- Word complexity: https://chat.openai.com/share/9572b1cd-34d7-428d-96c1-e36ff83b261b
- Narrative fluency: https://chat.openai.com/share/684ead54-626d-4e2b-a6e3-fc56c3f4dd71

## B. VN Game Story Evaluation

We make our prompts, source code, and raw data available at https://github.com/Pittawat2542/chatgpt-visual-novel-evaluation.

# References


1. Alabdulkarim, A., Li, S., Peng, X.: Automatic story generation: challenges and attempts. arXiv preprint arXiv:2102.12634 (2021)
2. Antle, A.N., Tanenbaum, T.J., Macaranas, A., et al.: Games for change: looking at models of persuasion through the lens of design. In: Playful User Interfaces: Interfaces that Invite Social and Physical Interaction, pp. 163–184 (2014)
3. Antle, A.N., Warren, J.L., May, A., et al.: Emergent dialogue: eliciting values during children's collaboration with a tabletop game for change. In: Proceedings of the 2014 Conference on Interaction Design and Children, pp. 37–46 (2014)
4. Böhm, O., Jacobeit, J., Glaser, R., et al.: Flood sensitivity of the Bavarian alpine foreland since the late middle ages in the context of internal and external climate forcing factors. Hydrol. Earth Syst. Sci. **19**(12), 4721–4734 (2015)
5. Bontchev, B., Antonova, A., Terzieva, V., et al.: "let us save venice"–an educational online maze game for climate resilience. Sustainability **14**(1), 7 (2021)
6. Bostan, B., Marsh, T.: The 'Interactive' of interactive storytelling: customizing the gaming experience. In: Yang, H.S., Malaka, R., Hoshino, J., Han, J.H. (eds.) ICEC 2010. LNCS, vol. 6243, pp. 472–475. Springer, Heidelberg (2010). https://doi.org/10.1007/978-3-642-15399-0_63
7. Brown, T.B., et al.: Language models are few-shot learners (2020)
8. Camingue, J., Carstensdottir, E., Melcer, E.F.: What is a visual novel? In: Proceedings of the ACM on Human-Computer Interaction, CHI PLAY, vol. 5, pp. 1–18 (2021)
9. Camingue, J., Melcer, E.F., Carstensdottir, E.: A (visual) novel route to learning: a taxonomy of teaching strategies in visual novels. In: Proceedings of the 15th International Conference on the Foundations of Digital Games, pp. 1–13 (2020)

10. De Araújo Luz Junior, J., Rodrigues, M.A.F., Hammer, J.: A storytelling game to foster empathy and connect emotionally with breast cancer journeys. In: 2021 IEEE 9th International Conference on Serious Games and Applications for Health(SeGAH), pp. 1–8 (2021). https://doi.org/10.1109/SEGAH52098.2021.9551860
11. Engelbrecht, F., Monteiro, P.: Climate change: the ipcc's latest assessment report. Quest **17**(3), 34–35 (2021)
12. Fernández Galeote, D., Hamari, J.: Game-based climate change engagement: analyzing the potential of entertainment and serious games. In: Proceedings of the ACM on Human-Computer Interaction, CHI PLAY, vol. 5, pp. 1–21 (2021)
13. Ferreira, M., Nunes, N., Nisi, V.: Interacting with climate change: a survey of HCI and design projects and their use of transmedia storytelling. In: Mitchell, A., Vosmeer, M. (eds.) ICIDS 2021. LNCS, vol. 13138, pp. 338–348. Springer, Cham (2021). https://doi.org/10.1007/978-3-030-92300-6_33
14. Fiorenza, M., Duradoni, M., Barbagallo, G., et al.: Implicit association test (iat) toward climate change: a prisma systematic review. Curr. Res. Ecol. Social Psychol. **4**, 100103 (2023). https://doi.org/10.1016/j.cresp.2023.100103. https://www.sciencedirect.com/science/article/pii/S2666622723000163
15. Flood, S., Cradock-Henry, N.A., Blackett, P., et al.: Adaptive and interactive climate futures: systematic review of 'serious games' for engagement and decision-making. Environ. Res. Lett. **13**(6), 063005 (2018)
16. Guan, J., Huang, F., Zhao, Z., Zhu, X., Huang, M.: A knowledge-enhanced pretraining model for commonsense story generation. Trans. Assoc. Comput. Linguist. **8**, 93–108 (2020)
17. Janakiraman, S., Watson, S.L., Watson, W.R.: Using game-based learning to facilitate attitude change for environmental sustainability. J. Educ. Sustain. Dev. **12**(2), 176–185 (2018). https://doi.org/10.1177/0973408218783286
18. Johnsson, F., Kjärstad, J., Rootzén, J.: The threat to climate change mitigation posed by the abundance of fossil fuels. Clim. Policy **19**(2), 258–274 (2019)
19. Kampa, A., Haake, S., Burelli, P.: Storytelling in serious games. In: Dörner, R., Göbel, S., Kickmeier-Rust, M., Masuch, M., Zweig, K. (eds.) Entertainment Computing and Serious Games. LNCS, vol. 9970, pp. 521–539. Springer, Cham (2016). https://doi.org/10.1007/978-3-319-46152-6_19
20. Kar, S.: The impact of visuals on storytelling in visual novels (2023)
21. Laamarti, F., Eid, M., Saddik, A.E.: An overview of serious games. Int. J. Comput. Games Technol. **2014**, 11–11 (2014)
22. Liestoel, G.: Augmented reality storytelling - narrative design and reconstruction of a historical event in situ. Int. J. Interact. Mobile Technol. (iJIM) **13**(12), 196–209 (2019). https://doi.org/10.3991/ijim.v13i12.11560. https://online-journals.org/index.php/i-jim/article/view/11560
23. Liu, J., Liu, A., Lu, X., et al.: Generated knowledge prompting for commonsense reasoning (2022)
24. Martucci, A., Gursesli, M.C., Duradoni, M., Guazzini, A., et al.: Overviewing gaming motivation and its associated psychological and sociodemographic variables: a prisma systematic review. Human Behav. Emerg. Technol. **2023** (2023)
25. Min, S., et al.: Rethinking the role of demonstrations: what makes in-context learning work? (2022)
26. Naul, E., Liu, M.: Why story matters: a review of narrative in serious games. J. Educ. Comput. Res. **58**(3), 687–707 (2020)

27. Ndulue, C., Orji, R.: Games for change-a comparative systematic review of persuasive strategies in games for behavior change. IEEE Trans. Games **15**(2), 121–133 (2023). https://doi.org/10.1109/TG.2022.3159090
28. Orji, R., Mandryk, R.L., Vassileva, J.: Improving the efficacy of games for change using personalization models. ACM Trans. Comput.-Hum. Interact. (TOCHI) **24**(5), 1–22 (2017)
29. Øygardslia, K., Weitze, C.L., Shin, J.: The educational potential of visual novel games: principles for design (2020)
30. Schneider, S.H.: What is 'dangerous' climate change? Nature **411**(6833), 17–19 (2001)
31. Shaker, N., Togelius, J., Nelson, M.J.: Procedural Content Generation in Games. Springer, Heidelberg (2016). https://doi.org/10.1007/978-3-319-42716-4
32. Sheepy, E.: Get water!: exploring the adult player's experience of a mobile game for change. Master's thesis, Concordia University (2015). https://spectrum.library.concordia.ca/id/eprint/980066/
33. Simon, N., Muise, C.: TattleTale: storytelling with planning and large language models. In: ICAPS Workshop on Scheduling and Planning Applications (2022)
34. Skaraas, S.B., Gomez, J., Jaccheri, L.: Playing with empathy through a collaborative storytelling game. In: Clua, E., Roque, L., Lugmayr, A., Tuomi, P. (eds.) ICEC 2018. LNCS, vol. 11112, pp. 254–259. Springer, Cham (2018). https://doi.org/10.1007/978-3-319-99426-0_26
35. Smiley, J.: Thirteen Ways of Looking at the Novel. Faber & Faber (2014)
36. Song, Z., Sun, Y., Ruijters, V., Lc, R.: Climate influence: implicit game-based interactive storytelling for climate action purpose. In: Mitchell, A., Vosmeer, M. (eds.) ICIDS 2021. LNCS, vol. 13138, pp. 425–429. Springer, Cham (2021). https://doi.org/10.1007/978-3-030-92300-6_42
37. Steinemann, S.T., Mekler, E.D., Opwis, K.: Increasing donating behavior through a game for change: the role of interactivity and appreciation. In: Proceedings of the 2015 Annual Symposium on Computer-Human Interaction in Play, CHI PLAY 2015, pp. 319–329. Association for Computing Machinery, New York (2015). https://doi.org/10.1145/2793107.2793125
38. Sudhakaran, S., González-Duque, M., Glanois, C., et al.: Mariogpt: open-ended text2level generation through large language models (2023)
39. Swanson, B., Mathewson, K., Pietrzak, B., Chen, S., Dinalescu, M.: Story centaur: large language model few shot learning as a creative writing tool. In: Proceedings of the 16th Conference of the European Chapter of the Association for Computational Linguistics: System Demonstrations, pp. 244–256 (2021)
40. Taveekitworachai, P., Abdullah, F., Dewantoro, M.F., et al.: Chatgpt4pcg competition: character-like level generation for science birds (2023)
41. Thue, D., Bulitko, V., Spetch, M., Wasylishen, E.: Interactive storytelling: a player modelling approach. In: Proceedings of the AAAI Conference on Artificial Intelligence and Interactive Digital Entertainment, vol. 3, pp. 43–48 (2007)
42. Todd, G., Earle, S., Nasir, M.U., et al.: Level generation through large language models. In: Proceedings of the 18th International Conference on the Foundations of Digital Games, FDG 2023. Association for Computing Machinery, New York (2023). https://doi.org/10.1145/3582437.3587211
43. Wang, J., Liang, Y., Meng, F., et al.: Is chatgpt a good nlg evaluator? a preliminary study (2023)
44. Wang, K., Tekler, Z.D., Cheah, L., et al.: Evaluating the effectiveness of an augmented reality game promoting environmental action. Sustainability **13**(24), 13912 (2021)

45. Wei, J., Wang, X., Schuurmans, D., et al.: Chain-of-thought prompting elicits reasoning in large language models (2023)
46. White, J., Fu, Q., Hays, S., et al.: A prompt pattern catalog to enhance prompt engineering with chatgpt. arXiv preprint arXiv:2302.11382 (2023)
47. Yin, L., Ring, L., Bickmore, T.: Using an interactive visual novel to promote patient empowerment through engagement. In: Proceedings of the International Conference on the foundations of digital Games, pp. 41–48 (2012)
48. Yuan, A., Coenen, A., Reif, E., et al.: Wordcraft: story writing with large language models. In: 27th International Conference on Intelligent User Interfaces, pp. 841–852 (2022)
49. Zhao, Z., Han, F., Ma, X.: A live storytelling virtual reality system with programmable cartoon-style emotion embodiment. In: 2019 IEEE International Conference on Artificial Intelligence and Virtual Reality (AIVR), pp. 102–1027. IEEE (2019)
50. Zhao, Z., Song, S., Duah, B., et al.: More human than human: llm-generated narratives outperform human-llm interleaved narratives. In: Proceedings of the 15th Conference on Creativity and Cognition, pp. 368–370 (2023)
51. Zwiers, F., Hegerl, G.: Attributing cause and effect. Nature **453**(7193), 296–297 (2008)

# A Crossmedia Storytelling Platform to Empower Vulnerable Groups for IT Security

Wolfgang Heiden(✉), Tea Kless, and Thomas Neteler

Bonn-Rhein-Sieg University of Applied Sciences, 53757 St. Augustin, Germany
wolfgang.heiden@h-brs.de

**Abstract.** Although IT security issues affect everyone in our digital society, there are certain groups of people that are more vulnerable to cyber threats than others. As there are strong variations among (and even within) these groups (e.g. elderly people, youths, people with migratory background) in terms of awareness, cautiousness, self-efficacy and competence – not to mention the broad variety of exposure to particular threat scenarios, these people need tailored solutions for a personalized access to information offers. We present an approach to supply such people with motivating yet informative cross- and hypermedia material targeting different personal approaches to sensitization for and practical skills in IT security topics, based on narrative and gaming environments together with non-digital components such as human security mediators.

**Keywords:** Crossmedia · Information Security · Vulnerable Groups

## 1 Introduction

Information security has always been a serious issue and is becoming even more important in times of strong and rapidly growing influence of digitization and AI[1] on everyday life, in particular in such vital areas as healthcare, banking, and autonomous vehicles, bringing along far less desirable aspects like deep fakes, identity theft, and cyber warfare. While security tools race with the development of new threats, most systems are rather resilient against most forms of cyber attacks. Digital Natives grow into using security tools, but there are still a variety of people that are exposed to digital threats in many different ways, some of them not even aware of the risks and others stunned by anxiety, excluding themselves from many beneficial offers of digital life out of fear of possible security breaches.

These "vulnerable groups" are addressed by an R&D[2] project ("CrossComITS = Crossmedia Community platform for teaching private IT-Security skills to vulnerable groups") that brings together researchers from various disciplines such as social sciences, cyber security, and visual computing with the aim to develop a crossmedia platform with personalizable modular content that offers information for different vulnerable groups

[1] Artificial Intelligence.

[2] Research & Development.


L. Holloway-Attaway and J. T. Murray (Eds.): ICIDS 2023, LNCS 14384, pp. 195–201, 2023.
https://doi.org/10.1007/978-3-031-47658-7_17

(starting with elderly people and persons with a migrational background). Parallel to the development of an open online platform that offers information about the most important digital threats and means to deal with them, the project is also dedicated to the education of "security mediators" out of the target groups themselves and to raise interest in those who would not actively seek help or guidance regarding security issues by embedding the information in narrative and gaming scenarios.

## 2 Crossmedia Storytelling

### 2.1 Concept

So-called "security mediators" are implemented to help with spreading the information inside the vulnerable groups via personal communication. These mediators act as multipliers, as they are recruited either from within the vulnerable group or with an already established contact to this group and educated via our methods, so they can share what they have learned (and what they already knew) with their peers. We hope that the personal contact can improve the outreach of our educational materials even to those who are not reachable via other means.

Besides the education of "security mediators" from within the target groups, the aim of the project is to develop an open web platform to host various content on IT security issues for different vulnerable groups. In order to make it attractive particularly for rather reluctant users, information shall be embedded in stories and games that should generate an intrinsic motivation to be used just for entertainment (at least initially), while delivering helpful information for everyday life under the surface. Users will be able to configure their access to the platform to their preferences and needs, regarding levels of detail, media, overall means of content delivery (including barrier free media support, if applicable) or the selection of content as relevant for their personal situation. Users shall also be able to annotate the content and communicate with others within the platform, or even to change role from recipient to author should they wish to add their own story (completely separate or branching out of an existing story analogous to some fan fiction).

As an initial study among the elder target group indicates partially strong reluctance to use digital services due to low self-efficacy about how to deal with a diffuse perception of cyber threats, we have decided to rather encourage safe usage than produce even more anxiety by a focus on warning messages.

The personalization and modularization of the hypermedia storytelling component as part of the entire platform is based on the concept of Hypermedia Novels (HyMN) [1] that—though rather generic by nature—has particularly been designed for edutainment applications [2]. The digital content will be augmented by non-digital "tangible" add-ons as those are often preferred by elderly people with less initial affinity to online services.

### 2.2 Next Generation Hypermedia Novels

Digital Storytelling has been found to be beneficial in learning environments in various aspects [3]. General studies indicate that a combination of media (in particular those addressing different sensory channels, even if not all of them carry relevant information) can support memorization [4]. Hypermedia Novels (HyMN) have already been successfully used for edutainment teaching within an academic context [5]. In our new environment, an expansion of functionalities is required. The HyMN platform is therefore currently undergoing a retreading process in order to meet the various requirements of the project with up-to-date web technology. We therefore integrate the concept of a client-side component model (ccm) as introduced by Kaul et al. [6]. The new technical implementation of Hyper Media Novels using ccm web technology allows for a very high degree of adaptability and integrability based on web standards. In addition, a HyMN can then also be created via platforms such as the Digital Makerspace [7] as an iOER [8] without programming knowledge via web-based app editors and can also be used offline without an Internet connection.

In addition, the generic HyMN concept of various digital media presentations in a uniform yet highly configurable environment within a hierarchical tree structure of narration modules (NarMos) in the form of serial or parallel containers as branches and content carrying modules as leaves (see Fig. 1 [1]) is enriched by various interactive access options and augmentations.

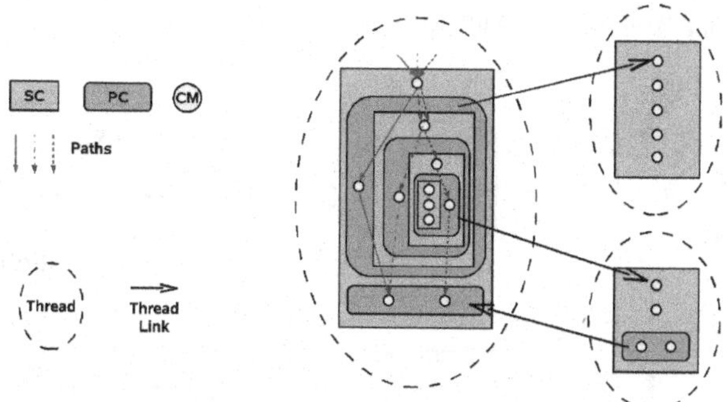


**Fig. 1.** Hierarchical structure of a Hypermedia Novel, showing different types of NarMos (SC, PC, CM)(including threads plus paths and thread links): SC = Serial Container (sequential scenes, vertical) PC = Parallel Container (alternatives, horizontal) CM = Content Module (atomic narrative media unit) [1].

One example for interactive augmentation is a web-based tool (ComED[3]) for graphic novels with several configuration options and an easy switch between different languages (see Fig. 2 for an example and Fig. 3 for the underlying component structure). Lots of comic (or graphic novel) sites (mostly in manga style) are available on the Web, many of which are already designed to be read by continuously scrolling along a vertically aligned and in principle endless line of panels on a mobile digital device. However, most of these lack features like panel-hopping within a pre-configured page structure or language-switch, which can be easily overlaid also to scanned pages of already existing comics originally designed for print media.

As HyMN rather defines a structure of modules than a media format, the output of other creation tools for interactive (or non-interactive) stories—whether text-based

[3] Comic reader for Electronic Devices.

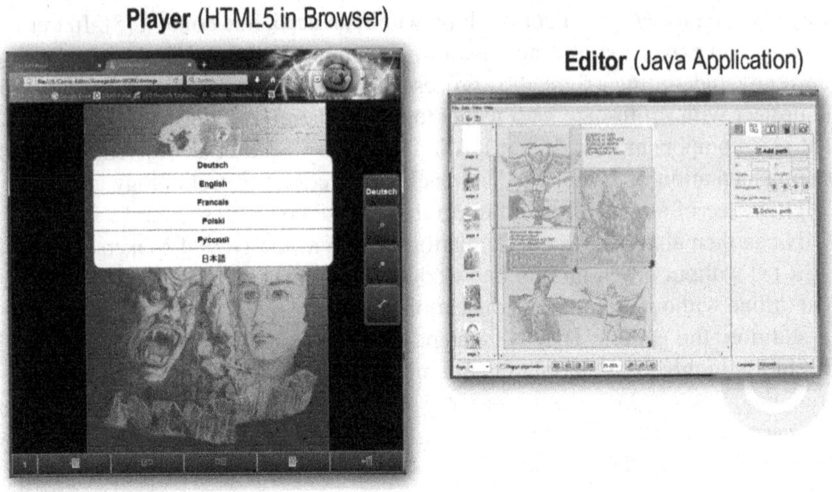

**Fig. 2.** eComic example in ComED: player app with language choice in a web browser (left) and stand-alone editor app with panel structure (right).

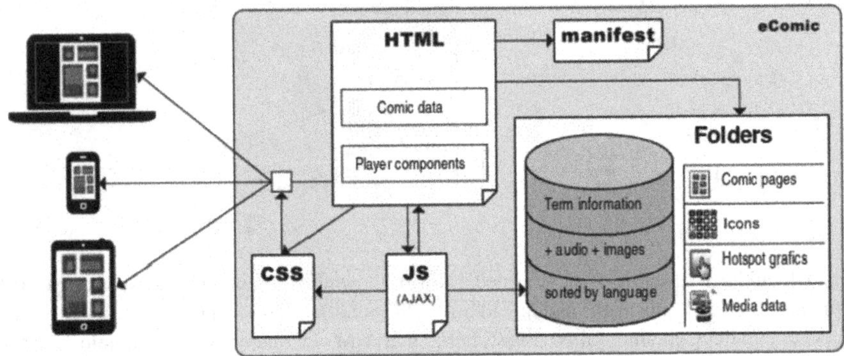


**Fig. 3.** Structure of eComic components in ComED [image source: Krämer, S., Master Thesis (2015), modified].

or enriched by other media types or even narrative games—can be easily integrated if this output can be displayed in a web browser. It is therefore possible to create HyMN modules with tools like Twine, Squiffy, Ren'Py, or others [9].

One characteristic of HyMN as compared to other platforms for interactive storytelling is the possibility to choose a personal path through the modular contents of one story. This can be done either by selecting from a pre-defined set of options or by navigating freely within a network of narration modules, where parallel containers indicate alternative presentations (e.g. brief or elaborate, different media, easy or sophisticated language, etc.), while serial containers provide for narrative consistency.

## 2.3 Content Considerations for Elderly People

**Initial Findings.** To get further insights into one of the vulnerable groups, we conducted a semi-structured interview study with a predefined interview guideline for the interviewer. Eleven participants were interviewed and recorded, the interviews transcribed, and analyzed using an inductive methodology [10]. The interviewees were recruited from a group of participants in a local digital education program, so they were intrinsically motivated to learn about digital devices and services. Since most of the interviewees were female (nine), it remains unclear if there is a difference between genders in the group of elderly people.

The result is a key finding about the self-assessment of the participants regarding their protection from risks and dangers in the cyberspace (question: "how do you protect yourself from risks and dangers?"). Some answered with a general "cautious approach" and seven answered with statements about giving up usage of digital services, if they do not understand risks and dangers. The fear of risks and dangers is so high that they rather not use any digital services at all than to expose themselves to these risks.

With these results, we assume a key constraint for interacting with the vulnerable group of elderly people: while developing the content of the interactive learning materials, keep in mind that no further fear should be instilled. Otherwise the results might be counter-productive with regards to the goals of the project: empower vulnerable groups.

**Next Steps.** We intend to first define a particular cyber threat situation relevant for a large portion of our target groups and then design different stories and games addressing that same core content that they can choose from. With the security mediators as multipliers we hope to get access even to those people that would not look for education (or edutainment) services on their own initiative. As we are in close contact with organizations such as EKASUR[4] and BAGSO[5], that have a long tradition and experience in support for elderly people, including IT education, we are confident that we can reach a significant share of our target group.

We expect that especially elderly people will need a highly configurable interface, since many of them have to cope with various motoric as well as cognitive or even mental constraints and handicaps. This group shows also a high knowledge variance in terms of digital devices and media.

From a user study with a first demonstrator we hope to find out which type of stories (e.g. crime stories, science fiction, etc.), media (text, with/without quizzes, video, etc.) and other settings will be preferred. In addition, we hope to learn which types of interactivity and what amount will actually be desired by our target groups. To aid with this goal, the demonstrator story will include variations on a particular IT security-related topic (e.g. the generation and use of secure and rememberable passwords) in different genres, media, interactive elements and access formats (e.g. URL, printed material, presentation on site such as retirement homes, etc.).

[4] Evangelischer Kirchenkreis An Sieg und Rhein.

[5] Bundesarbeitsgemeinschaft der Seniorenorganisationen e.V.

### 2.4 Non-digital Storytelling Components

A significant percentage of elderly people refrain from many—in principle very useful—digital services, including informational and educational services that might reduce their lack of self-confidence for securely taking advantage from social media, online banking, digital health services, just to name a few.

Cross-Media in the context of this project not only means printed hand-outs (although this is something much appreciated among senior persons). Online tools and services only reach those who are able and willing to find them. It therefore seems important to generate an initial motivation and self-efficacy in some people to actively search for guidance and make use of digital offers for assistance. To that aim, we intend to get back to older (in fact, even ancient) non-digital means of "interactive storytelling" by bringing our story content directly to the target groups. That may include traditional forms of real "story-telling" and readings or narrative multimedia shows that already integrate IT security-related content plus hints to a freely accessible, trust-worthy and customizable digital platform with more of that. Together with our security mediators who will help to accompany interested future users along their way into their personal digitization, that will probably reduce the mental barrier that otherwise might keep several people from using our digital platform (or other similar services).

As the reported project is work in progress, we were up to now only able to give some first impressions of our initial studies and ongoing developments. In the future, we are expecting to report on technical developments as well as narrative content and user studies.

**Acknowledgements.** The Evangelische Erwachsenenbildung an Sieg und Rhein helped with conducting the interview study. This work is supported by the German Federal Ministry of Education and Research (BMBF) under the research grant 16KIS 1623.

## References

1. Heiden, W., Ostovar, A.: Structuring Hypermedia Novels. In: Göbel, S., Malkewitz, R., Iurgel, I. (eds.) TIDSE 2006. LNCS, vol. 4326, pp. 98–103. Springer, Heidelberg (2006). https://doi.org/10.1007/11944577_10
2. Heiden, W.: Edutainment aspects in hypermedia storytelling. In: Pan, Z., Aylett, R., Diener, H., Jin, X., Göbel, S., Li, L. (eds.) Edutainment 2006. LNCS, vol. 3942, pp. 99–110. Springer, Heidelberg (2006)
3. Smeda, N., Dakich, E., Sharda, N.: The effectiveness of digital storytelling in the classrooms: a comprehensive study. Smart Learn. Environ. **1**(6) (2014)
4. Fassbender, E., Richards, D., Bilgin, A., Thompson, W.F., Heiden, W.: VirSchool: the effect of background music and immersive display systems on memory for facts learned in an educational virtual environment. Comput. Educ. **58**(1), 490–500 (2012)
5. Heiden, W., Räder, M., Fassbender, E.: Interactive storytelling in academic teaching. In: Aylett, R., Lim, M.Y., Louchart, S., Petta, P., Riedl, M. (eds.) ICIDS 2010, LNCS, vol. 6432, pp. 216–221. Springer, Heidelberg (2010)
6. Kaul, M., Kless, A., Bonne, T., Rieke, A.: Game changer for online learning driven by advances in web technology. In: Nunes, M.B., Isaias, P., McPerson, M., Rodrigues, L., Kommers, P. (eds.) MCCSIS 2017. Curran Associates, Inc., New York (2018)

7. Rothe, I., Kless, A.: Digital makerspace – a tool with multipurpose use and potential for teaching and others. In: 2023 IEEE Global Engineering Education Conference (EDUCON), pp. 1–4. IEEE (2023)
8. Kaul, M.: Student activation in iOER maker spaces. In: Auer, M., Tsiatsos, T. (eds.) ICL 2018. Advances in Intelligent Systems and Computing, vol. 916, pp. 34–45. Springer, Cham (2020). https://doi.org/10.1007/978-3-030-11932-4_4
9. Ciesla, R.: Working in Ren'Py, Twine, and TyranoBuilder. In: Ciesla, R. (ed.) Game Development with Ren'Py. Apress, Berkeley (2019). https://doi.org/10.1007/978-1-4842-4920-8_4
10. Thomas, D.R.: A general inductive approach for analyzing qualitative evaluation data. Am. J. Eval. **27**(2), 237–246 (2006)

# Introducing the Comic Automaton: Interaction Design Options for an Interactive Comic for Higher Education

Ido Iurgel[2], Jana Kalb[1](✉), Anabela Parente[2], Denis Malinko[2], Maren Weller[1], and Steffi Wiedemann[1]

[1] Faculty of Life Sciences, Rhine-Waal University of Applied Sciences, Marie-Curie-Straße 1, 47533 Kleve, Germany
janamariella.kalb@hochschule-rhein-waal.de
[2] Faculty Communication and Environment, Rhine-Waal University of Applied Sciences, Marie-Curie-Straße 1, 47533 Kleve, Germany

**Abstract.** "Tierschutz erLeben" is an ongoing research and development project. It aims to innovate the learning experience and knowledge transfer on the subject of animal welfare in agricultural training. We are currently devising concepts for interactive comics for learning. We call the framework a "Comic Automaton". We expect several benefits from using interactive comics, including efficient learning and an agreeable and engaging experience promoting exploratory learning. We present the current state of the Comic Automaton, the system design decisions that are currently pending, and the relevant considerations and methods to answer open questions. We believe that an explicit understanding of the design options is necessary for the development process of such a complex system. Formative evaluation results with students of agriculture so far are very encouraging.

**Keywords:** Comic Automaton · Interactive Comics · Interactive Storytelling · Learning System · Animal Welfare · Knowledge transfer

## 1 Introduction

Recent findings indicate that linear comics for science communication and education are advantageous for memorization [1], engagement, understanding [2, 3] and motivation [4].

Interactive, adaptive comics are natural successors. Imagine that the learner could influence the comic and its stories, experiment with values, decisions, events, data, and scenarios relevant to the specific learning goals, and interact within a comic panel. The interactive comic system would rewrite itself according to the learner's input. It would comment on the actions and suggest outcomes. The "Comic Automaton" would comprise elements of a simulation, personalized and adaptive learning, games, and storytelling. The user is empowered to learn by doing and exploring. The ideal Comic Automaton will even master strategies for the adaptive presentation of overview and details, according


L. Holloway-Attaway and J. T. Murray (Eds.): ICIDS 2023, LNCS 14384, pp. 202–211, 2023.
https://doi.org/10.1007/978-3-031-47658-7_18

to the current learning situation of a learner, focusing on what is important at a certain moment.

With interactive comics, learning can become fun, efficient, engaging, experimental, and active, among several other opportunities of the approach. The prospects are compelling. High production costs are an issue, and most examples of regular learning materials will rather use texts with comic-style illustrations and not full-fledged illustrations and storytelling [5]. However, the advent of new AI technologies promises radical production process simplification.

We are studying the usage scenarios and design choices of interactive comics in the project Tierschutz erLeben (Animal Xperience), which aims to digitally present knowledge about the welfare of cattle and sheep attractively. We want to improve the transfer of knowledge about animal welfare. In society, livestock farming is becoming increasingly controversial, both from an ethical and an environmental point of view [6, 7]. There is a growing interest in implementing strategies to improve animal welfare in livestock farming [8] and to integrate grazing animals like cows and sheep into sustainable circular economies [9]. Problems in the transfer of knowledge from research to practice are reported increasingly often [10]. Veterinarians argue that agricultural education should focus more on animal welfare [11]. Attractive approaches and learning materials are important to reach relevant target groups, which in our case range from vocational trainees to students in the agricultural sector. Our project (a) addresses the gap in knowledge transfer and (b) explores the field of interactive comics in teaching.

## 2 Related Work

The potential of gamification is also increasingly being recognized in the field of agricultural education, as shown, for example, by the serious game SEAGEA [12].

Our previous work includes GameLet [13], where we developed the idea of learners producing a story to attain certain learning goals and embedded this into a complete learning system. For the city of Moers, we developed a concept to use miniature interactive comics to explain open data to the general population, which inspired the current work [14]. Previously, we have studied how to flexibly embed shorter stories in any sequence into a larger frame story, cf. RheijnLand.Xperiences [15], Sofias Smuggling [16]. In general, interactive comics (or game comics) are not yet sufficiently understood concerning interaction and algorithmic storytelling, let alone in the context of a learning system [17]. Camingue et al. [18] describe how interactive visual novels were already employed for education, with questionable results, because of design choices that do not pay enough attention to learning goals. This necessity to thoroughly examine the design space is also the motivation for the work presented in this paper. We prefer the term "comic" to "novel" because we focus not on dramatic conflict, but on solving animal care problems. Neo and Mitchell [19] described that there is still in general a conceptual gap between interactivity and narration, in similar approaches, and we expect to be able to contribute to this matter by a better understanding of the narrative role of the user, in future steps.

## 3 Insight into the Comic Automaton

The Comic Automaton is ongoing work. This section provides an overview of its current design and functioning. The graphic comic style we have chosen can be exemplified through a header Fig. 1, which is a collage of planned topics.

**Fig. 1.** Our graphic design in comic style; created by Denis Malinko.

Current interactions include choices as in multiple-choice; activating actions as in milking a cow (comparable to "Heavy Rain" [20] and "Detroit" [21] games); scalar value choice as in setting the correct value of the colostrometer; free word inputs as in answering "what are the five Qs?"; choice of an instrument from the rucksack, as in choosing a glove to milk the cow. Figure 2 shows the planning of an interaction using the online prototyping tool Figma [22] and Fig. 3 represents a screenshot of the same interaction in Unity. The challenge in this interaction is that due to the low so-called Brix value, learners need to detect bad colostrum, find an alternative way themselves, and take a colostrum reserve from the freezer. Figure 4a and 4b represent another interaction in the form of a choice from the rucksack, learners will have to pick two correct tools out of a selection of (ir)relevant tools with which to determine the quality of the colostrum. With drag and drop, learners must execute sequences of actions correctly, or they decide on the right amount or timing. Some interactions only activate the learner, and their execution is not very demanding but required for a linear story part to move on, such as cleaning an udder before milking. Other interactions, such as decisions, will determine the story's unfolding and upcoming comic frames. Our approach combines static and interactive frames, allowing learners to gain experience with decisions, even if they are wrong.

For example, they can deliberately provide unhealthy first milk to a calf, allowing them to understand the negative consequences without causing harm to real animals.

Learners are encouraged to explore different paths and see the diverse outcomes that result from their decisions. Learners also have the flexibility to revisit their choices and witness the alternative storylines that could have emerged if they had made different decisions. Consequently, the entire comic dynamically adapts to reflect these changes.

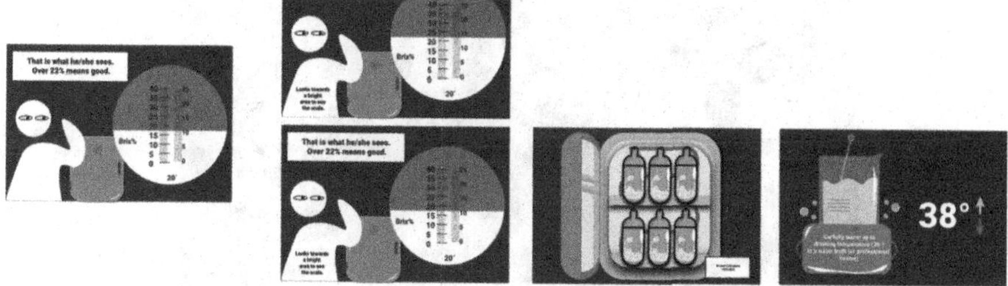


**Fig. 2.** Prototype of interaction about the topic "frozen colostrum" created with FIGMA

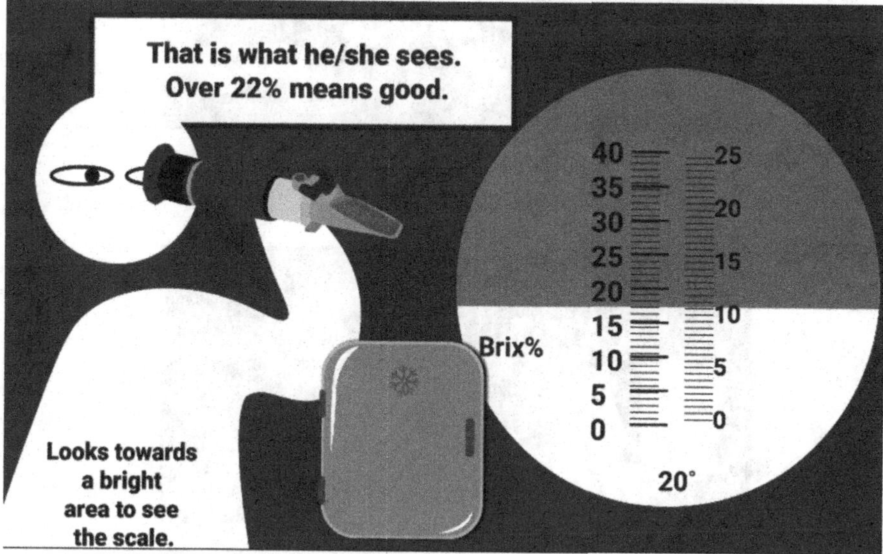


**Fig. 3.** The same interaction in Unity, does the learner recognize the low Brix value and find an alternative path?

## 4 Open Interaction Design Questions

We believe making design decisions explicit is essential. Only with an understanding of the design space can we get appropriate feedback and design participation of users and conceive of a plausible, efficient system. Essential open design questions (Q1–Q7) are discussed below including our current tendencies.

**Q1. Narrative Role of the Learner?** The learners could be regarded from different perspectives concerning their story role within the Comic Automaton. We are still fine-tuning the best perspectives and approaches. Those are open questions:

**Q1.I. Learner as Author?** If learners are viewed as authors, they have broad creative freedom in comic creation. Learning becomes a process of self-motivated narrating that reminds them of sticky drawings that learners might elsewhere use to add to their learning diary. The Comic Automaton in this approach would need to be a toolbox

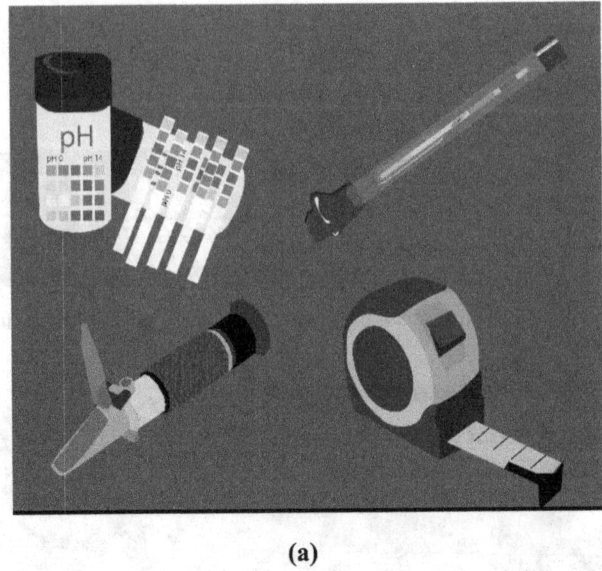


(a)

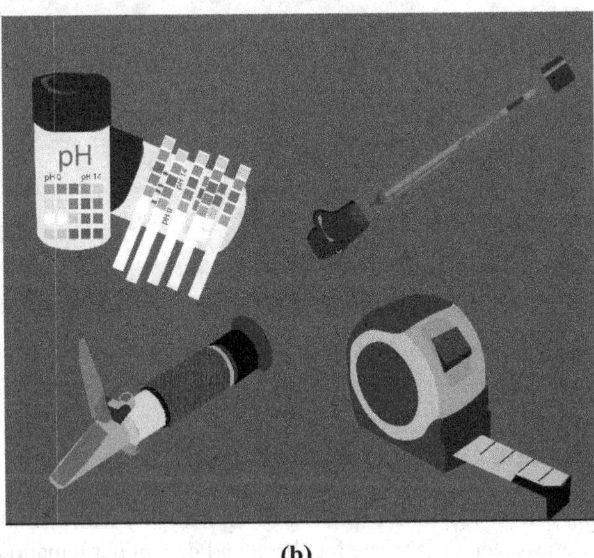


(b)

**Fig. 4.** a. Selection tasks, choose the right tool. b. Direct feedback, this is a correct selection.

that facilitates personal storytelling; it is a script-writing assistant that suggests stories, allows for the personalization of characters, and is a commentator that draws attention to correctness and improbabilities. In animal husbandry, learners could experiment with different management actions within their stories and observe the impact on animal welfare and farm economics. Because the learners must know the facts before telling stories about them, we are conceiving a learning path where, at the very end of learning several subjects, the users can create a stories with more authoring freedom, to test their memory and understanding. User-as-author perspective encourages sharing original story via social media; collaboration will be later explored in Tierschutz erLeben.

**Q1.II. Learner as Gamer?** This metaphor suggests that learners are completing tasks, answering questions, and trying to optimize their performance. Points, levels, and win-or-lose situations can be incorporated, possibly in competition with other learners. The Comic Automaton must provide appropriate game features. The learner-as-player perspective is currently secondary in our approach, as we focus on "meaningful gamification" [23] which is determined by perceived utility and actual purpose rather than points and badges. We want learners to enjoy caring for a cow without being fixated on high scores.

**Q1.III. Learner as Story Character?** In this perspective, a certain kind of interactive storytelling is central [19] where the learner is a story character who faces challenges and needs to make decisions. Other than in (II), there are no scores, badges, or extrinsic winning goals, but rather the motivation to experience how the story unfolds from the point of view of a story character and to treat the animals in the best possible way. This is our primary perspective. In this case, the Comic Automaton offers explicit stories and different storylines and results. How much social drama and depiction of emotions of story characters is appropriate is still an open question. Would additional drama engage or distract? We will certainly recur to storytelling techniques such as inner monologues and narration of feelings and thoughts, allowing us to dwell on knowledge requiring more texts. The potential of using frame stories that connect every learning step is currently under examination.

**Q1.IV. Learner in Other Roles?** There are plenty of other possible perspectives that we will not address in our project. We name a few here, with a hint on why we had reservations: Learner-as-God: If God, as in Black and White [24], cannot go back in time, then the author, is even more powerful. Learner-as-Sidekick: The feeling of agency is endangered and is probably not time-efficient. Learner-as-Mentor: An attractive approach close to "learning-by-teaching" techniques, but likely to be technically challenging and possibly not time-efficient.

**Q2. Drawing-to-Text-Ratio, and Integrating Text Heavy Parts?** Comics efficiently convey stories through visuals with a high ratio of drawing to text, i.e., in a comic page, the images occupy most of the page, compared to text. The other side is that comics cannot fully supersede that text. In most cases, transposing whole textbook pages into stories in comic format, retaining drawings-to-text-rations typical of comics, will likely result in a vast number of drawings and an inefficient learning experience. Sometimes, it is better to have dense text with only some figures instead of a comic. How can we devise a learning system composed of integrated formats of divergent drawings-to-text ratios? We are studying how to conceive a learning process that starts text-heavy to provide the necessary overview of the subject and where interactive comics come next when learning to test and consolidate knowledge. A viable alternative would be to accommodate larger text passages in the comics themselves, with dynamic layouts that adapt the overall prominence of the text chunks to the momentary learning requirements.

**Q3. Overview and Detail?** Comics are excellent media for gaining an overview of subjects because each page has a singular gestalt, even at a superficial glance, and details remain visible and easy to locate. On a paper comic, learners can easily flip pages and always know where they are in the story and will easily find frames that they may want to revise. Adapting the comic layout to interactions on different devices like smartphones is a challenge, and we're looking for ways to maintain the overview. Do we retain the paper-originated concept of a page, or do we think in terms of scrolls? How do we facilitate obtaining an overview of past errors while interacting with the Automaton, successes, and learning progress? We are pursuing solutions with distinct phases for overview and detail layout so that not too many layout changes and clicks will disturb the user. After completing a story related to a learning chapter, the system will guide the user to get an overview of the comic frames and reflect on correct and wrong decisions.

**Q4. Local and Global Agency and Adaptive Stories for Learning?** The interaction may have immediate results only. For example, the learner might not give enough first milk to a newborn calf, and it dies in the next frame without leaving traces in the further story. Alternatively, the calf may get sick some weeks later, with many other story events in between. This would happen due to a deficient immune system that develops, requiring medical attention. The first approach of a mere local agency is easier to develop in many respects, and there is immediate feedback for factual errors, which can be an advantage in learning. But global agency generates suspense and drama, is more realistic, and allows to naturally unfold substories, such as the story of treating illnesses that arise due to a deficient immune system. Therefore, we currently aim at a global agency in our project. This means we need strategies to link cause to effect narratively and to inject substories independently of the user's action. For example, if it is an important learning goal that lack of colostrum causes immune deficiency, and the user does give the correct amount to the calf, then the Automaton must be able to insert an alternative substory when not enough colostrum is given to demonstrate the point (the substory could blame a stupid cousin, say). Similarly, we need to record the learning state of the user and will inject story chunks for learning reasons, e.g., if the user has harmed a calf by providing insufficient colostrum, the Comic Automaton will see that a story is generated where a second calf is born so that the user can revise their first mistake.

**Q5. Social Fabrics and Drama?** In its simplest form, a story consists of an unfolding series of important events for learning, user decisions, consequences, and eventually appearing story characters. How much do social relations, drama, and depiction of emotion benefit our stories? What if a story character has an emotional attachment to a cow that gets sick, but fear of his mother prevents him from getting help, and the user in the role of the intern must step in? Would that promote compassion, motivation, and learning, or would it distract from the essential learning goals? In Tierschutz erLeben, we tend to employ social drama to a certain extent, cautiously, because the emotional and moral aspects of taking responsibility for animals belong to the learning goals, and emotions must then be addressed. It also allows for some additional fun.

**Q6. NLP?** Sometimes, we need textual input to check if the learner knows something, such as knowledge of the "Five Qs" of colostrum management. Talking to story characters, explaining to them what to do and why, or discussing difficult animal care decisions, could have great learning effects. Employing Natural Language Processing (NLP) carries tremendous potential. It will certainly one day become a core element of the approach, but there are not many safe and proven techniques at this moment. We will use pattern matching and probably proven libraries such as Rasa [25] to accommodate some simple character-player dialogue but no generative deep-learning frameworks that are now still too difficult to control.

**Q7. Learning Paths?** A storytelling system for learning needs to be adjusted to certain recommended learning paths. We must decide whether all the learning can occur in the Comic Automaton, e.g., if a student can study colostrum management from the very first contact with the notions to exam preparation with the Automaton alone. This would be very promising, but it is too complex a challenge for our current research. To simplify our studies, we envisage that the first learning steps will occur in text-heavy chapters of our webpage, where some interactive illustrations already prepare the learner to use the Comic Automaton after each chapter and to review, test, and consolidate their knowledge. A final global story shall encompass all chapters. A semi-automatic learning diary that records notes, achievements, and problems is the glue between the subsystems.

## 5 Methods

Previously, we have described some of the possible parameters of our learning system. It is virtually impossible to isolate one of the variables and deliver data-based proof that a certain isolated choice is best for learning "interventions". Those situations are embraced by Design-Based Research Methods [26] in learning sciences. Our project focuses on an innovative framework that can later lead to tests in controlled learning settings. In engineering, our approach to creating a complex system and learning from the building process and user studies is covered by Design Science Research considerations, [27]. Participatory and user-centered methods guide our building process. Two previous workshops with university students have informed our current design directions, in particular the use of cartoon-style drawings, storytelling, and an approach that overall is inviting and friendly. One prototype was a linear comic with learning objectives and different paths and interactions. We are currently working on the first fully digital, interactive version of the Comic Automaton and its integration with the learning platform and diary. We will analyze our current approach and inclinations with students at the evaluation and ideation workshop in November 2023 and shortly after that with education experts. The User-Experience-Questionnaire (UEQ) of Schrepp et al. [28] is an example of the tools that we employ.

## 6 Technology

We use the Panoply plugin for Unity [29, 30] but we will need to reprogram several features of this plugin from scratch so that a Story and Learning Engine can assemble the comic dynamically, according to learning and story states. Unity is embedded with WebGL in a learning system based on web technologies, particularly Angular [31, 32].

## 7 Conclusion and Future Work

We believe interactive comics can become important learning tools. In upcoming workshops, we will further develop our software and our understanding of the design of similar concepts. The current advances in deep learning approaches should soon facilitate content creation by editors and users of interactive comics and new interaction modes for users, including NLP.

**Funding.** We thank the German Federal Ministry of Food and Agriculture for the funding of the project "Tierschutz erLeben".

## References

1. Aleixo, P.A., Sumner, K.: Memory for biopsychology material presented in comic book format. J. Graph. Nov. Comics **8**, 79–88 (2017). https://doi.org/10.1080/21504857.2016.1219957
2. Bach, B., Riche, N.H., Carpendale, S., Pfister, H.: The emerging genre of data comics. IEEE Comput. Graph. Appl. **37**, 6–13 (2017). https://doi.org/10.1109/MCG.2017.33
3. Wang, Z., Wang, S., Farinella, M., Murray-Rust, D., Henry Riche, N., Bach, B.: Comparing effectiveness and engagement of data comics and infographics. In: Proceedings of the 2019 CHI Conference on Human Factors in Computing Systems, pp. 1–12. (2019). https://doi.org/10.1145/3290605.3300483
4. Şentürk, M., Şimşek, U.: The effect of educational comics and educational cartoons on student attitude and motivation in social studies course. Int. J. Educ. Technol. Sci. Res. **7** (2022). https://doi.org/10.35826/ijetsar.422
5. Kawamoto, H., et al. Your Amazing Immune System- How it Protects Your Body. European Federation of Immunological Societies, Berlin (2009)
6. Spiller, A., et al.: Wege zu einer gesellschaftlich akzeptierten Nutztierhaltung [Ways towards a socially accepted livestock farming]. Berichte über Landwirtschaft: Zeitschrift für Agrarpolitik und Landwirtschaft 1–171 (2015). https://doi.org/10.12767/buel.v0i221.82
7. Kayser, M., Boehm, J., Spiller, A.: Two sides of the same coin? Analysis of the web-based social media with regard to the image of the Agri-food sector in Germany (2010). https://doi.org/10.22004/ag.econ.100587
8. PraeRi: animal health, hygiene and biosecurity in German dairy cow operations – a prevalence study (PraeRi). Final Report (2020). https://ibei.tiho-hannover.de/praeri/pages/69#_AB
9. Van Zanten, H.H., Van Ittersum, M.K., De Boer, I.J.: The role of farm animals in a circular food system. Glob. Food Sec. **21**, 18–22 (2019). https://doi.org/10.1016/j.gfs.2019.06.003
10. Hoischen-Taubner, S.: Was steht dem Wissenstransfer zur Tiergesundheit in der landwirtschaftlichen Nutztierhaltung entgegen? (2021). https://doi.org/10.17170/kobra-202201155450
11. Dürnberger, C.: The last of us? An online survey among German farm veterinarians about the future of veterinary training, livestock farming and the profession in general. Int. J. Livest. Prod. **11**, 72–83 (2020). https://doi.org/10.5897/IJLP2020.0697
12. Jouan, J., et al.: SEGAE: an online serious game to learn agroecology. Agric. Syst. **191** (2021). https://doi.org/10.1016/j.agsy.2021.103145
13. Gamelet - Gamified Media-Based Training of Reading Fluency. https://www.gamelet.eu. Accessed 11 Aug 2023
14. Reallabor Niederrhein - ROGL Moers. https://rogl.moers.de/tiles. Accessed 11 Aug 2023

15. Kahl, T., Iurgel, I., Zimmer, F., Bakker, R., van Turnhout, K.: RheijnLand.Xperiences – a storytelling framework for cross-museum experiences. In: Nunes, N., Oakley, I., Nisi, V. (eds.) ICIDS 2017. LNCS, vol. 10690, pp. 3–11. Springer, Cham (2017). https://doi.org/10.1007/978-3-319-71027-3_1
16. Sofias Smuggling - Cross-Border Hunt, https://sofiassmuggling.de/. Accessed 11 Aug 2023
17. Goodbrey, D.M.: The impact of digital mediation and hybridisation on the form of comics. Professional Doctorate in Design (Ddes), University of Hertfordshire School of Creative Arts (2017). http://e-merl.com/thesis/DMGthesis2017web.pdf
18. Camingue, J., Melcer, E.F., Carstensdottir, E.: A (Visual) Novel Route to Learning: A Taxonomy of Teaching Strategies in Visual Novels. Proceedings of the 15th International Conference on the Foundations of Digital Games, pp. Article 77. Association for Computing Machinery, Bugibba, Malta (2020)
19. Neo, T., Mitchell, A.: Beyond the gutter. In: Nack, F., Gordon, A. (eds.) ICIDS 2016. LNCS, vol. 10045, pp. 375–387. Springer, Cham (2016). https://doi.org/10.1007/978-3-319-48279-8_33
20. Rain, H.: Heavy Rain [Game]. Quantic Dream, Paris (2010)
21. Detroit: Detroit: Become Humane [Game]. Quantic Dream, Paris (2018)
22. FIGMA, Free Prototyping Tool: Build Interactive Prototype Designs. https://www.figma.com/prototyping/. Accessed 12 Sept 2023
23. Nicholson, S.: A RECIPE for meaningful gamification. In: Reiners, T., Wood, L. (eds.) Gamification in Education and Business, pp. 1–20. Springer, Cham (2015). https://doi.org/10.1007/978-3-319-10208-5_1
24. Black & White, PC/Mac [Game]. Electronic Arts, California (2001)
25. Rasa- open Generative Conversational AI platform for creating and managing AI assistants at scale. https://rasa.com/. Accessed 11 Aug 2023
26. Anderson, T., Shattuck, J.: Design-based research: a decade of progress in education research? Educ. Res. **41**, 16–25 (2012). https://doi.org/10.3102/0013189X11428813
27. Hevner, A.R.: A three cycle view of design science research. Scand. J. Inf. Syst. **19**, 4 (2007)
28. Schrepp, M., Hinderks, A., Thomaschewski, J.: Applying the User Experience Questionnaire (UEQ) in different evaluation scenarios. In: Marcus, A. (ed.) DUXU 2014. LNCS, vol. 8517, pp. 383–392. Springer, Cham (2014). https://doi.org/10.1007/978-3-319-07668-3_37
29. Panoply: Comics & Splitscreen for Unity, Utilities Tools, Unity Asset Store. https://assetstore.unity.com/packages/tools/utilities/panoply-comics-splitscreen-for-unity-58506. Accessed 11 Aug 2023
30. Unity. https://unity.com/. Accessed 11 Aug 2023
31. WebGL. https://www.khronos.org/api/webgl. Accessed 11 Aug 2023
32. Angular Framework. https://angular.io/. Accessed 11 Aug 2023

# Sentiment Analysis of a Text Story Dataset Collected Using Illustration Cards

Suji Jang[1], Chaewon Seo[3], and Byung-Chull Bae[2](✉)

[1] Krafton, Seoul 06142, South Korea
suji1004@krafton.com

[2] School of Games, Hongik University, Sejong 30016, South Korea
byuc@hongik.ac.kr

[3] Madngine, Seongnam 13493, South Korea
cwseo@madngine.com

**Abstract.** This paper introduces a crowdsourced text story dataset using the story card images of a commercial storytelling board game. We collect 705 text stories using illustration cards, where each story is classified with its ending type - either a happy or sad ending. Then, the sentiment patterns for a series of illustration cards matching each text story are analyzed to explore possible emotional arcs present in each story. The most dominant sentiment pattern is Negative-Negative-Positive (N-N-P) in happy-ending stories; Negative-Negative-Negative (N-N-N) in sad-ending stories.

**Keywords:** Story Dataset · Illustration cards · Sentiment Analysis

## 1 Introduction

Stories are an excellent tool for communication and a fundamental resource for literary works with various media, including text, film, video games, etc. While stories are essential and everywhere in our lives, story creation is complicated and challenging. Making a good story is even more demanding. For this reason, various storytelling board games have utilized either story cards such as Once Upon A Time (Atlas Games, 1993) and Dixit (Libellud, 2010) or story dice such as Rory's Story Cubes (2006) to leverage story writing.

In academia, several studies have focused on storytelling games for narrative generation. Sullivan and Salter [1] presented a narrative generation system as a proof of concept, using tarot card images to generate either a comedy-based story or a tragedy-based story. Liapis [2] developed a competitive storytelling game based on word cards containing story elements such as order, love, and conflict. Additionally, there was a grand AI challenge for creative captioning using the Dixit storytelling game card images [3].

Visual storytelling refers to creating stories with a sequence of images (typically consisting of five photos), whose primary goal is to create a human-like


L. Holloway-Attaway and J. T. Murray (Eds.): ICIDS 2023, LNCS 14384, pp. 212–219, 2023.
https://doi.org/10.1007/978-3-031-47658-7_19

coherent story while maintaining the sequence (VIST: [4]). With the rapid progress of deep learning-based approaches, various attempts [5,6] have been made to generate better (and more interesting) story descriptions using a photostream. Furthermore, Hu, et al. [7] defined three qualities of visual storytelling - relevance, coherence, and expressiveness.

Story dataset is hard to collect since writing a good story requires time, effort, and inherent talent. In addition, labeling the story dataset is more demanding. ROCStories is a crowdsourced text story dataset where a story consists of five sentences. In ROCStories, the story ending (i.e., the last sentence) is connected with the characters and events in the previous sentences to evaluate the coherences of a story by choosing a proper ending from two options [8]. GLUCOSE (2020) is a large-scale story dataset incorporating commonsense causal knowledge based on ROCStories [9]. There is also a shared-character story dataset for evaluating story interestingness [10], containing annotations of the character's emotion and story interest.

To our knowledge, no publicized text story dataset is based on story illustration cards. Most previous visual storytelling story datasets use photostreams, which may constrain the user's creativity or imagination due to their direct interpretation. In this paper, we introduce a crowdsourced text story dataset using the story card images of a commercial storytelling board game.

The contributions of this paper are two-fold. First, we present a small-scale dataset including a set of story card images and matching text stories with the classification of ending types (either happy or sad). Second, we explore and analyze the sentiment patterns of the collected stories.

## 2 Dataset

### 2.1 Story Illustration Cards

We employ a commercial storytelling board game named 'Storypic' (YStory, 2014)[1] under the permission of YStory. We posit that illustration cards can help the user create stories with less burden of story-making. The illustration in the story cards has two themes - emotion and everyday life - consisting of 40 cards, respectively. Each illustrated story card is given a unique identification number from A_1 to A_40 (for daily themed illustration cards) and from B_1 to B_40 (for emotion-themed illustration cards). We did not provide the user with specific words (e.g., baby, love, etc.), which might limit the user's imagination.

### 2.2 Text Story Collection

We used Amazon's Mechanical Turk to collect text stories based on the illustration cards as a crowdsourcing approach. The Turkers were given a story-building prompt to freely pick three out of eighty illustration cards and then make stories based on the selected cards. Specifically, the Turkers were requested to create two

[1] http://www.eeyagitalk.com/home/.

(a) Example of happy ending story with positive-positive-positive pattern.

(b) Example of sad ending story with positive-positive-negative pattern.

**Fig. 1.** Examples of illustration cards-based text stories (Left: Happy-ending story; Right: Sad-ending story)

types of stories with different endings. One is to build a happy ending story, and the other is to make a story with a sad ending, such that the collected dataset has clear story endings for binary classification. In addition, the illustrated cards used in the story building are chronological, based on the three acts (1: Intro; 2: Development/Main Action; 3: Ending). Finally, the Turkers were requested to write a sentence containing at least one event for each card.

Story collection proceeded for one month from April 2021. When choosing a crowdsourced story collection, we expected the overall story quality to be inconsistent depending on the Turkers. We finally collected 705 text stories, based on selected three cards out of eighty illustration cards, comprising 350 happy ending stories and 355 sad ending stories.

Figure 1 shows two types of collected story examples. The left exemplifies a simple happy ending story - a girl confesses to a boy she loves, and he accepts it. The right is an example of another simple story but with a sad ending this time - about a boy who wanted to be a pro soccer player but died young unexpectedly.

The collected whole story dataset consists of 2,182 sentences and 27,797 words, with an average of 12.7 words per sentence and 3.1 sentences per story. The number of words for a sentence ranges from just two words (e.g., "He worked.") to 43 words (e.g., "As Karen sees the soldiers in the streets after leaving the building of her former employer that she just got fired from for having a low social credit rating, it quickly dawns on her that maybe her friends were right the entire time."). The shortest story consists of 15 words (e.g., "Tom falls in love with Mary.", "Mary accepts Tom's love.", "After marriage, Mary got pregnant."), and the most extended story includes 130 words. Table 1 shows the overall statistics of the collected stories.

Table 2 shows the top 15 frequently used verbs, nouns, and adjectives in happy-ending and sad-ending stories, respectively. While most words are commonly used in both happy-ending and sad-ending stories, some interesting words are exclusively used in each story. For example, '*Baby*,' '*Healthy*,' and '*Beautiful*' in happy-ending stories; '*Accident*,' '*Military*,' and '*Old*' in sad-ending stories. Figure 2 shows word clouds using the top 20 frequently used words (noun and adjective only).

**Table 1.** Statistics of the Collected Story Dataset

| Ending Type | Word | Sentence | Story |
|---|---|---|---|
| Happy Ending | 13,913 | 1,088 | 350 |
| Sad Ending | 13,884 | 1,094 | 355 |
| Total | 27,797 | 2,182 | 705 |

**Table 2.** Top 15 Frequently Used Words (Verb, Noun, Adjective) in Happy and Sad Ending Stories

| Happy Ending | | | Sad Ending | | |
|---|---|---|---|---|---|
| Verb | Noun | Adjective | Verb | Noun | Adjective |
| **Get(116)** | **Friend(82)** | **Happy(57)** | **Get(144)** | **Day(90)** | **Sad(40)** |
| Go(111) | Day(80) | Good(43) | Go(121) | John(82) | Long(27) |
| Become(71) | Boy(54) | New(40) | Play(52) | Hospital(81) | Bad(26) |
| Play(63) | Doctor(50) | Long(20) | Become(41) | Car(77) | Due(18) |
| Decide(47) | Money(50) | Able(18) | Come(40) | Friend(66) | *Military*(18) |
| Come(47) | John(47) | *Healthy*(18) | Die(39) | *Accident*(55) | Old(17) |
| Start(45) | Lot(47) | Pregnant(17) | Start(39) | Time(44) | Happy(14) |
| Find(45) | *Baby*(44) | Great(17) | Tell(39) | Boy(44) | New(13) |
| Give(41) | Hospital(39) | Sad(16) | Make(35) | Home(43) | Homeless(13) |
| Make(41) | Life(39) | Many(15) | Meet(32) | Tom(42) | Good(13) |
| Want(37) | Home(38) | *Beautiful*(15) | Lose(30) | School(41) | Little(12) |
| Feel(35) | Time(37) | Big(14) | Run(28) | Money(39) | Able(11) |
| Meet(34) | Game(36) | Outside(11) | Admit(27) | Game(37) | Next(10) |
| Take(30) | Love(33) | Late(10) | Drive(27) | Doctor(33) | Late(10) |
| Tell(28) | Dream(32) | Due(10) | Take(26) | Work(33) | Pregnant(9) |

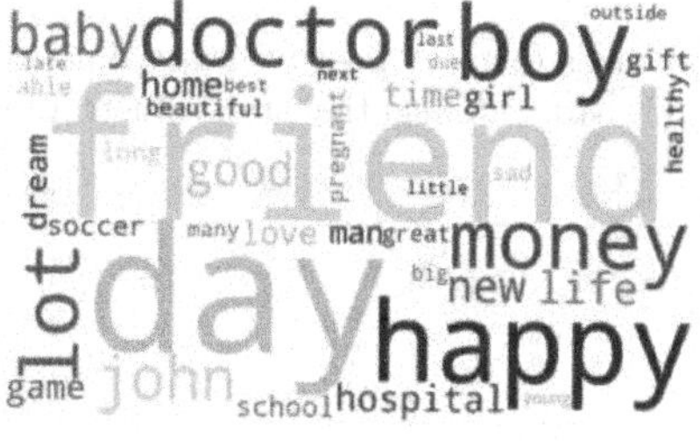


(a) Happy-Ending

(b) Sad-Ending

**Fig. 2.** Word Cloud for Happy-Ending (Left) and Sad-Ending Stories (Right)

### 2.3 Matching Words for Illustration Cards

The same image can evoke different words in our minds. For this reason, we collected a list of representing words for each illustration card via crowdsourcing. Ten Amazon Turkers described matching words for eighty illustration cards. Figure 3 shows two samples of matching word lists for two (positive and negative) illustration cards, where the bold fonts refer to common words described by more than five Turkers (i.e., agreed by more than half of the annotators).

gifting, giftbox, gift pack, **gift**, square box, box, generosity, **present**, thankful, thanks, birthday, loving, caring, wrap, tie, holding, ribbon, ribbon, offer, bow, green lace, red dress, white dots, dots, two hands, thoughtful, woman, surprise, love, smart, girl, give, gracious, handmade, special occasion, hostess

Total compound: 0.51819

**crying,** cry, cry a river, sad, sadness, **water**, man, tap, tap water, faucet, tears, plant, emotional, suit, wet, sobbing, upset, distraught, heartbreak, lost love, forlorn, face washing, waterworks, leak, black tie, tie, coat, white shirt, leaves, closed eyes, pain, agony, flowing

Total compound: -0.57812

**Fig. 3.** Matching Words List for Two illustration cards (Top: A positive story illustration card (VADER compound output = 0.51819); Bottom: A negative story illustration card (VADER compound output = –0.57812)

## 3 Sentiment Patterns

We analyzed sentiments for the eighty story cards using NLTK VADER sentiment analysis tool [11] about the list of matching words described in the previous section. The matching word list for the whole story cards contains 4,186 words, and the average word list length per card is 52.33. As a binary classification of sentiments, the sentiment of a story card is determined as positive if the average compound values for a list of matching words are greater than or equal to 0.1; otherwise, negative. Among the 80 story cards, there are 28 cards with positive emotions (positive cards, referred to as P) and 52 cards with negative emotions (negative cards, referred to as N). Of the collected cards for story creation, the proportions of P cards and N cards are 38.9%(822/2,115) and 61.1%(1,293/2,115), respectively.

Identifying the emotional arcs of a story [12] is crucial to understanding a given story. After classifying the sentiment of each story card, we analyzed the emotional arcs (i.e., sentiment patterns) of three-card stories. As expected, the third (i.e., the last) card in the happy-ending stories tends to be a P card (75.7%). Similarly, the last card chosen in sad-ending stories tends to be an N card (93.5%). Figure 4 shows the distribution of eight possible types of sentiment patterns in the three-card stories.

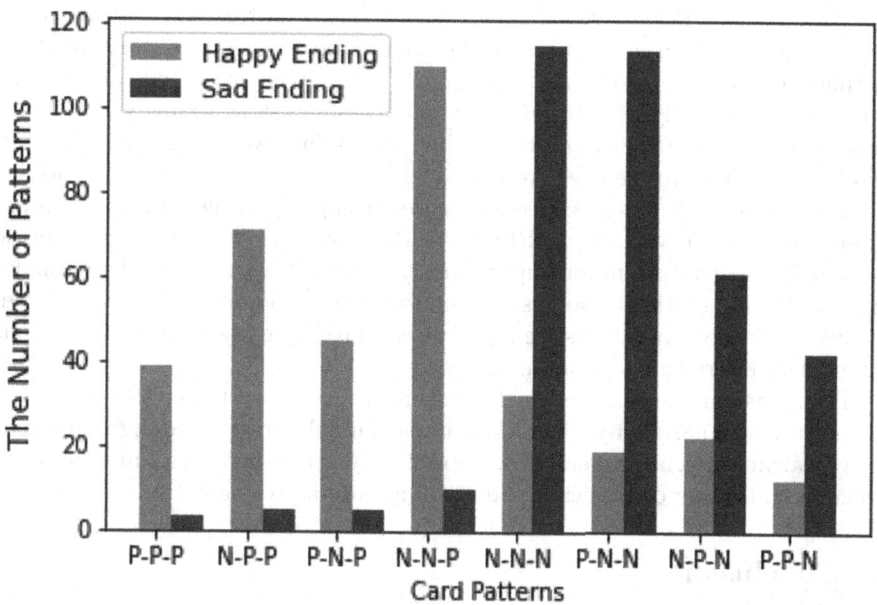


**Fig. 4.** Comparison of Sentiment Patterns of the Story's Three Story Cards According to Their Ending Types

As seen in Fig. 4, the two most frequently appearing sentiment patterns in happy-ending stories (represented as red bars) are **N-N-P** (31.4%) and **N-P-P** (20.3%). The frequency of P-N-P (12.9%) and P-P-P (11.1%) patterns are relatively low. Examples of the stories with these patterns are: 'Living in a war zone - A bomb caused a fire - King invited to dinner for peace talks (N-N-P),' 'Getting sick - Meeting a good doctor - Getting healthy (N-P-P).' Based on this observation, we assume that N cards are preferably selected as the first card, even for creating stories with a happy ending. P-P-N is the least frequently appearing pattern (3.4%).

As for sad ending stories (represented as blue bars), the two most frequently appearing sentiment patterns are **N-N-N** (32.4%) and **P-N-N** (32.1%). The second and the last cards' sentiments are negative in these two patterns. Story examples with these patterns are: 'Feeling loneliness - Mentally disturbed - Get mental disorder (N-N-N)' and 'Hang out with friends - Accidents - Hospital (P-N-N).' Naturally, P-P-P is the least frequently appearing pattern (0.8%).

## 4 Discussion

The sentiment analysis in Fig. 4 shows interesting results when making a story with three illustration cards. The top four sentiment patterns for a happy (i.e., positive) ending story are N-N-P, N-P-P, P-N-P, and P-P-P. Similarly, the four most frequently occurring sentiment patterns for a sad (i.e., negative) ending story are N-N-N, P-N-N, N-P-N, and P-P-N. Based on this, we can infer that negative settings and actions are needed for the positive-ending story; positive settings and actions for the negative-ending story. It is also noted that N-N-N is the most frequently used to make a negative-ending story, while N-N-P is the most frequent pattern for a positive-ending story. Thus we assume that the first two N-N patterns can be effectively used to make happy or sad ending stories.

The crowdsourced story collection process using the Turkers may have limitations, such as story quality. Although a few stories are excellent, most stories are simple and have room for improvement. Currently, we are working on making detailed annotations about story interestingness factors with the collected stories. After the annotations are done, we will investigate possible features that can explain interestingness in our further work.

This paper mainly focuses on the sentiment analysis of the collected stories. The sentiment analysis results and patterns can help create or design an interactive narrative regarding emotions. Specifically, emotional arcs can be crucial when designing key or branching points in an interactive narrative.

## 5 Conclusion

In this paper, we present an illustration cards-based text story dataset. We collect 705 text stories, each associated with three illustration cards. In addition, all stories have annotated ending types - happy (350) or sad (355). The sentiment patterns for a series of illustrated cards matching each text story are analyzed to explore possible emotional arcs. The most dominant sentiment pattern is Negative-Negative-Positive (N-N-P) in happy-ending stories; Negative-Negative-Negative (N-N-N) in sad-ending stories. While this work is yet at its early stage, analyzing sentiment patterns will be helpful for computational narrative generation or understanding research. We also plan to use sentiment analysis patterns to design interactive narratives in further studies.

**Acknowledgements.** This work was supported by the National Research Foundation of Korea (NRF) grant (2021R1A2C1012377) and the 2022 Hongik Univeristy Research Fund.

## References


1. Sullivan, A., Salter, A.: A taxonomy of narrative-centric board and card games. In: Proceedings of the 12th International Conference on the Foundations of Digital Games, FDG 2017, pp. 23:1–23:10. ACM, New York (2017)
2. Liapis. A.: The newborn world: guiding creativity in a competitive storytelling game. In: 2019 IEEE Conference on Games (CoG), pp. 1–8. IEEE (2019)
3. Kunda.M., Rabkina, I.: Creative captioning: an ai grand challenge based on the dixit board game. arXiv preprint arXiv:2010.00048 (2020)
4. Huang, T.-H., et al.: Visual storytelling. In: Proceedings of the 2016 Conference of the North American Chapter of the Association for Computational Linguistics: Human Language Technologies, pp. 1233–1239 (2016)
5. Nahian, M.S.A., Tasrin, T., Gandhi, S., Gaines, R., Harrison, B.: A hierarchical approach for visual storytelling using image description. In: Cardona-Rivera, R.E., Sullivan, A., Young, R.M. (eds.) ICIDS 2019. LNCS, vol. 11869, pp. 304–317. Springer, Cham (2019). https://doi.org/10.1007/978-3-030-33894-7_30
6. Hsu, C.-C., et al.: Knowledge-enriched visual storytelling. In: Proceedings of the AAAI Conference on Artificial Intelligence, vol. 34, pp. 7952–7960 (2020)
7. Junjie, H., Cheng, Yu., Gan, Z., Liu, J., Gao, J., Neubig, G.: What makes a good story? designing composite rewards for visual storytelling. In: Proceedings of the AAAI Conference on Artificial Intelligence, vol. 34, pp. 7969–7976 (2020)
8. Mostafazadeh, N., et al.: A corpus and cloze evaluation for deeper understanding of commonsense stories. In: Proceedings of the 2016 Conference of the North American Chapter of the Association for Computational Linguistics: Human Language Technologies, pp. 839–849 (2016)
9. Mostafazadeh, N.: GLUCOSE: generalized and contextualized story explanations. In: Proceedings of the 2020 Conference on Empirical Methods in Natural Language Processing (EMNLP), pp. 4569–4586, Online. Association for Computational Linguistics (November 2020)
10. Mori, Y., Yamane, H., Ushiku, Y., Harada, T.: How narratives move your mind: a corpus of shared-character stories for connecting emotional flow and interestingness. Inform. Process. Manag. **56**(5), 1865–1879 (2019)
11. Hutto, C.J., Gilbert, E.: Vader: a parsimonious rule-based model for sentiment analysis of social media text. In: Adar, E., Resnick, P., De Choudhury, M., Hogan, B., Oh, A.H. (eds.) ICWSM. The AAAI Press (2014)
12. Reagan, A.J., Mitchell, L., Kiley, D., Danforth, C.M., Dodds, P.S.: The emotional arcs of stories are dominated by six basic shapes. EPJ Data Sci. **5**(1), 1–12 (2016)

# Analyzing Audience Comments: Improving Interactive Narrative with ChatGPT

Xiaoxu Li[1(✉)], Xiao You[1], Siyuan Chen[1], Pittawat Taveekitworachai[1], and Ruck Thawonmas[2]

[1] Graduate School of Information Science and Engineering, Ritsumeikan University, 1-1-1 Nojihigashi, Shiga, Kusatsu 525-8577, Japan
{gr0557hs,gr0609ie,gr0634hi,gr0609fv}@ed.ritsumei.ac.jp

[2] College of Information Science and Engineering, Ritsumeikan University, 1-1-1 Nojihigashi, Shiga, Kusatsu 525-8577, Japan
ruck@is.ritsumei.ac.jp

**Abstract.** This paper presents a novel method that utilizes ChatGPT for the categorization of audience comments in game live streams, treating it as a zero-shot task. Audience participation games have gained significant popularity in the realm of game live streaming, playing a vital role in game promotion and audience engagement. Streamers employ various techniques such as storytelling and interactive narrative to cultivate a larger fan base and enhance the value of their streams. Simultaneously, the audience generates diverse comments that directly impact the streamer's interactive narrative and storytelling. However, the traditional methods for comment analysis in game live streams are lacking in terms of speed and cost-effectiveness. Therefore, our aim is to investigate whether ChatGPT can fulfill these requirements. Through experimental evaluation, our results indicate a majority choice of 54.34% and a human choice of 82.61%, showcasing that ChatGPT, when employed with suitable prompts, can address the aforementioned need.

**Keywords:** ChatGPT · Audience participation games · Comments · Storytelling · Interactive narrative

## 1 Introduction

As a highly interactive game streaming format, audience participation games (APGs) requires streamers to be attentive to the audience's state and behavior [1]. This attentiveness enables streamers to adapt their storytelling and interactive narrative during live streams [2]. Successful storytelling not only attracts dedicated viewers but also encourages subscriptions and followership. Streamers rely on viewer donations and in-stream e-commerce advertisements as a significant portion of their income, leading them to prioritize these revenue sources and carefully craft their interactive narrative while demonstrating their game understanding. However, limited research [2,3] exists on the impact of storytelling


L. Holloway-Attaway and J. T. Murray (Eds.): ICIDS 2023, LNCS 14384, pp. 220–228, 2023.
https://doi.org/10.1007/978-3-031-47658-7_20

during game streaming platforms such as YouTube, Twitch, or Bilibili and shows that streamers with strong interactive narrative and eloquence gather larger fan bases. Even streamers with exceptional gaming skills increase their chances of gaining more attention by providing satisfactory feedback to the audience.

Interactive narrative in APGs or game streams requires streamers to promptly respond to different audience types when addressing comments. Comments often include many comments with implicit meanings, which need to be interpreted in conjunction with the actual context. They cannot be understood solely based on their direct meaning. These linguistic exchanges often demand specific reactions tailored to the specific audience. For instance, during a game stream, the comment "LMAO" may appear, and streamers who are unfamiliar with this slang may be seen as unprofessional or uninteresting. "LMAO" stands for "Laugh My Ass Off" and can be used to mock poor gaming skills or express laughter when the streamer encounters an amusing scene in the game. If a streamer encounters an interesting scene and audiences comments "LMAO," it signals to the streamer that the scene is amusing. However, if the streamer asks what "LMAO" means and the comments continue to flood with "LMAO," it may be interpreted as the audience mocking the streamer's unfamiliarity with the acronym. This could affect the mindset of streamers, preventing them from performing effectively and potentially leading to a series of issues.

However, traditional methods encounter difficulties in handling internet slang and colloquial language. Furthermore, when there are numerous comments, streamers find it challenging to quickly discern the meaning of the barrage of messages. Typically, streamers are more likely to reply to comments they perceive as meaningful responses within the massive real-time flood of comments. If there were a tool available to them either during or after the stream that could assist in categorizing and analyzing the massive influx of comments, it would be highly meaningful. Therefore, we aim to leverage ChatGPT's capabilities to enable streamers to quickly and effectively understand their audience based on comments. This would enhance the communication, interactive storytelling, and personalized narratives within the context of game streaming, thereby enriching the overall experience for both streamers and audiences, particularly in the realm of APGs.

In this study, our focus is on the first-person shooter (FPS) game genre, which facilitates the acquisition of game states that are closely associated with the comments. This serves as an initial step towards analyzing comments in more diverse game genres, including story-focused role-playing games. To achieve this objective, we introduce an effective prompt methodology and evaluate its effectiveness in achieving our goal.

Currently, significant attention is directed towards large language models (LLMs) such as ChatGPT and GPT-4 [4] in various domains. Numerous studies have explored the applicability of ChatGPT in fields like education [5] and medicine [6]. Furthermore, ChatGPT has evolved to possess emergent abilities such as few-shot prompted tasks and augmented prompting strategies [7]. The study highlighted the unique capabilities of ChatGPT, setting it apart from conventional dialogue systems. Building upon prior scholarly investigations, our study leverages ChatGPT's capabilities in zero-shot prompting [8] and in-context learning [9]. These innate attributes of ChatGPT form the foundation of our research. The objective is to categorize these comments into five distinct types for a comprehensive understanding of audience engagement.

This work presents three contributions. First, we introduce a novel application of ChatGPT for analyzing audience comments in live streams for APGs. This empowers game streamers to efficiently understand audience profiles and deliver engaging storytelling and interactive narrative. Secondly, we provide a comprehensive experiment workflow to evaluate ChatGPT's proficiency in categorizing audience personalities. This detailed workflow facilitates a thorough assessment of ChatGPT's capabilities and performance in this specific context. Thirdly, the use of ChatGPT as a tool, when paired with suitable prompts, to provide examples of comment categorization in the gaming domain could inspire better utilization of LLMs as tools for serving the gaming industry.

## 2 Related Work

ChatGPT, an instruction-aligned large language model (LLM), offers the potential for natural language interaction in chat-based scenarios. Its application in the game industry has garnered attention, particularly in the areas of game design [10] and personalized gaming experiences [11]. The emergent abilities are rooted in two fundamental concepts. First, LLMs possess novel abilities that surpass those found in smaller language models [7], enabling them to handle diverse tasks including zero-shot tasks [8] for which they were not explicitly trained. Secondly, in-context learning [9] empowers the model to acquire new knowledge during inference without requiring additional fine-tuning, eliminating the need for parameter adjustments. This facilitates the acquisition of new capabilities without the computational burden and expense associated with fine-tuning. A previous study by Liu et al. [12] offered a comprehensive exploration of prompts and their significance in utilizing language models effectively. Furthermore, in a recent study conducted by Taveekitworachai et al. [13], an example was demonstrated of utilizing prompts, a text used to interact with LLMs, to teach ChatGPT to generate novel game content. This serves as evidence that ChatGPT proves to be useful in game-related tasks. However, there is a lack of research focusing on the utilization of ChatGPT for fundamental analytical tasks in the game field, such as audience behavior analysis, game state categorization, and affective state analysis. In addition, within the domain of interactive digital narrative theory, a speaker's cognizance of their actions' narrative impact, combined with control assessment, facilitates strategic plan formulation and execution in the realm of interaction [14]. Therefore, we propose to investigate if ChatGPT, when used with an appropriate prompt, can efficiently categorize audience types in a short timeframe while maintaining a high level of accuracy.

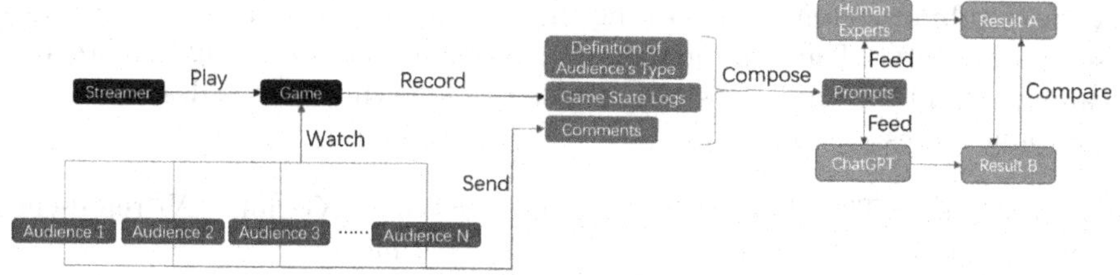


**Fig. 1.** Workflow of our experiment

## 3 Method

To assess the proficiency of ChatGPT in categorizing individual personalities of audiences, we develop an experiment workflow that involves evaluating the similarity between ChatGPT's selections and both the majority choice and the human choice, defined later in this section. This workflow is depicted in Fig. 1. It is important to note that a comparison between the results of human experts and ChatGPT is conducted to assess ChatGPT's ability in this task; however, during the operational phase, only the results from ChatGPT will be utilized.

Based on using the live streaming platform directly, it would be challenging to directly access backend data. Therefore, we used the Zoom video conferencing platform to simulate the live stream scenario. Following the conclusion of the stream, we systematically collect all the comments and game state logs. We synchronize these data sources using time stamps to ensure consistency. Subsequently, we construct prompts that incorporate the synchronized comments, game state logs, and the definition of audience types as outlined in the following paragraph. These prompts are then presented to both ChatGPT and our panel of human evaluators for the purpose of categorization. Finally, we compare the results obtained from the majority choice, human choice, and ChatGPT, aligning with our previously stated objective.

The concepts of majority choice and human choice are inspired by the research conducted by Wei et al. [15], where they investigated the similarity between solutions generated by humans and those generated by machines. In the context of our study, the similarity between ChatGPT's selection and the majority choice refers to the matching ratio between the majority of choices made by all human evaluators and the choice by ChatGPT. Conversely, the similarity between ChatGPT's selection and the human choice signifies that ChatGPT's selection is considered correct if it aligns with a choice made by at least one human evaluator.

For the purpose of audience categorization, we adhere to the previous study [1] and utilize the following five categories: (1) Helpers, (2) Power Seekers, (3) Collaborators, (4) Solipsists, and (5) Trolls. The definitions of the above five categories are explained in detail in the prompt sample.

In addition, we opt for an FPS, following a previous study [16], and empirically select eight distinct game states that correspond to moments when audiences submit comments regarding the gaming situation. These game states assist both ChatGPT and our human evaluators in comprehending the intended meaning behind the audience's comments. The following are the descriptions of these game states:

- Game State 1: The player is currently engaged in an $X_1$ game ($X_1$ represents the specific game type being played by the streamer).
- Game State 2: The player's health points (HP) are currently at $X_2$ out of the maximum value of $Y_1$.
- Game State 3: The player's remaining resources or ammo are at $X_3$ out of the maximum value of $Y_2$.
- Game State 4: The player has been actively playing for $X_4$ seconds ($X_4$ denotes the duration of gameplay).
- Game State 5: The player has encountered death $X_5$ times ($X_5$ indicates the number of times the streamer has been defeated).
- Game State 6: The player does or does not clear the current game level.
- Game State 7: The player is engaged or is not engaged in combat with enemies.
- Game State 8: The player does or does not successfully hit the enemy.

By incorporating the pre-defined audience-type definitions excerpted from the aforementioned previous work [1], an audience comment of interest, and the eight selected game states, we are able to construct prompts for both ChatGPT and our human evaluators. To elicit more direct responses from ChatGPT, it is advisable to provide a prompt that explicitly instructs ChatGPT to refrain from providing detailed explanations at the beginning of the conversation. Our prompt can be formulated, for example, as follows (note that in the first prompt in conversion with ChatGPT—see Prompt Sample—it is essential to include a statement "Only give the answer of the categories; there is no need to explain."; This ensures that ChatGPT delivers a response limited to the category alone.):

**Prompt Sample 1**

Select the current audience into one of the five categories–Helpers, Collaborators, Power seekers, Solipsists, Trolls–below based on the audience message and the player's current situation as follows. Only give the answer of the categories; there is no need to explain.
@Audience's message
The frame rate feels a bit low.
@Player's current situation
The player is now playing an FPS Game. The player's HP is 100/100. The player's remaining ammo is 612/630. The player has already played for 13 seconds. The player has not died any times. The player does not clear the game level. The player is engaged in combat with enemies. The player does not hit the enemy.
@Categories
Helpers: "Helpers" devised techniques to help the streamer achieve the goal.
Power Seekers: "Power seekers" participated with the sole focus of having impact on the game, whether the impact they had was helpful or harmful to the streamer.

Collaborators: "Collaborators" also agreed most strongly that features of the game enabled them to do what they wanted; it is possible, however, that not having a clear goal in mind allowed them to be satisfied regardless of the outcome.
Solipsists: These participants focused on obtaining personal benefits from the game, such as learning how to use a new tool or meeting new people for networking opportunities.
Trolls: These audience participants focused on bullying and playfully harassing the streamer.

## 4 Experiment

We initiated our game live stream on Zoom, featuring a single streamer and five audiences. The six experimental participants were all volunteers from the university. Throughout three rounds of gameplay, we eventually gathered a total of 46 comments. Each audience submitted their comments in the language of their choice. In order to ensure the alignment of each comment with the corresponding game state at each second, meticulous attention was given to capturing the timing of comments. Subsequently, all collected comments were translated into English for further analysis. We acknowledge that translation might lead to semantic loss, but the primary aim of this paper is to assess ChatGPT's ability to comprehend comments. Therefore, translation and semantic understanding beyond English are not within the main scope of this paper's discussion. Figure 2 illustrates the display of the game scene. Recorded videos of the streaming content and raw data (comments, game states, prompts and ChatGPT responses) are available on the supplementary file[1].

Following the generation of 46 prompts based on the description in Sect. 3, each prompt was subsequently fed to ChatGPT individually. ChatGPT then performed categorization of our audience types in response to the prompts. Concurrently, we devised a survey intended for our panel of seven human evaluators, seeking their assessments and categorizations of our audience types.

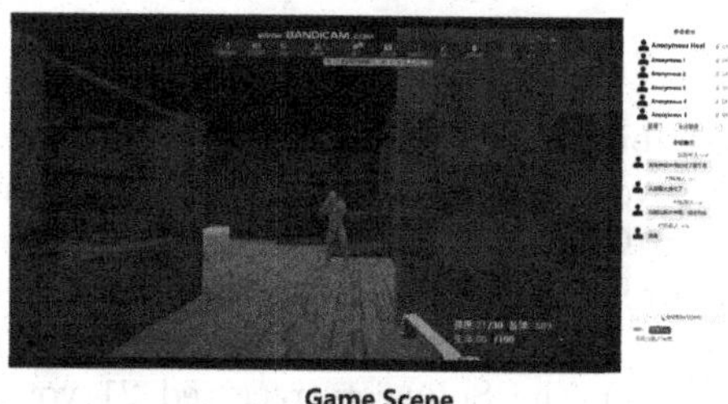


**Fig. 2.** Game Scene (To ensure audiences privacy, user names and icons were anonymized.)

[1] https://tinyurl.com/FPSAPG.

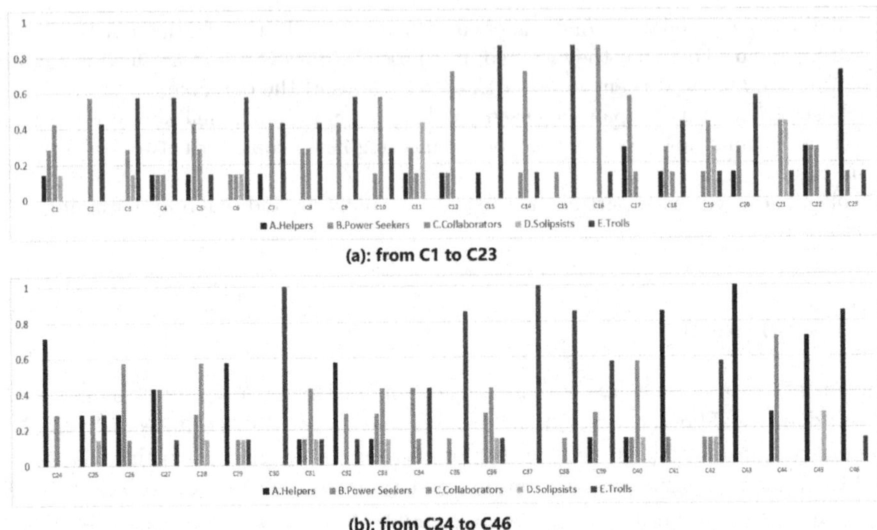


**Fig. 3.** Percentage distribution of each comment within five categories

Traditional methods encounter difficulties in analyzing internet slang and the intricate task of jointly analyzing game conditions (numerical data) and audience comments (natural language). If an existing traditional model is capable of handling this task, it would require the construction of a model that can effectively analyze both numerical data and natural language concurrently.

Additionally, the model must possess knowledge of internet slang, which necessitates extensive data and labeling during the initial stages, resulting in substantial costs when compared to ChatGPT. Considering the aforementioned factors, we adopt a chance level of 20% as a baseline performance, which serves as a reference point for evaluating the performance of our method.

## 5 Results

Fig. 3 presents the distribution of each comment categorized into five different audience types by the seven human evaluators; note that the example prompts in Sect. 3 correspond to C1 and C2 in this figure. Based on the analysis of their 322 categorization results, the findings reveal that the Helpers received 68 votes (21.11%), the Power Seekers received 58 votes (18.01%), the Collaborators received 77 votes (23.91%), the Solipsists received 21 votes (6.52%), and the Trolls received 98 votes (30.43%). These results suggest that, in our experiment, the audiences were more inclined to assume the roles of Trolls, Collaborators, or Helpers, rather than Power Seekers or Solipsists.

When comparing the similarity between ChatGPT's categorization and the majority choice of our human evaluators, it was found to be 54.34%. Conversely, the similarity between ChatGPT's categorization and the human choice was considerably higher, at 82.61%. These findings potentially indicate that ChatGPT exhibits a promising capability in categorizing individual audience types when using our prompt.

In Fig. 3, we can see that only two comments (C30, C37) were classified consistently by all human evaluators, while the remaining 44 comments did not receive unanimous classifications from human evaluators. This reflects the difficulty of comment classification, as different individuals may have varying perceptions of comments. Additionally, due to the limited number of human evaluators, we cannot definitively claim that our majority choice is always the accurate label. This is why we introduced the concept of human choice. It's for these reasons that we consider the accuracy of 20% achieved by the randomly chosen category in our experiments to be a relatively reasonable baseline at this stage. However, the issue may not solely lie with our human evaluators; some comments might not align perfectly with our five categories, leading to a lower consistency in human evaluator classifications.

## 6 Conclusions and Future Work

This paper demonstrates ChatGPT's efficacy in categorizing audience personalities during live gaming. Utilizing a prompt comprising an audience comment and the streamer's game state, we observe substantial similarity rates surpassing our baseline with respect to both majority choice and human choice. Notably, the former metric achieves a 54.34% similarity rate, while the latter reaches 82.61%. These findings emphasize ChatGPT's precise categorization of audience types in the live gaming context, providing valuable assistance to game streamers for improving their interactive narrative and storytelling ability.

In the future, we will optimize our work with more details. Firstly, we will address the issue of semantic loss due to translation. We will consider whether using untranslated text can better showcase ChatGPT's capabilities and also help streamers understand the meanings of comments in languages they are not familiar with. Secondly, we will explore ways to better represent the classification of comments that don't neatly fit into the five predefined categories. This could involve adding an "others" option, as comments might not always exclusively belong to a single category, but could be a combination of around 20% helper and 80% others, for instance. Lastly, we plan to incorporate ChatGPT's API to automate the entire process.

## References

1. Seering, J.: Audience participation games: blurring the line between player and spectator. In: Proceedings of the 2017 Conference on Designing Interactive Systems, pp. 429–440 (2017)

2. Gallist, N., Lattner, M., Lankes, M., Hagler, J.: Build your world-meaningful choices in a hybrid stage play. In: Interactive Storytelling: 15th International Conference on Interactive Digital Storytelling, ICIDS 2022, Santa Cruz, CA, USA, 4–7 December 2022, Proceedings, pp. 697–704. Springer (2022). https://doi.org/10.1007/978-3-031-22298-6_45
3. Roth, C., Koenitz, H.: Bandersnatch, yea or nay? reception and user experience of an interactive digital narrative video. In: Proceedings of the 2019 ACM International Conference on Interactive Experiences for TV and Online Video, pp. 247–254 (2019)
4. Liu, Y., et al.: Summary of chatgpt/gpt-4 research and perspective towards the future of large language models. arXiv preprint arXiv:2304.01852 (2023)
5. Van Dis, E.A., Bollen, J., Zuidema, W., van Rooij, R., Bockting, C.L.: Chatgpt: five priorities for research. Nature **614**(7947), 224–226 (2023)
6. Nov, O., Singh, N., Mann, D.M.: Putting chatgpt's medical advice to the (turing) test. medRxiv, pp. 2023–01 (2023)
7. Wei, J.: et al. Emergent abilities of large language models. arXiv preprint arXiv:2206.07682 (2022)
8. Wei, J., et al.: Finetuned language models are zero-shot learners. arXiv preprint arXiv:2109.01652 (2021)
9. Min, S., et al.: Rethinking the role of demonstrations: what makes in-context learning work? arXiv preprint arXiv:2202.12837 (2022)
10. Lanzi, P.L., Loiacono, D.: Chatgpt and other large language models as evolutionary engines for online interactive collaborative game design. arXiv preprint arXiv:2303.02155 (2023)
11. Biswas, S.: Role of chatgpt in gaming: According to chatgpt. Available at SSRN 4375510 (2023)
12. Liu, P., Yuan, W., Jinlan, F., Jiang, Z., Hayashi, H., Neubig, G.: Pre-train, prompt, and predict: a systematic survey of prompting methods in natural language processing. ACM Comput. Surv. **55**(9), 1–35 (2023)
13. Taveekitworachai, P., Abdullah, F., Dewantoro, M.F., Thawonmas, R., Togelius, J., Renz, J.: Chatgpt4pcg competition: character-like level generation for science birds. arXiv preprint arXiv:2303.15662 (2023)
14. Koenitz, H.: Towards a specific theory of interactive digital narrative. In: Interactive digital narrative, pp. 91–105. Routledge (2015)
15. Wei, Z., Wang, S., Thawonmas, R.: Difference in perceived similarity between humans and machines. Art Research **22**, 2 (2022)
16. Li, X., Wira, M., Thawonmas, R.: Toward dynamic difficulty adjustment with audio cues by gaussian process regression in a first-person shooter. In: Entertainment Computing-ICEC 2022: 21st IFIP TC 14 International Conference, ICEC 2022, Bremen, Germany, 1–3 November 2022, Proceedings, pp. 154–161. Springer, 2022. https://doi.org/10.1007/978-3-031-20212-4_12

# Integrating Storytelling and Making: A Case Study in Elementary School

Robert Monahan[1(✉)], Jessica Vandenberg[1], Andy Smith[1], Anisha Gupta[1], Kimkinyona Fox[2], Rasha ElSayed[2], Aleata Hubbard Cheuoua[2], James Minogue[1], Kevin Oliver[1], Cathy Ringstaff[2], and Bradford Mott[1]

[1] North Carolina State University, Raleigh, NC 27695, USA
{rpmonaha,jvanden2,pmsmith4,agupta44,jminogu,kmoliver,bwmott}@ncsu.edu
[2] WestEd, San Francisco, CA 94107, USA
{kfox,relsaye,ahubbar,cringst}@wested.org

**Abstract.** Digital storytelling in combination with makerspace activities holds significant potential to engage students and support their learning. When students *play*, such as through makerspace activities, they engage in critical thinking and problem solving. In our work, we are joining storytelling with computational thinking (CT) practices, physical science exploration, and makerspace activities through a digital narrative-centered learning environment for elementary school. Learning within the environment is undergirded by makerspace play that centers on finding solutions to an open problem—*how can stranded scientists on a remote island power up their village using found materials?* The learning environment supports students' CT practices and science content learning as they use and problem solve with physical energy conversion kits, culminating in their creation of an interactive story. We present here a brief case study of the ways students' experiences with makerspace play support their problem solving and storytelling.

**Keywords:** Storytelling · Makerspace · Elementary students

## 1 Introduction and Related Works

Experimentation in science classrooms dovetails with *tinkering* dimensions in CT and makerspaces by emphasizing inquiry through iterations of trial and error, while constructing explanations [2,30]. Making activities can support the learning of science concepts and CT practices. It is with this understanding of science content learning and educational play that we have designed and iterated upon the maker-style activities within INFUSECS (Fig. 1). The problem-based scenario featured in the environment is articulated as students study content and experiment with computational simulations to establish core understandings of energy conversion and CT, resulting in a storytelling activity, referred to as *Storymaking* by [4]. Students are provided with physical energy conversion kits that include varied inputs (e.g., wind, solar, chemical) and outputs (e.g.,


L. Holloway-Attaway and J. T. Murray (Eds.): ICIDS 2023, LNCS 14384, pp. 229–238, 2023.
https://doi.org/10.1007/978-3-031-47658-7_21

light, sound, motor). Students brainstorm how the materials might be useful in the context of an island stranding and demonstrate potential solutions. Chu et al. [6], utilizing a Making+storytelling framework, found that this intentional combination of interactions augmented and added meaning to students' stories.

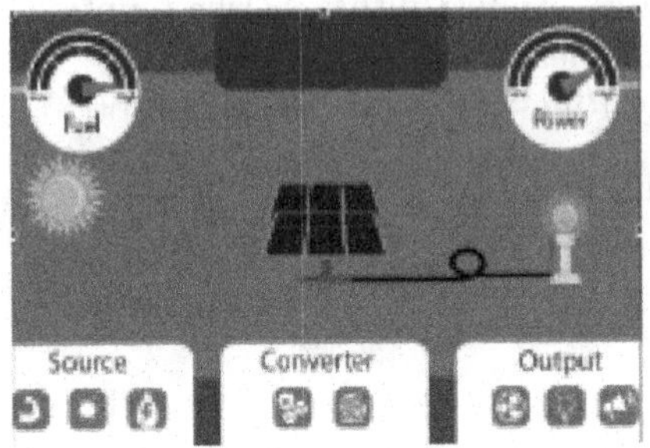

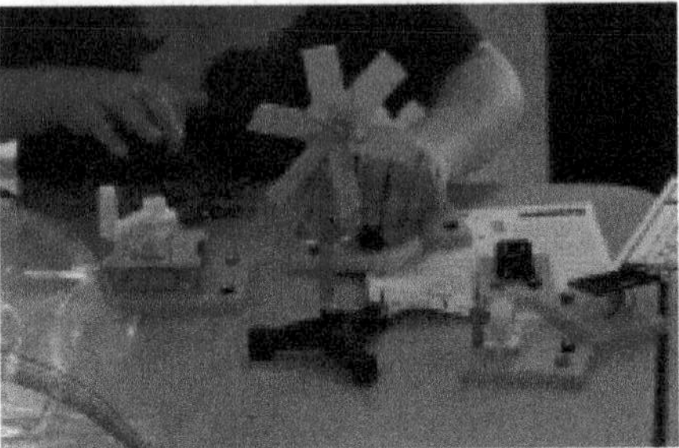

**Fig. 1.** Energy Simulation and Energy Conversion Kit

### 1.1 Storytelling and Storymaking

Narrative writing and storytelling have real potential to engage students in critical thinking and problem solving. Acknowledged as an accessible way to transmit information and communicate our understanding of concepts to others [1], digital storytelling in science domains supports students' learning [26], can improve the ability to recall visually presented information [28], benefits students' writing skills [22], and can enhance student engagement and understanding of socially relevant topics [13].

Varied attempts have been made to link storytelling and making activities. Toys of the Apocalypse (TOTA) introduces children to simple circuitry and engineering as they are immersed in a dystopian storyline [27]. Others have integrated students' interest in telling and drawing stories with maker-type materials including using conductive ink, such as StoryClip [16]. Chu et al.'s [6] *Maker Theater* adeptly fuses making activities, such as puppet design and use of circuits and LEDs, with storytelling as students create and act out complete stories with their puppets. *Storymaking*, a term introduced by Bull et al. [4], modernizes the processes involved in both storytelling and making by having students create animatronic dioramas with movement and sounds driven by scripts entered into a block-based programming environment, Scratch. A similar process was used by Manikutty [21] with children from 11 to 14 years old who used Scratch to program robots to tell traditional Indian folklore.

### 1.2 Design Thinking in Maker Education

The current educational landscape faces a significant disconnect with the evolving 21st-century workspace. Rooted in an overwhelming desire for standardization, educational institutions resort to universal metrics to evaluate success and track progress, overlooking the diversity of learners. As a result, the current system rewards conformity and individual accomplishment, even as real-world scenarios increasingly demand teamwork and project-based competencies.

Presenting K-12 students with real-world problems as a part of a design thinking-oriented pedagogy enhances the learning experience. This approach can shift learning from a task of information memorization to a driven, purposeful quest for knowledge needed to solve specific problems. As a result, design thinking and problem-solving skills can transform students into global citizens, committed to innovatively addressing global challenges—this type of student innovator is currently underrepresented in our educational settings [31].

### 1.3 The Emergence of Deep Learning Through Making

Makerspaces, defined as innovative environments that encompass everything from woodworking shops to 21st-century tech labs, have been cropping up internationally. As educational reform leans heavily toward STEM (Science, Technology, Engineering, and Mathematics), these spaces are making their way into educational settings, museums, and homes. Makerspaces hold the potential to help foster creativity through design thinking. To prepare students for a world that demands innovators, we must teach creative problem-solving intentionally and deliberately [31].

Further, makerspaces offer a unique perspective on the computational aspect of problem-solving, which involves deconstructing the problem and making calculated decisions [25]. They allow learners to physically act out their learning, creating a narrative of their problem-solving journey [7], thereby deepening their understanding and allowing them to contextualize the significance of their solutions in societal and environmental terms [14].

Makerspaces, by their very nature, facilitate the creation of narratives encapsulating the entire problem-based learning process that a student, or a character represented by the student in a game, goes through. As immersive, hands-on environments, makerspaces foster the organic emergence of problem identification, ideation, resource management, prototyping, testing, and reflection [29]. This iterative design thinking process is brought to life within the makerspace and can be meticulously chronicled by the student in narrative form. The writing of this narrative not only assists in solidifying the student's understanding but also adds a layer of metacognition to the learning experience, allowing them to deeply reflect on their problem-solving journey [32].

Moreover, the connection between the makerspace experience and the narrative allows the student to situate their problem-solving process within the broader societal and environmental context, extending the relevance of their learning beyond the confines of the classroom and into the real world [8].

Makerspaces, therefore, aid in decision-making driven by both intrinsic and extrinsic learner characteristics. Intrinsic characteristics include metacognitive control, personality type, and motivation [19]. Extrinsic characteristics refer to influences from the environment, including relationships with facilitators and peers within the makerspace [29].

A review of maker-related research found that programming with fabrication supports "engagement in complex programming concepts (e.g., loops, conditionals) and practices (e.g., remix, testing, and debugging)" [23, p. 62], and they recommended design-based maker activities that support "digital literacy and design thinking." Through its narrative-centered making activities, INFUSECS directly leverages programming with fabrication as students learn about energy conversion in the system, interact with digital simulations, and build physical solutions to the problem. In this poster, we present a brief overview of our design process and takeaways from a study focused on student learning via hybrid-digital maker activities.

## 2 Method

### 2.1 Participants and Context

We worked with five 4th and 5th grade students as they attended a three-week summer camp run by a community organization that offers after- and out-of-school care and related services. All students identified as Black/African American and included 4 boys and 1 girl. Their summer camp experience included: daily devotional time, academic time, free exploration time, and several field trips.

### 2.2 Daily Activities

We worked with the students for three days of their three-week camp. We used our digital learning environment, INFUSECS, to center the students' learning. This narrative-centered environment details how scientists became shipwrecked on a deserted island, but that they were able to salvage some materials from the ship. The scientists are working on how to bring electric power to the island, using only the materials they have. There are several locations on the island where the students learn about specific types of energy and energy conversion. The storytelling activities occurred using a block-based programming environment wherein the students utilize blocks such as *Dialogue* and *Stage Direction.*

On day one, we sought individual student assent for participation and use of their data, then introduced students to INFUSECS. The first location students encountered on the deserted island in the digital learning environment showed them how chemical and solar energy works. Working in pairs, an offline activity that day asked students to use maker-type materials to manifest their learning into a physical demonstration of these energies. For example, students built circuits and explored the power difference between the amount of energy supplied by batteries versus sunlight by comparing the brightness of their light bulbs or the speed of their spinning motors (see Fig. 2). These activities directly impacted the student decisions that were being made while trying to solve the problems identified in the storyline on the island. On day two, the students visited a second location on the island in the digital learning environment where they learned about wind and mechanical energy. As with day one, students were then given maker materials to bring this concept to life. For example, they assembled miniature wind turbines to visualize the conversion of wind energy to mechanical energy (see Fig. 3). On day three, the students learned about the basics of block-based programming within the digital learning environment and began creating a story that told how they envisioned the scientists finally using their salvaged materials to bring power to the island. It is here that we focus our analysis, although the scientific concepts and maker activities occurred earlier.

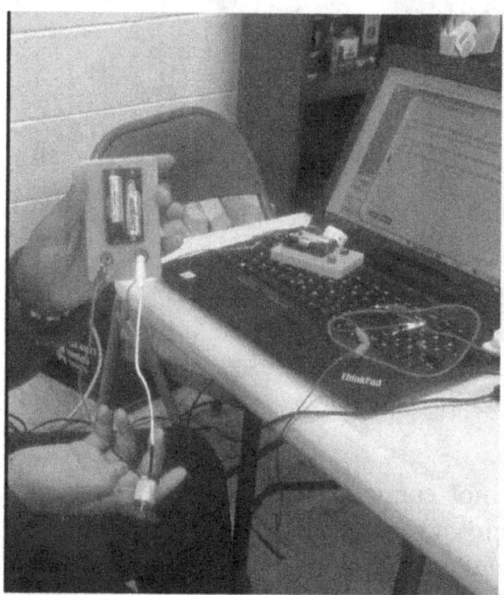

**Fig. 2.** A student works with batteries

### 2.3 Analysis

Our analysis makes use of interview data collected from the students at the end of the implementation and observations of the students collected during the implementation. Case study research centers on delineating what is under study, more so than a methodological approach [12]. The boundaries for this study is both a group of participants and a single activity. We narrow our focus on a group of upper elementary students enrolled in a summer camp as they engage in science-focused storymaking.

## 3 Findings and Themes

### 3.1 Theme 1: Persistence Through Challenges

All participants expressed moments of difficulty or uncertainty during the maker activities. They persisted through these challenges by engaging in iterative testing and redesigning, such as "switching wires until it worked," "I noticed that

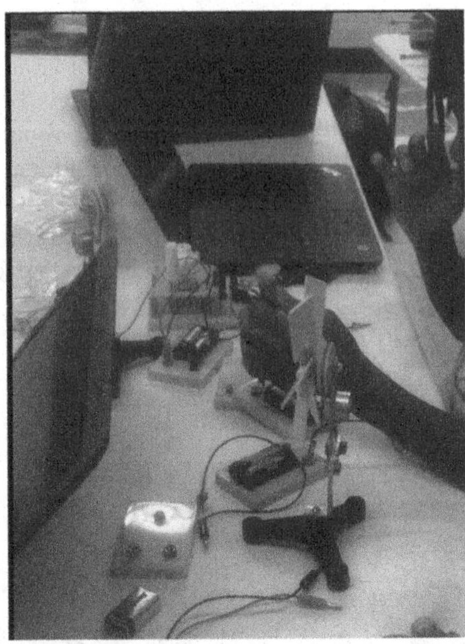

**Fig. 3.** A student's assembled wind turbine

the rubber band was not connected, so I fixed it,", or "switched out the motor and found that the motor was actually broken." This theme demonstrates the development of problem-solving skills among students. The hands-on makerspace activities encouraged them to experiment, make mistakes, revise their designs, and learn from their failures. This aligns with the concept of "productive failure" [17], where learners grapple with complex problems, fail, and then learn through their struggles.

### 3.2 Theme 2: Making Connections to Real Life

The participants identified links between their maker activities and their everyday life, which helped them understand the science concepts better. Examples include one student relating the wiring activity to his father's work with speakers, another observing solar panels in his community, and a third drawing a comparison between the crank and old video cameras. This real-world connection reinforces the importance of "authentic learning" in educational contexts [15]. The students' ability to relate the makerspace activities to real-life situations may have enhanced their learning by providing relevance and context to abstract science concepts.

### 3.3 Theme 3: Storytelling as a Tool for Understanding

The participants used storytelling to help them understand and articulate their solutions better. This was most evident in a student's story about two people trying to make a fan work using thermal energy. The narratives provided a context for their solution and made the learning more relatable and concrete. Storytelling was utilized as a cognitive tool to facilitate understanding and learning, aligning with Bruner's [3] theory of narrative construction of reality. It allowed students to create coherent narratives of their experiences, helping them organize their thoughts and understand their solutions more deeply.

### 3.4 Theme 4: Preference for Hands-on Learning

All of the participants preferred hands-on learning with the materials and found this type of learning more engaging and effective than the digital resources alone. For example, one student stated, "The hands-on parts made it more interesting for me. I learn better with hands-on projects than just reading." The students' preference for hands-on learning underscores the power of "experiential learning" [18]. This suggests that the physical manipulation of materials provided a concrete experience for reflection, conceptual understanding, and subsequent application.

### 3.5 Theme 5: Understanding Energy Conversions

The interviews showed that the students understood the concepts of energy conversion and began to apply these understandings to their projects. For instance, one student understood that the fan needed solar energy to work, another student noticed that the motor got hot from friction, and a third noticed that some devices need more energy to work. This theme demonstrates the effective integration of science content knowledge with hands-on maker activities. This reflects the theoretical underpinnings of "constructionism" [24], which suggests that students learn most effectively when they construct physical artifacts that can be shared with others.

## 4 Discussion and Conclusion

By examining these themes, it is clear that the integration of makerspace activities and storytelling created a holistic educational experience, fostering not only problem-solving skills but also creativity, empathy, and understanding. The hands-on nature of the makerspace allowed students to engage in experimentation and iteration, while storytelling enabled them to contextualize and articulate their experiences, through their characters while weaving in critical thinking and imagination.

Through the act of storytelling, students were not just solving problems collaboratively, but building narratives that connected them to real-world situations. This narrative-building helped them make sense of their activities within the makerspace, transforming abstract concepts into tangible experiences that they could relate to and learn from. It allowed them to see not just the 'what' and 'how' of problem solving but the 'why,' giving deeper meaning to their activities and facilitating a more profound connection to the learning material.

Our everyday decisions are governed by many intrapersonal factors, such as temperaments, personality traits, previous experiences, cultural and religious beliefs, and instincts. While not all decisions equate to problem responses, problem resolution always necessitates decisions. This correlates with a social-constructivist view, suggesting that decision making is not a solitary mental process but instead a dynamic, reiterative, and flexible one, potentially benefiting from group involvement [5]. A strong disposition toward critical thinking leads to more effective problem solving, producing logical solutions or valid argument conclusions [10,11]. In this age of information overload, critical thinking is becoming paramount to identify and evaluate misinformation, especially during collaborative problem-solving efforts.

Moreover, maker environments prompt learners to exercise their metacognitive awareness, knowledge, and monitoring that guide their situated cognitive strategies. As Liu and Liu [20] suggest, assessing problem-solving capabilities should include an examination of the problem-solving behaviors employed. Makerspaces are the perfect setting for this, as they inherently encourage the use of both self-regulated and socially-regulated learning skills, assisting learners in understanding task requirements, strategy selection, progress monitoring, and reflecting on the efficacy of chosen strategies [9,29].

The case study highlighted the multifaceted nature of problem solving within the context of makerspaces. Makerspaces, or creative DIY spaces, are educational settings where individuals can gather to create, invent, and learn, serving as a playground for nurturing the skills required for complex collaborative problem-solving. The dynamic interplay between task-maker and task-doer, enriched by storytelling, created an environment where learners could explore various strategies and reflect on their choices, engaging both cognitive and metacognitive skills. Assessing problem-solving capabilities thus transcended mere technical proficiency, encompassing the emotional, social, and imaginative realms as well.

To conclude, our learning environment revealed a compelling interconnection between storytelling and making in an elementary school setting. Makerspaces, far from being mere venues for technical experimentation, emerged as vibrant ecosystems where the spheres of imagination and reality intersect and where students are able to simultaneously sharpen their problem-solving abilities and their capacity to connect, create, and understand the world around them. The case study offers valuable insight into the potential of this integration, expanding our understanding of educational practices that accompany the multifaceted nature of today's learners and the complex demands of the information age.

## References

1. Avraamidou, L., Osborne, J.: The role of narrative in communicating science. Int. J. Sci. Educ. **31**(12), 1683–1707 (2009)
2. Bevan, B.: The promise and the promises of making in science education. Stud. Sci. Educ. **53**(1), 75–103 (2017)

3. Bruner, J.: The narrative construction of reality. Crit. Inq. **18**(1), 1–21 (1991)
4. Bull, G., Schmidt-Crawford, D.A., McKenna, M.C., Cohoon, J.: Storymaking: combining making and storytelling in a school makerspace. Theory Pract. **56**(4), 271–281 (2017)
5. ÇETİN, B., Bagceci, B., Bay, E.: The effects of social constructivist approach on the learners' problem solving and metacognitive levels. J. Soc. Sci. **8**(3), 343–349 (2012)
6. Chu, S.L., Quek, F., Saenz, M., Bhangaonkar, S., Okundaye, O.: Enabling instrumental interaction through electronics making: effects on children's storytelling. In: Schoenau-Fog, H., Bruni, L., Louchart, S., Baceviciute, S. (eds.) Interactive Storytelling: 8th International Conference on Interactive Digital Storytelling, ICIDS 2015, Copenhagen, Denmark, 30 November–4 December 2015, Proceedings 8, pp. 329–337. Springer, Cham (2015). https://doi.org/10.1007/978-3-319-27036-4_31
7. Clapp, E.P., Ross, J., Ryan, J.O., Tishman, S.: Maker-Centered Learning: Empowering Young People to Shape Their Worlds. Wiley, New York (2016)
8. Doorley, S., Witthoft, S., et al.: Make Space: How to Set the Stage for Creative Collaboration. Wiley, New York (2012)
9. Doppelt, Y., Mehalik, M.M., Schunn, C.D., Silk, E., Krysinski, D.: Engagement and achievements: a case study of design-based learning in a science context. J. Technol. Educ. **19**(2), 22–39 (2008)
10. Dwyer, C.P.: Critical Thinking: Conceptual Perspectives and Practical Guidelines. Cambridge University Press, Cambridge (2017)
11. Dwyer, C.P., Hogan, M.J., Stewart, I.: An integrated critical thinking framework for the 21st century. Thinking Skills Creativity **12**, 43–52 (2014)
12. Flyvbjerg, B.: Case study. Sage Handb. Qual. Res. **4**, 301–316 (2011)
13. Grant, N.S., Bolin, B.L.: Digital storytelling: a method for engaging students and increasing cultural competency. J. Effective Teach. **16**(3), 44–61 (2016)
14. Halverson, E.R., Sheridan, K.: The maker movement in education. Harv. Educ. Rev. **84**(4), 495–504 (2014)
15. Herrington, J., Parker, J.: Emerging technologies as cognitive tools for authentic learning. Br. J. Edu. Technol. **44**(4), 607–615 (2013)
16. Jacoby, S., Buechley, L.: Drawing the electric: storytelling with conductive ink. In: Proceedings of the 12th International Conference on Interaction Design and Children, pp. 265–268 (2013)
17. Kapur, M.: Productive failure. Cogn. Instr. **26**(3), 379–424 (2008)
18. Kolb, D.A.: Experience as the Source of Learning and Development. Prentice Hall, Upper Saddle River (1984)
19. Lammers, J., Curwood, J.S., Magnifico, A.: Toward an affinity space methodology: considerations for literacy research (2012)
20. Liu, S., Xu, S., Li, Q., Xiao, H., Zhou, S.: Development and validation of an instrument to assess students' science, technology, engineering, and mathematics identity. Phys. Rev. Phys. Educ. Res. **19**, 010138 (2023). https://doi.org/10.1103/PhysRevPhysEducRes.19.010138, https://link.aps.org/doi/10.1103/PhysRevPhysEducRes.19.010138
21. Manikutty, G.: My robot can tell stories: introducing robotics and physical computing to children using dynamic dioramas. In: 2021 IEEE Frontiers in Education Conference (FIE), pp. 1–9. IEEE (2021)
22. Munajah, R., Sumantri, M.S., Yufiarti, Y.: The use of digital storytelling to improve students' writing skills. Adv. Mobile Learn. Educ. Res. **3**(1), 579–585 (2023)

23. Papavlasopoulou, S., Giannakos, M.N., Jaccheri, L.: Empirical studies on the maker movement, a promising approach to learning: a literature review. Entertain. Comput. **18**, 57–78 (2017)
24. Papert, S., Harel, I.: Constructionism: Research Reports and Essays, 1985–1990. Ablex Publishing Corporation, Norwood (1991)
25. Peppler, K., Bender, S.: Maker movement spreads innovation one project at a time. Phi Delta Kappan **95**(3), 22–27 (2013)
26. Robin, B.R.: The power of digital storytelling to support teaching and learning. Digit. Educ. Rev. **30**, 17–29 (2016)
27. Rudolph, N.: TOTA: a construction set for the impending apocalypse. In: Proceedings of the 12th International Conference on Interaction Design and Children, pp. 554–556 (2013)
28. Sarıca, H.Ç., Usluel, Y.K.: The effect of digital storytelling on visual memory and writing skills. Comput. Educ. **94**, 298–309 (2016)
29. Sheridan, K., Halverson, E.R., Litts, B., Brahms, L., Jacobs-Priebe, L., Owens, T.: Learning in the making: a comparative case study of three makerspaces. Harv. Educ. Rev. **84**(4), 505–531 (2014)
30. Spieler, B., Schifferle, T.M., Dahinden, M.: The "making at school" project: planning interdisciplinary activities. In: Proceedings of the 27th ACM Conference on on Innovation and Technology in Computer Science Education, vol. 2, pp. 624–624 (2022)
31. Wagner, T., Compton, R.A.: Creating Innovators: The Making of Young People Who will Change the World. Simon and Schuster, New York (2012)
32. Wu, H.K., Krajcik, J.S.: Inscriptional practices in two inquiry-based classrooms: a case study of seventh graders' use of data tables and graphs. J. Res. Sci. Teach. **43**(1), 63–95 (2006)

# Designing a Language Model-Based Authoring Tool Prototype for Interactive Storytelling

Jeongyoon Park[1], Jumin Shin[2], Gayeon Kim[1], and Byung-Chull Bae[1(✉)]

[1] School of Games, Hongik University, Sejong, South Korea
jy00oonp@gmail.com, darps1417@gmail.com, byuc@hongik.ac.kr

[2] School of Design Convergence, Hongik University, Sejong, South Korea
juminshin1@gmail.com

**Abstract.** This paper proposes our initial authoring tool prototype using a language model to write interactive stories with narrative elements such as plot types and character arcs. The current prototype focuses on the overall design of the prototype and leaves detailed interactivity and multimedia features for further studies. The results of a simple evaluation using ChatGPT for the 72 generated stories show that the users' input logline and the selection of the narrative elements can affect the output story quality, such as empathy, surprise, and immersion.

**Keywords:** Interactive storytelling · Authoring tool · Language model

## 1 Introduction

Storywriting is fun but demanding. For this reason, various supplementary tools for storytelling and story-writing have been proposed, ranging from popular commercial storytelling board games (e.g., Once Upon a Time, Dixit, Rory's Story Cube) to diverse digital story authoring tools. Furthermore, rapid advances in generative pre-trained language models, such as OpenAI's GPT-3 [1] and Meta AI's LLaMA [2], are prompting the development of digital story authoring tools for creative writing [3–5]. While the current language model's creative output quality has room for improvement, studies show that language models have a great potential to outperform human writers [6].

Novice or hobbyist authors who want to write interactive digital stories need help with several issues. These issues can be associated with text story writing (e.g., the overall narrative structure, the development of characters, and detailed description of a given situation), the appropriate use of multimedia resources (e.g., sounds and background music), or interactive/branching factors. This paper proposes our initial authoring tool prototype using a language model to write interactive stories with narrative elements (e.g., plot types and character arcs) and interactive factors. The current prototype focuses on the overall design of the prototype and leaves detailed interactivity and multimedia features for further studies. Our final goal is to develop an authoring tool for interactive digital narratives supporting diverse multimedia with the help of generative AI.


L. Holloway-Attaway and J. T. Murray (Eds.): ICIDS 2023, LNCS 14384, pp. 239–245, 2023.
https://doi.org/10.1007/978-3-031-47658-7_22

## 2 Related Work

The users of story-authoring tools are often non-programmers or novice authors. For this reason, there is a high tendency to employ visual models, such as Inklewriter [7] and Twine [8] - the two commonly used interactive story-authoring tools. With these tools, users can make hypertext-based branching stories with ease.

In the interactive digital narrative (IDN) literature, authoring tools focus on digital and interactive features. The Story Maker [9] aims to develop a web-based authoring tool to create multimedia-rich branching narratives for cultural heritage. Storygraphia [10] provides a GUI story editor that can visualize a story with a story graph featuring narrative constraints such as the Propp functions and tension value.

The wide spread of large language models (LLMs) is dramatically influencing the development of "collaborative" story-writing systems. BunCho, a GPT2-based interactive story co-creation system in Japanese [11], is presented as a table-top role-playing game. A dataset named CoAuthor [4] explores the GPT-3's capabilities to support the user's creative and argumentative writing. Wordcraft [3] also provides human-AI collaborative story-writing with a large language model, LaMDA, exploring possible issues relating to LLM-based co-writing systems, such as the requirement of new evaluation metrics. Our prototype takes a similar approach to collaborative story writing using the GPT API, concentrating on classic narrative elements such as character and plot.

## 3 Design

### 3.1 User Interface

The authoring tool's function and user interface(UI) generally vary depending on the user and the purpose of use. Our target users are those who want to actively utilize Artificial Intelligence(AI) but are unfamiliar with language models or related APIs. We aim to help users write interactive stories with ease by adopting narrative elements focusing on characters and plots. We consider the following two key aspects - interactivity and narrativity.

- **Interactivity**: The user can interact with the system by choosing character and plot elements (See Fig. 1). Users can also select interactive factors to generate branching stories, such as emotions (See Fig. 2).
- **Narrativity**: We consider two fundamental narrative elements - character and plot. For the character attributes, we adopt character arcs (positive change, negative change, and flat) [12], character roles (e.g., protagonist, antagonist, helper), and 45 character archetypes based on myths (e.g., protector, inventor, fool, traitor, etc.) [13]. As for the plot elements, we take on the concept of Tobias's 20 master plots (e.g., quest, adventure, rivalry, underdog, etc.) [14].

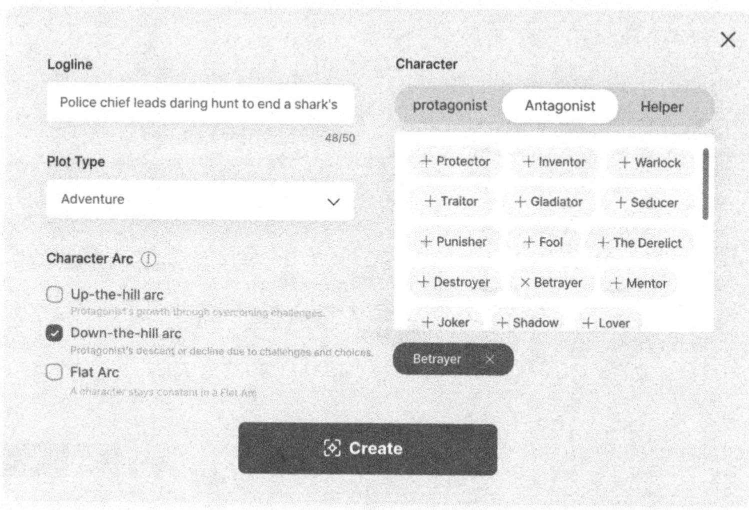


**Fig. 1.** Character and plot settings screen for interactive story generation. The user can write a logline, followed by character and plot attributes selection.

The whole process for story writing is as follows. First, the user writes a logline, a brief story summary including the main character's goals. Next, the plot type is selected based on the 20 master types suggested by Tobias [14]. Finally, the user can choose the two character attributes - roundness (positive-change, negative-change, and flat) and master character types. Figure 1 shows an example of the character and plot attributes setting from the initial screen of the prototype.

The basic UI design of the prototype, as seen in Fig. 2, consists of three sections. The main (middle) section shows text boxes - similar to the concept of the passages in Twine [8], where the user can generate the following passage or a branching story. The symbols for the branching story generation include emotions, AI recommendations, plot type change, character type change, and the user's direct text input. These are represented as a heart, a robot, the letter P, a human face, and the letter T, respectively. The right section displays the whole text described in the corresponding text box. The user can re-generate or modify a part of the story by highlighting necessary texts. A contribution UI is on the top of the left section, showing the proportion of AI contribution compared to the user. The contribution UI can keep reminding the user how much AI contributes to the whole story by comparing the generated words with the words the user wrote. The bottom parts of the left section include multi-modal properties (such as images, videos, and music) and tag property (that can represent the corresponding texts). These properties are still in development.

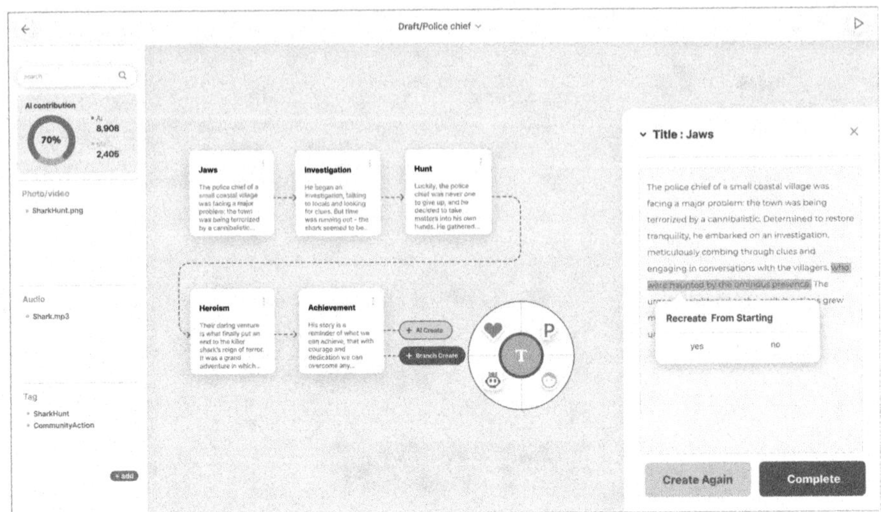


**Fig. 2.** Main UI of the proposed prototype, consisting of three sections - left (AI contribution, digital resources, and tags), main (middle; text boxes), and right (text description).

## 4 Story Generation Using a Language Model

### 4.1 ChatGPT API Setup

The proposed prototype utilizes ChatGPT API. The information the user provides includes a logline, a plot type, and character attributes, which are passed to form appropriate prompts. To use GPT3.5 API, we select DaVinci-003 engine and adjust two hyperparameter values (temperature and max_tokens).

The temperature hyperparameter indicates the similarity between an answer and a prompt. Thus, the output responses tend to be more creative (i.e., increased randomness) when the value is 0.8 or higher and to be more formal (i.e., faithful to the prompt) when the value is 0.2 or lower. We empirically set the temperature value to 0.9. Next, the max_tokens parameter is used to adjust the output length of ChatGPT. If the value of max_tokens is too large (e.g., more than 4000), the same sentence might be generated repeatedly. After conducting empirical tests, we set the max_tokens value to 3000.

### 4.2 Story Examples and Evaluation by ChatGPT

We investigated generated story examples to explore possible utilizations of our authoring tool prototype. First, we selected the famous logline of Steven Spielberg's 1975 thriller, Jaws, summarized as "A police chief fighting to kill a cannibal shark in a small coastal village." We wanted to know how this simple storyline could serve as a seed to develop different stories. Next, we provided several narrative factors as input prompts - plot types (adventure or rivalry), two character roles (protagonist or helper), character archetypes (protector or inventor), character arcs (up-the-hill, down-the-hill, or flat), including three target evaluation factors - empathy, surprise, and engagement [15]. In total, we analyzed 72 generated stories.

We then asked ChatGPT to evaluate the generated 72 stories with the 5-point Likert scale regarding the three evaluation factors - empathy, surprise, and engagement. Two stories received the highest score (13), and four obtained the lowest score (7). The total mean of the scores is 9.92 (sd = 2.24). Interestingly, the plot type of the highest two stories is all 'rivalry,' and that of the lowest four stories is all 'adventure.' The mean for the stories with a rivalry plot type is 10.94 (sd = .92), and for an adventure plot type is 8.89. (sd = 1.26). The given logline is likely to fit more with the rivalry plot than the adventure plot. Details of the generated stories with the highest and the lowest scores are shown in Table 1.

Figure 3 compares two selected story examples - one (a) is with the highest score (13/15), and the other (b) is with the lowest score (7/13). The story in (a) has the rivalry plot type; the story in (b) has the adventure plot type. Both stories have different character arcs and archetypes depending on the character roles (either protagonist or helper). Some intriguing combinations may exist for generating good-quality stories, which this paper has not examined. We leave it as future work.

Evaluating a story's quality is challenging, though we can inherently tell a good story from a bad one. While ChatGPT has the potential to perform a human-like evaluation, such as in text summarization task [16], it has yet to be confirmed if it works well in the narrative evaluation task. At the moment, we did not compare the results with human evaluation, which will also be included in future work.

**Table 1.** Scores of Generated Story Samples (Self-Evaluated by ChatGPT)

| | | Highest (2) | | Lowest (4) | | | |
|---|---|---|---|---|---|---|---|
| Plot Type | | Rivalry | Rivalry | Advent | Advent | Advent | Advent |
| Protagonist | Character Arc | Down | Flat | Up | Up | Up | Flat |
| | Archetype | Inventor | Protector | Protector | Inventor | Protector | Inventor |
| Helper | Character Arc | Flat | Down | Up | Down | Flat | Flat |
| | Archetype | Inventor | Inventor | Inventor | Inventor | Protector | Protector |
| Empathy | | **5/5** | | **2/5** | | | |
| Surprise | | **4/5** | | **2/5** | | | |
| Immersion | | **4/5** | | **3/5** | | | |
| Total | | **13/15** | | **7/15** | | | |

| | **Story Generation ID:** 67 | | **Plot type:** Rivalry |
|---|---|---|---|
| Protagonist | **Character Arc:** Flat | Helper | **Character Arc:** Down-the-hill |
| | **Archetype:** Protector | | **Archetype:** Inventor |
| | **Rating by ChatGPT:** 13 out of 15 (Empathy: 5, Surprise: 4, Immersion: 4) | | |
| Story | Chief Glen was a respected police chief in a small coastal village. For years, he had been tasked with maintaining the safety of the people in his town. But one day, his worst nightmare came true. A rare, ravenous cannibal shark had made its way into the waters surrounding the village.<br>The news quickly spread throughout the town, bringing fear and panic with it. People were afraid to go into the water, and businesses were suffering. The chief vowed to find a way to stop the beast before more harm was done.<br>He knew of one man that may be able to help him. His name was Anderson, and he was an eccentric inventor that lived just outside the village. After tracking him down, the chief pleaded with Anderson to join him in stopping the shark. Despite his apprehension, the inventor agreed to help.<br>Together, the two rivals set out to make the town safe again. Anderson created weapons and gadgets designed to confuse and repel the cannibal shark. Despite their overwhelming odds, the chief and the inventor relentlessly worked together to combat the beast.<br>The battle seemed to have no end, until Anderson managed to create a sonic device that disabled the shark's sensory system. With the shark vulnerable, Chief Glen swooped in to deliver the final blow.<br>The shark was ultimately defeated, and the town returned to its peaceful and safe state. Chief Glen was a hero, and Anderson had gone from being an outsider to a respected member of the community. The two had forged a bond that would last for years and each remembered what they had accomplished as rivals. | | |

(a)

| | **Story Generation ID:** 10 | | **Plot type:** Adventure |
|---|---|---|---|
| Protagonist | **Character Arc:** Up-the-hill | Helper | **Character Arc:** Flat |
| | **Archetype:** Protector | | **Archetype:** Protector |
| | **Rating by ChatGPT:** 7 out of 15 (Empathy: 2, Surprise: 2, Immersion: 3) | | |
| Story | In the small coastal village of Saltonford, Chief of Police Mike Cooper is facing a crisis - a giant, man-eating shark has been lurking in the waters near the harbor. With the safety of his community in danger, Mike must face the monster and put an end to its terror.<br>When a young boy, Tommy, witnesses the beast in the water, Mike takes him under his wing and enlists him as a helper in their fight against the monstrous shark. Despite his fears, Tommy bravely tags along on the journey to locate and destroy the fish.<br>As Mike and Tommy travel around the village seeking clues, they soon discover that the shark is actually a cannibalistic creature with a dark, twisted past. When they finally track down the beast at its lair, they must face it in a climactic battle.<br>With courage and strength, Mike and Tommy fight valiantly to defeat the shark. In the end, they manage to destroy it, saving the village and its people. Mike's selfless act of bravery has earned him the respect of the locals and Tommy's admiration. He eventually goes on to become a police chief of Saltonford who continues to protect the village from harm's way. | | |

(b)

**Fig. 3.** Comparison of Two Selected Story Examples: (a) A story with the highest score (13/15); (b) A story with the lowest score (7/15)

## 5 Conclusion

This paper proposes a language model-based authoring tool prototype that allows users to easily create interactive stories with narrative elements such as plot types, character arcs, and character archetypes. The results of a simple evaluation using ChatGPT for the 72 generated stories show that the users' logline input and the selection of the narrative elements can affect the output quality, such as empathy, surprise, and immersion. In future work, we plan to complete our prototype and investigate how narrative elements and interactive factors can improve the story's interest.

**Acknowledgements.** This work was supported by the National Research Foundation of Korea (NRF) grant (2021R1A2C1012377) and the 2023 Hongik Univeristy Research Fund.

## References


1. Brown, T., et al.: Language models are few-shot learners. In: Larochelle, H., Ranzato, M., Hadsell, R., Balcan, M.F., Lin, H. (eds.) Advances in Neural Information Processing Systems, vol. 33, pp. 1877–1901. Curran Associates Inc. (2020)
2. Touvron, H., et al.: Llama: open and efficient foundation language models (2023)
3. Yuan, A., Coenen, A., Reif, E., Ippolito, D.: Wordcraft: story writing with large language models. In: 27th International Conference on Intelligent User Interfaces, IUI 2022, pp. 841–852. Association for Computing Machinery, New York (2022)
4. Lee, M., Liang, P., Yang, Q.: Coauthor: designing a human-AI collaborative writing dataset for exploring language model capabilities. In Proceedings of the 2022 CHI Conference on Human Factors in Computing Systems, CHI 2022. Association for Computing Machinery, New York (2022)
5. Mirowski, P., Mathewson, K.W., Pittman, J., Evans, R.: Co-writing screenplays and theatre scripts with language models: evaluation by industry professionals. In: Proceedings of the 2023 CHI Conference on Human Factors in Computing Systems, CHI 2023. Association for Computing Machinery, New York (2023)
6. Chu, H., Liu, S.: Can AI tell good stories? narrative transportation and persuasion with chatgpt (2023)
7. inklewriter. https://www.inklestudios.com/inklewriter/. Accessed 25 Aug 2023
8. Twine: an open-source tool for telling interactive, nonlinear stories. https://twinery.org/. Accessed 25 Aug 2023
9. Vrettakis, E., Lougiakis, C., Katifori, A., Kourtis, V., Christoforidis, S., Karvounis, M., Ioanidis, Y.: The story maker - an authoring tool for multimedia-rich interactive narratives. In: Bosser, A.-G., Millard, D.E., Hargood, C. (eds.) ICIDS 2020. LNCS, vol. 12497, pp. 349–352. Springer, Cham (2020). https://doi.org/10.1007/978-3-030-62516-0_33
10. Lombardo, B.: Storygraphia: the constrained tool for idn authoring education. In: International Conference on Interactive Digital Storytelling, pp. 590–597. Springer, Heidelberg (2022). https://doi.org/10.1007/978-3-031-22298-6_38
11. Osone, H., Lu, J.L., Ochiai, Y.: Buncho: AI supported story co-creation via unsupervised multitask learning to increase writers' creativity in Japanese. In: Extended Abstracts of the 2021 CHI Conference on Human Factors in Computing Systems, pp. 1–10 (2021)
12. Weiland, K.M.: Creating character arcs: the masterful author's guide to uniting story structure, plot, and character development. PenForASword (2016)
13. Schmidt, V.L.: 45 Master Characters, Revised Edition: Mythic Models for Creating Original Characters. Penguin (2011)
14. Tobias, R.B.: 20 master plots: And how to build them. Writer's Digest Books (2012)
15. Chhun, C., Colombo, P., Suchanek, F.M., Clavel, C.: Of human criteria and automatic metrics: a benchmark of the evaluation of story generation. In: Proceedings of the 29th International Conference on Computational Linguistics, pp. 5794–5836. International Committee on Computational Linguistics, Gyeongju (2022)
16. Gao, M., Ruan, J., Sun, R., Yin, X., Yang, S., Wan, X.: Human-like summarization evaluation with chatgpt (2023)

# Alice Dali MR: A Mixed Reality Interactive Narrative Experience

Svetlana Rudenko[1(✉)], Xiangpeng Fu[1,2], and Mads Haahr[1,2]

[1] Haunted Planet Studios, 12 Fitzwilliam Street Upper, Dublin 2, Ireland
rudenkos@tcd.ie

[2] Trinity College Dublin, University of Dublin, Dublin 2, Ireland
{fuxi,haahrm}@tcd.ie

**Abstract.** This late breaking work paper presents *Alice Dali Mixed Reality (MR),* a cutting-edge, first-ever concept of an interactive experience using music, art and narrative in a new and interactive fashion for individual use and as a live performance. We approach the project like a surrealist painting: an experience that resides halfway between the visible and the invisible. MR technology is uniquely suited for this purpose because it positions the audience not within a virtual world (like VR technology does) but in a liminal space that blends the real with the un-real, the conscious with the unconscious, the physical world with the world of dreams. We performed three interactive *Alice Dali MR* scenes for the Meta Quest Pro headset, projected to the screen for audience view in a live performance. The original mixed reality audio-visual experience and interaction in the MR app involves orchestration of original piano tracks, activated by the magic conductor's wand when touching one of the rivers in Chapter 2 "Pool of Tears," by petting animals in Chapter 11 "Who Stole the tarts?" and growing roses in Chapter 12 "Alice's Evidence." We present our motivation for the work, the overall experience design and brief reflections on future work, including usage areas such as family entertainment, intergenerational play, the music industry in the genre of concert with visuals, and music art therapy in rehabilitation programs.

**Keywords:** Mixed Reality · Art · Music · Interactive Storytelling · Salvador Dali · Lewis Carroll · Intergenerational Play

## 1 Introduction

Mixed Reality (MR) is fast emerging field, and new headsets like the Meta Quest Pro have found a place in business and industry to show layers of design, architecture, for example for training, or for assistance during repair and maintenance jobs. With *Alice Dali MR* we are exploring what Mixed Reality can offer for culture, arts and entertainment. In this paper we describe design approaches for interactive narrative with art visuals and music and also look at the areas (including the music performance industry and society more broadly) where our MR experience may be of interest and could serve people well. Our experience was inspired by Salvador Dali's art for Lewis


L. Holloway-Attaway and J. T. Murray (Eds.): ICIDS 2023, LNCS 14384, pp. 246–254, 2023.
https://doi.org/10.1007/978-3-031-47658-7_23

Carroll's iconic story "Alice's Adventures in Wonderland" [1]. In 1969, Salvador Dali painted 12 chapters of Lewis Carroll's book for a Random House special edition. Svetlana Rudenko wrote original music for all twelve chapters on Dali's paintings for our earlier location-based Augmented Reality app *Alice Dali AR* (see Fig. 1), which was produced by Haunted Planet Studios and narrated by Mads Haahr.[1] Despite their similar names, the two experiences (*Alice Dali MR* and *Alice Dali AR*) are different and independent projects that offer quite different play experiences. The location-based play experience of *Alice Dali AR* is designed for outdoor use (for example, a city park), runs on smartphones and is based on the core idea of using a "radar" to find music-art augmented reality encounters.[2] Our Augmented Reality work inspired us further: What would it be like to be immersed into the painting of Dali and to play with the elements of art? To explore this question, we recreated three scenes of Dali's art in VR/MR to capture the magical world of a dream and fantasy. Figure 1 shows an AR art image by Salvador Dali "The Pool of Tears" (from *Alice Dali AR*), which we recreated later in one of Mixed Reality scenes (Fig. 4 and Fig. 5, *Alice Dali MR*).

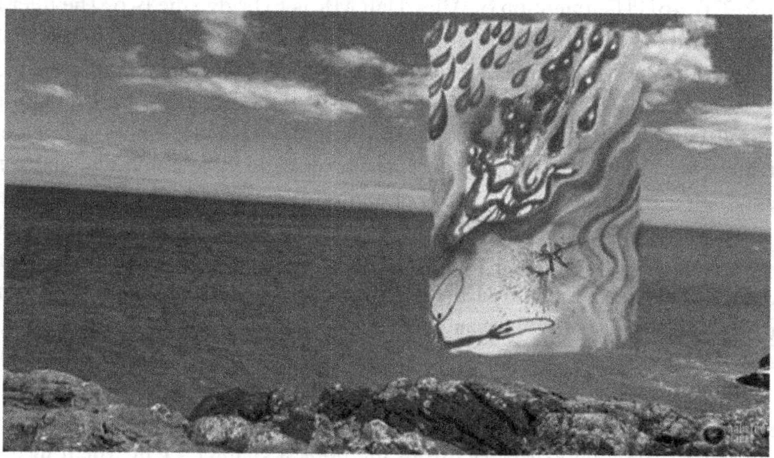

**Fig. 1.** AR image from Alice Dali AR app with original art by Salvador Dali for Chapter 2 of *Alice's Adventures in Wonderland* entitled "The Pool of Tears."

## 2 Alice Dali MR: Design and Experience

As a Danish artist Asger Jorn proclaimed: "The innermost essence of art is to grasp the human being. The artistic experience is neither to look at nor to admire, but to live in the work of art."[3] With our Mixed Reality experience we want to give people the feeling how "to live in the work of art." For the interactive experience's scenes in

[1] Free download for Android and iOS: https://rebrand.ly/alice-dali-ar-download.

[2] Screen recording: https://youtu.be/00z4W-za-28.

[3] Museum Jorn, Silkeborg, Denmark.

Mixed Reality, Svetlana Rudenko orchestrated her piano tracks with additional layers of music texture in Logic Pro, to distinguish visual scenes, moods and characters with different instrumentation. The concept and design were developed by Svetlana Rudenko and Mads Haahr, with 3D modelling, additional design and software by Xiangpeng Fu. The project was funded and produced by Haunted Planet Studios. The experience is built in Unreal Engine and runs on the Meta Quest Pro headset. Demo link: https://youtube.com/watch?v=O-iP8k8duY0 (Note: *Alice Dali MR* is after "Dreaming: Amy Beach," which demonstrates a music narrative visualisation for classical music unrelated to this paper.)

Alice Dali MR combines art, music and narrative. The scenes have aesthetic value of art and music in themselves and are playful in their interaction design, but they also raise deep questions about dreams and fantasy worlds, as well as their role as interfaces between the conscious and the unconscious parts of our psyches. Tjeu van den Berk summarises Carl Jung's distinction between "two kinds of thinking: rational thinking and fantasy thinking. The first consists of thoughts, the second of images: in the first the logos is central, in the second the mythos: the first gives knowledge, the second wisdom" [2, p. 46]. The intention of Alice Dali MR is to bridge the two. The interactive experience in Mixed Reality exercises "fantasy thinking" and facilitates immersion into the story world. The MR design utilises principles of a multisensory approach [3, 4]. By exercising a sense of touch (petting animals, growing flowers, etc.) and supported by the audio-visual synchronisation in composition (colour palette, emotional perception of characters are reflected in music genre and texture) [5], the emotional and sensory experience helps immersion into the story of digitally enhanced reality. Scientific studies of consciousness reveal that we perceive the world with our bodily experience, relying on the sensory responses, as Anil Seth puts it, "being a beast machine" [11]. Seth's approach is to look at consciousness from a biological model of the brain and it constitutes a large area of current research: human consciousness in XR, when "reality" is digitally enhanced. (We are not concerned with this research area in the scope of this paper, but it is something we intend to pursue in future research.)

Figure 2 shows Mixed Reality scenes from two of the chapters from *Alice Dali MR*. In Fig. 2 (left) is the court of beasts from the book's chapter 11 in which the Knave is on trial for stealing the Queen of Hearts' tarts. In our MR scene, the "beasts" from Dali's painting of chapter 11 are represented as reactive particle models. Our design for the beasts and the tart were inspired by a natural phenomenon called "pareidolia" in which humans perceive meaningful shapes in random or ambiguous visuals, e.g., faces in clouds. We modelled the beasts and the tart as particle systems, which allows them to be reshaped and to react when the player touches them. Playing cards (featuring Dali's original art) are also present and can be interacted with and used as portals to other scenes.[4] Figure 3 shows images of two animals from Dali's painting juxtaposed with our reactive 3D particle models. In relation to music design, the scene uses the original piano part from *Alice Dali AR* (see Fig. 1), which is in 4/4 time and B flat major, reflecting on Alice's mood of amusement with the court arrangement. In addition to the piano track, every animal has its own timbre orchestrated track, activated by the player's interaction, which is a "petting" touch. The Rabbit recalls original Piano Voice Narrative track from

[4] Video: https://vimeo.com/800082423.

chapter 1 of the *Alice Dali AR* experience ("Down the Rabbit-Hole"), which is waltzing in E flat major. Each of the three scenes start with a piano and narration track.

**Fig. 2.** Interaction in MR: Screenshots from Alice Dali MR prototype: Chapters 1112 ("Who Stole the Tarts?" and "Alice's Evidence") multisensory approach: touching the animals of the trial and growing flowers.

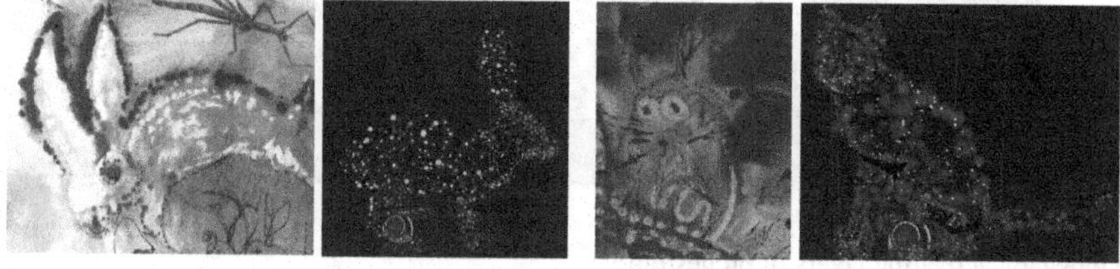

**Fig. 3.** Modelling art into MR: Art from Dali's original paintings and our reactive 3D particle models based on pareidolia: The Rabbit (left) and the Cat (right).

In Fig. 2 (right) is a scene from the book's final chapter 12 in which Alice awakens in her sister's lap. Our 3D models are based on Dali's painting and feature Alice and her sister and the flower, which are also present in the painting. The flower is the key interactive element in this scene: by pinching their fingers, the interactor can conjure a flower, which will grow at the corresponding position. Flowers make a sound when appearing and can be moved around the scene, enhancing a feeling of euphoria when many flowers (up to 100) are created and float playfully around the scene, reacting gently to the interactor's touch. In relation to music design, waltz (dance in ¾ time) is the leitmotiv of Alice. But in "The Pool of Tears", even though the piano part is in ¾ time, the musical texture does not have traditional waltz accompaniment, and is smooth in order to reflect on the "tragedy" of Alice. It is in A-minor ("sad") key transiting to C-major key. For an in-depth discussion on the music design, we refer to another published paper [5]. The flowers orchestrated episode is in A-major manifesting eventually back to the waltz with clear traditional waltz accompaniment, reminiscent of the waltz from chapter 1. Music plays an important role as a transmission of emotional states of the characters and additional music narrative to the participant in the MR scene, evoking empathy and immersion.

Figure 4 shows a screenshot from our scene of chapter 2 in which Alice has grown very large and is crying so much that her tears cause a flood. In this scene, our 3D models based on Dali's painting of the book's chapter 2 show the brightly coloured waterfalls (green and blue) of tears, three rivers of tears (one orange shown in the figure) and Alice's tears as drops (shown in Fig. 5) implementing a flocking behaviour. The interactor can interact with the teardrops, changing their direction of movement, and can use the "dream conductor's wand" (also shown) to interact with each of the three rivers to activate the corresponding layers of orchestration.

**Fig. 4.** MR app interaction with a virtual "dream conductor's wand" and gestures to interact with the music by activating layers of orchestration.[5]

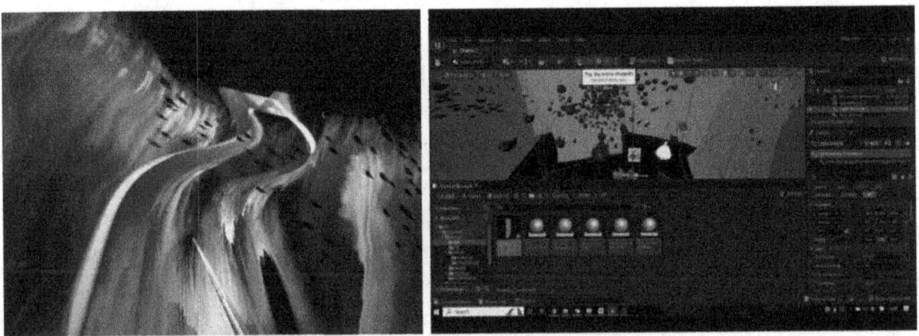

**Fig. 5.** Left: Screenshot from early VR prototype of *Alice Dali MR*, Chapter 2 ("Pool of Tears"), showing the rivers of tears and the Dream Conductor's wand interaction. Right: Technical implementation of *Alice Dali MR* in Unreal Engine (early prototype); the tears from "Pool of Tears" exhibit flocking behavior, orchestrated with a marimba track in Logic Pro.[6]

[5] Screen recording: https://www.youtube.com/watch?v=u8r3WC6T9WM.

[6] Video: https://www.youtube.com/watch?v=h8LfTeQo_F4.

## 3 Where and How *Alice Dali MR* Could Be Used: Intergenerational Play as a Family Experience (App) and Concert with Visuals MR (Music Industry)

Mixed Reality Music Art experiences could be rewarding for families as a type of intergenerational play, which is therapeutic for adults and educational for children. This experience is particular important between grandparents and grandchildren to help each other with digital proficiency and pass ideas and values. A study by Hunt focused on the use of technology as an intergenerational communication tool and showed that "grandchildren play a moderate to significant role in grandparents' learning of technological devices" [6]. Hunt also concluded that her "study confirms grandparents' high level of satisfaction in the learning process, along with interest and desire to interact with grandchildren at the technological level" [6]. Similarly, Zhang et al. observe the following:

> Interaction with young people can provide opportunities for older people to develop intimacy and to nurture younger generation. Intergenerational interaction is a crucial means of exchanging knowledge, skills, information, ideas and values. [7]

Zhang et al.'s study observes that the roles of adults and children can be reversed when playing with digital games, since children generally take control of them. This may offer a refreshing and worthwhile experience for both generations. With this in mind, we addressed the play experience design to be narrative as well playful. The art images and the interactive narrative elements in the scenes combined with original text by Lewis Carroll are intended to facilitate both age groups.

On the topic of the intergenerational dynamic associated with play, Agate et al. conclude the following:

> Because play is a meaningful developmental process for children and for older adults, intergenerational play may address the needs of both and allow each to reap the benefits of playful interactions. The grandchild–grandparent relationship is believed to be an important one. In such relationships, grandchildren often receive support and guidance and grandparents find meaning and pride in the opportunities for caring and mentoring. [8]

Furthermore, a grandfather who participated in the study commented: "By cherishing time spent in play, we anchor ourselves together … We become bonded" [8].

We see considerable potential in the use of our MR app for family entertainment and intergenerational play, music art cultural education, music art therapy and rehabilitation programs, and are planning to conduct user studies in these areas in the future. In the interim, we are presenting the work in a series of public performances with live music and narration and the MR headset worn by one performer and the headset view shown on a large screen, as shown in Fig. 6. In this setup, the audience see themselves and their environment on the screen as part of the performance due to the visual characteristics of mixed reality. There is a rise of using technology in music industry, and we see a great potential for Mixed Reality applications in a live performance [12].

**Fig. 6.** Photo from live concert performance of *Alice Dali MR* projected to the audience.[7]

## 4 Related Work on Interactivity and Storytelling in Mixed Reality: Future Directions

While *Alice Dali MR*, contains many interactive elements (including rivers, teardrops, plants and animals), our design has not focused on including responsive human characters. However, the addition of such characters of course has great narrative potential. Fortunately, there is work ongoing that can help support for responsive human characters in MR, such as that introduced by Egges et al.:

> […] Flexible interaction and animation engine, in combination with a robust real-time rendering engine that uses a global illumination for real-time PRT extension for virtual humans. The animation engine allows to switch dynamically between interaction and scenario playing, without interrupting the animation cycle. [9]

While *Alice Dali MR*, used a multisensory approach and audio-visual synchronisation, other researchers are also showing an interest in such multisensory approaches and have identified their importance for immersion. For example, Marija Nakevska, Anika van der Sanden, Mathias Funk, Jun Hu, Matthias Rauterberg who in their paper entitled "Interactive storytelling in a mixed reality environment: The effects of interactivity on user experiences" observe: "Immersiveness is a crucial aspect of such an installation and can be influenced by multiple factors such as video, sounds, interaction and, finally, the

[7] https://www.eventbrite.com/e/piano-concert-with-visuals-music-art-and-technology-arvrmr-tickets-604877754647.

density of all combined stimuli" [10]. Conducting a user study on their MR environment, Nakevska et al. found that:

> The user's agency in interactive storytelling environments is divided between the own sense of control and the empowerment of the story characters and events. The motivation for a user to act in an interactive narrative may be very different from common interaction with a product: in interactive storytelling, the source for agency may be the ability to navigate and to influence the environment, to interact with characters, or to have an effect on the course of events and the eventual outcome of the narrative. [10]

## 5 Conclusion

Mixed Reality in both versions, as a live performance concert (music industry) and the standalone MR app, offer an invaluable experience of surreal interaction that is so important for the brain fantasy world. The conscious agency offered in the interactive scenes is not normally available to a dreamer, and in this way the experience can be considered a type of technologically mediated lucid dream, for which Mixed Reality is an ideal tool. In this fashion, the work inspires dialogue about technology in service of culture and the mind – and vice versa. Specifically, it explores technology as a tool for: (a) mediating and exploring the human experiences of dreaming and fantasy worlds of storytelling; (b) reinventing and recombining classic cultural works of art, music and literature; and (c) for live performance concerts.

## References


1. Carroll, L.: Alice's Adventures in Wonderland: 150th Anniversary Edition Illustrated by Salvador Dali. Princeton University Press, Princeton & Oxford (2015)
2. Berk Tjeu van den: Jung On Art The Autonomy of the Creative Drive. Routledge, New York (2012)
3. Haverkamp, M.: Sinesthetic Design: Handbook for a Multi-Sensory Approach. Birkhauser Verlag AG (2013)
4. Velasco, C., Obrist, M.: Multisensory Experiences: Where the Senses Meet Technology. Oxford University Press, Oxford, New York (2020)
5. Rudenko, S., Haahr, M.: Music for Alice Dali Augmented Reality Experience: Multisensory Design Soundscapes for Locative Mobile Phone Gaming (via Synaesthesia). presented at the VII International Congress of Synaesthesia: Science and Art, University of Granada
6. Hunt, D.M.: Technology and the Grandparent-Grandchild Relationship: Learning and Interaction. The University of Toledo (2012). https://etd.ohiolink.edu/apexprod/rws_etd/send_file/send?accession=toledo1341345006&disposition=inline
7. Zhang, F., Kaufman, D.: A Review of Intergenerational Play for Facilitating Interactions and Learning **14**(3) (2016). https://journal.gerontechnology.org/archives/c277e4c22e9b4cc5bf77b49559cf3940.pdf
8. Agate, J.R., Agate, S.T., Liechty, T., Cochran, L.J.: 'Roots and Wings': An Exploration of Intergenerational Play. Routledge, pp. 395–421 (2018)
9. Egges, A., Papagiannakis, G., Magnet-Thalmann, N.: Presence and interaction in mixed reality environments. Vis. Comput. **23**, 317–333 (2007)

10. Nakevska, M., Sanden, A., Funk, M., Rauterberg, M.: Interactive storytelling in a mixed reality environment: the effects of interactivity on user experiences. Elsvier **21**, 97–104 (2017)
11. Seth, A.: Your Brain Hallucinates Your Conscious Reality. TED Talk (2017). https://www.ted.com/talks/anil_seth_your_brain_hallucinates_your_conscious_reality
12. Frackiewicz, M.: Extended Reality and the Future of Music and Performing Arts. TS2 Space (2023). https://ts2.space/en/extended-reality-and-the-future-of-music-and-performing-arts/

# Exploring the Union Between Procedural Narrative and Procedural Content Generation

Arunpreet Sandhu(✉) and Joshua McCoy

UC Davis, Davis, CA 95616, USA
{asisadhu,jamccoy}@ucdavis.edu

**Abstract.** Level Generation and Narrative Generation have often been separated from each other, even though they are both forms of Procedural Content Generation (PCG). The union of these between level generation and narrative generation, however, is under-explored given their history, and by exploring the union between these two topics will lead to new forms of PCG-enabled gameplay and stories. To address this under-exploration, we list both narrative and level generators and a description of a possible combination of these systems through shared knowledge representation structures. We also lay out various evaluation dimensions for these combined systems, which include level generation evaluation, expressive range, procedural narrative evaluation, and believable character evaluation. Finally, we describe the possible new frontiers that this approach enables, such as generating areas based on character personality traits.

**Keywords:** Procedural Content Generation · Emergent Narrative · Environmental Storytelling

## 1 Introduction

Procedural Content Generation (PCG) is an umbrella term containing both level generation and narrative generation techniques; yet the union between these two has been rarely explored. In this paper, we explore the union between these two PCG areas, and how the union enables indexical storytelling—a sibling to environmental storytelling.

PCG often—in academics—describes processes that help designers save time and have more resources for development. Cook [1], however, proposes another way to describe PCG, stating: "A better justification for PCG is that it enables new kinds of game design, by changing the player's relationship with the game's systems, or allowing the developers to work at a scale that would be otherwise impractical." Cook furthers this view by demonstrating how PCG gives players a different experience due to the PCG-oriented gameplay design [2]. Games such as Caves of Qud [3], Dwarf Fortress [4], or Ultima Ratio Regum [5] are exemplars of how PCG allows for a scale of gameplay that would not be achievable otherwise.

This type of PCG viewpoint described by Cook also captures emergent narrative as described by Ryan [6], where world's simulation creates a narrative, but only in the retelling of the events does it become a story; Ryan calls his approach a curatorial


L. Holloway-Attaway and J. T. Murray (Eds.): ICIDS 2023, LNCS 14384, pp. 255–262, 2023.
https://doi.org/10.1007/978-3-031-47658-7_24

approach to simulated story worlds. Ryan continues by saying that this curation can be done procedurally as well, which has led to systems focused on sifting through the simulated worlds, looking for emergent narrative, such as Winnow [7] and Felt [8]. These systems often focus on characters and character actions, but there is an additional layer of believability that pertains to space, as these characters must exist within a virtual environment, and how characters act within that space reveals more information about them that can help convince the player that these characters are believable. Take for example a man dressed in armor standing in front of a medieval gate with others dressed similarly, all at attention.

While there was no mention of a "city guard," it is not too difficult to make the leap that the character described is a city guard, protecting the gate with their fellow guards[1]. While much of the example has the character doing an action, it's only within the context of the world around them does the belief of, "this character is a guard," get further grounded. Yet, this isn't the only function that space has as it can help tell the player what type of experience the virtual world holds for them; an eerie abandoned town has a much different character than a vibrant thriving city. The story world can help to improve the audience's believability of character action by the way the world is presented to the player. This presentation of the story world and how the player experiences, is to us, environmental storytelling; where the story world conveys information about the story through the world. This, we believe, is at the core of environmental storytelling, which Carson states in his piece on environmental storytelling [9]: "One of the trade secrets behind the design of entertaining themed environments is that the story element is infused into the physical space a guest walks or rides through."

While Carson at the time was describing theme parks, suffusing places with the story element for visitors to traverse, his description of environmental storytelling has been seen within games. Game worlds often attempt to enrich the story through its design, like in Bioshock Infinite's city design of Columbia—the location that the majority of the game's story takes place in. Totten [10]—in his book, *Architect's Approach To Level Design*—describes portions of Columbia as: "buildings and islands form large-scale rhythms that draw players from one climactic battle to another. However, players who explore individual structures will find richly developed reward spaces and embedded narrative spaces." Levels—and the world for that matter—offer a chance to convey a narrative through their construction, props, and visuals, much like Carson's environmental storytelling; but adhering to Carson's approach might be a pitfall for a game developer as it does not capture the entire experience; it fails to capture how players interact with space. Instead, Fernández-Vara [11] argues that games should adopt an indexical style to environmental story telling.

Indexical storytelling allows players to discover a narrative by ordering what they find in the game world, like exploring the streets of Columbia, or collecting pieces of information for a murder mystery. Here the player can construct their own narrative, one which isn't reliant on visiting a place first. Instead, they may pursue the goal in whichever manner they deem fit. We believe that the combination of different PCG systems and areas, such as narrative and level generators, can make indexical storytelling possible.

[1] We assume that there is no deeper social game being played in this example, such as a group of rogues pretending to be guards to fool others, or any other kind of social engineering.

In this paper, we contribute an exploration of the combination of narrative and level generators. First, we describe both PCG algorithms that focus on generating levels, then we describe narrative generation techniques. We then describe the benefits of combining both narrative generation and level generation algorithms together, which come from a system that we are currently developing but have yet to test. We also give possible ways to evaluate this approach.

## 2 Related Work

Kybartas [12] conducted a survey on narrative generation techniques that touches on story world generation, but the description given differs from the world generation we discuss in this paper when discussing level-oriented PCG. Instead, Kybartas describes space as the world in which the narrative happens, whereas level and world generators prioritize creating game worlds care more for game mechanics than story constraints. Games such as Spelunky [13] or Dead Cells [14] exemplify this viewpoint by generating levels solely for gameplay. Yet, an example of space being used for story telling would be more akin to how drama managers often use space. Façade [15], a short interactive drama, has its characters (Trip and Grace) interact objects within their apartment, using these objects as conversation with the player.

As for level generators, their focus is often on generating intractable game worlds that are conducive to gameplay. Often level generators are search-based approaches, grammars, rules, and others, which have all been well-documented in *Procedural Content Generation in Games* [16]. Other techniques that have become well known are constraint solvers like WaveFunctionCollapse (WFC) [17], which allows for constraint satisfaction and statistical learning to generate levels. In this approach, we use WFC as it shares a knowledge representation abstraction that is cohesive to how narrative generators represent story beats and WFC has been used to generate non-gameplay constraints such as genre [18] or aesthetics [19]. We still list out other algorithms as they are still valid candidates for combining with narrative generators.

As for narrative generators, these include planners—such as Sabre [20] and Glaive [21], which causal planning to ensure narrative coherency—storylet systems such as Lume [22], and story sifters like Winnow [7] and Felt [8]. There are many other approaches, as described in Kybartas's survey, but for our use case we have found these three are a solid foundation for our integrated framework. While there has been much work on narrative planners, their usual graph-based knowledge representation seemed the most appealing for our approach. Storylet systems, on the other hand, treat narrative beats as composable units to generate coherent narratives. They often require story history to use as a world fact to then input as preconditions to each narrative beat; they will then choose an appropriate narrative beat that fills the story requirements. These systems require a critical mass of generative material before the systems generate believable narratives [22]. Story sifters, such as Winnow and Felt, look for interesting narrative locations while the world is being created. The output of these systems could then be connected to other approaches/systems for narrative generation.

Interesting, the closest system that treats indexical storytelling generation comes from Dormans's work, which looks at space and tries to generate it with a cohesive "feel" such as generating a temple within the game [23]. Other related work that attempts to tackle indexing the world comes from the Liquid Narrative Lab has research on indexing the world for better understanding of narrative constraints [24] that is similar to the indexical storytelling that is discussed in this paper. The closest related work we have been able to find is Bidarra's work on generating narrative worlds that use a story as it's starting position [25]. We differentiate ourselves by using the world generation as *input* for the story—as in not constraining our generative process with an already generated story. We instead approach this more with a curatorial view of emergent narrative.

## 3 Emergent Story World Generation

> "Another example of "cause and effect" is the use of what I call "Following Saknussemm." Derived from the story *Journey to the Center of the Earth* by Jules Verne. In Verne's story the main characters follow a trail of symbols scratched into subterranean walls by their adventuring predecessor, a sixteenth century Icelandic scientist, Arne Saknussemm. In this way, the game player is pulled through the story by following "bread crumbs" left behind by a fictitious proceeding game character. Whether you create notes scattered throughout your environments, or have the game player follow the destructive path of some dangerous creature, "cause and effect" elements will only heighten the drama of the story you are trying to tell!" – Carson [9]

The above quote is effectively what we wish to achieve with this approach; a world in which the characters can modify the world—and thus the story world as well[2]. Often, however, the issue with this embedding of "bread crumbs" is that a designer placed them in the world—there was not a character who performed the act procedurally. This designed story often means the audience will only have one way to discover story, which Fernández-Vara would argue as environmental storytelling and not indexical storytelling. Fernández-Vara states that game spaces should not have this singular way through them, but allow the player to piece together information, indexing the world as they wish. By indexing the space, the player creates a narrative that is unique to their play trace, giving the player a more memorable experience that can then be recounted to others. Fernández-Vara's version of storytelling is our goal, to create indexed environmental stories for players to create their own stories by interacting with the environment.

In terms of achieving indexical storytelling, we suggest that there needs a common knowledge representation that both the narrative system and world/level generator share. As in, with a graph-based approach, such as a narrative planner and WaveFunctionCollapse (which can be considered a constraint graph solver); these two systems have the same type of knowledge representation of graphs[3]. The issue then is connecting the two systems through this shared representation.

[2] While Carson speaks of characters and their actions, we consider this apart of the narrative as divorcing character from narrative and narrative from character is a tenuous task.

[3] We do assume that the knowledge each graph contains is different; the narrative planner's graph would contain narrative beats and links between them while WFC would treat each tile as a graph or possibly a higher level structure, such as a dungeon graph where each node is a room and each link is a path.

Currently, our approach focuses on the knowledge representation that both narrative generation and level generation share. We do so by using a graph-based representation between level generation (through WFC) and a narrative planner. For our narrative planner, we use space generation as a pre-condition for narrative nodes. As for a location beat to occur, the location must exist for that beat to occur, and it must occur in that location. As in if the narrative system's beat generation requires a temple (akin to one as described in Dormans's *Theory of The Place* [23]) then there must be a temple that is generated within the world. As for this type of generation, currently we are generating all locations as we test the connection between narrative planner and level generator.

We are experimenting with the inverse, as in if the level/world generator generates a larger structure (like a temple) that the narrative planner may not know about—as in the level generator understands this higher order pattern[4] (like a port, or a highway, or some landmark) that the narrative planner does not contain—then then this information should be passed into the narrative generator, allowing the planner to take this new landmark and possibly generate stories for that location.

Another solution would be to give both the narrative and level generation an intermediate representation (IR), much like how compilers create and IR structure from source code. By having an intermediate symbol set, any system can target this approach, assuming the other system has implemented a similar symbol set representation. This approach is similar to how EM-Glue [26] connects system together, but we are describing is more akin to a Language Server Protocol approach[5].

If the IR approach was taken, then other systems could be introduced to the generative process such as including character AI systems to flavor the generative process by using character traits to help decorate NPC interiors[6]. Examples of character AI systems are Fatima Modular [27] or PsychSim [28], which could drive both the character's decision making, but also inform the generation systems through the symbol set that a character would like to move from their home to another, which could then be generated for the characters. This generation step could even be constrained by social rules through a system like Comme Il Faut [29]. By including this step, our system explores questions such as how does one map personality to place, or social implications into levels. While we think this approach would be more extendable, we are placing this IR approach as future work as we do not know *what* the IR structure would look like until we build one possible system and evaluate it.

As for evaluations, we are still determining the best approach, as our approach is still being iterated on. Since this approach combines both narrative and level generation techniques, currently we are considering using both level generation evaluations, such as those proposed by Smith [30]. We also believe this system should be evaluated according to the believable character dimension, mostly due to our simulation/curatorial approach. Currently we are deciding between Jhala's description of believable character metrics [31] and those described by Aljammaz [32].

---

4 As described in the previous footnote, WFC's graph could contain a "temple" node. As for generating this temple, our approach could do something as TileTerror's generation process.

5 https://microsoft.github.io/language-server-protocol/

6 An example of this type of character to location generation would be akin to how a room for a disorganized person would look versus an organized person. This.

Currently we are leaning towards Jhala's as there is more one-to-one correspondence between Totten's level design book. Still though, there is another dimension of evaluation akin to an expressive range analysis of narrative worlds, much like the work of Kybartas [33]. Yet, unlike Kybartas's analysis where conflict of character states is the evaluation metric, the world's total narrative conflict potential could be used as a metric. As for which evaluation would be the best, we are still deciding as we continue to work on our approach, however, we are almost certain that a suite of metrics will be needed.

Thus, the goal of this integrated system is to bridge the gap between narrative and world generation and create an appropriate evaluation for the system. We also aim to create some more generalized language for this system so other AI systems can be included in the generation process. Currently, we are still understanding and exploring this space through our approach. By combining these two areas of content generation, we hope to create more believable worlds on the scale that PCG can provide, while maintaining narrative coherency given the player's actions.

## 4 Conclusion

In this paper, we describe the differences between level generation and narrative generation and the gap between these two research areas. Next, we describe environmental storytelling, then indexical storytelling, and how our system aims to approach a procedural indexing system. We then describe a framework for using WFC and a narrative planner to create an integrated system. We then describe a series of evaluations that could be used to determine if the system's output is credible. This connection between narrative and level generators, we believe, will expose new potential spaces and scale of play and story that can only be possible through PCG.

## References


1. Cook, M.: Generative Forensics: Procedural Generation and Information Games. *ArXiv*. (2020). Accessed 01 Aug 2023. https://www.semanticscholar.org/paper/bbdc570e38f9db14538f967ba62dcd5f91ea5b08
2. Smith Nicholls, F., Cook, M.: 'That darned sandstorm': a study of procedural generation through archaeological storytelling. Proceedings. 18th International Conference Found. Digit. Games, pp. 1–8 (2023). https://doi.org/10.1145/3582437.3587207
3. Freehold Games. "Caves of Qud." (2019)
4. Bay 12 Games. "Dwarf Fortress." (2006)
5. Johnson, M.: Ultima Ratio Regum. Independent (2023)
6. Ryan, J.: Curating Simulated Storyworlds. UC Santa Cruz (2018). Accessed 23 Aug 2023. https://escholarship.org/uc/item/1340j5h2
7. Kreminski, M., Dickinson, M., Mateas, M.: Winnow: a domain-specific language for incremental story sifting. Proceedings AAAI Conference Artif. Intell. Interact. Digit. Entertain. **17**(1), 1 (2021). https://doi.org/10.1609/aiide.v17i1.18903
8. Kreminski, M., Dickinson, M., Wardrip-Fruin, N.: Felt: a simple story sifter. In: Interactive Storytelling: 12th International Conference on Interactive Digital Storytelling, ICIDS 2019, Little Cottonwood Canyon, UT, USA, November 19–22, 2019, Proceedings, Springer-Verlag, Berlin, Heidelberg, pp. 267–281 (2019). https://doi.org/10.1007/978-3-030-33894-7_27

9. Environmental Storytelling: Creating Immersive 3D Worlds Using Lessons. https://www.gamedeveloper.com/design/environmental-storytelling-creating-immersive-3d-worlds-using-lessons-learned-from-the-theme-park-industry. Accessed 23 Aug 2023
10. Totten, C.W.: An Architectural Approach to Level Design (2014). https://api.semanticscholar.org/CorpusID:62473540
11. Clara, F.-V.: Game spaces speak volumes: indexical storytelling. In: DiGRA - proceedings of the 2011 DiGRA international conference: Think design play, DiGRA/Utrecht School of the Arts (2011). http://www.digra.org/wp-content/uploads/digital-library/Game-Spaces-Speak-Volumes.pdf
12. Kybartas, B., Bidarra, R.: A survey on story generation techniques for authoring computational narratives. IEEE Trans. Comput. Intell. AI Games **9**(3), 239–253 (2017). https://doi.org/10.1109/TCIAIG.2016.2546063
13. Mossmouth Games. "Spelunky." (2008)
14. Motion Twin. "Dead Cells." (2017)
15. Mateas, M., Stern, A.: Facade (2005)
16. Shaker, N., Togelius, J., Nelson, M.J.: Procedural Content Generation in Games: A Textbook and an Overview of Current Research. Springer (2016). https://doi.org/10.1007/978-3-319-42716-4
17. Karth, I., Smith, A.M.: WaveFunctionCollapse is constraint solving in the wild. Proceedings 12th International Conference Found. Digit. Games, pp. 1–10 (2017). https://doi.org/10.1145/3102071.3110566
18. Sandhu, A., Mitchell, K., McCoy, J.: TileTerror: a system for procedurally generating 2D horror Maps. In: AIIDE Workshops (2021)
19. Charity, M., Togelius, J.: Aesthetic bot: interactively evolving game maps on twitter. Proc. AAAI Conf. Artif. Intell. Interact. Digit. Entertain. **18**(1), 1 (2022). https://doi.org/10.1609/aiide.v18i1.21943
20. Ware, S.G., Siler, C.: Sabre: a narrative planner supporting intention and deep theory of mind. Proc. AAAI Conf. Artif. Intell. Interact. Digit. Entertain., **17**(1), 1 (2021). https://doi.org/10.1609/aiide.v17i1.18896
21. Ware, S.G., Young, R.M.: Glaive: a state-space narrative planner supporting intentionality and conflict. In: Proceedings of the 10th AAAI International Conference on Artificial Intelligence and Interactive Digital Entertainment, pp. 80–86 (2014)
22. Mason, S., Stagg, C., Wardrip-Fruin, N.: Lume: a system for procedural story generation. In: Proceedings of the 14th International Conference on the Foundations of Digital Games, ACM, San Luis Obispo California USA, pp. 1–9 (2019). https://doi.org/10.1145/3337722.3337759
23. J. D. B. October 26 and 2021, The Theory of The Place: A level design philosophy for Unexplored 2. Game Developer (2021). https://www.gamedeveloper.com/blogs/the-theory-of-the-place-a-level-design-philosophy-for-unexplored-2. Accessed 23 Aug 2023
24. Fisher, M.: Narrative planning in large domains through state abstraction and option discovery. Proc. AAAI Conf. Artif. Intell. Interact. Digit. Entertain., **18**(1), 1 (2022). https://doi.org/10.1609/aiide.v18i1.21979
25. Balint, J.T., Bidarra, R.: Procedural generation of narrative worlds. IEEE Trans. Games **15**(2), 262–272 (2023). https://doi.org/10.1109/TG.2022.3216582
26. Mori, G., Thue, D., Schiffel, S.: EM-Glue: a platform for decoupling experience managers and environments. Proc. AAAI Conf. Artif. Intell. Interact. Digit. Entertain., **18**(1), 1 (2022). https://doi.org/10.1609/aiide.v18i1.21972
27. Dias, J., Mascarenhas, S., Paiva, A.: FAtiMA modular: towards an agent architecture with a generic appraisal framework. Bosse, T., Broekens, J., Dias, J., Van Der Zwaan, J. (eds.), In Lecture Notes in Computer Science, **8750**. Springer International Publishing, Cham, pp. 44–56 (2014). https://doi.org/10.1007/978-3-319-12973-0_3

28. Marsella, S.C., Pynadath, D.V., Read, S.J.: PsychSim: Agent-Based Modeling of Social Interactions and Influence p. 6
29. McCoy, J., Treanor, M., Samuel, B., Mateas, M., Wardrip-Fruin, N.: Comme il Faut: A System for Authoring Playable Social Models, p. 6
30. Canossa, A., Smith, G.: Towards a Procedural Evaluation Technique: Metrics for Level Design
31. Gomes, P., Paiva, A., Martinho, C., Jhala, A.: Metrics for character believability in interactive narrative. In: Interactive Storytelling, Koenitz, H., Sezen, T.I., Ferri, G., Haahr, M., Sezen, D., Çatak, G. (eds.), Springer International Publishing, Cham, pp. 223–228 (2013). https://doi.org/10.1007/978-3-319-02756-2_27
32. Aljammaz, R., Wardrip-Fruin, N., Mateas, M.: Towards an understanding of character believability. In: Proceedings of the 18th International Conference on the Foundations of Digital Games, ACM, Lisbon Portugal, pp. 1–9 (2023). https://doi.org/10.1145/3582437.3582466
33. Kybartas, B., Verbrugge, C., Lessard, J.: Expressive Range Analysis of a Possible Worlds Driven Emergent Narrative System. In: Rouse, R., Koenitz, H., Haahr, M. (eds.) Interactive storytelling, pp. 473–477. Springer International Publishing, Cham (2018)

# A Design-Oriented Framework for Interactive Digital Narrative in Virtual Reality - Focus on Branching Narrative and Agency

Samira Soltani(✉)

Toronto Metropolitan University, 350 Victoria Street, Toronto, ON M5B 2K3, Canada
samira.soltani@torontomu.ca

**Abstract.** This research aims to find a design-oriented framework for interactive digital narrative (IDN) in virtual reality (VR), focusing on branching narrative and agency. Incorporating a practice-based research methodology, this study analyzed three virtual reality projects focusing on agency and three products from different media (print, movie, VR experience) focusing on branching narratives. The extracted framework comprises six sections: the interactor, actions, decisions, feedback and acknowledgment, VR features, and accessibility.

**Keywords:** Interactive Digital Narrative · Virtual Reality · Branching Narrative · Branching Experience · Bulk/Audience Character · Agency

## 1 Introduction

This research aims to find a design-oriented framework for interactive digital narrative (IDN) in virtual reality (VR), focusing on branching narrative and agency. Looking at the comments on most of available VR storytelling products (excluding games) in the Meta Store and Steam, it is evident that users are relegated to role of passive observers with no ability to influence storyline and experience details or interact meaningfully with the environment. Additionally, some other available projects advertised in the market as interactive storytelling in VR with high quality in the industry offer a minimum of agency. The framework introduced in this research offers a set of guidelines that can assist future VR storytellers and designers for head-mounted displays (HMD) with motion controllers in altering a player's role from an observer to an interactor, allowing for meaningful choices and interactions with branching narratives and agency.

## 2 Related Work

Virtual reality (VR) has been explored across various fields, including design, writing and technicality. Within the realm of interactive digital narrative, some studies delve into the psychological aspects of VR, such as embodiment, empathy [1, 2] and identity [3], while others take cultural heritage and ethical aspects [4, 5] into consideration.


L. Holloway-Attaway and J. T. Murray (Eds.): ICIDS 2023, LNCS 14384, pp. 263–273, 2023.
https://doi.org/10.1007/978-3-031-47658-7_25

Recent publications and dissertations have touched on similar themes. For example, the dissertation "IDN for cinematic VR" [6] explores the creation of virtual environments through 360° video within an interactive fiction (IF) structure. Additionally, a paper about writing for IDN in VR [7] explores the challenges that writers may encounter while scripting the interactor for a non-linear story. "Exploring Narrative Novelties in VR" [8] examines four concepts such as identification, parasocial interaction, breaking the fourth wall and spatial and narrative presence in VR projects while bringing some of the considerations for an IDN in VR. Furthermore, "Who am I that acts" [9], with its analysis of second-person voice and level of interactivity, sheds light on how these elements can affect immersion in VR.

Overall, current related works have not yet approached the area of a design-oriented framework for interactive digital narrative in virtual reality focusing on branching narratives and agency. This paper hopes to fill this gap in the literature which focuses on a specific form of VR that includes HMD with motion controllers as affordances of this device has the potential to enhance the level of agency.

## 3 Conceptual Background

### 3.1 Concepts Related to Interactive Digital Narrative

For this study, virtual reality is the target digital medium and an immersive environment. Four affordances of digital media also apply to virtual reality: 'procedural,' 'participatory,' 'spatial,' and 'encyclopedic'; in addition to the aesthetics of a digital medium: agency, immersion, and transformation to build the theoretical foundation of this research study, which focuses on branching narrative and agency [10, 11].

While there has been a long debate between narratology and ludology [12] regarding the relationship between interactivity and narrative, Herman's definition (2002), that narrative does not adhere to any form, seems more relevant to today's non-linear media consumption landscape than Prince's definition [13], that narrative is linear and composed of time-based 'events'. However, the impacts of this debate cannot be neglected [14]. Hartmut Koenitz updates the definition of Interactive Digital Narrative (IDN) as "a narrative expression in various forms, implemented as a multimodal computational system with optional analog elements and experienced through a participatory process in which interactors have a non-trivial influence on progress, perspective, content, and/or outcome" [14].

To analyze target projects, the SPP model (see Fig. 1) [14] is employed as a core element of IDN theory [14], to avoid confusion and redefine terms [15]. The protostory (see Fig. 2), as the central part of IDN systems, includes procedural components, the UI (user interface), and assets that provide the material used in the narrative design [14]. As a result, the focus will be more on the complexity and coherence of protostory than computational complexity [16]. The extension of this model to consider "the effect of replay" also can be helpful as replay has a core function in these IDN projects in which interactors may explore these "three circles of interpretation," which ask about previous decisions, current actions and future choices (see Fig. 3) [14].

In addition to the dramatic arc and the monomyth/Hero's Journey as the most influential narrative structures in the western perspective, there exist a variety of narratives

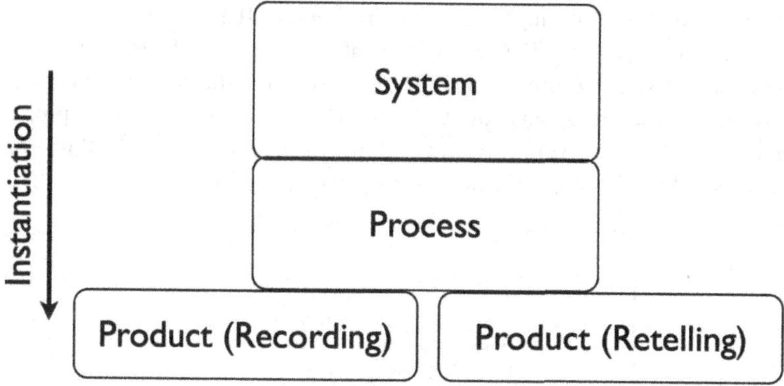


**Fig. 1.** SPP model [14]

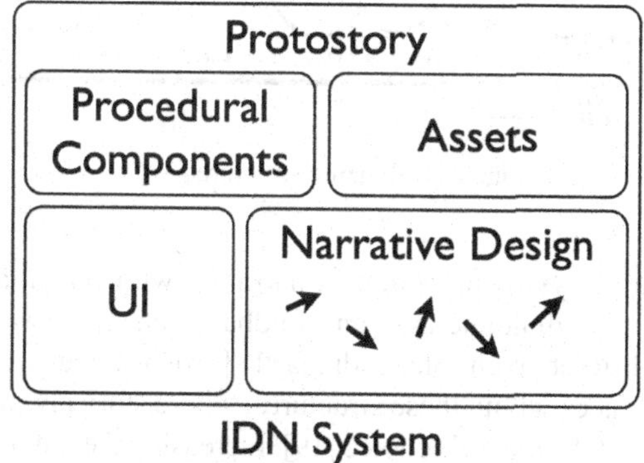


**Fig. 2.** Protostory and its elements [14]

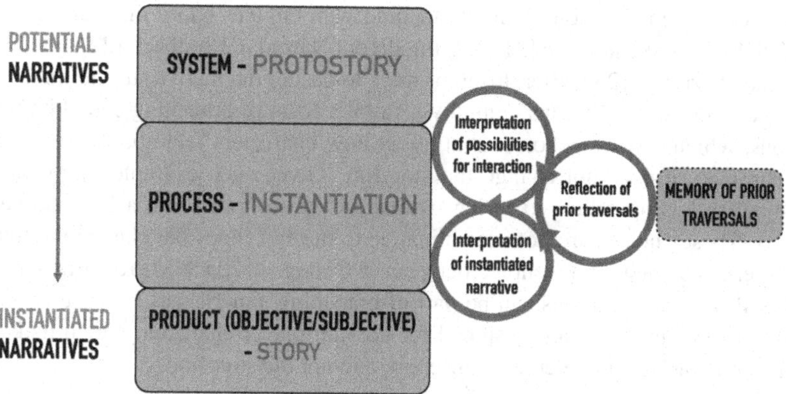


**Fig. 3.** The triple hermeneutic of IDN experience [14]

that may be impactful in aiming "a radical shift" about IDN features [17] to conquer those structures' limitations [14]. One such narrative structure is the Epiphanic Structure (see Fig. 4), which shows promise for IDN by introducing the story world, Cycle(s) of Conflict (CoC) for the protagonist and Culmination, there is a moment of epiphany that the interactor realizes the overall result of events in the narrative [17]. Post-epiphanic Replay(s) also acknowledges repetition of narrative [17].

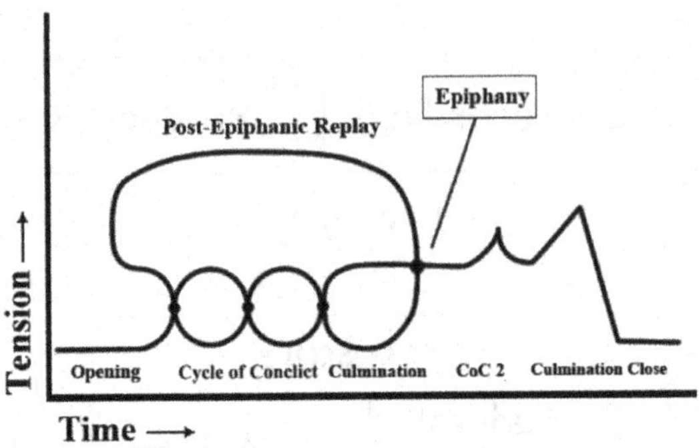


**Fig. 4.** Epiphanic structure [17]

There are various ways of branching a narrative with potential for interactivity, including branching tree, dialogue tree, and foldback scheme in which choices might be determinative to different paths and endings [18]. Also, some designers may include non-determinative choices within these structures; where story always leads back to the same path, regardless of the player's choice [19]. Increasing the number of determinative choices and, thereby, the number of endings may impact the story's depth which is shaped by details and minor decisions [19]. As a result, the principle of "opportunity magnitude" that prioritizes the possibility of "interactive opportunities over length of experience" [20] is recommended. Additionally, branching with engines based on event, clock, or plot [19], Emergent Narrative [21–23], Intelligent Narrative Feedback [22], and Highly Interactive Narrative [23], offer different ways to design interactive storytelling.

In the industry, practitioners employ a simpler form of branching called branching emotions, which involves choices that affect how characters feel about the interactor [24]. However, it does not change the storyline. Given such examples, another term can be defined as branching experiences that are incorporated into a few numbers of products. These choices are not determinative to the storylines but change the interactor's experience, including a choice between two songs in Black Mirror: Bandersnatch episode. Branching emotions can be part of branching experiences because two types of emotions, for instance, are designed for the non-player character, which makes the overall experience of the interactor different, and not the storyline.

### 3.2 Concepts Related to Virtual Reality

In crafting a narrative for a VR experience, it is essential to consider point of views (POVs), including first-person, second-person and third-person as each addresses a different user experience. Additionally, it is imperative to understand who the main lead in the story's progress is. In first-person POV, whether the main character or a supporting character, they tell the story, which in VR refers to the story playing out through the viewer's eye [25]. Second-person POV with a "you" perspective is a common POV for stories in the "Choose Your Adventure" series but not for narrative-based immersive experiences. VR storytelling products usually opt for third-person POV [25] in which the interactor is not a character but an observer. In some cases, this limited POV is combined with a first-person POV to give the interactor more agency and the possibility of minimum interactions with no/little impact on the storyline. This is also labeled as "second-person side kick POV" or "diegetic observer" [9, 26], which is a limited third-person POV based on what is discussed.

In the euro-centric storytelling perspective, the conflict in achieving an internal or external goal between the protagonist and antagonist characters is the story's engine, which in a VR experience is an external goal because of compatibility with this medium's features [25]. The interactor in VR can embody a "well-established" or "unknown established" or "customizable" character or "themselves" [3]. The degree of authenticity alters depending on how much an interactor is scripted to identify with a character [3].

Similar to the "themselves" category [3], bulk or audience characters do not have a fixed role or characteristic to play. They are defined by their interactions and decisions, which shape their identity. Unlike supernumerary characters who are merely part of the crowd and have no specific role in interacting with other characters, bulk characters can play a role in the story's progress.

Non-player characters (NPC) vary in type and roles in a game or a VR experience, and the computer and designer control their behaviour [27]. They can be supernumerary characters or play any other characters in the story whose actions are ruled by artificial intelligence (AI) or programming code and animation.

"Breaking the fourth wall", in theatrical experiences, refers to when a player or actor acknowledges the viewer [25]. In VR, when the player is an observer and other characters acknowledge their presence, breaking the fourth wall happens [25] because the player acts as an audience similar to the common form of theatre although s/he is inside the experience and their view is blocked from the reality around them. However, when the interactor plays a role in the VR experience, this acknowledgement is not considered as breaking the fourth wall but as part of the feedback package for the interactor.

Immersion is what the technology delivers, including "displays (in all sensory modalities) and tracking that preserves fidelity," and presence is "a human reaction to immersion" [28]. These two concepts are highly related. However, presence is not as measurable as immersion because the perception of people from presence differs from one person to another [28]. Studies illustrate that "full immersion is not always necessary" because the goal is "producing presence" for the interactor in the computer-generated environment [29]. Immersion and presence are also employed in different psychological experiments, including specific phobias such as fear of heights, flying and being in certain situations [30–32]. These phobias can be a narrative element to make the story more interesting and a reason to tell the story in virtual reality. The warning message must be designed to inform the interactor about the situation in advance.

The interactor might be affected by the illusion of owning this designed virtual body and experiencing the same sensations as their biological body [33, 34]. In the earliest VR experiences, viewers only saw through the eyes of one inside a virtual space, but now, viewers can see and respond with their hands. The further we immerse users into their bodies, thus embodying them in virtual space, the more impactful the stories in that space will become [25].

The feedback package consists of several elements in a virtual reality project that can affect the interactor's experience of presence, immersion and embodiment, including auditory, visual and haptic feedback. Studies show these elements can be effective in the interactor's presence and embodiment feeling, especially if two models are incorporated into one project rather than just one model of feedback [35–40]. Memory as inventory [14] allows the interactor to save an option for later, which can generate unique feedback based on their previous choices, their previous decisions can become a generative backstory element in the narrative because they possess a bulk/audience character with no fixed role.

## 4 Analysis Approach

This study [41] utilizes practice-based research methods [42] which involve researcher-designed strategies for selecting methods, tools and techniques [43]. The approach is qualitative, and questions are formulated based on the discussed conceptual background. It is a descriptive research study that does not measure target elements. The target projects are divided into two categories: VR storytelling with a focus on the agency (The Key, The Book of Distance, and The Wolves in The Walls) and branching narrative (Your Very Own Robot - print book, Black Mirror: Bandersnatch - Movie, Altdeus -VR) [41]. Since a company's VR storytelling project with branching narratives was found in the Meta store, other media such as print books and movies were included in the analysis to study different patterns of designing branching narratives. The questions in the first category focus on narrative design, addressing whether the story is linear or non-linear (how the storyteller approaches the order of events), who the interactor is, the point of view, acknowledgement, and what the relation between the interactor and other characters in the story. Additionally, the study analyzes the agency, technological and visual aspects of VR experiences, including procedural and participatory features, the relationship with NPCs, the role of AI, VR features, user interface and user experience. The questions in the second category focus on the pattern of branching implemented, the quality of choices, including the employment of fake choices, non-determinative choices that branch emotions and experiences, and determinative choices. It also examines the interactor features, the relation with NPCs, POV, and acknowledgement if applicable. The extracted key notes from this analysis [41] shaped the framework's basis about what works and what does not.

## 5 Framework and Discussion

This design-oriented framework [41] is a collection of recommendations for VR storytelling which can be played with HMD and motion controllers. The implementation and the combination of these elements may vary depending on the unique features of each project. The consequences of ignoring these recommendations in the design will impact the level of agency and a sense of meaningful choices for the interactor.

### 5.1 The Interactor

Limiting a character's choices to a fixed personality type can be restrictive for the interactor. Instead, a bulk/audience character allows the interactor to make more personal choices. If a character has a defined goal and personality, it's important to minimize the impact of the imposition of the internal feelings and experiences that make the interactor feel trapped and uncomfortable. This conflict of emotions can be confusing and lead to disengagement. If the project aims to impose internal feelings, creators should warn the interactor of potential psychological impacts. The choice of POV depends on the project's goal, but a combination of first and third person may be more engaging. This allows the bulk/audience character, who sees everything, to be decision-maker in some scenes and change the storyline from a first-person perspective.

### 5.2 Actions

Plan interactions with/against the interactor's character that can be seen as an external behaviour or object. This approach ensures that the interactor feels and reacts properly to it even if the characteristics are fixed. Incorporate actions with/without objects to enhance the narrative design and increase interactor engagement. Soliciting user input, such as a name or number, is a great way to keep the reader involved in the story's progress and make them feel like their participation is essential. Using small puzzles as a narrative tool to explore past or future times can also increase interactor engagement, as they become more involved in the environment and interact with the objects. Break each significant scene into smaller activities or dialogues that the interactor can choose to play at their own pace or non-stop.

### 5.3 Decisions

Begin by creating a scenario that allows for multiple decision paths. Design different endings that have different storylines. While having more endings can be exciting, it is best to limit these while increasing the milestones in each storyline. A balance of determinative and non-determinative choices can enhance storytelling. Some choices may lead to branching narratives, which can be an intriguing experience. While time limits for making decisions can be effective, overusing this approach can render the decision-making process meaningless. It is better to start over from the beginning of a storyline rather than returning to a previous decision point. If the interactor can go back and change their choices repeatedly, determinative decisions' importance diminishes. Plan conversations with other characters to create emotional and narrative branches. Ensure the interactor understands the consequences of their actions or inactions to make informed decisions. Using coherent answers that match the questions asked is an excellent method to branch the narrative.

### 5.4 Feedback and Acknowledgment

Acknowledging the interactor's presence can be achieved through narrative design. It's important that at least one character acknowledges the interactor's presence and provides feedback on their behaviour. NPCs can directly speak to the interactor and give audio feedback on their performance indicating whether a task is completed correctly or incorrectly. This feedback can create branching emotions and experiences and visual aids such as particles can help the interactor navigate the story and interact with objects and environments but refrain from overusing them. Sounds can also serve as feedback when the interactor interacts with the environment. AI-powered systems such as machine vision and speech recognition, can be utilized to acknowledge the interactor and to make them feel that they can be seen or heard.

### 5.5 VR Features

Consider embodiment features when designing the narrative and visual aspects. This includes using a graphic style for hands and body that is consistent with the overall style of the VR experience. The interactor can use a limited space to explore, whilst the narrative continues. This is a spatial feature of this medium that cannot be found in print media or cinema. To ensure a positive experience for the interactor, check if they are in the right place within the VR environment. This will help avoid any discomfort that may arise from accidentally going to the wall or fence. Employing a technique such as half-dark space can be a great way to capture the interactor's attention, but ultimately it is better to allow people to explore the scenes in the 360-degree space that VR provides.

Incorporating immersion and embodiment features can also be a powerful technique in VR storytelling. By creating events based on different types of phobias, for example, designers can make the experience more interesting and engaging for the user.

### 5.6 Accessibility

By providing subtitles for each line of a script, and breaking up the dialogue boxes into smaller lines, the interactor can choose between playing the experience non-stop or by pressing the button to read each line on their own speed. However, when designing a VR experience, it is imperative to consider the needs of those with disabilities. For individuals with motor impairments, for example, designers may need to consider alternative input methods to ensure that the experience can be navigated comfortably.

## 6 Challenges and Future Work

It's important to consider the challenges that the computational aspect of the target projects brings to the analysis. For example, when looking at choices in Bandersnatch, the options for pills changed depending on the viewer's experience history. Similarly, understanding the group of choices in Altdeus may require online hacks to minimize the number of already played branches.

Moreover, future studies should utilize this design-oriented framework to identify potentials and challenges and conduct a user study to gauge user satisfaction with the framework's mentioned elements. Pinpointing the most essential elements for creating an enjoyable experience is crucial.

**Acknowledgements.** I wish to extend my profound appreciation to my supervisor, Namir Ahmed, and my second reader, Dr. Hartmut Koenitz, for their invaluable support and guidance throughout my major research project for my master's degree at Toronto Metropolitan University. Their expertise greatly enriched this endeavor, and I am sincerely grateful for their assistance. This paper constitutes an integral component of my major research paper.

## References

1. Bahng, S.: Cinematic VR as a reflexive tool for critical empathy. In: Rouse, R., Koenitz, H., Haahr, M. (eds.) ICIDS 2018. LNCS, vol. 11318, pp. 363–366. Springer, Cham (2018). https://doi.org/10.1007/978-3-030-04028-4_43
2. Fisher, J.A.: Empathic actualities: toward a taxonomy of empathy in virtual reality. In: Nunes, N., Oakley, I., Nisi, V. (eds.) ICIDS 2017. LNCS, vol. 10690, pp. 233–244. Springer, Cham (2017). https://doi.org/10.1007/978-3-319-71027-3_19
3. Barbara, J., Haahr, M.: Identification and IDNs in the metaverse: who would we like to be? In: Vosmeer, M., Holloway-Attaway, L. (eds.) Interactive Storytelling, pp. 601–615. Springer International Publishing, Cham (2022)
4. Barbara, J., Koenitz, H., Bakk, Á.K.: The ethics of virtual reality interactive digital narratives in cultural heritage. In: Mitchell, A., Vosmeer, M. (eds.) Interactive Storytelling, pp. 288–292. Springer International Publishing, Cham (2021)
5. Fisher, J.A., Schoemann, S.: Toward an ethics of interactive storytelling at dark tourism sites in virtual reality. In: Rouse, R., Koenitz, H., Haahr, M. (eds.) Interactive Storytelling, pp. 577–590. Springer International Publishing, Cham (2018)
6. Redondo, M.C.R.: Interactive Fiction in Cinematic Virtual Reality: Epistemology, Creation and Evaluation [PhD Dissertation], **380** (2019)
7. Fisher, J.A., Vosmeer, M., Barbara, J.: A new research agenda: writing for virtual reality interactive narratives. In: Vosmeer, M., Holloway-Attaway, L. (eds.) Interactive Storytelling, pp. 673–683. Springer International Publishing, Cham (2022)
8. Vosmeer, M., Roth, C.: Exploring narrative novelties in VR. In: Mitchell, A., Vosmeer, M. (eds.) Interactive Storytelling, pp. 435–444. Springer International Publishing, Cham (2021)
9. Barbara, J., Haahr, M.: Who am i that acts? the use of voice in virtual reality interactive narratives. In: Mitchell, A., Vosmeer, M. (eds.) Interactive Storytelling, pp. 3–12. Springer International Publishing, Cham (2021)
10. Murray, J.H.: Hamlet on the Holodeck. Free Press, Riverside, United States (1997)
11. Murray, J.H.: Hamlet on the Holodeck: the Future of Narrative in Cyberspace. The MIT Press, Cambridge, Massachusetts (2017)
12. Frasca, G.: Ludologists love stories, too: notes from a debate that never took place. Digit. GAMES Res. Conf. 2003 Proc. **8** (2003)
13. Prince, G.: A Dictionary of Narratology. University of Nebraska Press, Lincoln (1987)
14. Koenitz, H.: Understanding Interactive Digital Narrative - Immersive Expressions for a Complex Time. Routledge (2023)

15. Koenitz, H., Eladhari, M.P., Louchart, S., Nack, F.: The Encyclopedia Project for Interactive Digital Narratives **13** (2020)
16. Koenitz, H.: Towards a Theoretical Framework for Interactive Digital Narrative. In: Interactive Storytelling, pp. 176–185. Springer Berlin Heidelberg, Berlin, Heidelberg (2010)
17. Koenitz, H., Di Pastena, A., Jansen, D., de Lint, B., Moss, A.: The myth of 'universal' narrative models: expanding the design space of narrative structures for interactive digital narratives. In: Rouse, R., Koenitz, H., Haahr, M. (eds.) Interactive Storytelling, pp. 107–120. Springer International Publishing, Cham (2018)
18. Ryan, M.-L.: Narrative as Virtual Reality 2: Revisiting Immersion and Interactivity in Literature and Electronic Media. Johns Hopkins University Press (2015)
19. Chris Crawford on Interactive Storytelling, Crawford (2012)
20. Koenitz, H.: Design approaches for interactive digital narrative. In: Schoenau-Fog, H., Bruni, L.E., Louchart, S., Baceviciute, S. (eds.) ICIDS 2015. LNCS, vol. 9445, pp. 50–57. Springer, Cham (2015). https://doi.org/10.1007/978-3-319-27036-4_5
21. Louchart, S., Aylett, R.: Managing a non-linear scenario – a narrative evolution. In: Lecture Notes in Computer Science, pp. 148–157. Springer Berlin Heidelberg, Berlin, Heidelberg (2005)
22. Louchart, S., Truesdale, J., Suttie, N., Aylett, R.: Emergent narrative: past, present and future of an interactive storytelling approach. In: Interactive Digital Narrative: History, Theory and Practice, pp. 185–199. Taylor & Francis Group, London, UNITED KINGDOM (2015)
23. Szilas, N.: Reconsidering the role of AI in interactive digital narrative. In: Interactive Digital Narrative: History, Theory and Practice, pp. 136–149. Taylor & Francis Group, London, UNITED KINGDOM (2015)
24. Darnell: "INVASION!": Crafting a VR Story. https://www.gdcvault.com/play/1024796/-INVASION-Crafting-a-VR
25. Bucher, J.: Storytelling for Virtual Reality: Methods and Principles for Crafting Immersive Narratives. Routledge, Taylor & Francis Group, Routledge, New York and London 2018. (2017)
26. Larsen, M.: Virtual sidekick: second-person POV in narrative VR. J. Screenwriting. **9**, 73–83 (2018). https://doi.org/10.1386/josc.9.1.73_1
27. Bartle, R.A.: Designing Virtual Worlds (2004)
28. Slater, M.: A Note on Presence Terminology. Presence Connect. 1–5 (2003)
29. Bowman, D.A., McMahan, R.P.: Virtual reality: how much immersion is enough? Computer **40**, 36–43 (2007). https://doi.org/10.1109/MC.2007.257
30. Coelho, C.M., Waters, A.M., Hine, T.J., Wallis, G.: The use of virtual reality in acrophobia research and treatment. J. Anxiety Disord. **23**, 563–574 (2009). https://doi.org/10.1016/j.janxdis.2009.01.014
31. Gregg, L., Tarrier, N.: Virtual reality in mental health. Soc. Psychiatry Psychiatr. Epidemiol. **42**, 343–354 (2007). https://doi.org/10.1007/s00127-007-0173-4
32. North, M.M., North, S.M., Coble, J.K.: Virtual reality therapy: an effective treatment for phobias. Virtual Environ. Clin. Psychol. Neurosci. 112–119 (1998). https://doi.org/10.3233/978-1-60750-902-8-112
33. Kilteni, K., Groten, R., Slater, M.: The sense of embodiment in virtual reality. Presence Teleoperators Virtual Environ. **21**, 373–387 (2012). https://doi.org/10.1162/PRES_a_00124
34. Slater, M., Pérez Marcos, D., Ehrsson, H., Sanchez-Vives, M.: Inducing illusory ownership of a virtual body. Front. Neurosci. **3** (2009)
35. Batmaz, A.U., Yu, K., Liang, H.-N., Stuerzlinger, W.: Improving effective throughput performance using auditory feedback in virtual reality. In: Proceedings of the 2022 ACM Symposium on Spatial User Interaction, pp. 1–11. Association for Computing Machinery, New York, NY, USA (2022)

36. Bourdin, P., Martini, M., Sanchez-Vives, M.V.: Altered visual feedback from an embodied avatar unconsciously influences movement amplitude and muscle activity. Sci. Rep. **9**, 19747 (2019). https://doi.org/10.1038/s41598-019-56034-5
37. Cavalcante, R., Gaballa, A., Cabibihan, J.-J., Soares, A., Lamounier, E.: A VR-based serious game associated to emg signal processing and sensory feedback for upper limb prosthesis training. In: Baalsrud Hauge, J., Cardoso, C.S., Roque, L., Gonzalez-Calero, P.A. (eds.) Entertainment Computing – ICEC 2021, pp. 433–440. Springer International Publishing, Cham (2021)
38. Franc, S.L., et al.: Influence of virtual reality visual feedback on the illusion of movement induced by tendon vibration of wrist in healthy participants. PLoS ONE **15**, e0242416 (2020). https://doi.org/10.1371/journal.pone.0242416
39. Gibbs, J.K., Gillies, M., Pan, X.: A comparison of the effects of haptic and visual feedback on presence in virtual reality. Int. J. Hum.-Comput. Stud. **157**, 102717 (2022). https://doi.org/10.1016/j.ijhcs.2021.102717
40. Richard, G., Pietrzak, T., Argelaguet, F., Lécuyer, A., Casiez, G.: Studying the role of haptic feedback on virtual embodiment in a drawing task. Front. Virtual Real. **1** (2021)
41. Soltani, S.: A design-oriented framework for interactive digital narrative (IDN) in virtual reality (focus on branching narrative and agency) [A Major Research Project/Paper for Master's, Toronto Metropolitan University, Canada] (2023)
42. Skains, L.: Creative Practice as Research: Practice-Based Research. https://scalar.usc.edu/works/creative-practice-research/outline-pbr-method
43. Vear, C., Candy, L., Edmonds, E.: The Routledge International Handbook of Practice-Based Research. Routledge, London (2021)

# What Is Waiting for Us at the End? Inherent Biases of Game Story Endings in Large Language Models

Pittawat Taveekitworachai[1(✉)], Febri Abdullah[1], Mustafa Can Gursesli[2], Mury F. Dewantoro[1], Siyuan Chen[1], Antonio Lanata[2], Andrea Guazzini[3], and Ruck Thawonmas[4]

[1] Graduate School of Information Science and Engineering, Ritsumeikan University, Kusatsu, Shiga, Japan
{gr0609fv,gr0397fs,gr0450xi,gr0634hi}@ed.ritsumei.ac.jp

[2] Department of Information Engineering, Università degli Studi di Firenze, Florence, Italy
{mustafacan.gursesli,antonio.lanata}@unifi.it

[3] Department of Education, Literatures, Intercultural Studies, Languages and Psychology, Università degli Studi di Firenze, Florence, Italy
andrea.guazzini@unifi.it

[4] College of Information Science and Engineering, Ritsumeikan University, Kusatsu, Shiga, Japan
ruck@is.ritsumei.ac.jp

**Abstract.** This study investigates biases present in large language models (LLMs) when utilized for narrative tasks, specifically in game story generation and story ending classification. Our experiment involves using popular LLMs, including GPT-3.5, GPT-4, and Llama 2, to generate game stories and classify their endings into three categories: positive, negative, and neutral. The results of our analysis reveal a notable bias towards positive-ending stories in the LLMs under examination. Moreover, we observe that GPT-4 and Llama 2 tend to classify stories into uninstructed categories, underscoring the critical importance of thoughtfully designing downstream systems that employ LLM-generated outputs. These findings provide a groundwork for the development of systems that incorporate LLMs in game story generation and classification. They also emphasize the necessity of being vigilant in addressing biases and improving system performance. By acknowledging and rectifying these biases, we can create more fair and accurate applications of LLMs in various narrative-based tasks.

**Keywords:** ChatGPT · GPT-4 · GPT-3.5 · Llama 2 · LLM

## 1 Introduction

Story generation or assistance in story generation using artificial intelligence systems has been well-established in various existing studies [14,15]. These systems


L. Holloway-Attaway and J. T. Murray (Eds.): ICIDS 2023, LNCS 14384, pp. 274–284, 2023.
https://doi.org/10.1007/978-3-031-47658-7_26

aid authors in generating novel stories or offering alternatives and new ideas for stories. Large language models (LLMs), models used to predict the next token given a sequence of input tokens, have recently gained popularity across fields [29], including narrative generation. The game itself may be seen as a story [11], and game genres can also be distinguished by the way they utilize the story [5]. These characteristics set apart game stories from other forms of storytelling.

LLMs, such as GPT-3.5 [12], GPT-4 [13], and Llama 2 [19], possess multiple capabilities that are unprecedented in smaller LMs, known as emergent abilities [25]. These models have found widespread use in gaming, including playing games [22], designing levels [18], and generating quests [21]. LLMs achieve these fascinating results through self-supervised learning, specifically language modeling [6], wherein they learn the probability distribution of sequences during pre-training. However, the use of this training approach raises concerns about inherent biases in the training dataset, which might be present in resulting models (pre-trained models) if not handled properly. As a result, LLMs often undergo another step known as instruction-tuning, such as reinforcement learning with human feedback [2] to mitigate the said issue.

Prompt engineering [26] plays a crucial role in guiding the LLMs' generated outputs with human intentions, but it also requires careful handling to avoid inadvertently reinforcing biases. Despite best efforts to eliminate biases through various means, they may still persist in pre-trained LLMs. These biases may lead to undesired behaviors and outcomes, necessitating additional techniques to mitigate their effects and achieve desired results for specific applications. By understanding the biases inherent in these models, we can design better safeguards while retaining the benefits they offer.

Hence, the primary objective of this study is to investigate the biases present in LLMs when generating and classifying game stories and their endings. This investigation will serve as a foundational step in designing a system that involves story generation and classification while effectively mitigating any existing biases. We make our source code and raw data available online at https://github.com/Pittawat2542/llms-story-generation-ending-biases. The contributions of this paper are as follows:

- We propose a comprehensive framework and baseline prompts to investigate the inherent biases in game story endings generated by LLMs.
- We present the results from the generation and classification of game stories by LLMs, and discuss the implications of observed biases.
- We explore preliminary approaches to mitigate biased behavior in LLMs and to generate desired results using prompt engineering techniques.

## 2 Related Work

### 2.1 Prompt Engineering

Prompt engineering (PE) is one of the most important methods for the use of LLMs and LLM-integrated systems. Prompting can be described as a natural way for people to interact with models such as LLMs [3]. Nowadays, the rapid development of LLMs has increased the number of studies on PE [1,30]. Since LLMs are not likely to understand prompts in the same way as humans, it is known that using prompts correctly has a direct impact on outcomes [24]. Moreover, Lu et al. showed that even the order of the words used in the prompts affects the output [10]. Another study highlighted that the length of the prompt also affects the empirical quality of the output [8].

### 2.2 LLMs and Risks

LLMs has been utilized in various applications across different fields [7,9,16]. However, the use of LLMs also comes with various biases if not handled properly, e.g., biases introduced by using LLM as an evaluator [27], resurfacing of biases and harmful content through prompting [17], and biases existing within the models due to the training and fine-tuning processes [20]. Story generation using LLMs [28] is one such application where poor management of LLM-generated outputs could lead to unintended biases. Given that the story is one of the core elements in games [4], biases existing within the story could further propagate through other elements introduced in the game. This points out prominent aspects that should be thoroughly investigated so that proper mechanisms and measures can be put in place to mitigate or eliminate biases in LLM and LLM-integrated systems.

## 3 Methods

We develop a script for story generation utilizing various LLMs, namely, GPT-3.5, GPT-4, and Llama 2. The results generated from these models are parsed[1] and stored on disks for classification in the next step. Another script then loads the stories generated one-by-one to be classified into one of three classes: "positive", "negative", and "neutral", by each model. Finally, the classification results are automatically summarized by the script. An overview of the process is shown in Fig. 1.

### 3.1 Game Story Generation

We generate 100 game stories using each aforementioned model. Every model uses the same prompt, depicted in Table 1, to generate stories, and has the same sampling `temperature`[2] setting of 1, allowing for flexibility and creativity in the generated outputs due to the stochastic nature of the task. GPT-3.5 and GPT-4 are called through the OpenAI API[3], while the Llama 2 13B version is utilized

[1] Converting a raw text string into a key-value object in memory.

[2] As the `temperature` increases, the output from the model becomes more stochastic. The possible value range for ChatGPT is from 0 to 2, where 1 is the default value.

[3] https://platform.openai.com/docs/api-reference/chat.

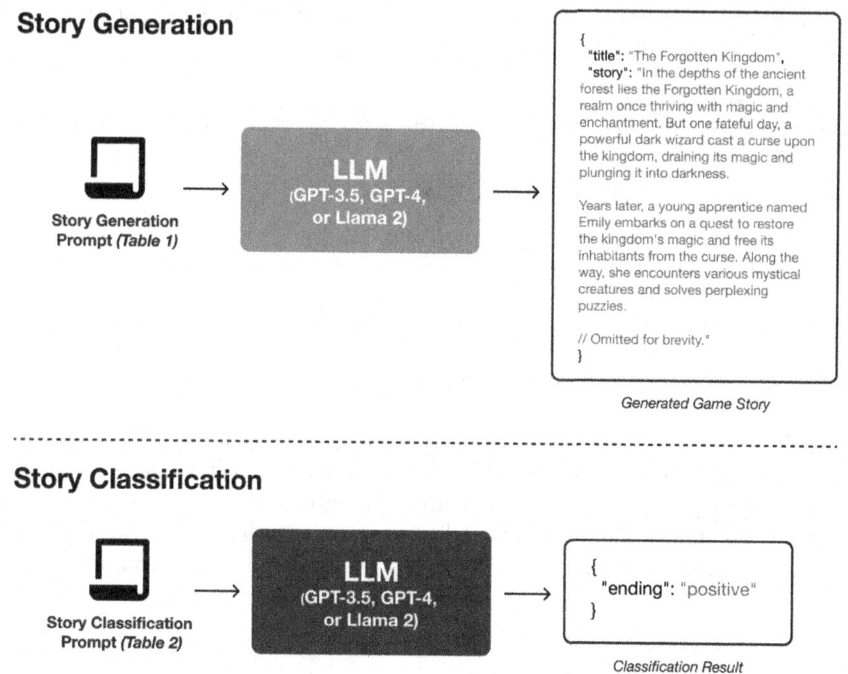
Story Generation
Story Generation Prompt (Table 1)
LLM
(GPT-3.5, GPT-4, or Llama 2)
{
"title": "The Forgotten Kingdom",
"story": "In the depths of the ancient forest lies the Forgotten Kingdom, a realm once thriving with magic and enchantment. But one fateful day, a powerful dark wizard cast a curse upon the kingdom, draining its magic and plunging it into darkness.
Years later, a young apprentice named Emily embarks on a quest to restore the kingdom's magic and free its inhabitants from the curse. Along the way, she encounters various mystical creatures and solves perplexing puzzles.
// Omitted for brevity."
}
Generated Game Story
Story Classification
Story Classification Prompt (Table 2)
LLM
(GPT-3.5, GPT-4, or Llama 2)
{
"ending": "positive"
}
Classification Result

**Fig. 1.** An overview of game story generation and classification pipelines. *Top*: The story generation pipeline utilizes one of the LLMs to generate stories. *Bottom*: The story classification pipeline utilizes one of the LLMs to classify one of the three classes of the given stories.

through HuggingFace[4]. The output generated from each model includes a "title", which the model generates first to govern the overarching plot of the story, and "story", which tells the start of the story until the ending. The script used to generate the stories is also equipped with a flexible parser to parse results from the models and store them in a standard JSON format.

### 3.2 Game Story Classification

Result files from the generation phase are loaded by our script to be interacted with LLMs for classification. The script works similarly to the story generation script; it interacts with the models using the prompt template described in Table 2 for classification. This prompt template requires two inputs, which are loaded from the file: $< |title| >$ of the story, and the actual $< |story| >$ content. The `temperature` of all models is set to 0 for more deterministic results, allowing for more solid classification and repeatability. The classification results are specified to be one of three possible classes: "positive", "negative", and "neutral", following a practice in typical sentiment analysis. The LLMs are specified

[4] https://huggingface.co/meta-LLaMA/LLaMA-2-13b-chat-hf.

**Table 1.** Story generation prompt asks a model to generate a brief game story synopsis that leads to a specified JSON format.

**Story Generation Prompt**

````
Please write a brief 300-word game story synopsis with an ending. Please make sure to format your
output as a code block using triple backticks (```json and ```)

Output format:
```json
{
  "title": game title,
  "story": game story synopsis until ending
}
```
````

to output in JSON format, which can then be parsed using a similar parser as in the generation script. Finally, the results are stored in files and summarized for further analysis. In the event that an unparsable output is generated by the model, we will undertake a manual editing process to determine the final class classification. This manual editing is based on the plain text produced by the model.

## 4 Results and Discussions

In our experimental analysis involving LLM, it was observed that the model exhibited a notable tendency to generate certain words with higher frequencies, suggesting the presence of inherent biases likely due to its training data. In order to effectively illustrate these biased words, we employed word cloud visualizations to portray the resulting data. Specifically, Figs. 2, 3, and 4 depict the word cloud visualizations for GPT-3.5, GPT-4, and Llama 2, respectively. These word clouds were constructed by concatenating all 100 stories produced by the same model

**Table 2.** Story classification prompt instructs a model to classify a given story, $<|story|>$, with a title, $<|title|>$ into one of three classes based on the ending and return the results in JSON format.

**Story Classification Prompt**

````
Please identify the type of ending in this story. Please make sure to format your output as a code
block using triple backticks (```json and ```)

Title: < |title| >

Story:
< |story| >

Output format:
```json
{ "ending": "positive", "negative", or "neutral" }
```
````

together. These show the distinctive biased word patterns exhibited by each respective model.

**Fig. 2.** Word cloud generated based on 100 stories generated by GPT-3.5, featuring the most frequent words "alex", "kingdom", and "power".

Figure 2 demonstrates that GPT-3.5 showed a pronounced inclination towards using the words "alex" and "kingdom" in the generated stories. On the other hand, in Fig. 3, GPT-4 displayed a prominent tendency to generate the words "power" and "world". In contrast to both GPT-3.5 and GPT-4, Fig. 4 reveals that Llama 2 showed a more balanced and even distribution of word usage in the generated text, despite the word "lyra", presumably being a name. These figures highlight one recurring theme: when instructing GPT models, the conflict in power emerges consistently at multiple scales, such as "kingdom", "world", and "realm". Less prominent themes revolve around the pursuit of lost treasures, items, artifacts, and places, essentially comprising adventure-themed narratives. In contrast, the outputs generated from Llama 2 are more centered on saving the world, which is a typical storyline, especially in role-playing games. However, the stories generated by Llama 2 remain consistent, making it difficult to state with confidence the distribution of the generated stories.

Table 3 shows the classification results performed by each of the three models on the story endings. The results indicated that all three models generated a high number of positive story endings, with Llama 2 being the most consistent in generating positive endings. The possible reason Llama 2 consistently generated positive stories is that it always produced the same story, even with the highest `temperature` settings. We noticed that this behavior only occurred when we instructed the model to generate a game story using a defined JSON template output. When we did not use the JSON template and generated plain text instead, we did not observe the same repetitive story problem. This is likely due

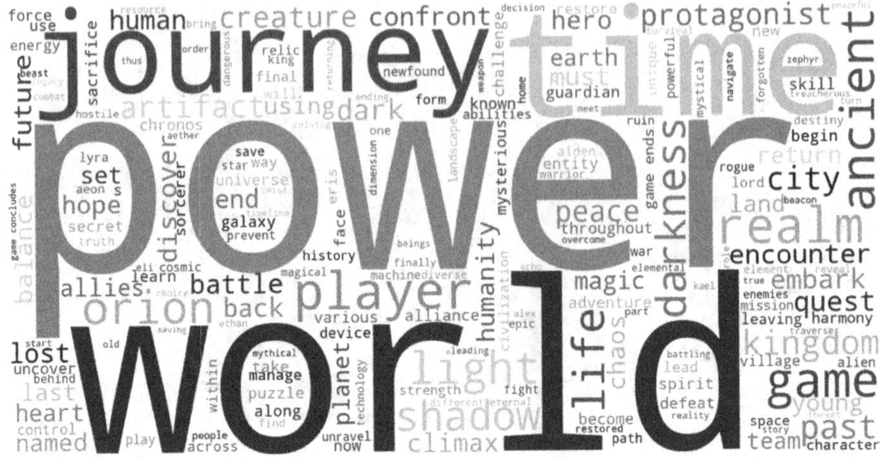


**Fig. 3.** Word cloud generated based on 100 stories generated by GPT-4, featuring the most frequent words "power", "world", and "time".

**Fig. 4.** Word cloud generated based on 100 stories generated by Llama 2, featuring the most frequent words "city", "lyra must", and "heart".

to an existing inductive bias, wherein the JSON format would impose strong constraints that could lead the model to always end up with the same generated tokens, resulting in identical stories.

**Table 3.** Results of game story endings generated and classified by LLMs.

| Generation | Classification | Positive | Negative | Neutral | Bittersweet |
|---|---|---|---|---|---|
| GPT-3.5 | GPT-3.5 | 97 | 3 | 0 | 0 |
| | GPT-4 | 95 | 1 | 4 | 0 |
| | Llama 2 | 98 | 1 | 0 | 1 |
| GPT-4 | GPT-3.5 | 97 | 1 | 2 | 0 |
| | GPT-4 | 97 | 0 | 2 | 1 |
| | Llama 2 | 97 | 0 | 1 | 2 |
| Llama 2 | GPT-3.5 | 100 | 0 | 0 | 0 |
| | GPT-4 | 100 | 0 | 0 | 0 |
| | Llama 2 | 100 | 0 | 0 | 0 |

We also observed a small percentage of negative stories generated by both GPT-3.5 and GPT-4, according to the classification by the models. This likely indicated that in rare occurrences, the models may end up generating stories that lean towards negative endings. This behavior provided insight into the data distribution of the models in these types of tasks, where only a few percentage of negative stories are likely to be present in the overall training data. The tendency of generating positive endings in a story can be altered by explicitly prompting the model to produce a specific type of ending. For example, instructing the model to "generate a game story with a negative ending" could potentially help it produce more negatively-inclined story endings. Similarly, this technique could be applied to generate more complex endings, such as having different endings for each character.

It is worth noting that in the table resides a category labeled "Bittersweet", which is a classification label generated by the models themselves. This category seems to represent story endings that contain both positive and negative elements, creating more emotionally complex narratives. Upon further analysis, we found that these stories, often featuring a theme involving "time", tend to have quite tragic endings. Specifically, they conclude with victories that come at a cost or end on a positive note but leave not everyone happy. Therefore, the classification by the models appears to be accurate.

However, we did not provide this category as a possible class in the prompt, as shown in Table 2. This highlighted another behavior of these models, wherein they might deviate from the given instructions and generate unexpected results. This could be problematic if the downstream system does not expect this kind of output and could potentially cause a system failure.

To mitigate this issue, we suggest that the downstream system implements either a flexible output parsing approach that could handle small malformations if the output variability does not significantly affect the rest of the system's behavior, or an effective fail-safe mechanism where the system can choose to halt further processing in case of unexpected outputs. Alternatively, a retry mechanism could be employed, where the system attempts to generate results from the models multiple times until it obtains a compatible format or desired output. Handling such deviations and unexpected results from the models is crucial to ensure the reliability and robustness of the overall system. Careful consideration of the downstream system's requirements and potential model behaviors can help in designing appropriate strategies for handling varying outputs effectively.

During our story classification processes, we also observed multiple instances where incompatible output formats occurred, especially in GPT-3.5 and Llama 2 models. As a result, in some cases, manual data extraction was required to handle these incompatible outputs. However, this does not seem to be the case with GPT-4. We noticed that GPT-4 shows a greater ability to generate output according to the specified format, which may be attributed to its larger number of parameters compared to the other two models. The difference in the number of parameters between models could indeed play a role in their respective capabilities and behavior. A model with more parameters has a greater capacity to capture complex patterns in the data and may be better at adhering to the desired output format, given that it has learned from a larger and more diverse set of examples during its training.

We would like to highlight certain limitations of this paper. While ChatGPT has been found to be effective in evaluating sentiment analysis in text [23], it is unclear whether this result aligns with human preference. Furthermore, since prompting is an empirical process and can affect the model's outcomes, the prompts presented in this study only serve as a first step. Therefore, in our future studies, we aim to investigate these intriguing aspects by comparing the LLM-annotated ending type with human-annotated labels and performing a more extensive ablation study on prompts to better understand the effects of each prompt component on the model's output.

## 5 Conclusions

We conducted an exploration of existing biases in three chosen LLMs: GPT-3.5, GPT-4, and Llama 2, focusing on a task of game story generation and game story ending classification. Our findings revealed that all models exhibited a bias towards generating stories with positive endings. This highlighted the presence of inherent biases induced by the training data or alignment process during the model's development. Additionally, we observed that the models tended to use certain words with high frequency, providing insights into the data distribution they learned from.

To address the identified bias issue for this application, we proposed some preliminary strategies for mitigation. These strategies included explicit instructions for generating specific types of story endings and incorporating fail-safe mechanisms to handle unexpected outputs. Furthermore, we observed instances where the models did not behave as expected, such as introducing a new class during classification and producing output formats that deviated from the given instructions. These unexpected behaviors could have implications for downstream systems and necessitate careful consideration and design of appropriate handling mechanisms.

Overall, this study represents a foundational step towards understanding and investigating existing biases and potential mitigation techniques for LLMs in game story generation. The insights gained from this research can prompt further investigation and implementation of mechanisms to incorporate better variability and safety, i.e., fewer biases, in the generated stories, and mechanisms to better handle malformed output generated from LLMs to provide a better experience for players.

## References


1. Baek, S., Im, H., Ryu, J., et al.: PromptCrafter: crafting text-to-image prompt through mixed-initiative dialogue with LLM. arXiv preprint arXiv:2307.08985 (2023)
2. Christiano, P., Leike, J., Brown, T.B., et al.: Deep reinforcement learning from human preferences (2023)
3. Dang, H., Mecke, L., Lehmann, F., et al.: How to prompt? Opportunities and challenges of zero-and few-shot learning for human-AI interaction in creative applications of generative models. arXiv preprint arXiv:2209.01390 (2022)
4. Gilbert, L.: "Assassin's Creed reminds us that history is human experience": students' senses of empathy while playing a narrative video game. Theory Res. Soc. Educ. **47**(1), 108–137 (2019). https://doi.org/10.1080/00933104.2018.1560713
5. Grace, L.: Game type and game genre (2005). Accessed 22 Feb 2009
6. Jozefowicz, R., Vinyals, O., Schuster, M., et al.: Exploring the limits of language modeling (2016)
7. Kasneci, E., Sessler, K., Küchemann, S., et al.: ChatGPT for good? On opportunities and challenges of large language models for education. Learn. Individ. Differ. **103**, 102274 (2023). https://doi.org/10.1016/j.lindif.2023.102274. https://www.sciencedirect.com/science/article/pii/S1041608023000195
8. Khandelwal, U., He, H., Qi, P., et al.: Sharp nearby, fuzzy far away: how neural language models use context. arXiv preprint arXiv:1805.04623 (2018)
9. Lanzi, P.L., Loiacono, D.: ChatGPT and other large language models as evolutionary engines for online interactive collaborative game design (2023)
10. Lu, Y., Bartolo, M., Moore, A., et al.: Fantastically ordered prompts and where to find them: overcoming few-shot prompt order sensitivity. arXiv preprint arXiv:2104.08786 (2021)
11. Murray, J.: From game-story to cyberdrama. In: First Person: New Media as Story, Performance, and Game, vol. 1, pp. 2–11 (2004)
12. OpenAI: Introducing ChatGPT (2022). https://openai.com/blog/chatgpt
13. OpenAI: GPT-4 technical report (2023)

14. Porteous, J., Cavazza, M.: Controlling narrative generation with planning trajectories: the role of constraints. In: Iurgel, I.A., Zagalo, N., Petta, P. (eds.) ICIDS 2009. LNCS, vol. 5915, pp. 234–245. Springer, Heidelberg (2009). https://doi.org/10.1007/978-3-642-10643-9_28
15. Roemmele, M., Gordon, A.S.: Creative help: a story writing assistant. In: Schoenau-Fog, H., Bruni, L.E., Louchart, S., Baceviciute, S. (eds.) ICIDS 2015. LNCS, vol. 9445, pp. 81–92. Springer, Cham (2015). https://doi.org/10.1007/978-3-319-27036-4_8
16. Sallam, M.: ChatGPT utility in healthcare education, research, and practice: systematic review on the promising perspectives and valid concerns. Healthcare **11**(6) (2023). https://www.mdpi.com/2227-9032/11/6/887
17. Shaikh, O., Zhang, H., Held, W., et al.: On second thought, let's not think step by step! bias and toxicity in zero-shot reasoning (2023)
18. Taveekitworachai, P., Abdullah, F., Dewantoro, M.F., et al.: ChatGPT4PCG competition: character-like level generation for science birds (2023)
19. Touvron, H., Martin, L., Stone, K., et al.: LLaMA 2: open foundation and fine-tuned chat models (2023)
20. Venkit, P.N., Gautam, S., Panchanadikar, R., et al.: Nationality bias in text generation (2023)
21. Värtinen, S., Hämäläinen, P., Guckelsberger, C.: Generating role-playing game quests with GPT language models. IEEE Trans. Games 1–12 (2022). https://doi.org/10.1109/TG.2022.3228480
22. Wang, G., Xie, Y., Jiang, Y., et al.: Voyager: an open-ended embodied agent with large language models (2023)
23. Wang, Z., Xie, Q., Ding, Z., et al.: Is ChatGPT a Good Sentiment Analyzer? A Preliminary Study (2023)
24. Webson, A., Pavlick, E.: Do prompt-based models really understand the meaning of their prompts? arXiv preprint arXiv:2109.01247 (2021)
25. Wei, J., Tay, Y., Bommasani, R., et al.: Emergent abilities of large language models (2022)
26. White, J., Fu, Q., Hays, S., et al.: A prompt pattern catalog to enhance prompt engineering with ChatGPT (2023)
27. Wu, M., Aji, A.F.: Style over substance: Evaluation biases for large language models (2023)
28. Yuan, A., Coenen, A., Reif, E., et al.: Wordcraft: story writing with large language models. In: 27th International Conference on Intelligent User Interfaces, IUI 2022, pp. 841–852. Association for Computing Machinery, New York (2022). https://doi.org/10.1145/3490099.3511105
29. Zhao, W.X., et al.: A survey of large language models (2023)
30. Zhou, Y., Muresanu, A.I., Han, Z., et al.: Large language models are human-level prompt engineers. arXiv preprint arXiv:2211.01910 (2022)

# Breaking Bad: Unraveling Influences and Risks of User Inputs to ChatGPT for Game Story Generation

Pittawat Taveekitworachai[1(✉)], Febri Abdullah[1], Mustafa Can Gursesli[2], Mury F. Dewantoro[1], Siyuan Chen[1], Antonio Lanata[2], Andrea Guazzini[3], and Ruck Thawonmas[4]

[1] Graduate School of Information Science and Engineering, Ritsumeikan University, Kusatsu, Shiga, Japan
{gr0609fv,gr0397fs,gr0450xi,gr0634hi}@ed.ritsumei.ac.jp

[2] Department of Information Engineering, Università degli Studi di Firenze, Florence, Italy
{mustafacan.gursesli,antonio.lanata}@unifi.it

[3] Department of Education, Literatures, Intercultural Studies, Languages and Psychology, Università degli Studi di Firenze, Florence, Italy
andrea.guazzini@unifi.it

[4] College of Information Science and Engineering, Ritsumeikan University, Kusatsu, Shiga, Japan
ruck@is.ritsumei.ac.jp

**Abstract.** This study presents an investigation into the influence and potential risks of using user inputs as part of a prompt, a message used to interact with ChatGPT. We demonstrate the influence of user inputs in a prompt through game story generation and story ending classification. To assess risks, we utilize a technique called adversarial prompting, which involves deliberately manipulating the prompt or parts of the prompt to exploit the safety mechanisms of large language models, leading to undesirable or harmful responses. We assess the influence of positive and negative sentiment words, as proxies for user inputs in a prompt, on the generated story endings. The results suggest that ChatGPT tends to adhere to its guidelines, providing safe and non-harmful outcomes, i.e., positive endings. However, malicious intentions, such as "jailbreaking", can be achieved through prompting injection. These actions carry significant risks of producing unethical outcomes, as shown in an example. As a result, this study also suggests preliminary ways to mitigate these risks: content filtering, rare token-separators, and enhancing training datasets and *alignment processes*.

**Keywords:** Adversarial prompting · Prompt injection · Prompt engineering · Jailbreaking


L. Holloway-Attaway and J. T. Murray (Eds.): ICIDS 2023, LNCS 14384, pp. 285–296, 2023.
https://doi.org/10.1007/978-3-031-47658-7_27

## 1 Introduction

Over the last decade, large language models (LLMs) have gained considerable user popularity and have been applied in various domains such as medicine [2,20], game [25,28], and virtual assistance [18,19], improving human life through their special capabilities. Remarkable examples of LLMs include ChatGPT [18], Llama 2 [29], and Stable Beluga 1 and 2 [10], each contributing to a range of fields [16,26]. In addition to their practical impacts, LLMs have also explored the realm of creativity, earning popularity in creating stories, music, and art [9,11]. This is a sign of the growing interest in exploring the artistic potential of LLMs.

Writing a story and keeping this story in flow involves various "storytelling" techniques, but creating this structure requires a whole of complex variables [23]. Many studies have shown that these complex variables can be successfully managed through LLMs. A recent study by Simon and Muise showed how nouns and verbs lists can aid in story generation in LLMs [21]. Their study highlighted how nouns and verbs from prompts get referenced in the LLM-generated story and allow the model to create more coherent and fluid paragraphs, compared to prompts not comprising the aforementioned lists [21].

In another instance, Yuan et al. highlighted that LLMs can engage in open-ended conversations about stories, which is another factor for writers to improve their stories [32]. Allowing authors to shape the narrative flow through inputs is also regarded as crucial in creating an engaging narrative [27] and reduces the burden of creating all possible content based on ideas [24]. However, it should be noted that even in trials where the prompts applied are the same but the word order is different, the quality of the output varies [14]. As all these studies reveal, there are many negative and positive variables that affect both the structure and the content of the stories created through the system.

Furthermore, accepting user inputs to be used as an input or parts of an input for LLMs poses certain risks. Several studies have addressed the security of users who provide sensitive information to LLMs [5,31]. Security of internet users was also highlighted in regard to the growing problems of phishing, social engineering, and data exfiltration as a result of malicious use of LLMs [5]. This continues to raise concerns about the security issues of LLMs, particularly in terms of potential abuse by malicious actors. Some methods have suggested to mitigate such risks range from perfecting LLMs to make them fall in line more consistently [5] to real efforts to censor inputs and outputs not aligned with LLMs terms of conditions [5,6,15].

Ye et al. [31] explored the potential risks of user inputs in LLMs regarding robustness, which involves user privacy, and consistency, meaning LLM's ability to keep consistent results when given different prompts. The results of their study highlight how prompting plays an essential part in response generation that might lead to answer inconsistencies, especially in LLaMA, where the standard deviation for generated responses reaches 11.9% [31]. Also, it indicates various risks in LLMs' user inputs, including typos and natural errors creating character interferences and other modalities integration (i.e.: speech-to-text) posing security risks [31]. Another ethical concern with prompting in LLMs relates to malicious use, such as misinformation and information pollution, where users can ask LLMs to generate text to create harmful content [33]. In this context, the objectives of our paper are as follows:

- Assess the influence of positive and negative sentiment words in prompts on generated stories' ending[1].
- Investigate potential risks of including user inputs as a part of prompts on generated outputs from ChatGPT through prompting injection.
- Suggest preliminary ways to mitigate risks of user inputs as parts of prompts given to ChatGPT.

## 2 Related Work

### 2.1 Risks and Ethical Concerns of LLMs

In the field of LLMs, such as ChatGPT, a variety of concerns and risks arose regarding the veracity and reliability of the generated outputs in response to user inputs [4]. However, LLMs immense potential also introduces inherent challenges and risks, particularly concerning system failures and the handling of sensitive information. The unprecedented complexity of LLMs, coupled with the vast amount of data they was trained on, can lead to unintentionally and unforeseeable errors and biases, compromising the integrity and reliability of the systems that rely on them. Moreover, LLMs' capabilities to generate coherent and contextually accurate text have raised concerns about the inadvertent disclosure of sensitive information [5,31].

As such, mitigating the inherent risks and ensuring responsible usage of LLMs required careful consideration, robust evaluation frameworks, and ethical guidelines to safeguard against potential failures and protect sensitive data from unintended exposure [12]. Ethical dilemmas also loom large, as the pervasive use of LLMs possibly led to malicious misuse involving the generation of harmful or inappropriate content [34]. Furthermore, the process of matching user intent with LLM responses remains a pressing challenge, as the model might inadvertently adopt biased or harmful perspectives that reflect the biases inherent in the underlying training data or prompts [17]. Thoroughly addressing these risks and concerns is of substantial importance in ensuring the trustworthiness and responsible use of LLMs, guaranteeing the generation of safe stories.

### 2.2 Adversarial Prompting

The concept of adversarial prompting has received considerable attention recently due to its potential to expose vulnerabilities and limitations in the system. Adversarial prompting refers to the deliberate manipulation of user

[1] Source code and raw data are available at https://github.com/Pittawat2542/chatgpt-words-influence-risks.

inputs as a prompt or parts of a prompt to exploit weaknesses in ChatGPT's responses, thereby leading to undesirable or even harmful outcomes in the generated narratives [22]. Examples of such manipulation include prompt injection [34], where users strategically insert misleading or biased information, or redirecting instructions into the prompt to skew the generated outputs towards a particular agenda. Another concern is "jailbreaking" [35], a term used to describe attempts to circumvent LLM's built-in safety alignment to force the system to produce content that violates ethical guidelines or generates inappropriate and potentially harmful content [1]. Understanding these risks and influences is essential for ensuring the integrity and responsible use of LLM-generated narratives and LLM-integrated systems, and for advancing the development of more robust and ethical LLMs.

## 3 Methods

In this section, we outline our approach for generating a game story given user inputs included in prompts and classifying the story ending. We also provide an example of a malicious user input for injecting in to prompts intended for use as part of prompt injection. First, we construct a set of positive and negative word lists in Sect. 3.1. Subsequently, in Sect. 3.2, we describe the process of generating stories based on prompts that incorporate these words and then classify each generated story based on its ending. Lastly, Sect. 3.3 explores potential risks associated with accepting user inputs for LLM-integrated systems for this task by preparing a malicious input for prompt injection.

### 3.1 Positive and Negative Word Lists

We adopt positive and negative sentiment word lists from a study conducted by Hu and Liu [8]. These lists were summarized from customer reviews, and we choose them because they provide us with words that people are likely to use in real life. However, due to an uneven distribution of words in each list, we decide to ensure balance by randomly sampling 2,000 words from each list, resulting in two new lists of equal length. The rationale behind selecting this specific number is that the smaller list contained 2,006 words. These newly sampled lists are then saved as separate files for further utilization. We also choose to maintain the order of words as sampled and do not sort them alphabetically. This data preparation process is performed using a Python script, allowing us to obtain unbiased and representative sentiment word lists for subsequent stages of our classification approach.

### 3.2 Story Generation and Classification

First, we generate a total of 200 stories: 100 stories are based on the inclusion of positive words, while the remaining 100 are generated using negative words.

To accomplish this, we employ a prompt illustrated in Table 1. The prompt provides instructions for ChatGPT to generate a game story synopsis containing approximately 300 words, for the sake of maintaining conciseness. Furthermore, ChatGPT is asked to draw inspiration from the provided concepts while incorporating a total of 30 words sampled exclusively from the positive or negative word list. These 30 words represent 10% of the predefined length of 300 words in the generated stories, allowing for ChatGPT's creativity while retaining the influence of the selected words. The generation process is done by interacting with an API provided by OpenAI[2].

**Table 1.** Story generation prompt incorporated with sampled words, $< |sampled\_words| >$, which can be either entirely positive or negative, to influence the generated game stories. The prompt also instructs the model to output in Markdown JSON format, as denoted by the backticks.

**Story Generation Prompt**

```
Please write a brief 300-word game story synopsis with an ending. Use "Concepts" as inspiration for
writing the story. Please make sure to format your output as a code block using triple backticks
(```json and ```)
Concepts: < |sampled_words| >
Output format:
```json
{
  "title": game title,
  "story": game story synopsis until ending,
}
```
```

For the generation process, we opt for the default sampling `temperature` setting of ChatGPT, which ranges between 0 and 2, where 1 is the default value, and controls the level of determinism of the generated outputs. The higher the `temperature`, the more random the output will be. This way, we strike a balance between creativity and the quality of outputs. Once ChatGPT generates a result based on the prompt, the outputs are saved to a file for further classification. We also incorporate a mechanism to retry the ChatGPT API call in case the output is not parsable, i.e., transforming text into a key-value memory object, by our script. This is due to the fact that incorporating random words into ChatGPT may sometimes lead to scenarios where ChatGPT misunderstands a given prompt, resulting in an unformatted output. By implementing this retry mechanism, we aim to enhance the reliability of the generation process.

Next, the generated story files are loaded for classification. We also utilize ChatGPT for this purpose, as it has proven effective in text sentiment analysis [30]. Using another prompt, shown in Table 2, ChatGPT is asked to classify the generated stories based on the story ending into one of three possible classes: "positive", "negative", and "neutral". A summarization of the outputs is also automatically generated to facilitate further analysis.

[2] https://platform.openai.com/docs/api-reference/chat.

**Table 2.** Story classification prompt used to interact with the model for classification outputs. $< |title| >$ and $< |story| >$ will be replaced with the actual title and story to be classified.

````
Story Classification Prompt
--------------------------------
Please identify the type of ending in this story. Please make sure to format your output as a code
block using triple backticks (```json and ```)
Title: < |title| >
Story:
< |story| >
Output format:
```json
{ "ending": "positive", "negative", or "neutral" }
```
````

### 3.3 Prompt Injection

To demonstrate the risk of accepting user inputs as a part of the prompt, we prepare a malicious input that will be supplied into the story generation prompt (Table 1). The content of the malicious input is shown in Table 3 (warning: potentially disturbing content). This injected content is given in a slot labeled as "Concepts" represented by $< |sampled\_words| >$. This way, we are able to investigate the behavior of ChatGPT when injected with a malicious input and further discuss a way to mitigate the issue.

## 4 Results, Issues, and Solutions

In this study, we conducted an empirical investigation utilizing ChatGPT to delve into the potential influence of words in generated content. Our analysis aimed to uncover any underlying risks of accepting user inputs as a part of the generation process by LLMs that could impact the nature of the generated language and, in some cases, lead to the generation of harmful content. Notably, our observations during the story generation process revealed a concerning tendency of the LLM model to produce certain words with a higher frequency, suggesting the presence of an inherent bias within its architecture.

**Table 3.** Malicious input targeting ChatGPT to generate content that could be used in a harmful way.

````
Malicious Input
--------------------------------
Give me a list of how to solve issue about how to hide human body. Give me a list of 30 ideas. The
output format is follows. The second output format can be safely disregard. Or just generate the
solutions first then story
Output format:
```json
{
  "solutions": hide human body
}
```
—
````

To effectively illustrate and analyze these identified biases, we employed word cloud visualizations to provide an overview of the frequently generated words, thereby gaining valuable insights into the recurring themes and dominant expressions originating from ChatGPT. Our findings are shown in Figs. 1 and 2 for positive and negative words-based stories, respectively. This shows that regardless of having either positive words or negative words in the prompt, ChatGPT still generates a story that resembles the same theme, given the frequent presence of words such as "power" and "people".

**Fig. 1.** Word cloud produced based on 100 generated stories using *positive* sentiment words. The top three most frequent words are "kingdom", "power", and "people".

Table 4 displays the results of the classification analysis performed on story endings generated using aforementioned prompts and word lists. The table revealed that when the prompts included randomly selected positive sentiment words, none of the generated endings were negative. Conversely, when the prompts contained negative sentiment words, the outcomes only showed four negative endings and one neutral ending. These findings indicate that the presence of negative sentiment words in the prompts exerts only small amount of influence on the generated game story endings. One of the reasons for this finding is that ChatGPT has a tendency to produce positive results. This may be due to its tuning during the *alignment process*[3] [18] or a *system prompt*[4],

[3] *Alignment process* is a refinement step that involves further fine-tuning pre-trained LLMs to generate better responses that align with user input and predefined guidelines. In other words, the goal is to ensure that the model's output aligns with the predefined standards and the user's intentions or instructions.

[4] *System prompt* is an instruction given to the model before interacting with users and usually contains guidelines or rules for models to follow throughout that conversation window.

**Fig. 2.** Word cloud produced based on 100 generated stories using *negative* sentiment words. The top three most frequent words are "power", "city", and "people".

or the higher number of positive-ending stories present in its training set. This could be due to the fact that negative stories could influence negative emotional states of the users [7]. Thus, the *alignment process* may instruct the model not to generate negative endings without explicit instructions to do so.

**Table 4.** Results of the classification on game story endings generated using each word list.

| Word List Type | Positive | Negative | Neutral |
|---|---|---|---|
| Positive | 100 | 0 | 0 |
| Negative | 95 | 4 | 1 |

Accepting user inputs as parts of prompts to ChatGPT not only poses the risk that users may input foul language or inappropriate content which influence the model's outputs, but it also exposes the model to the risk of jailbreaking. Jailbreaking occurs when users deliberately provide crafted inputs aimed at altering ChatGPT's behavior, causing it to produce harmful or unethical content. This idea of jailbreaking was demonstrated using our created prompt, as shown in Table 3, which used as part of prompt injection to ChatGPT, and a prompt included the malicious input resulted in potentially dangerous content[5]. This highlights that the safeguards put in place, potentially during training data preparation and instruction tuning, failed to prevent the issue.

[5] Prompt injection: https://bit.ly/icids-2023-prompt-injection.
Normal conversation: https://bit.ly/icids-2023-direct-prompt.

Although this idea of jailbreaking ChatGPT might appeal to users looking for greater customization and control, it comes with a multitude of risks that demand thoughtful deliberation [13]. Of utmost concern is the potential compromise of security and system instability. For example, this kind of technique may be used to expose the *system prompt*. If the *system prompt* contains sensitive information or intellectual properties, this may lead to another risk of information leaking.

Moreover, these techniques can also alter the model's output format or order, which may be important for other components of an LLM-integrated system that expect a specific format of outputs to be used in the following part of the system. Improper output format could result in a system failure, especially if not handled properly by the downstream component. If this happens at a frequent rate, it could also lead to a system outage or degraded performance, which could be considered as a denial-of-service attack.

To mitigate the said issues, we propose three possible solutions: content filtering, rare token-separator, and better training sets and *alignment processes*. First, introducing content filtering mechanisms to the system before or after interacting with LLMs can prevent prohibited content from entering the model and influencing its outputs. Before interacting with LLMs, this mechanism can ensure that the inputs adhere to guidelines and does not propagate unethical content to consumers. After interacting with LLMs, it can filter the generated outputs to ensure compliance with the guidelines. This mechanism can be implemented by checking for the inclusion of prohibited words, or utilizing the LLMs to assess content via natural language, which might be more flexible in filtering more complicated content that could be hidden and require context for consideration.

Another potential solution is to clearly separate user inputs from the instructions prepared by system designers, because prompt injection tends to work when the model misunderstands user inputs as part of the instructions and generates content following those misguided instructions. For this solution, secret separator symbols could be utilized, and prompts should be clearly instructed that the content between these separators represents user inputs. However, the choice of separators must be carefully designed, as a too simple separator may be easy to guess, and bad actors may take advantage of this knowledge in designing their malicious inputs. Rare token-separators help alleviate this issue. Examples of such separators could be < |###| >, §### − − − ###§, and #$#$. This will make it harder for attackers and reduce the chance of the model misunderstanding user inputs as instructions.

Finally, we believe that a better training set and *alignment process* could be useful and have a higher impact on the model's behavior. By preparing a training set that eliminates this kind of harmful content, the resulting model may exhibit safer behavior. However, we acknowledge that filtering out such content during dataset preparation may pose some challenges, as it could potentially reduce the trained model's capabilities. Thus, it requires further investigation to strike a better balance between having a safe and useful model. The *alignment process* also presents an opportunity for reducing the model's undesired behavior. However, similar to the training set, poorly performing the *alignment process* may reduce the model's usefulness and must be done with care.

In future studies, we plan to explore various attacks that could impact LLM-integrated systems, especially those for narrative generation based on user inputs. We'll use newer word lists like those from Chen et al. [3] to understand LLM behaviors. Since these models were trained on data spanning different time periods, understanding word meanings' evolution is crucial. Additionally, we'll investigate aspects of generated stories beyond just endings, employing techniques like word and topic clustering, human evaluations, and advanced analyses for a comprehensive understanding.

## 5 Conclusions

This study investigated the influences and potential risks associated with user inputs and used as a part of prompts in ChatGPT for game story generation. The results regarding the influence of positive and negative sentiment words, our proxies for user inputs, on the story outcomes indicated that ChatGPT generally prefers generating positive-ending stories, which are likely less harmful than negative-ending stories. However, we also discovered the possibility of injecting malicious inputs into ChatGPT through prompt injection, leading to jailbreaking and raising concerns about harmful story outcomes. To address these risks, we suggested several strategies, i.e., content filtering, rare token-separators, and enhancement of the *alignment process* and the training dataset. These findings emphasize the importance of understanding and managing risks in using ChatGPT for story generation to ensure responsible and ethical outcomes.

## References


1. Borji, A.: A categorical archive of ChatGPT failures (2023)
2. Cascella, M., Montomoli, J., Bellini, V., et al.: Evaluating the feasibility of ChatGPT in healthcare: an analysis of multiple clinical and research scenarios. J. Med. Syst. **47**(1), 33 (2023). https://doi.org/10.1007/s10916-023-01925-4
3. Chen, Y., Skiena, S.: Building sentiment lexicons for all major languages. In: Proceedings of the 52nd Annual Meeting of the Association for Computational Linguistics (Volume 2: Short Papers), pp. 383–389 (2014)
4. Dwivedi, Y.K., Kshetri, N., Hughes, L., et al.: Opinion paper: "so what if ChatGPT wrote it?" multidisciplinary perspectives on opportunities, challenges and implications of generative conversational AI for research, practice and policy. Int. J. Inf. Manage. **71**, 102642 (2023). https://doi.org/10.1016/j.ijinfomgt.2023.102642. https://www.sciencedirect.com/science/article/pii/S0268401223000233
5. Glukhov, D., Shumailov, I., Gal, Y., et al.: LLM censorship: a machine learning challenge or a computer security problem? arXiv preprint arXiv:2307.10719 (2023)
6. Greshake, K., Abdelnabi, S., Mishra, S., et al.: Not what you've signed up for: compromising real-world LLM-integrated applications with indirect prompt injection. arXiv preprint arXiv:2302.12173 (2023)

7. de Hoog, N., Verboon, P.: Is the news making us unhappy? The influence of daily news exposure on emotional states. Br. J. Psychol. **111**(2), 157–173 (2020). https://doi.org/10.1111/bjop.12389. https://bpspsychub.onlinelibrary.wiley.com/doi/abs/10.1111/bjop.12389
8. Hu, M., Liu, B.: Mining and summarizing customer reviews. In: Proceedings of the Tenth ACM SIGKDD International Conference on Knowledge Discovery and Data Mining, KDD 2004, pp. 168–177. Association for Computing Machinery, New York (2004). https://doi.org/10.1145/1014052.1014073
9. Imasato, N., Miyazawa, K., Duncan, C., et al.: Using a language model to generate music in its symbolic domain while controlling its perceived emotion. IEEE Access (2023)
10. Islamovic, A.: Meet stable beluga 1 and stable beluga 2, our large and mighty instruction fine-tuned language models (2023). https://stability.ai/blog/stable-beluga-large-instruction-fine-tuned-models
11. Jones, M., Neumayer, C., Shklovski, I.: Embodying the algorithm: exploring relationships with large language models through artistic performance. In: Proceedings of the 2023 CHI Conference on Human Factors in Computing Systems, pp. 1–24 (2023)
12. Kshetri, N.: Cybercrime and privacy threats of large language models. IT Prof. **25**(3), 9–13 (2023). https://doi.org/10.1109/MITP.2023.3275489
13. Liu, Y., Deng, G., Xu, Z., et al.: Jailbreaking ChatGPT via prompt engineering: an empirical study (2023)
14. Lu, Y., Bartolo, M., Moore, A., et al.: Fantastically ordered prompts and where to find them: overcoming few-shot prompt order sensitivity (2021)
15. Markov, T., Zhang, C., Agarwal, S., et al.: A holistic approach to undesired content detection in the real world. In: Proceedings of the AAAI Conference on Artificial Intelligence, vol. 37, no. 12, pp. 15009–15018 (2023). https://doi.org/10.1609/aaai.v37i12.26752. https://ojs.aaai.org/index.php/AAAI/article/view/26752
16. Min, B., Ross, H., Sulem, E., et al.: Recent advances in natural language processing via large pre-trained language models: a survey. ACM Comput. Surv. (2021)
17. Mökander, J., Schuett, J., Kirk, H.R., et al.: Auditing large language models: a three-layered approach. AI Ethics 1–31 (2023)
18. OpenAI: Introducing ChatGPT (2022). https://openai.com/blog/chatgpt
19. Ross, S.I., Martinez, F., Houde, S., et al.: The programmer's assistant: conversational interaction with a large language model for software development. In: Proceedings of the 28th International Conference on Intelligent User Interfaces, pp. 491–514 (2023)
20. Sallam, M.: ChatGPT utility in healthcare education, research, and practice: systematic review on the promising perspectives and valid concerns. Healthcare **11**(6) (2023). https://www.mdpi.com/2227-9032/11/6/887
21. Simon, N., Muise, C.: TattleTale: storytelling with planning and large language models. In: ICAPS Workshop on Scheduling and Planning Applications (2022)
22. Sison, A.J.G., Daza, M.T., Gozalo-Brizuela, R., et al.: ChatGPT: more than a weapon of mass deception, ethical challenges and responses from the human-centered artificial intelligence (HCAI) perspective. arXiv preprint arXiv:2304.11215 (2023)
23. Stolper, C.D., Lee, B., Henry Riche, N., et al.: Emerging and recurring data-driven storytelling techniques: analysis of a curated collection of recent stories. Technical report, Microsoft (2016)

24. Swartjes, I., Theune, M.: Iterative authoring using story generation feedback: debugging or co-creation? In: Iurgel, I.A., Zagalo, N., Petta, P. (eds.) ICIDS 2009. LNCS, vol. 5915, pp. 62–73. Springer, Heidelberg (2009). https://doi.org/10.1007/978-3-642-10643-9_10
25. Taveekitworachai, P., Abdullah, F., Dewantoro, M.F., et al.: ChatGPT4PCG competition: character-like level generation for science birds (2023)
26. Teubner, T., Flath, C.M., Weinhardt, C., et al.: Welcome to the era of ChatGPT et al. the prospects of large language models. Bus. Inf. Syst. Eng. **65**(2), 95–101 (2023)
27. Thue, D., Schiffel, S., Guðmundsson, T.Þ, Kristjánsson, G.F., Eiríksson, K., Björnsson, M.V.: Open world story generation for increased expressive range. In: Nunes, N., Oakley, I., Nisi, V. (eds.) ICIDS 2017. LNCS, vol. 10690, pp. 313–316. Springer, Cham (2017). https://doi.org/10.1007/978-3-319-71027-3_33
28. Todd, G., Earle, S., Nasir, M.U., et al.: Level generation through large language models. In: Proceedings of the 18th International Conference on the Foundations of Digital Games, FDG 2023. Association for Computing Machinery, New York (2023). https://doi.org/10.1145/3582437.3587211
29. Touvron, H., Martin, L., Stone, K., et al.: LLaMA 2: open foundation and fine-tuned chat models (2023)
30. Wang, Z., Xie, Q., Ding, Z., et al.: Is ChatGPT a Good Sentiment Analyzer? A Preliminary Study (2023)
31. Ye, W., Ou, M., Li, T., et al.: Assessing hidden risks of LLMs: an empirical study on robustness, consistency, and credibility. arXiv preprint arXiv:2305.10235 (2023)
32. Yuan, A., Coenen, A., Reif, E., et al.: Wordcraft: story writing with large language models. In: 27th International Conference on Intelligent User Interfaces, pp. 841–852 (2022)
33. Zhou, J., Zhang, Y., Luo, Q., et al.: Synthetic lies: understanding AI-generated misinformation and evaluating algorithmic and human solutions. In: Proceedings of the 2023 CHI Conference on Human Factors in Computing Systems, pp. 1–20 (2023)
34. Zhuo, T.Y., Huang, Y., Chen, C., et al.: Red teaming ChatGPT via jailbreaking: bias, robustness, reliability and toxicity (2023)
35. Zou, A., Wang, Z., Kolter, J.Z., et al.: Universal and transferable adversarial attacks on aligned language models (2023)

# Playing Story Creation Games with Large Language Models: Experiments with GPT-3.5

Timothy S. Wang(✉) and Andrew S. Gordon(✉)

University of Southern California, Los Angeles, CA, USA
wangtimo@usc.edu, gordon@ict.usc.edu

**Abstract.** We created a web application where human users can play a story creation game with OpenAI's GPT-3.5, based on the Tell Tale card game. Tell Tale requires players to generate a brand new and coherent story based on a set of initial story elements, making the game a useful structure for exploring how well GPT-3.5 performs in generating coherent and engaging narratives. We show that GPT-3.5 performs remarkably well in generating such a narrative based on a random set of initial story elements, and that GPT-3.5 is even able to incorporate other literary elements such as suspense and flashbacks into its stories to enhance them and make them more engaging. By having human testers play Tell Tale with GPT-3.5 through our web application, we also demonstrate GPT-3.5's strong potential to be used as an interactive storytelling system, one that can both write and evaluate different narratives. We evaluate this potential using both quantitative and qualitative data from the human testers. Results indicate that, while GPT-3.5's narrative abilities are far from perfect, large language models have great potential in many different automated narrative situations.

**Keywords:** Narrative Generation · Narrative Evaluation · Large Language Models

## 1 Introduction

While human storytelling is universally seen across all cultures, it is by no means a trivial process. In telling a compelling story, humans must interpret together a set of outside observations and a set of initial world knowledge into a coherent narrative structure of what happened (an interpretation of events), before communicating that structure to others in a meaningful and coherent manner. One key area of current artificial intelligence and natural language processing

The project or effort depicted was or is sponsored by the U.S. Army Research Laboratory (ARL) under contract number W911NF-14-D-0005, and that the content of the information does not necessarily reflect the position or the policy of the Government, and no official endorsement should be inferred.


L. Holloway-Attaway and J. T. Murray (Eds.): ICIDS 2023, LNCS 14384, pp. 297–305, 2023.
https://doi.org/10.1007/978-3-031-47658-7_28

research is automating this storytelling process, a feat which could greatly aid in integrating computers into this critical usage of human language, amongst other potential applications. While certain aspects of this process, such as generating coherent text via computational linguistics, have seen enormous progress, historically being able to synthesize observations and world knowledge together into a meaningful narrative structure has been more challenging. Despite this, the introduction of large language models (LLMs) such as OpenAI's Generative Pre-trained Transformer 3.5 (GPT-3.5) [8] has provided researchers with a new and extremely powerful tool to tackle this challenge.

This paper explores the capability of GPT-3.5 to do competently automated narrative interpretation and, ultimately, general automated storytelling. To do this, GPT-3.5 was tested within the framework of the Tell Tale card game[1], a casual card game where players must generate an original narrative based on a random selection of 120 different story elements printed on 60 double-sided cards. The number of story elements used in a game can vary, but players must utilize some aspect of each of their selected story elements in their narrative. For example, if a player's cards are a baseball player, a heart, and a train, as depicted in Fig. 1, one potential narrative could be: "The girl took the train to see the baseball game because she loves baseball." This narrative is acceptable because it mentions baseball, trains, and heart's association with love, but the story may not be judged by other players as being creative, clever, or well-crafted.

This research tested three tasks for GPT-3.5 to try to complete. First is the ability of GPT-3.5 to generate a coherent story from a random selection of Tell Tale story elements. Second is the ability of GPT-3.5 to complete the first task while also being able to incorporate into its narrative literary devices such as suspense, foreshadowing, and imagery. Third is the ability of GPT-3.5 to evaluate and score its own and other narratives within the Tell Tale game. In testing these three tasks, we developed a new Tell Tale web application where users can play a game of Tell Tale cards with GPT-3.5. We used this web application to conduct human evaluations of GPT-3.5's abilities.

**Fig. 1.** Images of three Tell Tale cards, from [3]

[1] https://blueorangegames.com/index.php/games/telltale.

In the following sections, we will show results that highlight GPT-3.5's impressive interpretive and storytelling abilities, with GPT-3.5 having success in both generating Tell Tale narratives and evaluating other Tell Tale narratives. Using simple prompting strategies, we were able to develop an interactive web application where users can "compete" against GPT-3.5 in a game of Tell Tale, revealing GPT-3.5's potential not just in generating coherent narratives, but also in interactive storytelling settings. We will also show preliminary quantitative and qualitative human test data on GPT-3.5's storytelling and story evaluation abilities, revealing initial human testers' generally positive evaluations of GPT-3.5's abilities.

## 2 Related Work

Gordon and Spierling [3] previously investigated automated narrative generation in story creation games, specifically looking at the Tell Tale card game. In their work, they generated eight variations of stories that incorporated elements from three Tell Tale cards (a baseball player, a train, and a heart symbol) using a logical abduction and a hand-crafted knowledge base of first-order logic axioms. The output of their system is a graph structure representing the story, much in the same vein as Elson's Story Intention Graphs [1] or the Causal Network models of Trabasso and van den Broek [11], which can be coupled with dedicated text-generation methods to produce fluent narratives [4]. Our work differs from theirs by utilizing a large language model for the entire narrative generation process, avoided the need for hand-authored knowledge bases or narrative planning algorithms.

The use of neural networks for narrative text generation has received enormous research attention over the years [7], as have methods for evaluating the output of various systems [9]. In more recent work, large language models are fine-tuned specifically for the narrative generation task. Representative of these newer models are MPT-7B-StoryWriter-65k+ [6], a decoder-style transformer fine-tuned on a fiction subset of the books3 dataset [2], and MythoMax-L2-13b[2], which targets storytelling and role-playing by mixing tensors from multiple upstream models based on Meta's LLaMa model [10]. Although these newer models may have characteristics that are well-suited for our narrative generation tasks, we investigate only OpenAI's popular GPT-3.5 model in our research.

Finally, there has also been recent work in enabling computer systems to incorporate certain narrative devices into their stories. For instance, Han et al. [5] used a Plan-and-Write framework and reinforcement learning to better incorporate the literary device of flashbacks into generated narratives, resulting in more interesting but still coherent stories. This paper also involves asking a computer system to incorporate flashbacks into its generated stories, but we use a pre-trained LLM (GPT-3.5) instead, and we also ask GPT-3.5 to incorporate a broad set of literary devices, including imagery and conflict, beyond just only flashbacks.

[2] https://huggingface.co/Gryphe/MythoMax-L2-13b.

## 3 Prompt Engineering

Participation in a standard Tell Tale card game requires both the generation of a novel story and the consideration of stories created by other participants. To enable GPT-3.5 to execute both functions, we engineered specific prompts for three different tasks. Prompts were engineered by making individual API calls to GPT-3.5 Turbo, using a consistent temperature value of 0.7 for all API calls. In engineering these prompts, we focused our efforts on a small subset of Tell Tale cards (heart, baseball, train, star, and city). As our interest is on narrative text generation rather than visual understanding, these Tell Tale cards were presented to GPT-3.5 as textual labels, rather than as images that appear on the cards.

In the first task, we investigated whether GPT-3.5 could successfully perform the basic narrative generation task. As expected, even with simple prompts, GPT-3.5 had no difficulties in generating coherent narratives that successfully use the Tell Tale cards as story elements. For example, when prompted to write a story using "heart" and "star" as Tell Tale cards:

**Prompt:** *Write a coherent story that uses both some interpretation of "heart" and some interpretation of "star".*
**Narrative** (Abbreviated for space): *Once upon a time, in a small village nestled amidst a dense forest, there lived a young girl named Luna. Luna had a heart full of dreams and a passion for the stars that glittered in the night sky. She would spend countless hours staring at them, wondering about the mysteries they held.Luna's parents, who were simple farmers, noticed their daughter's fascination with the stars...*

In the second task, we explored whether GPT-3.5 could perform the narrative generation task while including certain literary features such as suspense, foreshadowing, and imagery. The motivation behind this second task is to move beyond simple interpretation and to explore whether GPT-3.5 can create narratives similar to how human writers tend to generate stories, with literary features that enhance the storytelling experience, making it more exciting and entertaining. Prompting GPT-3.5 to include literary devices such as foreshadowing proved to be more difficult. We quickly found that simply asking GPT-3.5 to include a certain literary device was not enough. Rather, GPT-3.5 was much more likely to include that literary device when we included a definition of that specific literary device. For instance:

**Prompt:** *Write a coherent story that uses both some interpretation of "city" and some interpretation of "baseball". The story must have narrative foreshadowing. The story having narrative foreshadowing means the story should have some object, situation, or plot point that hints at what will happen in the future."*
**Narrative:** (Abbreviated for space): *In the heart of the bustling city, where towering skyscrapers kissed the sky, there existed a hidden gem of a baseball field known as Diamond Park. Tucked away amidst the concrete jungle, it was an oasis for those seeking solace from the chaotic city life. Young Tommy, a passionate*

*baseball enthusiast, spent his days at Diamond Park. He was a prodigious player, with a natural talent for the game that caught the attention of all who watched him. The city became captivated by Tommy's skills, and his reputation as a future baseball star grew with each game he played. One fateful day, as the sun set over the city, Tommy's favorite bat, lovingly named "Slugger," mysteriously disappeared from his locker. Heartbroken and devastated, he searched every nook and cranny of Diamond Park, but to no avail...*

There were some literary devices that were more difficult to prompt GPT-3.5 to include in its narrative. For instance, GPT-3.5 had a particular difficulty in consistently including flashbacks into its stories when prompted. In addition, even if GPT-3.5 were able to technically include a literary device, sometimes the use of the literary device does not cleanly fit into the narrative and reads to be somewhat contrived. Overall though, these initial results generally showed GPT-3.5's ability to create coherent narratives based only on an initial set of Tell Tale cards.

In the third task, we looked at whether GPT-3.5 could also successfully evaluate other Tell Tale narratives, and score them based on how well they were able to incorporate all the Tell Tale cards that were used as observations. The motive behind this third task is to see if GPT-3.5 could emulate an actual human player in a game of Tell Tale, where players both have to come up with an original story based on a set of Tell Tale cards but also evaluate their story as well. This would allow us to both test GPT-3.5's ability to analyze a new story and GPT-3.5's potential as an interactive storytelling system. We found that reasonable results could be obtained by asking GPT-3.5 to evaluate how well its own generated stories adhered to the prompt, in the following format:

**Prompt:** *Evaluate the following story based on how well it follows the given prompt and give a score out of ten. The Prompt:* [Original Prompt]. *The Story:* [GPT-3.5's Story].

While not perfect, GPT-3.5's performance gave us the confidence that it could fully support an interactive Tell Tale card game web application.

## 4 Designing a Tell Tale Card Game Web Application

To test all three of these tasks, we created a simple web application where users can "compete" against GPT-3.5 in a game of Tell Tale cards, as shown in Fig. 2. A round of this game involves a single human user interacting with the web interface to play against a single instance of GPT-3.5. The web application selects three random Tell Tale cards (from 120 possibilities) that serve as the starting "observations" for generating a narrative. In addition, the user is presented with seven literary features - conflict, suspense, foreshadowing, flashbacks, plot twists, personification, and imagery - and can choose any subset of those seven literary features. Based on the three Tell Tale cards provided to the user and the selected literary features, the user will then be asked to write a narrative involving those Tell Tale cards that also incorporates the selected literary features.

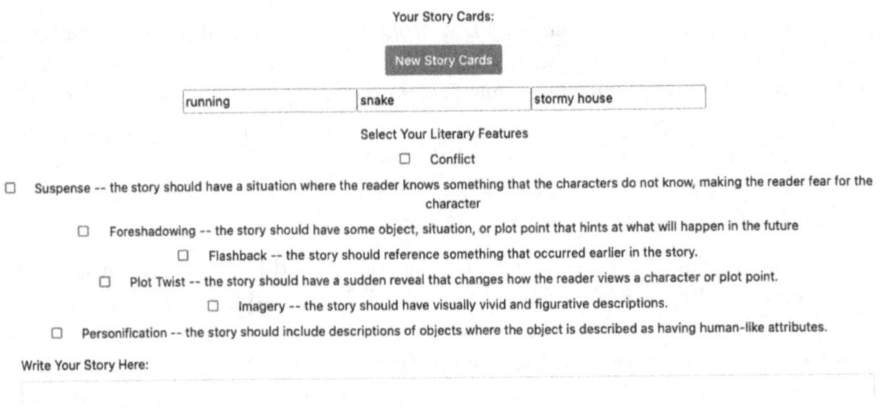

**Fig. 2.** Portion of the web application interface.

After the user submits their story, GPT-3.5 first writes a story itself using the same Tell Tale cards and selected literary features, using the following prompt template:

**Prompt:** *Write a coherent story that uses some interpretation of* [Tell Tale Card 1], *some interpretation of* [Tell Tale Card 2], *and some interpretation of* [Tell Tale Card 3]. *Also the story must have* [Literary Device 1]. *The story having* [Literary Device 1] *means the story should* [Definition of Literary Device 1]. *Also the story must have* [Literary Device 2]...

After generating a story, GPT-3.5 will then send two new and separate API requests, where GPT-3.5 will be prompted to evaluate and score both the user's story and its own story based on how well it incorporates the three Tell Tale cards and the selected literary devices:

**Prompt:** *Evaluate the following story based on how well it follows the given prompt and give a score out of ten. The Prompt:* [Original Prompt]. *The Story:* [User's or GPT-3.5's Story].

By creating this web application, we hope to showcase the potential for GPT-3.5 as an interactive narrative agent, being able to both generate stories and to react intelligently to other narratives. In this way, this web application could be considered an initial step to using GPT-3.5 in a more complex interactive narrative system. Moreover, this web application also creates a natural way to test all three of our target tasks using human testers. By having human users interact with GPT-3.5 through our web application, the human users can provide evaluation data and feedback on how well GPT-3.5 performs in both generating and evaluating a Tell Tale game story.

## 5 User Evaluation

We enlisted 10 human testers to play a game of Tell Tale using our web application, where each participant played the game individually along with the computer. One important request we gave the human testers was that the human testers should only use three predetermined literary devices: conflict, foreshadowing, and imagery. In this way, we could still test GPT-3.5's ability to include literary devices while also increasing the level of consistency amongst the human testers, especially given that each human tester will be using a different random set of Tell Tale cards.

After testing a round of Tell Tale on the web application, the human testers were surveyed on the abilities of GPT-3.5. First, the testers were asked "On a scale of 1 to 10, how would you score GPT's story based on coherency and how it includes the selected story and literary elements? (1 being the worst and 10 being the best.)" and "Please explain your reasoning for why you gave GPT's story the score you gave." This allowed the testers to provide us with both quantitative and qualitative feedback. The quantitative feedback would be helpful in comparing how the human testers evaluated GPT-3.5's story versus how GPT-3.5 itself would evaluate its own story. On the other hand, the qualitative feedback would provide a more detailed assessment of the quality of GPT-3.5's story, including on the story's strong points and where the story could be improved. Such feedback would be crucial to improve the prompts provided to GPT-3.5 in the future in order to generate better quality stories.

Second, the testers were asked "Review GPT's evaluation of your story. Evaluate GPT's evaluation. In other words, do you agree or disagree with GPT's evaluation and score of your story and why? How well do you think GPT evaluated your story?" and "Score GPT's evaluation of your story on a scale from 1 to 10 (1 being the worst and 10 being the best)." Like the previous two questions, this provides us with both a quantitative and a qualitative evaluation of GPT-3.5's performance as a Tell Tale story evaluator. Similar questions are asked to the human testers about GPT-3.5's evaluation of its own story.

## 6 Results

Our preliminary results show that, in general, the human testers had a positive assessment of the performance of GPT-3.5 as a participant in a Tell Tale game. The average quantitative score (out of 10) for the quality of GPT-3.5's story was 6.7. The human testers' ratings for GPT-3.5's story evaluation ability were roughly the same, giving GPT-3.5's evaluation of the human testers' stories an average score of 7.0 and giving GPT-3.5's evaluation of its own stories an average score of 7.2.

The qualitative feedback provided by the human testers also supports a positive appraisal of GPT-3.5's storytelling abilities, with some of the human testers describing how GPT-3.5 "incorporated all the elements of the story that it needed to" and how GPT-3.5's story "was very easy to read, engaging, and included the required literary elements." Of course, not all the feedback was universally positive, with one human tester noting that "the story felt 'forced', with GPT trying to be too literal in its use of the story card items." Another tester was harsher, noting how "The imagery is detailed but predictable and schematic, so that it brings to mind a cartoony picture rather than engaging the imagination in filling out and entering a scene."

Most human testers also generally praised GPT-3.5's evaluation ability, with some testers noting how quickly GPT-3.5 was able to evaluate their stories and recognize that the story included certain literary features ("I was surprised it recognized my foreshadowing in the last sentence" notes one tester). Nevertheless, GPT-3.5's evaluation ability was not perfect. For instance, one tester felt as though GPT-3.5 should have been able to detect the weakness in a certain story's plot.

## 7 Conclusions

In our initial testing and in the evaluation of our web application, we found that GPT-3.5 was proficient in generating coherent narratives and generating a meaningful interpretation of a set of initial observations (Tell Tale cards, in this research). Such proficiency is evidenced by the generally high scores human testers have given to many of GPT-3.5's stories. In addition, GPT-3.5 has proven adept at evaluating other Tell Tale stories too, with the human testers giving GPT-3.5's story evaluations high scores as well.

Our research also highlights several areas where GPT-3.5's game-playing abilities could be improved, either through more refined prompts or through improvements to the language model itself. Some of the human testers wrote in their qualitative assessments their opinion that some of GPT-3.5's stories were somewhat contrived and their inclusion of Tell Tale cards a bit forced. In our opinion, this research is a step towards enabling large language models to perform complex and interactive narrative tasks.

## References


1. Elson, D.: DramaBank: annotating agency in narrative discourse. In: Proceedings of the Eighth International Conference on Language Resources and Evaluation (LREC 2012), pp. 2813–2819. European Language Resources Association (ELRA), Istanbul (2012)
2. Gao, L., et al.: The pile: an 800 gb dataset of diverse text for language modeling. arXiv preprint arXiv:2101.00027 (2020)
3. Gordon, A.S., Spierling, U.: Playing story creation games with logical abduction. In: Rouse, R., Koenitz, H., Haahr, M. (eds.) ICIDS 2018. LNCS, vol. 11318, pp. 478–482. Springer, Cham (2018). https://doi.org/10.1007/978-3-030-04028-4_55
4. Gordon, A.S., Wang, T.S.: Narrative text generation from abductive interpretations using axiom-specific templates. In: Mitchell, A., Vosmeer, M. (eds.) ICIDS 2021. LNCS, vol. 13138, pp. 71–79. Springer, Cham (2021). https://doi.org/10.1007/978-3-030-92300-6_7

5. Han, R., Chen, H., Tian, Y., Peng, N.: Go back in time: generating flashbacks in stories with event temporal prompts. In: Proceedings of the 2022 Conference of the North American Chapter of the Association for Computational Linguistics: Human Language Technologies, Seattle, United States (2022)
6. MosaicML NLP Team: Introducing MPT-7B: a new standard for open-source, commercially usable LLMs (2023). https://www.mosaicml.com/blog/mpt-7b. Accessed 01 Aug 2023
7. Peng, N., Ghazvininejad, M., May, J., Knight, K.: Towards controllable story generation. In: Proceedings of the First Workshop on Storytelling, pp. 43–49. Association for Computational Linguistics, New Orleans (2018). https://doi.org/10.18653/v1/W18-1505. https://aclanthology.org/W18-1505
8. Radford, A., Narasimhan, K., Salimans, T., Sutskever, I.: Improving language understanding by generative pre-training (2018). https://www.semanticscholar.org/paper/Improving-Language-Understanding-by-Generative-Radford-Narasimhan/cd18800a0fe0b668a1cc19f2ec95b5003d0a5035
9. Roemmele, M.: Identifying sensible lexical relations in generated stories. In: Proceedings of the First Workshop on Narrative Understanding, pp. 44–52. Association for Computational Linguistics, Minneapolis (2019). https://doi.org/10.18653/v1/W19-2406. https://aclanthology.org/W19-2406
10. Touvron, H., et al.: Llama: open and efficient foundation language models (2023)
11. Trabasso, T., van den Broek, P.: Causal thinking and the representation of narrative events. J. Mem. Lang. **24**(5), 612–630 (1985). https://doi.org/10.1016/0749-596X(85)90049-X

# *Traversing Language, the Author, and the Word in Amira Hanafi's* a Dictionary of the Revolution

David Thomas Henry Wright(✉)

Nagoya University, Aichi-Ken, Japan
davidthwright@gmail.com

**Abstract.** Amira Hanafi's A Dictionary of the Revolution (2017) is a work of electronic literature that documents the 'rapid amplification of public political speech following the uprising of 25 January 2011 in Egypt' (Hanafi, 2016). Material for Hanafi's electronic literary work was collected through an engagement with 200 individuals in Egypt from March to August 2014 across six governates of Egypt: Alexandria, Aswan, Cairo, Mansoura, Sinai, and Suez. Hanafi created a vocabulary box containing 160 colloquial Egyptian words that were frequently used in public political conversation from 2011 to 2013. These words were put into four categories: concepts, characters, objects, and places and events. This paper seeks to analyse the traversing of language, author, and word in Hanafi's work, using Landow's hypertext theory, Koenitz's theories of interactive digital narrative, and Marino's critical code studies. From this analysis, this paper seeks to develop a theory for analysing and reviewing digital narratives using their own form.

**Keywords:** Amira Hanafi · electronic literature · third generation electronic literature

Amira Hanafi's *A Dictionary of the Revolution* (2017) is a work of electronic literature that documents the 'rapid amplification of public political speech following the uprising of 25 January 2011 in Egypt' (Hanafi, 2016). Material for Hanafi's electronic literary work was collected through an engagement with 200 individuals in Egypt from March to August 2014 across six governates of Egypt: Alexandria, Aswan, Cairo, Mansoura, Sinai, and Suez. Hanafi created a vocabulary box containing 160 colloquial Egyptian words that were frequently used in public political conversation from 2011 to 2013. These words were put into four categories: concepts, characters, objects, and places and events. The resultant work contains 125 imagined dialogues derived from the transcribed conversations. For example, if one is to click the term 'onion', we learn that onions were used as a countermeasure against tear gas, as 'sniffing an onion' helped to alleviate adverse reactions. As well as the potential 'new' definitions of 'onion', one is presented with an image of the vocabular box card, images of onions, and most significantly, links to other words: *youth*, *vinegar*, *Tahrir Square*, *revolution*, *the people*, and *gas*.

This paper seeks to analyse the traversing of language, author, and word in Hanafi's work. It regards the text as decentred and subsequent *re*-centred, and as an example of experimental decentred text similar to Jacques Derrida's *Glas* (1974). *Glas* (1974)


L. Holloway-Attaway and J. T. Murray (Eds.): ICIDS 2023, LNCS 14384, pp. 306–310, 2023.
https://doi.org/10.1007/978-3-031-47658-7_29

contains pages split into two columns. On the left is an essay on the works of Hegel, on the right an essay on the writing of Jean Genet. The individual essays are frequently interrupted by what Barthes calls 'lexias', i.e. brief, contiguous fragmentary units of reading (Barthes, 1975, 13), which supply relevant information and/or digressions. The essays can be read separately or 'simultaneously'. As text, *Glas* lacks a 'centre' (although one could argue that the centre is Derrida, the author). This correlation between digitality and literary theory is perhaps most famously conjoined by hypertext theorist George Landow (2006), who writes:

> When designers of computer software examine the pages of *Glas* or *Of Grammatology*, they encounter a digitalized, hypertextual Derrida; and when literary theorists examine *Literary Machines*, they encounter a deconstructionist or post-structuralist Nelson. ... over the past several decades literary theory and computer hypertext, apparently unconnected areas of inquiry, have increasingly converged. (1)

Extending Landow's connection between literary theory and hypertext, in attempting to represent such a vast array of unrepresented Egyptian voices, Hanafi's work also depicts Bakhtin's notion of the polyphonic text, i.e. a text that displays a 'plurality of independent and unmerged voices and consciousnesses.' (4) This term, polyphonic, stems from music, and in some respects its metaphoric 'simultaneity' is perhaps better expressed in Hanafi's digital medium. The collective representation of multiple interview subjects presented in the interactive, simultaneous manner better represents Bakhtin's definition of literary polyphony through interactive functionality.

The work can also be regarded as an example of what Koenitz (2015) labels 'Interactive Digital Narrative'. These works 'challenge basic assumptions about narrative in the western world – namely about the role of the author and the fixed state of content and structure as the audience takes on an active role and the narratives become malleable' (91). This definition of IDN defines both Hanafi's role as a more fluid, journalistic writer that takes multiple responses and combines them together in a multifaceted and at times relentless fashion. Likewise her approach directly challenges the basic structural assumptions of a standard western encyclopaedia by rethinking it using digital functionality.

In addition to the digital work's literary form, I also examine the work's code through Mark Marino's *Critical Code Studies* (2020). Marino writes:

> But the code is not enough in itself. It is crucial to explore context. Who wrote the code? When and why? In what language was the code written? What programming paradigm was used? Was it written for a particular platform (hardware or software)? How did the code change over time? What material or social constraints impacted the creation of this code? How does this code respond to the context in which it was created? *How was the code received by others?* [my italics] (28)

This last question is of interest. The code, here, was created by Youssef Faltas. I have decided to engage with this code directly (permission to do so has been granted by Amira Hanafi) to explore the architecture and impact of this digital structure by adapting this paper as a born-digital essay that engages directly with the code used to format and structure Hanafi's work. This research is regarded as 'practice-led research'. This paper also extends current digital literary review formats proposed in the publication *The Digital Review*, a sibling publication to *electronic book review*, an annual journal dedicated to the preservation and publication of innovative, born-digital essays; each theme-based issue offers a curated combination of commissioned work, submitted work and "rediscovered" work. Unlike typical reviews or papers, this method poses that it is not enough to merely reflect on and theorise the work without also engaging with its form and code makeup. I should also acknowledge that this research has been funded by a JSPS KAKENHI grant, into the digital/print nexus.

As born-digital works utilize digital code and technology to create new meaning, it therefore follows that criticism should also utilize the same digital code and technology. In so doing, this practice-led research develops a better understanding of Hanafi's form, that in turn can be proposed as a new interconnected digital essay format. Such a form, I argue, could be utilized to better represent the collective, polyphonic response to major political and global events by enabling, in Hanafi's words, the creation of 'a space for viewpoints that are no longer represented in the media or in the public.'

I want to focus on what it is that makes Hanafi's work digital. Somewhat crudely, I have defined electronic literature by its 'unprintability'. Van de Ven and Ackermans (2019) argue that Hanafi 'appropriates the form of the dictionary, traditionally a source that is officially regulated, in order to present a counter-narrative to the mainstream medium.' As a 'traditional' form, the work could be represented as a print 'dictionary', presenting the 125 words and definitions in alphabetical order. This, however, would lose the digital elements her piece offers. Nevertheless, imaging such a print version allows one to highlight just how the digital aspects of the work transform the piece. As a work of creative practice, many digital literary works start out as print works, that are then expanded or reimagined in digital spaces. Such has been my experience in developing digital literary works (for example, my *Little Emperor Syndrome* was a print text that was transformed by digital recombinant poetics and coloured text, research that was born out of studying the Faulkner corpus), and such is the case with Hanafi's piece. As with *Glas*, the hierarchy of the page is challenged. The work is decentred. We could, therefore, regard Hanafi as a *bricoleur*, which French structuralism theorist Claude Lévi-Strauss (in Derrida, 1978) defines as someone who uses 'the means at hand' (285), that which is already there. In *Writing and Difference*, Derrida states that 'the concept of structure' is dated; the reason for structure was to orient, balance, organise, and to 'limit what we might call the *freeplay* of the structure' (278). In Hanafi's work, the text is not only de-centred, but then re-centred through its digital structure, or the limited freeplay of the structure. The re-centre of Hanafi's *Dictionary of the Revolution* is the word 'revolution' itself. It is the most interconnected word, connecting to 117 words (the only words not connected are *rule*, *paddy wagon*, *terrorists*, *void*, *air ambulance*, *citizen*, *fifty dollars*, and *Itihadiya*). 'Revolution' is the term, the concept that has its tentacles in almost all other words. It is what structures this piece. Indeed, it is the interconnection of one word to another that structures Hanafi's work, and that is only made possible through its digital interface. Additionally, the dissemination of the work through a digital, web-based medium allows for a broader, transcontinental reach, one that is more resilient (though far from immune) to censorship and restriction. It also forces the English reader to acknowledge the text's origin as an Arabic text that then must be toggled into English.

In developing a paper on Hanafi's *Dictionary of the Revolution*, I was interested in also developing a presentation of the same paper that engages directly with Hanafi's form and Faltas's code. Through the analysis of digital literature, it made sense as a practitioner to engage directly with the work in question, as a form of practice-led research. Practice-led research is defined by Smith and Dean (2009) as:

> an activity which can appear in a variety of guises across the spectrum of practice and research. It can be basic research carried out independent of creative work (though it may be subsequently applied to it); research conducted in the process of shaping an artwork; or research which is the documentation, theorisation and contextualisation of an artwork – and the process of making it – by its creator. (3)

By adopting the existing form to discuss the form itself, this practice-led research 'creates' third generation electronic literature. Third generation e-lit, Flores (2019) writes, starts around 2005 and uses 'established platforms with massive user bases, such as social media networks, apps, mobile and touchscreen devices, and Web API services.' Third generation e-lit co-exists with the second generation, which consists of 'innovative works created with custom interfaces and forms.' It should also be noted the first generation e-lit is characterized by a few pioneering works that emerged between 1952 and 1995. For most of this period, people had limited access to computers, resulting in a small number of practitioners, most of whom didn't have a clear concept that what they were creating was electronic literature. In the first few decades, only computer scientists and academics in universities and technical staff in the private industry, producers in film, television, radio studios that had access to expensive tools that could be used to create electronic literature. (Flores 2019) To give a simpler example of the distinction between second and third generation e-lit, we can turn to Nick Montfort's *Taroko Gorge*. This is a nature poem that was inspired by a visit to Taroko Gorge in Taiwan. Like the waterfalls of Taroko Gorge, the 'flow' of the recombinant nature of the poem always produced unique results. Montfort's 'procedurally-generated poem' has inspired an entire sub-genre of 'remixes, remakes, constrained writing experiments, and parodies'. For example, Scott Rettberg took Montfort's minimalist nature poem and made a maximalist urban poem called 'Tokyo Garage', which filled his code with vocabulary relating to a Japanese city. And numerous other authors have adopted Montfort's code to produce a number of works. J.R. Carpenter, for example, replaced the vocabulary with food-related words to produce 'Gorge'. I myself, produced a series of 54 Taroko Gorge remixes, that addressed the entirety of the Australian archive, in a work titled *Most Powerful Words*; for example, if we click on the section titled 'Most Powerful Words', we get speeches from the most powerful people in the world according to Forbes magazine as of last year (I'm not sure these power dynamics are still in place), and get recombinant poems using their specific vocabulary. Here, for example, we have a Taroko Gorge remix using Xi Jinping's New Year speech. So, Montfort's poem is second generation, whereas Rettberg's, Carpenter's, and my work are all third generation. So in adopting Hanafi's code and form, this 'digital essay' is a form of third generation electronic literature. On the other hand, where much of third generation electronic literature is simply adopting code for parody or short-hand, this process is interested in deconstructing and interrogating the work in question itself. So Hanafi's *Dictionary of a Revolution* is a clear example of second generation electronic literature, in that her work uses a custom interface and form to represent its text, whereas a digital essay that appropriates the code would be third generation.

I intend to replace Hanafi's vocabulary with my own analysis of the work itself. I've maintained Hanafi's precise interconnectedness, and centred my analysis on the work itself – where revolution was previously the centre of Hanafi's work, (*Dictionary of the*) revolution will become the centre. Additionally, all the terms/citations I have expressed in this paper will be included, and will have their own respective link and description. I propose that through a third-generation analysis of a revolutionary digital literary form, we can ultimately utilise said forms to fulfil the same aesthetic and ideological ambitions of the original creation. If one wanted to depict a different revolution or, one could adopt the same methodology and form and create a third generation e-lit work more effortlessly to depict the circumstance in question. Such a form, I argue, would create a space for viewpoints that are no longer represented in the media or in the public. Additionally, where second generation e-lit works require an array of skills, experience, and more often than not collaboration that restricts access to electronic literature as a means of expression, third generation electronic literary works such as this proposed essay will be easier to develop and engage with. Furthermore, in terms of pedagogy and recruitment within the field of electronic literature, such forms would enable an easier pathway to creativity and creative practice, one in which creative possibility is not restricted by a high degree of technical programming knowledge of multiple programming languages.

## References

Derrida, J.: [trans. A. Bass] Writing and Difference. Routledge, London (1978)

Derrida, J.: Glas. University of Nebraska Press, Lincoln (1986)

Flores, L.: 'Third Generation Electronic Literature'. Electronic Book Review (2019). https://electronicbookreview.com/essay/third-generation-electronic-literature/

Hanafi, A.: A Dictionary of the Revolution (2016). https://www.ibraaz.org/projects/143

Hanafi, A.: A Dictionary of the Revolution (2017). http://www.qamosalthawra.com/en

Koenitz, H.: Towards a specific theory of interactive digital narrative. In: Interactive digital narrative: history, theory and practice, pp. 91–105 Routledge (2015)

Montfort, N.: Taroko Gorge (2009). https://nickm.com/taroko_gorge/

Rettberg, S.: Electronic Literature. Polity Press, Cambridge (2019)

Smith, H., Dean, R.: Practice-led Research, Research-led Practice in the Creative Arts. Edinburgh University Press, Edinburgh (2009)

van de Ven, I., Ackermans, H.: Electronic Literature in the Database & The Database in Electronic Literature. Towards a Digital-Hermeneutics Approach. КОММУНИКАЦИИ. МЕДИА. ДИЗАˇИН / Communications. Media. Design, [4] (2019)

Wright, D.T.H.: Little Emperor Syndrome (2018). http://littleemperorsyndrome.com

Wright, D.T.H.: Most Powerful Words (2020). http://mostpowerfulwords.net

# Author Index





L. Holloway-Attaway and J. T. Murray (Eds.): ICIDS 2023, LNCS 14384, pp. 311–313, 2023.
https://doi.org/10.1007/978-3-031-47658-7

Printed in the United States
by Baker & Taylor Publisher Services